"Matthew Barrett is one of the brightest young theologians on the scene today, and he is amazingly productive. His newest work on salvation is simply superb. Barrett marches through various topics on salvation, and even though the book is brief, the answers are thorough, rooted in Scripture, informed by church history, and, most important, faithful to the faith once for all delivered to the saints. I should also add that the answers are remarkably clear and lucid, and it is hard to imagine a better primer for students to become acquainted with the doctrine of alvation in Scripture."

—Thomas Schreiner,
James Buchanan Harrison Professor of
New Testament Interpretation and Associate Dean,
The Southern Baptist Theological Seminary

"When the Philippian jailer asked Paul and Silas "What must I do be saved?" he uttered humanity's most important question. The answer to that question requires on the one hand only childlike understanding, but on the other hand it can surpass the depths of human comprehension. Indeed, when one examines all that God has revealed in the Bible regarding salvation, many other questions arise, and yet all reveal the marvelous kindness and glorious complexity of God. Thus, it is an exercise of worship to seek to ask and answer those questions, and therefore it is my joy to commend such an exploration in Matthew Barrett's *40 Questions About Salvation*. This book will strengthen your faith and help you to grow in your understanding and admiration of the God who saves."

—Jason G. Duesing,
Provost and Associate Professor of Historical Theology,
Midwestern Baptist Theological Seminary

"The doctrine of salvation strikes a personal chord in the hearts of God's people, even though many Christians struggle to comprehend its deeper dimensions. In view of this challenge, Matthew Barrett has rendered the church a great service. An extraordinary teacher with a knack for clarifying complexity, Barrett explores forty of the most crucial questions of salvation, providing answers that inform the mind and animate the heart."

—Chris Castaldo,
Lead Pastor of New Covenant Church, Naperville,
and author of *Talking with Catholics about the Gospel.*

"Barrett accessibly and faithfully presents what the whole Bible teaches about salvation."

—Andy Naselli,
Associate Professor of New Testament and Theology at Bethlehem College &
Seminary in Minrem Baptist Church

40 QUESTIONS ABOUT
Salvation

Matthew Barrett

Benjamin L. Merkle, Series Editor

Kregel
Academic

40 Questions About Salvation
© 2018 Matthew Barrett

Published by Kregel Publications, a division of Kregel Inc., 2450 Oak Industrial Dr. NE, Grand Rapids, MI 49505-6020.

This book is a title in the 40 Questions Series edited by Benjamin L. Merkle.

The Greek font GraecaU is available from www.linguistsoftware.com/lgku.htm, +1-425-775-1130.

ISBN 978-0-8254-4285-8

Printed in the United States of America

18 19 20 21 22 / 5 4 3 2 1

To Cassandra

It has been a joy to watch salvation within your heart sprout like a fruit tree in rich soil, with lots of sunshine and water. I hope that when you put down this book, you will sit in awe of our great God and the salvation he has brought about within you by his grace alone.

Salvation belongs to the Lord!
—Jonah 2:9

Contents

Part 5: Sanctification, Perseverance, and Glorification

Preface: How to Read This Book

When I begin reading a book, I always appreciate a word of insight from the author as to why he wrote the book and how I, the reader, should approach the book. So I will do the same.

I have written each chapter so that you can read it on its own. Some readers who already have knowledge in certain topics may find it most helpful to just skip to those sections of interest. However, one will notice that in most chapters I reference other chapters. This is because each chapter builds upon the others. The reason for this is simple: This book is about the *ordo salutis* (order of salvation), in which each stage in the salvation process is very much connected to that which comes before and after. So one will be best served to read the book from beginning to end since salvation is not something that comes in nice, neat compartments but is more like a chain in which each link is connected to the next. Should one link break (and be misunderstood), the whole chain of salvation will regrettably be affected.

One other important thought: Some readers may wish this book explored the numerous views out there on any given topic, as the innumerable "views books" do today. It should be stated at the start, however, that this is not the purpose of this book. While "views books" are valuable and have their place, this is not one of them. Rather, my purpose in this book is to present what the Bible teaches about salvation. So while I will refer to various views from time to time when necessary, I do not intend to interact with all the views (that would take another book in itself!) but to simply and concisely present what Scripture teaches about each step in salvation. This format is best suited for beginning students, churchgoers, and pastors—to whom this book is directed. That said, one should consult the bibliography where I point readers to more advanced resources (and list books according to topic and reading level).

Finally, I wrote this book not for the academic or advanced student, but at an introductory level. If you have not studied the doctrine of salvation before, or at least not in tremendous depth, this book is for you. It is meant to be a concise primer to each aspect of the order of salvation. Serious Bible-studying churchgoers, novice students, and pastors were in view as I wrote. I hope and pray that this book will act as a theological jump-start, motivating you to explore each subject in more depth as you grow in your love for God and his great plan of salvation.

Abbreviations

BDAG	W. Bauer, F. W. Danker, W. F. Arndt, and F. W. Gingrich. *Greek-English Lexicon of the New Testament and Other Early Christian Literature.* 3rd ed. Chicago: University of Chicago Press, 2000.
BECNT	Baker Exegetical Commentary on the New Testament
CNTC	Calvin's New Testament Commentaries
EBC	Expositor's Bible Commentary
EDT	*Evangelical Dictionary of Theology*
ICC	International Critical Commentary
ISBE	*International Standard Bible Encyclopedia*
JSNT	*Journal for the Study of the New Testament*
LCC	Library of Christian Classics
NACSBT	NAC Studies in Bible and Theology
NIB	The New Interpreter's Bible
NICNT	New International Commentary on the New Testament
NIGTC	New International Greek Testament Commentary
NSBT	New Studies in Biblical Theology
NTC	New Testament Commentary
OTL	Old Testament Library
PNTC	Pillar New Testament Commentary
REDS	Reformed Exegetical Doctrinal Studies
TDNT	Theological Dictionary of the New Testament
TrinJ	*Trinity Journal*
TNTC	Tyndale New Testament Commentary
TynBul	*Tyndale Bulletin*
WBC	Word Biblical Commentary
WTJ	*Westminster Theological Journal*
ZECNT	Zondervan Exegetical Commentary on the New Testament

PART 1

Sin and the Need
for Salvation

What Is Sin?

"None is righteous, no, not one; no one understands; no one seeks for God. All have turned aside; together they have become worthless; no one does good, not even one."

—Romans 3:10–12

Paul's message is loud and clear: Every single person is a sinner, guilty before a holy God. No one is righteous, no, not even one. All of us like sheep have gone astray. We have all turned to our own way (Isa. 53:6). There can be no doubt about it: Sin is real, and each and every one of us is a rebel against God. That raises the most basic of questions, however: What is sin?

What Is Sin?

Sin Is a Failure to Obey God's Moral Law

Man as lawbreaker captures the essence of sin. Sin "may be defined as lack of conformity to the moral law of God, either in act, disposition, or state."[1] Man's disobedience of God's moral law is a theme that runs from Genesis to Revelation. Beginning in Genesis, God commanded Adam and Eve not to eat of the tree of the knowledge of good and evil lest they die (Gen. 2:17). However, Adam and Eve chose to listen to the serpent rather than God, violating his covenant stipulation. As a result, Adam and Eve lost their original righteousness and moral innocence when they broke God's command. Suddenly they were guilty before God for their disobedience and they were morally corrupt. As we will learn in Questions 2 and 3, Adam's guilt and corruption would not be limited to himself but would be inherited by his progeny as well, since he acted as their representative (i.e., original sin). But here our focus is restricted to the act of sin (i.e., actual sin) so that we can identify its essential nature or character.

---

1. Louis Berkhof, *Systematic Theology* (Edinburgh: Banner of Truth, 2003), 233.

Satan's deceptive and murderous ways (John 8:44), unfortunately, would not stop with Adam but can be seen once again with Adam's first child, Cain. Cain and his brother Abel both made an offering to the Lord, but while Abel's offering pleased the Lord, Cain's did not (Heb. 11:4). Anger and jealousy consumed Cain, though the Lord warned him that if he did what was right he would be accepted. Yet, sin was crouching at Cain's door and its desire was for him. Cain, God warned, must rule over it (Gen. 4:7). Like his father Adam, rather than obeying God and submitting to his moral instruction, Cain in his anger killed his brother Abel, so that his blood cried out to the Lord (4:8–10). As you can see, the first chapters of Genesis vividly (and painfully) demonstrate that sin is a violation of God's moral commands.

Sin would characterize all of Adam's children thereafter as well. In Genesis 6 we read that the earth was corrupt in God's sight and filled with violence (6:11–12). The intentions of man's heart were evil from youth (8:21), so God sent a flood to destroy the whole earth, with the exception of Noah and his family, whom God graciously spared. The corruption of man did not disappear after the flood, however. God's just wrath was once again unleashed when he destroyed Sodom and Gomorrah with sulfur and fire from heaven (19:23–29), for their sin was "very grave" (18:20).

The history of Israel is tainted by lawbreaking as well. One would think that God delivering his chosen people from an oppressive dictator like Pharaoh would result in steadfast obedience. And yet, even while Moses was on Mount Sinai receiving the Ten Commandments from God himself, Israel had already rejected Yahweh as her God and instead crafted a golden calf to worship (Exod. 32). Israel defiled herself, turning against the commands of Yahweh, and exchanged the one true God for an idol made by the hands of men. Consequently, God's righteous wrath, which burned hot that day, came down against his people, demonstrating his holiness and intolerance for sin.

Sin pervades the rest of the story line of Scripture as well. The history of Israel is one of perpetual disobedience. As God's covenant people, under God's covenant law, they were commanded to love the Lord their God with all their heart (Deut. 6:5). This is the greatest commandment they received. Yet, throughout the Old Testament Israel repeatedly failed to uphold this commandment. The book of Judges summarizes the OT: "Everyone did what was right in his own eyes" (17:6b).

No act reflects the sinfulness of man more than the crucifixion of Christ himself. The sinfulness Paul speaks of in Romans 3 is put on full display when Jesus, the Son of God, was nailed to the cross by wicked men (Acts 2:23). It is tempting to think that if we were there we would have acted differently. Yet, many of those who put Jesus on the cross were the *religious* leaders in Israel. Though they looked clean on the outside, on the inside they were "full of greed and self-indulgence" (Matt. 23:25–26). Many of the religious leaders were hypocrites, full of lawlessness, like whitewashed tombs, "which outwardly appear beautiful, but within are full of dead people's bones and all uncleanness" (Matt. 23:27–28). They transgressed the commandments of God for the sake of their traditions (Matt. 15:2–3).[2]

The words of Jesus in Matthew 23 are important, for they demonstrate that sin, or lawlessness, is not merely a disobedient *act* but is a corruption of the *heart*. In other words, external behavior is the outflow of one's internal disposition.[3] This much was evident in Cain's murder of Abel. While Cain's murder was a sin, his actions stemmed from the anger within his heart (Gen. 4:7). Jesus makes such a point in his Sermon on the Mount: "You have heard that it was said to those of old, 'You shall not murder; and whoever murders will be liable to judgment.' But I say to you that everyone who is angry with his brother will be liable to judgment" (Matt. 5:22). The Heidelberg Catechism reiterates the words of Jesus precisely: "By forbidding murder God teaches us that he hates the root of murder: envy, hatred, anger, vindictiveness. In God's sight all such are murder" (A. 106). Therefore, sin is not only a violation of God's moral law in one's external behavior, but it is first and foremost a violation of God's moral law in one's *internal* attitude and desires. [4]

The internal nature of sin is a reminder that sin not only is rooted in one's internal motivations and desires—whereby the sinner fails to conform to what God has commanded—but sin is first and foremost due to our *corrupt moral nature* (see Questions 2 and 3). Our nature (that which is our very essence) does not escape the grip of sin. In short, we are sinners *by nature*. As Paul says in Ephesians 2:3, we "were by nature children of wrath, like the rest of mankind." Or as David acknowledges, we were "brought forth in iniquity" and we were conceived in sin (Ps. 51:5). In the end, when we rebelliously break God's moral law (Rom. 1:18–23; 2:23; 1 John 3:4), such an action is ultimately rooted in who we are as children of Adam in a post-Fall world. Most fundamentally, this means that sin does not first and foremost have to do with the bad things we do, but with our inherent condition as those in solidarity with Adam. Our sinful *actions* stem from our sinful *condition*.[5] Our wicked decisions reflect our polluted identity.

---

2. "Transgression" is another word that appropriately conveys the meaning of lawbreaking (see Num. 14:41–42; Deut. 17:2; 26:13; Jer. 34:18; Dan. 9:11; Hos. 6:7; 8:1; Rom. 2:23–27; Gal. 3:19; 1 Tim. 2:14; Heb. 2:2; 9:15).

3. Cornelius Plantinga Jr., *Not the Way It's Supposed to Be: A Breviary of Sin* (Grand Rapids: Eerdmans, 1995), 13.

4. For an extensive treatment of this point, see John Owen, *Overcoming Sin and Temptation* (Wheaton, IL: Crossway, 2015).

5. "The basic assumption is that we become bad people by doing bad things and we can correct this by doing good things instead. By contrast, Scripture locates sin deep within the fallen heart and treats it first of all as an all-encompassing *condition* that yields specific actions" (Michael Horton, *Pilgrim Theology: Core Doctrines for Christian Disciples* [Grand Rapids: Zondervan, 2011], 151).

Sin Is a Failure to Live in Covenant with God

This second point is a helpful qualification to the first point for this reason: Sin is not an impersonal violation of law but most fundamentally a violation against God himself. Remember, it is *God's* law that has been transgressed. Given that God is our covenant Lord, we can describe sin as covenant unfaithfulness. Ultimately, sin is not just a rupture in our covenantal relations with others but is most importantly a rupture in our covenantal relation with God (Ps. 51:4). Sin's offense is first vertical, then horizontal.

In the Old Testament God entered into a covenant relationship with his chosen people. As seen already, however, Israel's entire history was one of covenant infidelity. Though God's covenant was made with Abraham and confirmed with the patriarchs (Gen. 15:1–21; 17:1–14; 22:15–18; 26:24; 28:13–15; 35:9–12), and while God later covenanted with Israel through Moses (Exod. 6:2–8) and then Joshua (Josh. 24:1–27), nevertheless, Israel failed to keep the covenant God made with her at Sinai, despite the fact that God even sent prophets to warn them of the punishment that would result. Unquestionably, Israel's covenantal treachery was characterized by her habitual attitude of ingratitude toward God, her Savior and Redeemer.[6]

But God, in his great mercy and grace, spoke through his prophets of a day to come when he would establish a *new* covenant (Heb. 1:1–4). In this new covenant God would put his law within and write it on the heart. "I will be their God, and they shall be my people," he promised through Jeremiah (Jer. 31:33). In the new covenant all would know the Lord, for he promised to forgive their iniquity and remember their sin no more (31:34). Furthermore, God would give his people a new heart and a new spirit. He even promised to put *his* Spirit within, causing his people to walk in his statutes (Ezek. 36:26–27). Of course, this new covenant was accomplished through the blood of Jesus Christ, the great high priest (Heb. 8–10), and applied by the Holy Spirit (Acts 2:1–41; cf. Joel 2:28–32). New covenant believers, therefore, have been cleansed of all their uncleanness and idolatry (Ezek. 36:25). What great news: While man failed to live in covenant with God, God himself established a new covenant so that his redeemed people now live in communion with their Creator and Savior.

Sin Is Unbelief

So far we have looked at sin as the breaking of God's law and as covenant unfaithfulness, which really are the essence of sin. But describing sin *as unbelief* takes us deeper still into the inner chambers of the heart where we see the root reason and cause of man's transgressions. At the center of Adam and Eve's first sin is unbelief, a failure to trust in God.

---

6. David Smith, *With Willful Intent: A Theology of Sin* (Eugene, OR: Wipf and Stock, 1994), 317.

In Scripture unbelief is a central motif when describing sin. Those who receive eternal life are those who believe in Christ (John 3:16), while those who are condemned are those who do not believe in the name of God's one and only Son (John 3:18). According to Jesus, those who do not believe are spiritually blind (John 9:39–41). The sinner who rejects Christ and his words will be condemned by those same words on the last day (John 12:48). Additionally, when Jesus describes the Helper, the Spirit, Jesus states that he will "convict the world concerning sin and righteousness and judgment: concerning sin, because they do not believe in me" (John 16:6–9). In each of these passages, unbelief is sin, a sin that will bring judgment. And what sin could be greater than unbelief in God's own Son (John 10:25–38; 12:37–39; Matt. 12:22–32)?

Sin Is Idolatry

Sin as unbelief is a natural segue into sin as idolatry.[7] Those who do not believe in the one true God have instead turned to idols, idols of their own making. As we have already seen, certainly this was the case with Israel.[8] Indeed, the first commandment makes clear Yahweh's stance on idolatry: "You shall have no other gods before me" (Exod. 20:3). Nevertheless, from Sinai to Israel's exile, God's people chose to worship the idols of neighboring nations (Exod. 32:1–35; Num 25:1–5), despite the attempt of some to lead Israel in worshiping Yahweh alone (2 Chron. 15:8–18; 2 Kings 18:1–4; 23:4). In fact, idolatry was one of the major reasons God gave Israel over to her enemies resulting in her exile.[9]

Idolatry, however, is not limited to those who have special revelation (like Israel did). Those who only have general revelation commit idolatry as well. As Paul explains, though what can be known about God is "plain to them" (Rom. 1:19–20), they did not "honor him as God or give him thanks" but "exchanged his glory" for images of mortal man and animals (Rom. 1:22–23). They "exchanged the truth about God for a lie and worshiped and served the creature rather than the Creator, who is blessed forever! Amen" (Rom. 1:25). Idolatry is the height of *selfishness* because rather than loving, serving, obeying, worshipping, and giving one's Creator the honor that is reserved for him alone, one has elevated another, perhaps even oneself, instead. As R. Stanton Norman explains, "If love of God is the essence of all virtue, then the antithesis is the choice of self as the supreme end."[10]

---

7. Idolatry is when someone worships or exalts an object, person, and especially themselves in the place of God. Idolatry is trusting in a false god. In short, idolatry is worship of the creature (or created) instead of the Creator (see Gen. 11:4–9; Exod. 20:3; Deut. 5:7; Ps. 115:4–8; Isa. 40:18–20; Jer. 10:1–5; Mark 12:30; Rom. 1:22–25).

8. For an extensive study of idolatry, see G. K. Beale, *We Become What We Worship: A Biblical Theology of Idolatry* (Downers Grove, IL: InterVarsity Press, 2008).

9. Smith, *With Willful Intent*, 317.

10. R. Stanton Norman, "Human Sinfulness," in *A Theology for the Church*, ed. Daniel L. Akin, rev. ed. (Nashville: B&H Academic, 2007), 348.

The temptation for us today, in the twenty-first century, is to look back on the biblical time period and laugh: "How ridiculous to bow down and worship something you made with your own hands." There are two problems with such an attitude. (1) Millions of people all around the world today still practice such a form of idolatry (e.g., Eastern religions). In other words, the hands-on, very material/physical idolatry we see in biblical times is very much alive today. Therefore, it should not be dismissed or taken lightly. (2) Such an attitude overlooks the definition of idolatry—namely, the elevation and worship of *anything*, material or non-material, above God and instead of God. While some may choose to bow down to a god they have made out of wood or stone, for others their idolatry is far more sophisticated, worshipping sex, drugs, money, fame, politics, ideologies, etc. In short, no unbeliever escapes idolatry. There is something or someone he is placing on the throne of his or her life other than God himself. There is something or someone he loves *more* than God. Naturally, then, idolatry is the very opposite of the greatest commandment: "You shall love the Lord your God with all your heart and with all your soul and with all your mind" (Matt. 22:37–38; cf. Mark 12:30).

Sin as Pride

If idolatry reveals the selfishness of sin, pride will be exposed as well. Pride and selfishness go hand in hand, and both are present at the very start of mankind's history.[11] Many of the early church fathers, medieval theologians, and Reformers made such a point. For example, Augustine, in his commentary on Psalm 19:15, saw pride behind the first sin in the garden. John Calvin comments on Augustine's point, saying, "Hence it is not hard to deduce by what means Adam provoked God's wrath upon himself. Indeed, Augustine speaks rightly when he declares that pride was the beginning of all evils. For if ambition had not raised man higher than was meet and right, he could have remained in his original state."[12] If pride is an exalted view of oneself or a trust in one's own understanding (rather than God's wisdom), then it is not hard to see why pride is sin.[13]

In Scripture, pride lurks behind the sinful actions of both individuals and nations at every turn. When God pronounces his judgment on Edom, it is because of her pride that he sends invaders to destroy her (Jer. 49:16). Pride deceives the human heart, making it think it is safe when in reality the judgment of God is at hand. Consider Daniel 4:28, where Nebuchadnezzar boasts,

---

11. We can even go further and say pride, selfishness, idolatry, and rebellion all go hand in hand. See Norman, "Human Sinfulness," 351–53.
12. John Calvin, *Institutes of the Christian Religion*, ed. John T. McNeil, trans. Ford Lewis Battles, LCC, vols. 20–21 (Philadelphia: Westminster, 1960), 2.1.4.
13. Gerald B. Stanton, "Pride," *Baker's Dictionary of Theology* (Grand Rapids: Baker, 1973), 419; Donald K. McKim, "Pride," *Westminster Dictionary of Theological Terms* (Louisville: Westminster John Knox, 1996), 220.

claiming credit for the "great Babylon" which he built by his "mighty power" and for the glory of his majesty. What was God's response? God brought him to his knees, to crawl on all fours, to eat grass like an ox. When God restored him, Nebuchadnezzar gave glory and honor to God alone (4:34–37) and acknowledged that those who "walk in pride he [God] is able to humble" (4:37; cf. Ps. 73:6). Nebuchadnezzar experienced firsthand the wisdom of the proverb: "Pride goes before destruction, and a haughty spirit before a fall" (Prov. 16:18; cf. 28:5; Jer. 50:32).

Truly pride, as Proverbs 16:5 states, "is an abomination to the Lord" and will not go "unpunished" (cf. 6:17). It is no surprise that pride is considered the mother of other forms of sinfulness, including discontent, ingratitude, presumption, sensuality, perversion, treachery, extravagance, bigotry, hopelessness, indifference (apathy), and much more.[14] This is not to say that pride is the essence of sin, but nonetheless pride is encompassing and acts in many ways as a parent to other types of sinfulness.

The Viciousness of Sin

No matter how hard we try to escape it, the reality is that sin is destructive, vicious, dangerous, and deadly. Why? Not merely because sin threatens our very existence, both physically and spiritually, but first and foremost because sin ruins our relationship with God, our Creator. If our chief end in life is to glorify God and enjoy him forever, then sin dismantles such a purpose. We fail to give glory to God and instead, as Calvin said, become idol factories.[15] Our delight, treasure, and satisfaction in life is no longer in our Maker but in the things he has made. In short, the sinner is one who has "displaced God as the primary Object of his affection."[16] And we have done this, Paul states, by exchanging the "glory of the immortal God for images resembling mortal man" (Rom. 1:23). As a result, the one relationship we were made to live for has been destroyed. As seen with Adam and Eve, so also is it true with each and every one of us: Sin results in alienation. We live east of Eden.

Is this not a sobering reminder that sin's grip is just as tight as ever? In every way we transgress God's law, disbelieve his commands and promises, reject his covenant love, whore after false gods, and revel in our pride and self-righteousness. Sin is all around us. But worse, sin is everywhere within us. It defines us, our thoughts, our actions, and even our inclinations. There is no aspect of us that escapes sin. Paul's words are our words: "Wretched man that I am! Who will deliver me from this body of death?" (Rom. 7:24–25).

---

14. Smith, *With Willful Intent*, 155–334; Norman, "Human Sinfulness," 339–51.
15. Man's "nature is a perpetual factory of idols" (Calvin, *Institutes* 1.11.8).
16. Smith, *With Willful Intent*, 316.

Summary

Most fundamentally, sin is a failure to obey God's moral law. Sin, however, is not only a breach of God's moral law by one's external actions, but is rooted in one's internal attitude, motives, disposition, and ultimately is due to one's sinful nature inherited from Adam. Sin can also be defined as covenant unfaithfulness, unbelief, idolatry, and pride, among other things.

REFLECTION QUESTIONS

1. In what ways have you failed to uphold God's moral law?

2. What does Scripture say are the consequences of rebelling against God's commands?

3. What is idolatry and why is it so offensive to the God who not only created all things but deserves our exclusive worship?

4. How does pride act as a mother that gives birth to other sins?

5. Do you think non-Christians understand what a personal offense it is to live for themselves rather than God's glory (review Romans 1–2)?

Do We Inherit the Guilt and Corruption of Adam's Sin? (Part 1)

Few doctrines are as offensive to modern sensibilities as the evangelical doctrine of original sin. How is it that Adam's children can be guilty of a sin they did not commit? Is it not unjust for God to credit or impute the guilt of Adam's sin to our account? Surely Scripture does not teach such a doctrine as this!

Such cries of protest have been voiced not only by those outside of the Christian tradition but also by those within the Christian tradition.[1] However, as we will discover in this chapter and the next, the doctrine of original sin is taught in Scripture. Yes, it does strike against our modern sensibilities, but this is because it is a sobering reminder of our identity in Adam, an identity that exposes our guilt and corruption before a holy God.

Defining Original Sin

It is best to begin by defining what original sin is not. Original sin is not *actual* sin. Actual sin refers to man's choice to violate God's moral law in his thoughts and actions (see Question 1). Original sin refers to the state or condition man is born into. The doctrine of original sin consists of two aspects: guilt and corruption.[2] Guilt is a judicial and legal concept, depicting man's relationship to the law of God. Guilt means that man has broken and violated God's holy law and is liable to be punished, as was the case with Adam in Genesis 3.

---

1. Examples include: Karl Barth (1886–1968), Emil Brunner (1889–1966), Rudolf Bultmann (1884–1976), Reinhold Niebuhr (1892–1971).
2. "Original sin" is not referring to the first sin of Adam. Rather, the doctrine refers to the guilt and corruption all of mankind inherits from Adam. See Anthony A. Hoekema, *Created in God's Image* (Grand Rapids: Eerdmans, 1986), 143.

In regard to original sin, however, we must speak of the *hereditary* nature of Adam's guilt. Theologians have titled such a doctrine *inherited guilt*, meaning that all of mankind is counted guilty because of Adam's first sin. Adam's guilt, in other words, is *imputed* to all mankind. "Imputation" means to "reckon" to another person's "account."[3] When Adam sinned, the guilt he acquired was reckoned to all his progeny. As will be argued in what follows, Adam, acting as our representative, sinned and when he did so his guilt was transferred to his posterity so that all mankind is born into a state of condemnation and corruption. All of humanity stands in corporate solidarity with Adam.

On the other hand, corruption is a moral concept or category. The word "pollution" can be used as well since it describes our moral condition. In other words, while guilt addresses our status in relation to God's law, corruption or pollution addresses our moral nature.[4] In reference to original sin, not only is Adam's guilt imputed to his progeny, but as a result so is his corrupt nature.

The question before us now is whether or not these components of original sin are imputed to Adam's race, and if so, then, how exactly. In what follows, we will first discuss several theories concerning the transmission of original sin and then we will turn to Scripture to see which one is best supported.

The Transmission of Original Sin

Historically there have been four major theories concerning the "transmission" of Adam's sin:

1. *Pelagianism.* Pelagianism is a rejection of original sin and instead argues that Adam merely set a bad example. Each person after Adam is born neutral. Sin in our world today can be explained by man imitating Adam's sinful example.[5]

2. *Mediate Imputation.* Mankind has inherited Adam's corruption. By means of such corruption (i.e., mediate) mankind stands guilty in Adam. Guilt, therefore, is based on corruption, not vice versa lest God be arbitrary.[6] As Berkhof explains the view, "They are not born corrupt because they are guilty in Adam, but they are considered guilty because they are corrupt.

---

3. Charles Hodge, "Imputation," *ISBE* (Grand Rapids: Eerdmans, 1982), 2:812; R. K. Johnston, "Imputation," in *EDT*, ed. Walter A. Elwell (Grand Rapids: Baker, 1984), 554–55.
4. Hoekema, *Created in God's Image*, 149–50.
5. E.g., Pelagius (c. 350), Albert Barnes (1798–1870), C. K. Barrett (1917–2011), Emil Brunner (1889–1966), and Rudolph Bultmann (1884–1976). Two Catholics include Daryl Domning and Monika Hellwig whose view is dependent upon their denial of Adam's historicity.
6. E.g., Josué De La Place (or Josua Placeaus; 1596–1655), Samuel Hopkins, Timothy Dwight, Nathan Emmons, Henry Boynton Smith (1815–1877).

Their condition is not based on their legal status, but their legal status on their condition."[7]

3. *Realism*. Advocates of realism argue that God has created us as one human race with one generic human (or seminal) nature.[8] Physical presence, in other words, is the rope that ties us to Adam. When Adam sinned, therefore, human nature fell with him. Man is guilty since he shares in this generic human nature which was wholly in Adam when he sinned. This view especially appeals to Hebrews 7:9–10.

4. *Immediate Imputation (or Federalism)*. Advocates of immediate imputation argue that Adam's guilt is not mediated through corruption (as in mediate imputation), nor is our solidarity with Adam solely based on a realist conception of human nature.[9] Instead, Adam's guilt is immediate. We inherit his guilt *directly* and, logically speaking, our inherited corruption follows as a result. Adam is not only mankind's physical (natural) head, but federal representative as well. Therefore, when Adam sinned he represented his progeny. As a result, Adam's guilt was imputed directly to all of his children. And since his guilt is credited to mankind, each person is born into a state of pollution. The federalist view appeals especially to Romans 5:12–21.

While we cannot enter into a detailed critique of each view, a couple of observations are necessary.[10] First, the Pelagian view is out of the question as it is in direct conflict with passages like Romans 5:12–21, 1 Corinthians 15:21–22, and Ephesians 2:3 where Paul does connect our fallen identity to Adam not by Adam's imitation but by Adam's representation. In other words, Scripture does affirm original sin, whereas Pelagianism denies it. Out of all the positions mentioned above, the Pelagian position is unorthodox, declared heretical by early church councils (e.g., Carthage [418], Mileve [418], Ephesus [431]).

Second, the mediate imputation view struggles to explain why the guilt of Adam's first sin *alone* is imputed to us if it is mediated through the corruption we receive at birth. Also, texts like Romans 5:12–21 never indicate that

---

7. Louis Berkhof, *Systematic Theology* (Edinburgh: Banner of Truth, 2003), 243.
8. E.g., Tertullian (c. 160–220), Augustine (354–430), John Calvin (1509–1564), William G. T. Shedd (1820–1894), James H. Thornwell (1812–1862), and Augustus H. Strong (1836–1921).
9. E.g., Francis Turretin (1623–1687), the Westminster Confession of Faith (1647), the Savoy Declaration (1658), the Second London Confession (1689), Charles Hodge (1797–1878), Herman Bavinck (1854–1921), J. Gresham Machen (1881–1937), John Murray (1898–1975), Louis Berkhof (1873–1957).
10. For a full critique, see Hoekema, *Created in God's Image*, 156–67; Berkhof, *Systematic Theology*, 241–43.

Adam's guilt is mediated through corruption.[11] The word Paul uses to say that many were made sinners (*hamartōloi*) does not refer to being made corrupt or becoming corrupt. And last, the mediate view does not explain how it actually rids "guilt" from the original sin equation. Even if we merely say original sin means mankind inherits Adam's corruption, the very idea of corruption implies guilt's presence.[12]

Third, as attractive as the realist view is, it is incomplete. Yes, texts like Hebrews 7:9–10 show us that there is a unity at play between Adam and mankind in regards to a common human nature. However, Paul's analogy in Romans 5:12–21 says nothing of a generic human nature nor does he make this *the* rope that ties us to Adam and then to Christ.[13]

Additionally, the Adam-Christ language in Romans 5 is a parallel. Adam's federal representation results in the imputation of guilt, but Christ's federal representation results in the imputation of righteousness. Realism, however, breaks the parallel in Romans 5. On the one hand we are seminally united to Adam and in Adam, but it makes no sense to say that we are seminally united to Christ and in Christ. The realist has to concede, if his view is correct, that sinners are not identified with Christ in the same way as they are identified with Adam. By contrast, in the immediate imputation view the "means by which humanity participates in Adam's sin," says Fesko, "is the same manner in which believers participate in Christ's act of righteousness."[14] We are legally

---

11. Hoekema, *Created in God's Image*, 157. Berkhof acutely exposes other problems: "(1) A thing cannot be mediated by its own consequences. The inherent depravity with which the descendants of Adam are born is already the result of Adam's sin, and therefore cannot be considered as the basis on which they are guilty of the sin of Adam. (2) It offers no objective ground whatsoever for the transmission of Adam's guilt and depravity to all his descendants. Yet there must be some objective legal ground for this. (3) If this theory were consistent, it ought to teach the mediate imputation of the sins of all previous generations to those following, for their joint corruption is passed on by generation. (4) It also proceeds on the assumption that there can be moral corruption that is not at the same time guilt, a corruption that does not in itself make one liable to punishment. (5) And finally, if the inherent corruption which is present in the descendants of Adam can be regarded as the *legal* ground for the explanation of something else, there is no more need of any mediate imputation" (*Systematic Theology*, 243).
12. For a book-length treatment of this point, see J. V. Fesko, *Death in Adam, Life in Christ: The Doctrine of Imputations*, REDS (Fearn, Ross-shire, Scotland: Mentor, 2016).
13. Berkhof adds several other critiques in need of mention: "(1) By representing the souls of men as individualizations of the general spiritual substance that was present in Adam, it would seem to imply that the substance of the soul is of a material nature, and thus to land us inevitably in some sort of materialism. . . . (3) It does not explain why Adam's descendants are held responsible for his first sin only, and not for his later sins, nor for the sins of all the generations of forefathers that followed Adam. (4) Neither does it give an answer to the important question, why Christ was not held responsible for the *actual* commission of sin in Adam, for He certainly shared the same human nature, the nature that *actually* sinned in Adam" (*Systematic Theology*, 241–42).
14. See Fesko, *Death in Adam, Life in Christ*, 211.

guilty in Adam, yet declared legally righteous in Christ, thanks to his righteousness being reckoned or imputed to our account.

Out of all the views, the immediate imputation view is biblical for a variety of reasons. First, we will discuss a theological argument for immediate imputation, one rooted in the flow of redemptive history. Second, and in the next chapter, we will turn to the more detailed exegetical support for immediate imputation.

Theological Argument from Redemptive History

Adam: Our First Covenantal Head

The point we must begin with is this: Immediate imputation provides the proper categories for interpreting the narrative that unfolds in Genesis 3, specifically the covenant of works Adam enters into at creation. As we will see in Question 7, the Genesis narrative, and especially Paul's interpretation of that narrative in Romans 5:12–21, assumes that God has established a covenant with Adam. This covenant has stipulations (do not eat of the tree of the knowledge of good and evil), a sanction (death), and a promised reward (eternal life and communion with God). It also has a covenant maker (God) and a covenantal recipient (Adam) who represents his progeny (mankind).[15] The covenant maker has condescended, stooped down to Adam, in order to enter into this covenant with him.

It is called a covenant of works because Adam's entrance into a permanent state of life, holiness, and communion with God is conditioned upon his obedience to God's command. Others call it a covenant of creation since this covenant is situated within the creation narrative. Regardless of what we label it, God had promised Adam (and by consequence, his progeny) life, though it is conditioned upon flawless obedience to his command during this testing period.[16] Obedience, in other words, would have been rewarded with unlimited access to the "Tree of Life" (2:9; 3:22, 24; cf. Rev. 2:7). Submission to God's will would have resulted in Adam's justification.[17]

---

15. The covenant of/with creation shows similarities to other ancient Near Eastern treaties, which only strengthens the case for a covenant in Genesis 1–3. See Peter J. Gentry and Stephen J. Wellum, *God's Kingdom through God's Covenants: A Concise Biblical Theology* (Wheaton, IL: Crossway, 2015), 47–56.

16. "The first covenant made with man was a covenant of works (Gal. 3:12), wherein life was promised to Adam; and in him to his posterity (Rom. 5:12–20; 10:5), upon condition of perfect and personal obedience (Gen. 2:17; Gal. 3:10)" ("The Westminster Confession of Faith [1646/1647]," in *Reformed Confessions of the Sixteenth Century and Seventeenth Centuries in English Translation, Volume 4, 1600–1693*, ed. James T. Dennison Jr. [Grand Rapids: Reformation Heritage, 2014], 7.2).

17. Geerhardus Vos, *Reformed Dogmatics*, 5 vols., ed. Richard B. Gaffin, Jr. (Bellingham, WA: Lexham Press, 2012–2015), 4:138. Cf. Fesko, *Imputation*, 242–58.

Law and Gospel

In what we have outlined so far, notice the contrast between law and gospel. The covenant of creation tests Adam: Will he obey God's command, God's law? God's instruction has been made clear to Adam; it has been communicated by God to Adam verbally. And the moral obligation to obey one's Maker is something that inherently resides within Adam's own heart (and all since Adam), characterizing his moral DNA, since he is a creature made in the image of God. Since law is present, justice hangs in the balance, awaiting Adam's choice. As we will see soon enough, Adam's violation of God's law results in condemnation and the grave need for an external Word (a *verbum externum*) from God, an announcement of good news, news that can change Adam's status and condition (Gen. 3:15).[18]

The point is, at the very start of the Bible there is a contrast between law and gospel. The law holds us accountable and exposes our transgression before God our judge. The law brings us face to face with the righteousness *of* God. However, in the gospel God acts as our Savior and as a result we receive, as a gift, a righteousness *from* God.

Christ: Our New Covenantal Head

As we will see in the next chapter, Adam acts as our federal representative in this covenant of works, which Paul assumes in Romans 5 as he contrasts Adam's headship with Christ's headship. Unlike the Pelagian view, Adam is not acting for himself alone. No, he is our father, our head, our *covenantal* head in fact, and his choice has ramifications for us all. And unlike the realist view, Adam's tie to his progeny is not primarily biological but most fundamentally covenantal and forensic, as is apparent in how Paul parallels Adam's legal inheritance to Christ's.

Covenantal headship proves to be a crucial component. When Adam sinned, God imputed the guilt of the first sin of our covenant head to us, Adam's children.[19] Why? Because we are legally (forensically) represented by Adam.[20] As a result, we are not only born inheriting guilt but Adam's depravity as well. Adam's corrupt nature becomes our own at birth. In contrast

---

18. For a comparison between the *verbum externum* (external word) of the gospel and the *verbum internum* (internal word) of the law, see Horton, *Pilgrim Theology*, 133.

19. When I say God imputed the guilt of Adam's sin, I assume under such a phrase both *reatus culpa* and *reatus poenae*. In other words, imputation includes both guilt and penalty, not merely the former. See John Calvin, *Institutes of the Christian Religion*, ed. John T. McNeil, trans. Ford Lewis Battles, LCC, vols. 20–21 (Philadelphia: Westminster, 1960), 2.1.8; Zacharias Ursinus, *The Commentary of Dr. Zacharias Ursinus on the Heidelberg Catechism*, trans. G. W. Williard (1852; Phillipsburg, NJ: P&R, n. d.), 40; idem, *Corpus Doctrinae Christiane* (Hanoviae: Jonas Rosae, 1651), 43; Francis Turretin, *Institutes of Elenctic Theology*, 3 vols., ed. James T. Dennison Jr., trans. George Musgrave Giger (Phillipsburg, NJ: P&R Publishing, 1992–97), 1:640–58.

20. Berkhof, *Systematic Theology*, 242.

to the mediate imputation view, man is not born guilty because he is corrupt, but he is born corrupt because he is guilty in Adam.

The major advantage of the immediate imputation view is that it provides a rationale for *why* only Adam's first sin, and not all his subsequent sins, is imputed to our account. Adam's headship and representation applies only within the probationary period of the covenant of works. After that, the covenant has been broken; Adam and the rest of mankind now suffer the consequences. Adam's guilt is the basis for the corruption that follows. Mankind's only hope is the arrival of a second Adam, whose righteousness (instead of guilt) can be imputed to Adam's children. As Paul explains in Romans 5, this second Adam comes in the person of Christ. As our new covenant head, Christ represents us, obeying the law perfectly on our behalf, as well as suffering the penalty of the law that we have broken. While we were united to the first Adam and as a result inherited his condemned legal standing, we have now been united to the second Adam whose representation has resulted in the imputation of his righteousness, giving us a right legal standing before God. As Paul concludes with enormous excitement, "For if, because of one man's trespass, death reigned through that one man, much more will those who receive the abundance of grace and the free gift of righteousness reign in life through the one man Jesus Christ" (Rom. 5:17).

Conclusion

The insights of the realist view should not be cast aside, but adopted as far as they are biblical (e.g., Heb. 7:9–10). Yet at the same time, the realist position is insufficient in and of itself. Realism must be accompanied by, and grounded in, a federalist-immediate imputation view. In the next chapter we shall see why, biblically speaking, this is the case.

Summary

There have been many attempts to explain the transmission of original sin. The major views come down to four: (1) Pelagianism, (2) Mediate imputation, (3) Realism, and (4) Immediate Imputation. The immediate imputation position makes the best biblical sense of the covenantal structure described in Genesis 1–3 and Romans 5:12–21.

REFLECTION QUESTIONS

1. What consequences does the Pelagian view have for how we view mankind after the Fall?

2. What are the major weaknesses to the realist position?

3. In light of the differences between mediate and immediate imputation, should our inherited corruption stem from our inherited guilt, or should it be the other way around?

4. Which position best fits the context of Genesis 1–3 and Romans 5:12–21?

5. In what ways does Genesis 2 indicate that a covenant may be present in God's conversation with Adam?

Do We Inherit the Guilt and Corruption of Adam's Sin? (Part 2)

Now that original sin as immediate imputation has been defined, the question remains: Is such a doctrine taught in Scripture? Several biblical texts warrant a positive answer and demonstrate that far from a speculative doctrine, original sin stands upon a firm biblical foundation, one that will be key for the future conclusions we draw concerning salvation.

Scriptural Support for Immediate Imputation

Union with Adam vs. Union with Christ: Romans 5:12–21

Romans 5:12–21 is the *locus classicus* on original sin. Paul writes in verse 12, "Therefore, just as sin came into the world through one man, and death through sin, and so death spread to all men because all sinned." The "one man" referred to is Adam. Sin came into the world through Adam, and likewise death entered the world through Adam's sin (Gen. 2:17; 3:19).[1] Paul says, "death spread to all men because all sinned."[2] But what does Paul mean when he says "because all sinned."[3] He cannot have in mind

---

1. "Death" here is both physical and spiritual, as becomes evident in Romans 5:18–19 with the mention of "condemnation" (Thomas R. Schreiner, *Romans*, BECNT [Grand Rapids: Baker, 1998], 272).

2. John Murray, *The Epistle to the Romans*, NICNT (Grand Rapids: Eerdmans, 1968), 182.

3. ἐφ' ᾧ πάντες ἥμαρτον (*eph hō pantes hēmarton*). It is not accurate to render Paul's phrase "in whom all sinned" but rather "because all sinned." Augustine (354–430) made the mistake of translating verse 12 as if Paul had said that "in" Adam we all sinned, basing his interpretation on the Latin phrase *in quo omnes peccaverunt*. However, the Greek is ἐφ' ᾧ (*eph hō*), translated "on the basis of which." Nevertheless, as Schreiner observes, dismissing Augustine's grammatical mistake does not refute his view or "invalidate his exegesis of the text." "Many interpreters understand Romans 5:12 to say that death spread to all people because all people sinned in Adam. They do not derive such

the Pelagian view, namely, that Paul is referring to the *actual, personal* sins of all men, as if man sins by imitating Adam's example.[4] The *context* of Romans 5 demonstrates that Paul is comparing Adam and Christ (cf. Rom. 5:12–21). Adam stands in our stead, as our representative. In 5:12, and especially in 5:15–19, the death and condemnation of mankind is because of Adam's sin. Therefore, a reference to actual sins is precluded. "God views all of humanity as guilty of sin," asserts Fesko, "because of Adam's one transgression."[5]

Such solidarity in the sin of Adam is elaborated on when we consider the verses that follow next: "Therefore, just as sin came into the world through one man, and death through sin, and so death spread to all men because all sinned—for sin indeed was in the world before the law was given, but sin is not counted where there is no law. Yet death reigned from Adam to Moses, even over those whose sinning was not like the transgression of Adam, who was a type of the one who was to come" (Rom. 5:12–14). Paul acknowledges that from Adam to Moses there was no written law from God, as we see in the Ten Commandments for example.[6] Nevertheless, people still died. How can this be if sin is not counted where there is no law? Answer: On the basis of Adam's sin, all men who came thereafter were counted as guilty before God. As those guilty in Adam, death followed, even to those without the written Law.

One objection, however, to such an interpretation of Romans 5:12–14 is that Paul cannot be arguing that all those prior to Moses died because of Adam's sin, for it was their own sin that was the cause of their condemnation and death. After all, doesn't Paul argue in Romans 2:12 that those who sin without the law perish without the law? They perish because they have violated the law written on their hearts. How then can Paul be teaching in Romans 5 that death came because of Adam's sin, or more specifically, because Adam's guilt was imputed to all mankind?[7]

---

an interpretation from the prepositional phrase in Romans 5:12. They maintain that the parenthetical comments in Romans 5:13–14 compel such an interpretation" (Thomas R. Schreiner, *Paul, Apostle of God's Glory in Christ: A Pauline Theology* [Downers Grove, IL: InterVarsity Press, 2006], 146; cf. Douglas Moo, *The Epistle to the Romans*, NICNT [Grand Rapids: Eerdmans, 1996], 321–22).

4. Schreiner, *Romans*, 289.

5. See J. V. Fesko, *Death in Adam, Life in Christ: The Doctrine of Imputation*, REDS (Fearn, Ross-shire, Scotland: Mentor, 2016), 209.

6. Hence, when Paul says that "sin is not counted where there is no law" and the sinning of those before the Law "was not like the transgression of Adam, who was a type of the one who was to come," Paul means that the sins of those after Adam were not like Adam's sin. Those who came after Adam were not functioning in the unique role of a representative, having a typological function as the head of all humanity.

7. This question is raised in Thomas R. Schreiner, "Original Sin and Original Death: Romans 5:12–19," in *Adam, the Fall, and Original Sin: Theological, Biblical, and Scientific*

In response, it must be acknowledged that it is true that all those living before the coming of the Mosaic Law were condemned before God as transgressors of the law written on their hearts. This much is obvious from the story of the flood in Genesis 6–8, the Tower of Babel in Genesis 11, and countless other examples of sin before the advent of the Law at Sinai. But to affirm the doctrine of imputed guilt from a text like Romans 5 is *not* to deny that all those before Moses added to their condemnation by the actual sins they committed.

That said, appealing to the actual sins committed before Sinai as a *comprehensive* explanation (or as the *sole* explanation) as to why "death spread to all men" in Romans 5 is insufficient for it does not account for (1) how it is that through one man death spread to all men "because all sinned" (Rom. 5:12), (2) how it is that Adam's sin results in a *universal reign* of sin, or (3) how it is that Paul can compare Adam to Christ and say "as one trespass led to condemnation for all men, so one act of righteousness leads to justification and life for all men" (Rom. 5:17). Yes, all those who came before Moses did commit grave acts of sin that only furthered their condemnation before a holy God, and they did so in defiance against the law written on their hearts. Nevertheless, the fundamental reason for death and condemnation before Sinai is because Adam represented all men when he sinned and his guilt was imputed to all men as a result. Stated otherwise: In Romans 5, the ultimate basis for death before the advent of the written Law is the fact that all men have inherited the guilt of their father Adam. It is this inherited guilt ("condemnation"; cf. Rom. 5:17) that inevitably leads to and results in the corruption of man's nature and the practice of wickedness, not vice versa.[8]

The case for inherited guilt is only strengthened when we read what Paul says in 5:16–19:

> And the free gift is not like the result of that one man's sin. For the judgment following one trespass brought condemnation, but the free gift following many trespasses brought justification. For if, because of one man's trespass, death reigned through that one man, much more will those who receive the abundance of grace and the free gift of righteousness reign in life through the one man Jesus Christ. Therefore, as one trespass led to condemnation for all men,

---

Perspectives, eds. Hans Madueme and Michael Reeves (Grand Rapids: Baker Academic, 2014), 271–88, though Schreiner comes to a different conclusion.

8. Some, however, reject such an interpretation of Romans 5:12–14, but nonetheless still think imputed guilt is affirmed by Paul in Romans 5:15–19. For example, see Schreiner, "Original Sin and Original Death," 272–81.

so one act of righteousness leads to justification and life for all men. For as by the one man's disobedience the many were made sinners, so by the one man's obedience the many will be made righteous.

Paul is completing and elaborating upon the comparison he started in verse 12. Because of Adam's trespass, all men are condemned before God. The language of "condemnation" is significant. The judgment unto condemnation for all men was based on the one trespass of Adam. As Murray argues, "The [judicial] sentence needed only the one trespass to give it validity and sanction; in fact, the one trespass demanded nothing less than the condemnation of all."[9] What is shocking here is that "condemnation" (*katakrima*) is not limited to Adam. "The surrounding context (5:15–19) demonstrates that the condemnation extends to all people because of Adam's one sin." Therefore, says Schreiner, "Here we see the "scandal of original sin."[10] The text never says we are condemned because of our own individual sin (though this is true in general), but rather the text conveys how we enter this world guilty, condemned because of Adam's sin. And notice, observes Schreiner, "Paul does not defend or apologize for such a notion," but "simply asserts it."[11] Everyone is born into this world condemned before a holy God because of Adam's one transgression.

Moreover, Paul is comparing and contrasting condemnation and justification. Paul could not be clearer than he is in verses 18–19. Just as Christ's one act of righteousness results in *justification*, so did Adam's one act of disobedience result in *condemnation*.[12] The former resulted in the abundance of grace and the free gift of righteousness because of the one man, Christ, while the latter resulted in death and judgment because of the one man, Adam. We must not shy away from the *forensic* language Paul uses (sin, transgression, judgment, condemnation, justification, righteousness).[13] In Adam we are constituted guilty, but in Christ we are constituted righteous. "We are constituted sinners in Adam," says Turretin, "in the *same way* in which we are constituted righteous in Christ."[14]

---

9. Murray, *The Epistle to the Romans*, 196.
10. Schreiner, "Original Sin and Original Death: Romans 5:12–19," 283.
11. Ibid.
12. Ibid., 285–86.
13. Murray, *Romans*, 205; Richard C. Gamble, *God's Mighty Acts in the Old Testament*, The Whole Counsel of God, vol. 1 (Phillipsburg, NJ: P&R, 2009), 210.
14. Emphasis added. Francis Turretin, *Institutes of Elenctic Theology*, 3 vols., ed. James T. Dennison Jr., trans. George Musgrave Giger (Phillipsburg, NJ: P&R Publishing, 1992–97), 1:618 Hodge is just as insightful: "In virtue of the union, representative and natural, between Adam and his posterity, his sin is the ground of their condemnation, that is, of their subjection to penal evils; and that, in virtue of the union between Christ and his people,

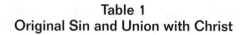

Table 1
Original Sin and Union with Christ

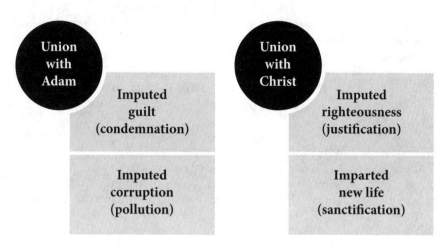

Also, it is impossible to avoid the language of representation in Romans 5. Adam acted as our representative when he sinned. On the other hand, Christ acted as our representative when he obeyed God.[15] In other words, Adam was a type of Christ in that he acted as our head, just as Christ did.[16] Again, the language of representation inevitably leads us to the doctrine of imputation. "It can only be that of imputation," claims Murray, "that by reason of representative unity the sin of Adam is reckoned to our account and therefore reckoned as ours with all the entail of implication and consequence which sin carries with it. In the judicial judgment of God the sin of Adam is the sin of all."[17] Because of our solidarity with Adam, his guilt is imputed to our account (see Questions 24 and 25). Yet, because of our solidarity with Christ, his righteousness is imputed to our account; similarly because of our relation to Adam, his disobedience is reckoned to us, but because of our relation to Christ, his obedience is reckoned to us. While the former led to our condemnation, the latter has led to our justification.[18]

Additionally, the phrase "the many were made sinners" (Rom. 5:19) refers to an action completed in the past. God considered all people guilty

his righteousness is the ground of their justification" (Charles Hodge, *A Commentary on the Epistle to the Romans* [New York: Robert Carter & Brothers, 1880], 135).

15. Murray, *The Epistle to the Romans*, 202.

16. Anthony A. Hoekema, *Created in God's Image* (Grand Rapids: Eerdmans, 1986), 149.

17. Murray, *The Epistle to the Romans*, 205.

18. One might object that if we affirm imputation then we must also believe that all of Adam's sins are imputed to his progeny. But this is not what Paul says. Paul attributes our death only to Adam's first sin.

(sinners) when Adam sinned. Though we did not yet exist, we were guilty like Adam. Paul is arguing that it was through *Adam's* sin that "all sinned." Due to our union with Adam, when Adam sinned we fell with him in God's sight. Therefore, it is Adam's sin that serves as the ground upon which death penetrates to all of mankind.[19]

Such a mystery can be better understood when we compare the reverse, namely, salvation in Christ. Paul says in Romans 5:8, "but God shows his love for us in that while we were still sinners, Christ died for us" (2 Cor. 5:21). The assumption, therefore, is that God saw us in Adam as *guilty sinners* in need of salvation through his Son.

The First Man Adam: 1 Corinthians 15:45–49

Besides Romans 5, the doctrine of original sin can also be supported by passages like 1 Corinthians 15, where Paul again conveys that Adam was our representative when he sinned. Like Romans 5, Paul contrasts Adam and Christ in 1 Corinthians 15:21–22, "For as by a man came death, by a man has come also the resurrection of the dead. For as in Adam all die, so also in Christ shall all be made alive." Later on, Paul states, quoting from Genesis 2:7, that "'The first man Adam became a living being'; the last Adam became a life-giving spirit" (1 Cor. 15:45).

What does Paul intend to convey by calling Christ the "last Adam"? Paul is implying that Adam's representation of us is analogous to Christ's representation of us. Both Adam and Christ serve as our head, though in different senses, the former being our head unto condemnation and the latter being our head unto justification.[20] Just as in Adam we all die, in Christ we are made alive.[21] All those in Adam share his banishment, alienation, guilt, corruption, and death. Such is the meaning of being Adam's posterity, bound to him in corporate solidarity. What was his is now ours. Likewise, with our union with Christ. Those in Christ share his victory, righteousness, and resurrection life. Though in Adam we received condemnation, in Christ we receive new life and justification. Therefore, the fate of the group is determined by the representative.[22]

Conclusion

What then are we to conclude from these key biblical passages? We should conclude that Adam represented all of mankind when he sinned, so much so that his guilt was imputed to our account. Just as we were counted just on the

---

19. Murray, *The Epistle to the Romans*, 182.
20. Hoekema, *Created in God's Image*, 149.
21. Roy E. Ciampa and Brian S. Rosner, *The First Letter to the Corinthians*, PNTC (Grand Rapids: Eerdmans, 2010), 763.
22. David Garland, *1 Corinthians*, BECNT (Grand Rapids: Baker, 2003), 707; Anthony C. Thiselton, *The First Epistle to the Corinthians*, NIGTC (Grand Rapids: Eerdmans, 2000), 1225.

basis of the one act of righteousness by Christ, so also were we counted guilty on the basis of Adam's one act of disobedience.

Summary

When Adam sinned he acted as our representative. As a result, all of mankind was counted guilty because of Adam's sin. Because there is corporate solidarity in Adam, his guilt was imputed to all his posterity. Such a doctrine is analogous to our union with Christ (e.g., Rom. 5:12–21). Adam acted as our covenant representative resulting in our guilt and condemnation; Christ has acted as our new covenant representative resulting in our righteousness and justification.

REFLECTION QUESTIONS

1. How does the doctrine of imputed guilt make sense of the world of sin and wickedness we live in?

2. Do you feel as though it is unfair for you to be counted guilty because of Adam's sin?

3. In what ways has an individualistic mindset influenced our reading of the biblical text when it comes to the doctrine of imputed guilt?

4. How does the concept of imputed guilt assist you in better understanding the imputed righteousness of Christ?

5. Does imputed guilt give you a greater hatred for sin and a greater longing to see Christ return?

Are We Totally Depraved?

In the previous chapter we discovered that all of mankind inherits Adam's guilt. Because of Adam's sin, guilt is imputed to our account, since Adam acted as our covenantal representative. However, not only do we inherit guilt from Adam, but as a result we also inherit a sinful nature from Adam. "Everyone who is guilty in Adam is, as a result, also born with a corrupt nature," observes Louis Berkhof.[1] Theologians call this doctrine "inherited corruption" or "inherited pollution."[2] These phrases convey the idea that because of Adam's sin, all of us are born with a depraved nature. But that raises a question: Just how corrupt are we? And are we, as some say, totally depraved? Does this inherited pollution extend to every aspect of our being?

What Total Depravity Does and Does Not Mean

Because we have inherited a depraved nature from Adam, no aspect of our nature escapes depravity. Calvin summarizes Scripture eloquently: "All parts of the soul were possessed by sin after Adam deserted the fountain of righteousness. For not only did a lower appetite seduce him, but unspeakable impiety occupied the very citadel of his mind and pride penetrated to the depths of his heart." The consequence is devastating: "None of the soul remains pure or untouched by that moral disease." And "the mind is given over to blindness and the heart to depravity."[3] In other words, we are totally

---

1. Louis Berkhof, *Systematic Theology* (Edinburgh: Banner of Truth, 2003), 233.
2. Berkhof adds several important qualifications: "Original pollution includes two things, namely, the absence of original righteousness, and the presence of positive evil. It should be noted: (1) That original pollution is not merely a disease. . . . (2) That this pollution is not to be regarded as a substance infused into the human soul, nor as a change of substance in the metaphysical sense of the word. . . . (3) That it is not merely a privation . . . it is also an inherent positive disposition toward sin" (ibid., 246).
3. John Calvin, *Institutes of the Christian Religion*, ed. John T. McNeil, trans. Ford Lewis Battles, LCC, vols. 20–21 (Philadelphia: Westminster, 1960), 2.1.9.

depraved, meaning that every part of our being (mind, will, emotions, etc.) is polluted by sin.

Regretfully, many have misunderstood the doctrine of total depravity. So, it is wise to begin by explaining what total depravity does *not* mean. First, total depravity does not mean we are as depraved as we possibly can be—an unfortunate misinterpretation of the word "total." Due to God's common grace, unbelievers do not indulge in every form of sin or even the worst of sins. God graciously restrains evil in the world (Gen. 9:6; Rom. 13:4). Second, total depravity does not mean that man cannot discern between good and evil. Man does possess a conscience, knowing right from wrong. Total depravity doesn't preclude man from possessing innate knowledge of God's will (Rom. 2:14–15). Third, total depravity does not mean man fails to act in ways that benefit others, or in ways that show his appreciation for the good deeds of others. Thanks to common grace, there is civil good that remains in society, despite the corruption that simultaneously exists (2 Kings 12:2; 2 Chron. 24:2; Luke 6:33; Rom. 13:4).

Now that we have clarified what total depravity does *not* mean, what exactly *does* it mean for man to be pervasively depraved? First, total depravity means that the corruption we have inherited from Adam has penetrated to *every* aspect of our nature. All of our faculties have been polluted, not just a limited few. Total depravity, in other words, is the internal corruption of the whole human being. For this reason, some prefer to speak of "pervasive" or "radical" depravity.

Second, total depravity means that we cannot do any spiritual good that pleases God. Instead, we are slaves to sin (see Question 5). As the Heidelberg Catechism asserts, we "are wholly incapable of doing any good, and inclined to all evil" (Q. 8). While unbelievers may accomplish civil good in society, these deeds are never done out of a love, reverence, and devotion to God. The "good" unbelievers do towards their fellow man is never done out of faith in Christ. The "good" deeds of unbelievers before a perfect and holy God are but filthy rags (Isa. 64:6), empty of any saving merit, failing to proceed from faith.

Total Depravity in Scripture

The doctrine of total depravity colors the storyline of the Bible from beginning to end. Not long after the fall we read of Adam's descendants: "The Lord saw that the wickedness of man was great in the earth, and that every intention of the thoughts of his heart was only evil continually" (Gen. 6:5; cf. 8:21). Notice, not only man's actions but even the intentions of the thoughts of his heart were evil continually. In Hebrew anthropology the heart is the very nucleus, the center, of man's being (Gen. 31:20; Ps. 33:11; 1 Sam. 10:26).[4] Man's depravity is not superficial but has penetrated to the very core of his

---

4. Kenneth A. Mathews, *Genesis 1–11:26*, NAC, vol. 1a (Nashville: B&H, 1996), 341.

essence. Furthermore, the text says the thoughts of man's heart were "only" evil continually. Not even a drop of good was mixed in with it.[5]

Even after God blots man out by means of a flood (Gen. 6:7), the depravity of man continues to show itself, as the Tower of Babel (Gen. 11:1–9) and the obliteration of Sodom and Gomorrah demonstrate (Gen. 18–19). Sadly, even Israel, God's chosen people, did what was right in their own eyes (Judg. 21:25), revealing the venality of their heart (Deut. 12:8). King David's words are blunt and sobering: "They are corrupt, they do abominable deeds, there is none who does good. The Lord looks down from heaven on the children of man, to see if there are any who understand, who seek after God. They have all turned aside; together they have become corrupt; there is none who does good, not even one" (Ps. 14:1–3; cf. Rom. 3:10). Based on Psalm 14, two observations deserve mention: (1) David says man is "corrupt," meaning he is sour, rotten, infected, vile, and polluted (cf. Ps 53:3).[6] Depravity is not limited to one aspect of man's being but has infiltrated every facet. (2) Do not miss the repetition: "all," "together," "none," and "not even one." Depravity is not only pervasive in its impact on man's being, but it is *universal*, leaving no person untouched. As David says in Psalm 143:2, "no one living is righteous before you."

Additionally, David believes such depravity characterizes man from birth. In 2 Samuel 11, for example, David commits adultery with Bathsheba, the wife of Uriah the Hittite. When David discovers Bathsheba is pregnant, he conspires to have Uriah struck down by the enemy in battle in order to cover his sin (2 Sam. 11:15). The Lord was very displeased, so he sent Nathan to confront David of his sin (12:9). David, pierced to the heart, responds to Nathan, confessing, "I have sinned against the LORD" (12:13). In Psalm 51:1–4 we receive further insight into David's distress. David cries out to God for mercy, asking God to blot out his transgressions and wash him of his iniquity. Notice what David says in verse 5: "Behold, I was brought forth in iniquity, and in sin did my mother conceive me." Overwhelmed by his own sinfulness, David confesses that from conception he was sinful before the Lord. Even in his mother's womb he had a sinful nature, a disposition and inclination toward sin. Hence, he can say he was "brought forth in iniquity." As David says in Psalm 58:3, "The wicked are estranged from the womb; they go astray from birth, speaking lies."

Of course, David is not alone in his outlook. We read in Job 15:16 that men are "abominable and corrupt," drinking "injustice like water!" Job concludes, "Man who is born of a woman is few of days and full of trouble. . . . Who can bring a clean thing out of an unclean? There is not one" (Job 14:1, 3; cf. Ps. 143:2). And Solomon asks rhetorically, "Who can say, 'I have made my

5. John Calvin, *Commentaries on the First Book of Moses Called Genesis*, trans. John King (Grand Rapids: Baker, 1996), 1:248.

6. Willem A. VanGemeren, *Psalms*, EBC, vol. 5 (Grand Rapids: Zondervan, 2008), 176–77.

heart pure; I am clean from my sin?'" (Prov. 20:9). Answer: no one! Also observe the words of Ecclesiastes: "Surely there is not a righteous man on earth who does good and never sins" (Eccl. 7:20; cf. Ps. 143:2). Likewise Ecclesiastes 9:3 reads, "The hearts of the children of man are full of evil, and madness is in their hearts while they live, and after that they go to the dead." Isaiah says the same: "All we like sheep have gone astray; we have turned—every one—to his own way" (Isa. 53:6). And again: "We have all become like one who is unclean, and all our righteous deeds are like a polluted garment" (Isa. 64:6a). The prophet Jeremiah agrees: "The heart is deceitful above all things, and desperately sick; who can understand it?" (Jer. 17:9; cf. Ezek. 36:26).

The New Testament affirms total depravity as well. When Jesus confronts the Pharisees over ritual cleanliness (i.e., washing one's hands before a meal), he explains that it is what comes out of man that defiles him, not what goes into him. "For from within, out of the heart of man, come evil thoughts, sexual immorality, theft, murder, adultery, coveting, wickedness, deceit, sensuality, envy, slander, pride, foolishness. All these evil things come from within, and they defile a person" (Mark 7:21–23; cf. Exod. 20:13–15; John 5:42–44). Man's problem is not that his hands are dirty but that his heart, his innermost nature, is defiled. In piling one sinful characteristic upon another, Jesus communicates just how wicked man is. Man's depravity is not qualified, but it is radical indeed. The love of God is not within any man; each and every one of us has rejected the supremacy of God over our lives, and we have instead sought glory from one another (John 5:42). This theme runs throughout the teachings of Jesus and the Gospel writers (John 1:13; 3:6; 5:42; 6:44; 8:34; 15:4–5).

As straightforward as these passages are, no one paints man's corruption as dimly as Paul in Romans 1:

> For although they knew God, they did not honor him as God or give thanks to him, but they became futile in their thinking, and their foolish hearts were darkened. Claiming to be wise, they became fools, and exchanged the glory of the immortal God for images resembling mortal man and birds and animals and reptiles. Therefore God gave them up in the lusts of their hearts to impurity, to the dishonoring of their bodies among themselves, because they exchanged the truth about God for a lie and worshiped and served the creature rather than the Creator, who is blessed forever! Amen. For this reason God gave them up to dishonorable passions. For their women exchanged natural relations for those that are contrary to nature; and the men likewise gave up natural relations with women and were consumed with passion for one another, men committing shameless acts with men and receiving in themselves the due penalty for their error. And since they did not see fit to

acknowledge God, God gave them up to a debased mind to do what ought not to be done. They were filled with all manner of unrighteousness, evil, covetousness, malice. They are full of envy, murder, strife, deceit, maliciousness. They are gossips, slanderers, haters of God, insolent, haughty, boastful, inventors of evil, disobedient to parents, foolish, faithless, heartless, ruthless. Though they know God's decree that those who practice such things deserve to die, they not only do them but give approval to those who practice them (Rom. 1:21–32).

If there was any doubt that man has inherited a corrupt nature, or any doubt that this nature is pervasively depraved, then Paul has removed it. The wrath of God burns hot because man has refused to give honor and glory to God. His heart is dark, exchanging divine glory for created images, engaging himself in despicable passions of the flesh. Man is filled with every "manner of unrighteousness." Like Jesus, Paul piles one evil characteristic on top of another, demonstrating the pervasive nature of man's depravity. Wickedness, covetousness, and maliciousness "accentuates the totality of the depravity involved and the intensity with which it had been cultivated."[7] We are left with only one conclusion: man is hopeless, lost, corrupt, and condemned before God (cf. Rom. 3:9–20; 8:5–7). Paul's striking words to the Ephesians seem to say it all: "And you were dead in the trespasses and sins in which you once walked, following the course of this world, following the prince of the power of the air, the spirit that is now at work in the sons of disobedience—among whom we all once lived in the passions of our flesh, carrying out the desires of the body and the mind, and were by nature children of wrath, like the rest of mankind" (2:1–3). Every single person is corrupt, lost in darkness, futility, alienation from God, hardness of heart, and bondage to sin.[8] Naturally, in Ephesians 2 there is a heavy sense of condemnation. By nature man stands under divine wrath.

Total Depravity and the Gospel

What implications does a doctrine like total depravity have for the Christian life?

1. Unbelievers are not neutral. One of today's most common misconceptions about our human condition is that we are born into this world morally neutral. Nothing could be further from the truth. What we have seen in this chapter is that each and every one of us is born into this world having inherited the corruption of Adam, our covenant head.[9] On a practical level,

---

7. John Murray, *The Epistle to the Romans*, NICNT (Grand Rapids: Eerdmans, 1979), 1:50.
8. Frank Thielman, *Ephesians*, BECNT (Grand Rapids: Baker, 2010), 127.
9. This also means that, fundamentally, we sin because we are sinners, not the other way around.

what this means is that we enter this world with a sinful disposition. To make matters worse, no part of us escapes the pollution of sin. Our corruption is so pervasive that even our innermost, secret thoughts are not exempt.

Therefore, we must realize that there are no good people in God's eyes (Rom. 3:10–12). Should we be like the Pharisee, claiming our own righteousness, then we will be condemned, for there is no self-righteousness to lean on (Luke 18:11–12, 14). Everything we have is stained crimson. Only he who is like the tax collector, beating his chest, crying out, "God, be merciful to me, a sinner!" will be justified before God (Luke 18:13–14). Such a biblical reality should completely change how we view the world around us, which leads to our next point.

2. Gospel-centered evangelism takes into account man's corrupt condition. If we view unbelievers as morally neutral, or as injured but nonetheless still very spiritually capable, then the gospel makes little to no sense. Men do not need a Savior, but merely a moral reformer *par excellence*. "If we are merely inhibited by Adam's poor example," says Horton, "then all that we need is a better example, not a divine-human Redeemer."[10] But what we see in Scripture differs considerably. Man is not neutral, nor is he merely in need of improvement or assistance. Man is spiritually dead. What lost sinners need is a spiritual resurrection (see Questions 15–17).

The implications for evangelism and salvation are significant. Consider two: First, the gospel we preach is a gospel *for sinners*. As Jesus himself said, he came to seek and save the lost (Luke 10:19). Hence, the religious leaders of his day looked at Jesus and called him a drunkard and a glutton, a friend of tax collectors and sinners (Luke 11:19). Why? In part, it was because these are the types of people Jesus spent his time with. For example, after calling Matthew, a tax collector, the Pharisees question Jesus's actions, to which he responds, "Those who are well have no need of a physician, but those who are sick. . . . For I came not to call the righteous, but sinners" (Matt. 9:12–13b). When we share the gospel let's be clear: We are not trying to give people a moral improvement plan to better enhance their lives. Nor are we trying to persuade them to simply add Jesus on top of their own good works or efforts. Quite the contrary, we walk in the midst of a graveyard yet we do so knowing that the Spirit is able to resurrect the dead through the preached Word (Ezek. 37). In short, we come with a gospel that saves sinners. We adopt Paul's mindset: "For I am not ashamed of the gospel, for it is the power of God for salvation to everyone who believes, to the Jew first and also to the Greek" (Rom. 1:16).

Second, man's corrupt condition means we must preach the bad news *before* we preach the good news. Sometimes the unbeliever is given the impression that Jesus is available to make his/her life better. But such an approach fails to take into consideration the awful plight of every unbeliever. Unless the

---

10. Michael Horton, *For Calvinism* (Grand Rapids: Zondervan, 2011), 51.

unbeliever first sees the condemned and polluted condition he is in, he will never see his need for a Savior. "The gospel does not center on whether God has some exciting plans for our lives," clarifies Horton, "but on whether we will be alienated from him for eternity."[11] Unless we take seriously the corrupt condition man is in, we run the risk of misunderstanding what the gospel is all about. The message of the gospel must begin with bad news. If it does not, the good news seems irrelevant and unnecessary.

Grace is just not amazing if conviction of sin does not precede the message of the cross. Therefore, the starting point must be a vertical one: You are a sinner, guilty and corrupt, and you have offended God who is perfectly holy and just. Your only hope is to be reconciled to God through Christ Jesus his Son.[12] Therein lies your salvation.

Summary

All of humanity is born with a sinful, corrupt nature, inherited from Adam our representative. Man is totally depraved, meaning that the corruption he has inherited extends to all of his faculties (intellect, will, affections, etc.). Therefore, sinners can in no way do anything spiritually good toward God since they are slaves to sin.

REFLECTION QUESTIONS

1. Review the biblical passages in this chapter. Is total depravity central to understanding the storyline of Scripture?

2. Since everyone is by nature a child of wrath (Eph. 2:1–3), how serious then is the sinner's need for divine grace?

3. Looking back on your life before you became a Christian, how was total depravity evident in the way you lived?

4. Does the doctrine of total depravity resonate with your everyday experience with people in the world?

5. How does a biblical understanding of total depravity lead you to pray differently for the salvation of unbelievers?

---

11. Michael Horton, *Putting Amazing Back into Grace: Embracing the Heart of the Gospel* (Grand Rapids: Baker, 2011), 86.
12. Ibid., 87.

Do We Need God's Grace to Be Freed from Sin?

Can the Ethiopian change his skin or the leopard his spots? Then also you can do good who are accustomed to do evil.
—Jeremiah 13:23

Perhaps this seems like an odd question from the prophet Jeremiah. Actually, by turning our eyes to the Ethiopian's skin and the leopard's spots, Jeremiah draws a creative illustration about our depravity. The wicked can in no way do what is right and good in the sight of God. It is as impossible as changing one's skin color. It's as unthinkable as removing the leopard's spots. Jeremiah's point is well taken: Evil is entrenched in man's character. He is like a diseased tree that cannot bear any good fruit (Matt. 7:18). Or as Calvin humorously said, "Faced with God's revelation, the unbeliever is like an ass at a concert."[1] The unbeliever, due to his inherited depravity, is enslaved to the foolishness of this world. He cannot even begin to understand the spiritual things of God in a saving way. If the sinner is to be born again it will be due to God alone, not to "the will of man" (John 1:12–13; 3:5).

Defining Spiritual Inability

Man's bondage, or spiritual inability, must be carefully defined, lest we risk misunderstanding it entirely.

First, spiritual inability means that the sinner can in no way meet the perfect demands of God's holy law, nor is he able to turn toward God in faith and repentance.

---

1. Calvin is commenting on 1 Corinthians 1:20. John Calvin, *Opera quae supersuni omnia* (Brunsvigae: C. A. Schwetschke, 1863-98), 49:325.

Second, spiritual inability means that the sinner is unable to overcome or change his inclinations for sin in order to love God instead. Due to being born with a corrupt nature, the sinner is inevitably predisposed toward sin, unable to perform any deed that is spiritually pleasing in God's sight. This does not mean that man has lost his rational faculties (knowledge, reason, conscience, will, etc.). Those remain intact. However, it does mean that man, by nature, has an irresistible predisposition for evil. Therefore, though man's rational faculties remain, they are inclined toward sin.

Third, spiritual inability is not only bondage to sin, but it is *willful* bondage. Many object to spiritual inability, arguing that if man is unable to obey God then he cannot be held responsible. However, as we will see, Paul sees no such inconsistency. Man is held responsible for his sin even though he cannot keep God's law.[2] How can this be? The tension is resolved when we realize that while man is enslaved to sin, nevertheless, this slavery is a willful one. In short, man loves sin. It is not as if man wants to come to God but is prohibited by the chains of his sinful nature. No, the sinner hates God and wants nothing more than to indulge himself in sin. Yes, sin is his master, but he would not have it any other way. The sinner is not forced against his will, but he gladly falls before the altar of sin, doing its bidding, willfully making sin his master.

"No one can come to me": Jesus on Total Depravity

Man's impotence is explicitly affirmed by Jesus. In John 6:44 Jesus states without qualification, "No one can come to me unless the Father who sent me draws him." The sinner is spiritually incapable of coming to Jesus. He is not merely hindered but actually enslaved to sin. As Jesus says in John 8:34, "Truly, truly, I say to you, everyone who commits sin is a slave to sin" (cf. Rom. 6:6, 17, 19–20; 2 Peter 2:19). Man's imprisonment to sin is not only evidenced in the fact that he practices sin, but his practice of sin actively enslaves him.[3] Furthermore, this enslavement to sin is habitual in nature.[4] "At issue here is not so much the commission of distinct acts of sin, but remaining in a state of sin," says Andreas Köstenberger.[5]

Likewise, in John 8 Jesus gets to the very reason for man's disbelief and bondage to sin. "Why do you not understand what I say? It is because you cannot bear to hear my word. You are of your father the devil, and your will is to do your father's desires. . . . But because I tell the truth, you do not believe me. Which one of you convicts me of sin? If I tell the truth, why do you

---

2. "Paul apparently did not believe that people were only culpable for sin if they had the 'moral' ability to keep commandments" (Thomas R. Schreiner, *Romans*, BECNT [Grand Rapids: Baker, 1998], 412–13).
3. D. A. Carson, *The Gospel According to John* (Grand Rapids: Eerdmans, 1991), 350.
4. Anthony A. Hoekema, *Created in God's Image* (Grand Rapids: Eerdmans, 1986), 232–33.
5. Andreas J. Köstenberger, *John*, BECNT (Grand Rapids: Baker, 2004), 263.

not believe me? Whoever is of God hears the words of God. The reason why you do not hear them is that you are not of God" (John 8:43–47). The words of Jesus here are shocking. Jesus's listeners do not understand because they cannot bear to hear his saving message. Moreover, Jesus is blunt: They belong to the devil, who is their father.

Cannot Please God: Paul on Total Depravity

The apostle Paul is as bleak as Jesus is concerning man's slavery to sin. He writes to the Romans, "For those who live according to the flesh set their minds on the things of the flesh, but those who live according to the Spirit set their minds on the things of the Spirit. For to set the mind on the flesh is death, but to set the mind on the Spirit is life and peace. For the mind that is set on the flesh is hostile to God, for it does not submit to God's law; indeed, it cannot. Those who are in the flesh cannot please God" (Rom. 8:5–8). Paul's stark statement demonstrates that it is not only the case that man won't submit to God's law, but that he cannot as it is impossible for him to please God. In other words, the corruption of man's nature includes the bondage of man's will.

When we consider the many texts in Paul's letters on man's bondage to sin, the case for spiritual inability becomes even more overwhelming. Consider how Paul uses the imagery of slavery throughout his epistles:

> Do you not know that if you present yourselves to anyone as obedient slaves, you are slaves of the one whom you obey, either of sin, which leads to death, or of obedience, which leads to righteousness? (Rom. 6:16).

> The natural person does not accept the things of the Spirit of God, for they are folly to him, and he is not able to understand them because they are spiritually discerned (1 Cor. 2:14).

> In their case the god of this world has blinded the minds of the unbelievers, to keep them from seeing the light of the gospel of the glory of Christ, who is the image of God (2 Cor. 4:4).

> Now before faith came, we were held captive under the law, imprisoned until the coming faith would be revealed (Gal. 3:23).

> In the same way we also, when we were children, were enslaved to the elementary principles of the world (Gal. 4:3).

> Formerly, when you did not know God, you were enslaved to those that by nature are not gods. But now that you have

come to know God, or rather to be known by God, how can you turn back again to the weak and worthless elementary principles of the world, whose slaves you want to be once more? (Gal. 4:8–9; cf. 4:25–31).

God may perhaps grant [unbelievers] repentance leading to a knowledge of the truth, and they may come to their senses and escape from the snare of the devil, after being captured by him to do his will (2 Tim. 2:25–26).

To the pure, all things are pure, but to the defiled and unbelieving, nothing is pure; but both their minds and their consciences are defiled. They profess to know God, but they deny him by their works. They are detestable, disobedient, unfit for any good work (Titus 1:15–16).

For we ourselves were once foolish, disobedient, led astray, slaves to various passions and pleasures, passing our days in malice and envy, hated by others and hating one another (Titus 3:3).

Paul not only uses the imagery of slavery to convey man's utter inability, but the imagery of death and darkness as well.

And you were dead in the trespasses and sins in which you once walked, following the course of this world, following the prince of the power of the air, the spirit that is now at work in the sons of disobedience-among whom we all once lived in the passions of our flesh, carrying out the desires of the body and the mind, and were by nature children of wrath, like the rest of mankind (Eph. 2:1–3).

Now this I say and testify in the Lord, that you must no longer walk as the Gentiles do, in the futility of their minds. They are darkened in their understanding, alienated from the life of God because of the ignorance that is in them, due to their hardness of heart. They have become callous and have given themselves up to sensuality, greedy to practice every kind of impurity (Eph. 4:17–19).

He has delivered us from the domain of darkness and transferred us to the kingdom of his beloved Son (Col. 1:13).

> And you, who were dead in your trespasses and the uncir-
> cumcision of your flesh, God made alive together with him,
> having forgiven us all our trespasses (Col. 2:13).

Enslaved, blind, captive, imprisoned, captured, darkened, defiled, alienated, callous, futile, dead—these words and many others demonstrate that
Paul does not depict sinners as merely disinclined, but as having absolutely no
spiritual ability to respond to the gospel.[6] It is erroneous, therefore, to argue
that the sinner is like a man who is wallowing in the waters in need of God
to throw him a life preserver, leaving it up to the drowning victim to choose
whether or not he will grab hold of it. Rather, man is dead, lifeless, rotting
away at the bottom of the ocean. He does not need a life preserver but a resurrection! He is like Lazarus, dead in the tomb. He stinketh. What Lazarus
needed was the resurrection words of Jesus, "Lazarus, come out" (John 11:43).

Willfully Inclined to Sin

So far, we have seen that Scripture teaches that man's will is in bondage
to sin. Yet, it is commonly objected that if man's will is in bondage to sin and
he cannot do otherwise, then he does not have a choice in the matter and
therefore cannot be held culpable. Such reasoning fails for several reasons.
Indeed, man is a slave to sin and his will is in bondage. But man's bondage is
voluntary and willful. It is not as if man does not want to commit sin but is
forced to kicking and screaming. Not at all. The unbeliever loves sin and has
made it his master.

It is concerning the complexity of spiritual inability and human responsibility that the great American pastor-theologian Jonathan Edwards is most
helpful. The human will, according to Edwards, "is that faculty or power or
principle of mind by which it is capable of choosing: an act of the will is the
same as an act of choosing or choice."[7] Man's will is considered free when
he chooses that which *he most desires*. "A man never, in any instance, wills
anything contrary to his desires, or desires anything contrary to his will."[8] It
follows that a person will always choose according to whatever his strongest
desire or motive may be at the moment of decision. Man's choice is necessitated or determined by his strongest desire or motive.[9] Consequently, never is
there an act of the will that is uncaused. Free will, in other words, does not entail a freedom to act to the contrary (i.e., freedom of indifference or contrary

---

6. Thomas R. Schreiner, *Paul: Apostle of God's Glory in Christ* (Downers Grove, IL: InterVarsity Press, 2001), 138; Harold W. Hoehner, *Ephesians: An Exegetical Commentary* (Grand Rapids: Baker, 2002), 308.
7. Jonathan Edwards, *Freedom of the Will*, ed. Paul Ramsay, vol. 1, The Works of Jonathan Edwards (New Haven, CT: Yale University Press, 1970), 137.
8. Ibid., 139.
9. Ibid., 141–42.

choice), as if the will were uncaused. Instead, every act is caused by the will's strongest motive (i.e., freedom of inclination).

So what is it that the unbeliever most desires in regard to spiritual matters? What is the unbeliever's strongest motive, causing him to act? As we have seen from Scripture, the answer must be sin. When faced with choosing Christ or choosing to remain in sin, the unbeliever, apart from the work of the Spirit, will always choose the latter. As Edwards explains, man "is depraved and ruined by propensities to sin," that is, an "unfailing propensity" to moral evil.[10] Due to the corruption inherited from Adam, man's nature is polluted and his inclinations are evil. What this means for the will is that its "strongest motive" after the fall is toward sin. Man's will is necessitated by his sinful nature so that he chooses that which is evil. Nevertheless, since this is the will's strongest motive, it is exactly what he most wants to choose.[11] Man is not forced or coerced to sin but sins willingly because his will finds its strongest desire not in the things of God but in sinful pleasures.

Natural versus Moral Inability

Does this not conflict with the many commands in Scripture where the sinner is instructed to repent and believe? And if the sinner cannot fulfill such a duty, how then can he be held responsible? Once again, Edwards is one step ahead when he distinguishes between natural and moral inability.[12] If it is the case that man's will is physically constrained, then we cannot deny that man's will lacks genuine freedom. In this case, he is coerced. But if man's bondage is not natural but moral, then he is most free indeed.

In other words, man's inability is not one of nature (as if he physically lacked the faculty of a human will), but his inability is spiritual.[13] Man's moral ability consists of a "want of inclination." The difficulty, however, is that, after the fall, no man wants or is inclined toward righteousness. When the unbeliever chooses to sin, he does so out of necessity, and yet his choice is free because he is choosing according to his strongest inclination, namely, sin.[14] Therefore, every sinner is in desperate need of God's sovereign work in regeneration, whereby the Spirit changes the sinner's disposition and reorients

---

10. Jonathan Edwards, *The Great Christian Doctrine of Original Sin Defended*, The Works of Jonathan Edwards (Edinburgh, PA: Banner of Truth, 1979), 1:145, 152.
11. Edwards, *Freedom of the Will*, 152.
12. Ibid., 159.
13. I cannot emphasize enough how key this distinction is. Affirming natural ability avoids a Manichaean view, which makes sin a necessary and essential component of the created order. In this view, sin is no longer accidental to being human. On the other hand, affirming spiritual inability avoids Pelagianism and Semi-Pelagianism, both of which compromise total depravity. See Michael Horton, *Pilgrim Theology: Core Doctrines for Christian Disciples* (Grand Rapids: Zondervan, 2011), 153.
14. Edwards, *Freedom of the Will*, 164.

his inclinations, liberating him from his willful bondage to sin so that he will love, delight in, and cherish Christ rather than sin.

Freedom Biblically Illustrated

In order to see these important distinctions in action, consider two texts: 1 Corinthians 2:14 and 2 Thessalonians 2:9–12.

> The natural person does not accept the things of the Spirit of God, for they are folly to him, and he is not able to understand them because they are spiritually discerned (1 Cor. 2:14).

> The coming of the lawless one is by the activity of Satan with all power and false signs and wonders, and with all wicked deception for those who are perishing, because they refused to love the truth and so be saved. Therefore God sends them a strong delusion, so that they may believe what is false, in order that all may be condemned who did not believe the truth but had pleasure in unrighteousness (2 Thess. 2:9–12).

In 1 Corinthians 2:14 Paul says unbelievers are not able to accept the things of the Spirit. Here the sinner's spiritual inability exists before he even hears the truth of the gospel. However, in 2 Thessalonians 2 Paul merely says sinners do not accept the truth (i.e., "they refused to love the truth"). Here the sinner's delusion is a consequence of forsaking the gospel.[15] The contrast can be stated as follows: In 1 Corinthians 2:14 the sinner is incapable of obeying, whereas in 2 Thessalonians 2 the sinner chooses not to obey. So which is it? Is Paul contradicting himself?

Actually, Paul affirms both! Unbelievers cannot respond to the message of the gospel due to their inability. Yet unbelievers actively reject and refuse to respond to the gospel as well.[16] If we utilize our understanding of free will as a freedom of inclination, then the tension is further resolved. To refresh, freedom of inclination means that while the sinner's decisions are necessitated or determined by his strongest motive, he still chooses that which he most desires and so his choice remains a free one. Scripture tells us that man's strongest desire or motive is for sin. The sinner's choice is necessitated by his corrupt nature. Nevertheless, since committing sin is what the sinner most wants to do, his choice remains free.

Now, consider 1 Corinthians 2:14 and 2 Thessalonians 2:10–12 once again. In 1 Corinthians 2:14 the sinner is not able to submit and obey because he is a natural man, not a spiritual man. He is determined by his polluted

---

15. Schreiner, *Paul*, 137.
16. Ibid.

nature, and he is in bondage to sin. However, in 2 Thessalonians 2:10–12 we learn that the sinner willfully and voluntarily chooses sin as that which he most wants to do. Notice the complementary nature of these passages. The sinner is not able to accept the things of the Spirit since he is not spiritual, and at the same time the sinner does not accept the things of the Spirit because he refuses to love the truth. The former indicates that man's free will is determined by his corrupt nature, but the latter indicates that man sins voluntarily as his strongest inclination is toward sin.[17]

In summary, man's will is in bondage to sin, and yet such a bondage is willful since it is what he most desires.

Totally Dependent upon God

What should the bondage of the will teach us today? First, it reminds us that our only hope is God. Such a doctrine should drive us to the foot of the cross. We dare not stand before the cross even trusting in the slightest upon something within us. Instead, we come with nothing and we leave with everything. As Edwin Palmer wrote, "When anyone learns from the Bible about the enormity of his sin, he should want to run to God and plead, 'Help me, Jesus. I'm bad and sinful. I've done wrong. I'm no good. Save me, Jesus.'"[18] We are totally and entirely dependent upon God for our salvation.

Second, should an unbeliever find himself with a sudden desire to trust in Christ for salvation, it is only due to God's grace at work within. Total depravity and spiritual inability remind us that the new life we have is not something we initiated or willed into being, but something God accomplished according to his good pleasure (see Questions 16–17).

Third, for Christians the bondage of the will should result in a grateful heart. At first, such a statement sounds puzzling. But remember, this bondage to sin is very much a willful bondage. God would have been perfectly just to leave us in our slavery to sin. Contrary to the popular attitude of entitlement, whereby we believe that God was obligated to save us, Scripture teaches everywhere, as we have seen, that we deserve only divine wrath and condemnation. "God would be perfectly just at this point to pull a sheet over the lifeless corpse of humanity. He could have pronounced the judgment about which he clearly warned Adam and Eve without providing a means of redemption."[19] In that light, how astonishing it truly is that though we were enslaved, God liberated us from sin and gave us a new identity in Christ (John 8:36).

---

17. Ibid., 139.
18. Edwin H. Palmer, *The Five Points of Calvinism* (Grand Rapids: Baker Book House, 1972), 20.
19. Michael Horton, *Putting Amazing Back Into Grace: Embracing the Heart of the Gospel*, rev. ed. (Grand Rapids: Baker, 2011), 53.

Summary

Scripture teaches that unbelievers are slaves to sin. As a result of inheriting a corrupt nature from Adam, man's will is in bondage to sin and he is incapable of pleasing God. Nevertheless, man's slavery to sin is a willful slavery. While the sinner is held captive to sin, unable to do otherwise, his captivity is voluntary since sinning is what he most wants to do. Only God can liberate the sinner from his captivity to sin.

REFLECTION QUESTIONS

1. Has the doctrine of spiritual inability increased your appreciation and gratitude for God's grace and mercy in liberating sinners from their bondage to sin?

2. In what ways do you see unbelievers enslaved to sin and incapable of understanding the things of the Spirit?

3. Do you think unbelievers can change from being hostile to God to loving God apart from the saving work of the Holy Spirit?

4. What kind of human freedom do you believe to be most consistent with the biblical affirmation of spiritual inability?

5. How might the doctrine of spiritual inability positively change your assumptions when sharing the gospel with an unbeliever?

PART 2

Salvation and Union with Christ

What Is Meant by Salvation?

What is "salvation"? In its broadest sense, salvation refers to being rescued from danger. More specifically, in Scripture salvation refers to being "rescued" from the wrath of God, sin, and the devil.[1] Salvation is being rescued from the wrath of God because we are sinners deserving only eternal punishment and condemnation (Matt. 25:41; Rom. 1:18; 5:16; Eph. 2:1–3). Salvation also means being rescued from sin because (as we saw in Question 4) each and every one of us is corrupt by nature and therefore a slave to sin (Rom. 8:8; John 8:34; Eph. 2:1–3). Additionally, salvation means being rescued from the devil because, as Paul says, unbelievers are in the snare of the devil, captured by him to do his will (2 Tim. 2:26). However, as has yet to be seen, salvation not only means being saved *from* something, but *to* something as well. God not only delivers us from sin and condemnation but gives us eternal life. As Jesus explains in John 3:16, "For God so loved the world, that he gave his only Son, that whoever believes in him should not perish but have eternal life." Salvation in Christ means *not* perishing, but it also means *receiving* life everlasting.

Salvation in the Context of Redemptive History

The Old Testament is filled with examples of God rescuing sinners from impending doom and destruction. God saved Noah and his family from the flood, which God brought upon the earth in his righteous anger against wicked men (Gen. 6–8). God delivered Israel out of Egypt, saving his people from Pharaoh (Exod. 14:13; 15:2; Ps. 106:8–10). And when God's wrath came down on the firstborn of Egypt, God passed over the Israelites thanks to God's own provision of a sacrificial lamb (Exod. 11–12). God raised up judges to rescue his people from their enemies (Judg. 2:16; 3:9, 31; 6:14). The Psalms are filled with

---

1. Thomas R. Schreiner and Ardel B. Caneday, *The Race Set Before Us: A Biblical Theology of Perseverance and Assurance* (Downers Grove, IL: InterVarsity Press, 2001), 48.

songs of salvation. King David cries out, "Turn, O LORD, deliver my life; save me for the sake of your steadfast love" (Ps. 6:4). And again, "O LORD my God, in you do I take refuge; save me from all my pursuers and deliver me" (Ps. 7:1).

Additionally, God is a God who *promises* to save. For example, the Lord says in Isaiah 35:4, "Say to those who have an anxious heart, 'Be strong; fear not! Behold, your God will come with vengeance, with the recompense of God. He will come and save you.'" Yahweh's promise in Isaiah 46:13 is no less adamant, "I bring near my righteousness; it is not far off, and my salvation will not delay; I will put salvation in Zion, for Israel my glory." Or consider Isaiah 45:17, "But Israel is saved by the LORD with everlasting salvation; you shall not be put to shame or confounded to all eternity." Jonah's prayer in the belly of the great fish captures the message of the entire Bible: "Salvation belongs to the Lord!" (Jonah 2:9; cf. Ps. 2:9).

Many other Old Testament passages exhibit the promise of salvation (Isa. 49:6, 25; 52:10; Jer. 31:7–9; Ezek. 36:36), but it is essential to acknowledge that the promise of salvation made in the Old Testament comes to fruition in the New Testament, in the person and work of Jesus Christ. In the old covenant Israel had to offer up sacrifices for sin continually. But, as the author of Hebrews explains, these sacrifices repeatedly offered every year could not "make perfect those who draw near" (Heb. 10:1). If they could then there would be no need to offer them again and again, for the worshiper would be cleansed of his sin and no longer have any consciousness of sins (Heb. 10:2). Therefore, these sacrifices were a reminder of sins every single year (Heb. 10:3). "For it is impossible for the blood of bulls and goats to take away sins" (Heb. 10:4). However, Christ Jesus, the Lamb of God who takes away the sin of the world (John 1:29), came into the world so that we would be "sanctified through the offering of the body of Jesus Christ once for all" (Heb. 10:10). The author of Hebrews explains, "And every priest stands daily at his service, offering repeatedly the same sacrifices, which can never take away sins. But when Christ had offered for all time a single sacrifice for sins, he sat down at the right hand of God, waiting from that time until his enemies should be made a footstool for his feet. For by a single offering he has perfected for all time those who are being sanctified" (Heb. 10:11–14).

Moreover, Jesus himself knew he had come to offer himself up as a sacrifice, as an atonement for sin. Jesus said of himself, "the Son of Man came not to be served but to serve, and to give his life as a ransom for many" (Matt. 20:18; cf. Mark 10:45). And just before Jesus was about to undergo crucifixion, he shared a Passover meal with his disciples, and holding up the bread he said, "This is my body, which is given for you. Do this in remembrance of me." Likewise, Jesus took the cup, saying, "This cup that is poured out for you is the new covenant in my blood" (Luke 22:19–20). In that light, the New Testament authors affirm that God, out of his great love for us, put forward Christ Jesus to be a propitiation by his blood (Rom. 3:25; Heb. 2:17; 1 John 2:2; 4:10). In so doing, God shows himself to be both just and the justifier of the one who has faith in Jesus. He shows his righteousness "because in his divine forbearance he had passed over former sins" (Rom. 3:25), but now his wrath has been satisfied by the blood of Christ.[2] And he shows himself to be the justifier because, though we have all sinned and fallen short of the glory of God, through the blood of Christ we are "justified by his grace as a gift" (Rom. 3:24). It is no surprise then that Peter, after Jesus has risen and ascended to heaven, says to the elders and scribes in Jerusalem, "And there is salvation in no one else, for there is no other name under heaven given among men by which we must be saved" (Acts 4:12).

It is crucial to keep in mind that the death of Christ for our salvation was planned and determined by the Father before the foundation of the world. Peter made this abundantly clear when he first started preaching the gospel:

> Men of Israel, hear these words: Jesus of Nazareth, a man attested to you by God with mighty works and wonders and signs that God did through him in your midst, as you yourselves know—this Jesus, delivered up *according to the definite plan and foreknowledge of God*, you crucified and killed by the hands of lawless men (Acts 2:22–23, emphasis added).

> For truly in this city there were gathered together against your holy servant Jesus, whom you anointed, both Herod and Pontius Pilate, along with the Gentiles and the peoples of Israel, *to do whatever your hand and your plan had predestined to take place* (Acts 4:27–28, emphasis added).

In both of these texts we see that the death of Jesus was no accident, but predestined to take place according to the sovereign will of the Father. While what these evil men did was wicked, nevertheless, God had planned it from the beginning for the sake of our salvation.

While our salvation was *planned* by the Father and *accomplished* by the Son, it is *applied* by the Holy Spirit. Not only was the death of Jesus a fulfillment of the salvation promised in the Old Testament (see Isa. 53), but so also was the advent of the Holy Spirit (see Ezek. 36:26–28). As we will see in later chapters, it is the Holy Spirit who causes sinners to be born again (John 3:5–8; cf. 6:63), justifies those who believe (1 Cor. 6:11), sanctifies God's children

---

2. On Christ as our wrath-bearing substitute, see John Stott, *The Cross of Christ* (Downers Grove, IL: InterVarsity Press, 1986); Leon Morris, *The Apostolic Preaching of the Cross* (Grand Rapids: Eerdmans, 1956); Steve Jeffery, Michael Ovey, and Andrew Sach, *Pierced for Our Transgressions: Rediscovering the Glory of Penal Substitution* (Wheaton, IL: Crossway, 2007).

(Rom. 8:4–8; 2 Cor. 3:12–18; Gal. 5:22–23; Eph. 3:14–19), seals those who believe in the gospel (Eph. 1:18), indwells believers (John 14:17; Acts 2:4; Rom. 5:5), bears witness to the Son (John 15:26), intercedes on our behalf before the Father (Rom. 8:26), leads us to walk in righteousness (Gal. 5:16, 22), and one day will grant us resurrected bodies (Rom. 8:11).

Salvation: Past, Present, or Future?

Is salvation a past, present, or future reality? The answer is all three. The Bible speaks of salvation in diverse ways. Sometimes Scripture speaks of salvation as a reality that has occurred in the past. For example, Paul says in Ephesians 2:

> But God, being rich in mercy, because of the great love with which he loved us, even when we were dead in our trespasses, made us alive together with Christ—by grace you *have been saved*—and raised us up with him and seated us with him in the heavenly places in Christ Jesus, so that in the coming ages he might show the immeasurable riches of his grace in kindness toward us in Christ Jesus. For by grace you *have been saved* through faith. And this is not your own doing; it is the gift of God, not a result of works, so that no one may boast (Eph. 2:4–9, emphasis added).

According to Paul, salvation is something that has already been accomplished. The believer *currently possesses* salvation. Paul says the same elsewhere:

> But when the goodness and loving kindness of God our Savior appeared, *he saved us*, not because of works done by us in righteousness, but according to his own mercy, by the washing of regeneration and renewal of the Holy Spirit, whom he poured out on us richly through Jesus Christ our Savior, so that being justified by his grace we might become heirs according to the hope of eternal life (Titus 3:4–7, emphasis added).

> Therefore do not be ashamed of the testimony about our Lord, nor of me his prisoner, but share in suffering for the gospel by the power of God, who *saved us* and called us to a holy calling, not because of our works but because of his own purpose and grace, which he gave us in Christ Jesus before the ages began (2 Tim. 1:8–9, emphasis added).

> For in this hope we *were saved*. Now hope that is seen is not
> hope. For who hopes for what he sees? But if we hope for
> what we do not see, we wait for it with patience (Rom. 8:24–
> 25, emphasis added).

Paul's use of the past tense tells us that the believer has already been saved.

Although salvation is referred to as a reality in the present and as something currently possessed by believers, a strong case can be made that the New Testament writers primarily thought of salvation as a future reality. In Matthew 10, Jesus warns his disciples that they are being sent out as sheep among wolves. Warning his disciples of the persecution to come, Jesus says one must endure to the end to be saved (10:17–18, 21–22; cf. Mark 24:13). Jesus does not say that they have been saved or that their perseverance is evidence that they are saved. Rather, when the day of the Lord comes, those who have endured will be saved.[3]

Much like Jesus, the apostle Paul also refers to salvation as a future reality. Consider Romans 5:9–10: "Since, therefore, we have now been justified by his blood, much more shall we be saved by him from the wrath of God. For if while we were enemies we were reconciled to God by the death of his Son, much more, now that we are reconciled, shall we be saved by his life." Schreiner and Caneday comment, "Paul does not say that we can be sure that we are saved but that we *will* be saved. He thinks of salvation as a future blessing that we shall receive."[4]

Similarly, consider Paul's first letter to the Thessalonians: "But since we belong to the day, let us be sober, having put on the breastplate of faith and love, and for a helmet the hope of salvation. For God has not destined us for wrath, but to obtain salvation through our Lord Jesus Christ" (1 Thess. 5:8–9). Salvation is something to be obtained. It is a destiny we Christians have yet to reach but one day will reach through our Lord Jesus Christ. Unlike unbelievers, we are not destined for wrath on the last day, but for salvation and eternal life. In the meantime, we have the hope of salvation. Therefore, salvation is both a present reality and a future gift.

Paul sees salvation as a future reality in Romans 13:11–14 as well. Paul tells believers that the hour has come to wake from sleep since "salvation is nearer to us now than when we first believed." Using the imagery of day and night, Paul writes that the night is "far gone" but the "day is at hand." We are to "cast off the works of darkness and put on the armor of light." Much like 1 Thessalonians 5, Paul is using the soldier's armor to explain to Christians that they are not to put on sin but instead are to put on the Lord Jesus Christ. The point is clear: Christians are to press on in godliness, looking ahead to the

---

3. Schreiner and Caneday, *The Race Set Before Us*, 49.
4. Ibid., 50.

salvation that awaits all those in Christ. In so doing, our salvation is nearer now than when we first believed.

Sadly, not all those who profess the name of Christ "put on the Lord Jesus Christ, and make no provision for the flesh, to gratify its desires" (Rom. 13:14). There are some in our midst who refuse to repent and turn from sin. Such was the case in Corinth, where a man was committing incest. Paul instructs the church to "deliver this man to Satan for the destruction of the flesh, so that his spirit may be saved in the day of the Lord" (1 Cor. 5:5). Once again, Paul refers to being saved in the future (in the day of the Lord). Paul uses similar language in 1 Corinthians 3 as well. "If anyone's work is burned up, he will suffer loss, though he himself will be saved, but only as through fire" (1 Cor. 3:15). Paul is referring to believers who are saved in the end, though their works are consumed due to insufficiency. Notice, once again, that salvation is referred to as a future reality. After all, the fire that consumes is said to burn on the day of the Lord (see v. 13).

Paul's letters to Timothy also demonstrate that salvation is to be received in the future. Paul encourages Timothy, telling him not to let others despise him for his youth, but to set an example in all that he does. Paul tells Timothy to devote himself to the public reading, exhortation, and teaching of Scripture. Furthermore, says Paul, "Keep a close watch on yourself and on the teaching. Persist in this, for by so doing you will save both yourself and your hearers" (1 Tim. 4:16). By preaching and teaching God's Word, Timothy ensures future salvation.[5]

One might think that Paul would surely have considered salvation something entirely past by the end of his life. Not so! Paul confesses to Timothy, "The Lord will rescue me from every evil deed and bring me safely into his heavenly kingdom. To him be the glory forever and ever. Amen" (2 Tim. 4:18). Or as the NRSV says, "The Lord will rescue me from evil attack and *save me* for his heavenly kingdom." Again, Paul refers to salvation on the last day as something he will attain as he enters into God's "heavenly kingdom."[6]

Paul is not alone in referring to salvation as a future reality. The author of Hebrews does as well. In Hebrews 1:14 we learn that "ministering spirits" are sent out to serve for the "sake of those who are to inherit salvation." Or consider Hebrews 9:28: "Christ, having been offered once to bear the sins of many, will appear a second time, not to deal with sin but to save those who are eagerly waiting for him." From texts like these we discover that salvation is to be inherited at the second coming of Christ.

---

5. Also consult 1 Timothy 2:15: "Yet she will be saved through childbearing—if they continue in faith and love and holiness, with self-control."

6. "The verb *sōsei* is rightly translated by the NRSV as 'save,' and it is a future tense verb. That the salvation is on the last day is clear since it will involve induction into the Lord's heavenly kingdom" (Schreiner and Caneday, *The Race Set Before Us*, 51).

One of the clearest texts in this regard is 1 Peter 1:3–9.

> Blessed be the God and Father of our Lord Jesus Christ! According to his great mercy, he has caused us to be born again to a living hope through the resurrection of Jesus Christ from the dead, to an inheritance that is imperishable, undefiled, and unfading, kept in heaven for you, who by God's power are being guarded through faith *for a salvation ready to be revealed in the last time.* In this you rejoice, though now for a little while, if necessary, you have been grieved by various trials, so that the tested genuineness of your faith—more precious than gold that perishes though it is tested by fire—may be found to result in praise and glory and honor at the revelation of Jesus Christ. Though you have not seen him, you love him. Though you do not now see him, you believe in him and rejoice with joy that is inexpressible and filled with glory, *obtaining the outcome of your faith, the salvation of your souls* (emphasis added).

It cannot be denied that Peter regards salvation in this passage as eschatological. The goal (*telos*) or outcome of our faith is the salvation of our souls (v. 9). And it is this salvation that will be revealed in the "last time." Until then, believers are being "guarded through faith" by God's power.[7]

In light of these passages, it does not do justice to Scripture's witness to argue that salvation is only something we received in the past or possess in the present. Salvation is also considered a future, eschatological gift that those in Christ will one day receive. True, believers have been saved, but they are also being saved and will be saved. There is an already/not-yet dimension to our salvation. As followers of Christ, we wait eagerly for the hope of salvation, pressing on in the faith knowing that he who began a good work in us will bring it to completion (Phil. 1:6).

Summary

Scripture describes salvation in three different ways: past, present, and future. Salvation is not only what God has accomplished already through his Son, nor is salvation something the Spirit has presently brought about in conversion, but salvation is also described as a future reality and one that provides the believer with tremendous hope.

---

7. Also consider James 1:21: "Therefore put away all filthiness and rampant wickedness and receive with meekness the implanted word, which is able to save your souls."

REFLECTION QUESTIONS

1. Scripture refers to the "hope of salvation." What role should this future-oriented hope play in the Christian life?

2. In the midst of life's trials and hardships, how does the promise of salvation to come help you press on in your present circumstances?

3. Salvation is not only a future reality but a past and present reality. In what sense has salvation been accomplished by Christ in the past?

4. If salvation is something that was planned by God, then what kind of assurance can you have now that you have been united to Christ?

5. How does this chapter inform how you talk about salvation when sharing the gospel?

What Is the Order of Salvation?

Theologians throughout the centuries, looking to Pauline passages like Romans 8:28–30, have recognized that there is biblical justification for an order of salvation. Simply put, the order of salvation is that which structures the proper relationship between the various aspects of salvation to one another in the Spirit's application of Christ's redeeming work.[1] In this chapter we will explain the order of salvation, as well as its importance, and our discussion here will set the agenda for the rest of this book.

The Trinity and the Big Picture of Salvation

If we are to properly understand the order of salvation, we should begin with the "big picture of salvation." Consider the following diagram:

Table 2: The Trinity and the Big Picture of Salvation[2]

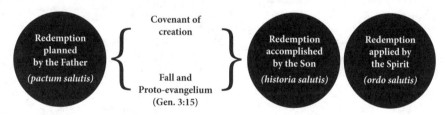

Let's explore each of the stages or steps in this "big picture of salvation."

---

1. Sinclair Ferguson, *The Holy Spirit* (Downers Grove, IL: IVP, 1996), 96. For a history of the order of salvation, see Herman Bavinck, *Reformed Dogmatics*, ed. John Bolt, trans. John Vriend (Grand Rapids: Baker Academic, 2006), 3:485–595.
2. One weakness of this diagram is that it doesn't picture how all three persons of the Trinity are at work at each stage in redemptive history (perhaps we need a 3D diagram). Nonetheless, that the three persons work inseparably will be emphasized in what follows.

The Covenant of Redemption (Pactum Salutis)

Before we can begin discussing the order of salvation—that is, the application of Christ's work to the believer in time by the Holy Spirit—it is paramount to recognize our salvation and redemption was planned by God before the foundation of the world (a point we will explore in depth in Questions 10–11 when we look at election). Salvation has to do with God saving or rescuing sinners. Naturally, then, such a great work of salvation does not accidentally happen when the Son becomes incarnate or when the Spirit descends at Pentecost. It's not as if mankind made a mess of the world for centuries only for God to come on the scene, like a Johnny-come-lately, and concoct a plan to save man. Not at all. Instead, salvation was planned by God in eternity, and this plan involved all three persons of the Trinity: the Father appointing the Son to become incarnate to redeem fallen mankind, as well as the Spirit being appointed to apply the work of Christ to God's elect in conjunction with the proclamation of the gospel. Theologians have sought to capture this eternal appointment in the Trinity by appealing to the "covenant of redemption" (also referred to as the *pactum salutis*).[3]

Richard Muller defines the covenant of redemption as the "pretemporal, intra-trinitarian agreement of the Father and the Son concerning the covenant of grace and its ratification in and through the work of the Son incarnate."[4] J. V. Fesko offers a similar definition, explaining how the covenant of redemption is "the eternal intra-trinitarian covenant to appoint the Son as covenant surety of the elect and to redeem them in the temporal execution of the covenant of grace."[5] Or consider the great Puritan theologian John Owen, who describes the covenant of redemption as that "compact, covenant, convention, or agreement, that was between the Father and the Son, for the accomplishment of the work of our redemption by the mediation of Christ, to the

---

3. To clarify, the covenant of redemption and election are not the same thing, though not unrelated. The covenant of redemption specifically has to do with the appointment of the Son (and Spirit) in eternity, but election has to do with the triune God's unconditional selection of certain individuals to eternal life. The covenant of redemption addresses the means by which redemption is accomplished. Logically speaking, then, election precedes the covenant of redemption because, as Berkhof explains, "the suretyship of Christ, like His atonement, is particular." "If there were no preceding election, it would necessarily be universal. Moreover, to turn this around would be equivalent to making the suretyship of Christ the ground of election, while Scripture bases election entirely on the good pleasure of God" (Louis Berkhof, *Systematic Theology* [Edinburgh: Banner of Truth, reprinted 2003], 268).
4. "The Son covenants with the Father, in the unity of the Godhead, to be the temporal sponsor of the Father's testamentum (q.v.) in and through the work of the Mediator. In that work, the Son fulfils his sponsio (q.v.) or fideiussio (q.v.), i.e., his guarantee of payment of the debt of sin in ratification of the Father's testamentum" (Richard A. Muller, *Dictionary of Latin and Greek Theological Terms: Drawn Principally from Protestant Scholastic Theology* [Grand Rapids: Baker, 2004], s.v.).
5. J. V. Fesko, *The Covenant of Redemption: Origins, Development, and Reception*, Reformed Historical Theology 35 (Göttingen: Vandenhoeck & Ruprecht, 2015), 15.

praise of the glorious grace of God."[6] Owen goes on to explain that it was the will of the Father to appoint the Son to be the "head, husband, deliver[er], and redeemer of his elect, his church, his people, whom he did foreknow," to which the Son responded voluntarily, "freely undertaking that work and all that was required thereunto."[7]

Our purpose here is not to enter into a biblical defense of the covenant of redemption (Zech. 6:13; Pss. 2:7; 110; Eph. 1; 2 Tim. 1:9–10; etc.), though one should note (1) how the covenant of redemption is assumed in the language Scripture uses to speak of God's eternal decree (Eph. 1:4–12; 3:11; 2 Thess. 2:13; 2 Tim. 1:9; James 2:5; 1 Peter 1:2), and (2) how Jesus refers back to his pre-incarnate existence and the mission the Father gave to him, as well as the appointment he has received (Luke 22:29; John 5:30, 43; 6:38–40; 17:4–12).[8] At this point we merely desire to grasp the "big picture" of salvation, noting first of all that its genesis is to be located in the covenant of redemption in eternity. For our purposes, however, we should pay special attention to the Spirit in this covenant of redemption. As mentioned already, in eternity the Father appoints the Son to accomplish redemption and the Son voluntarily agrees and assents for the sake of the salvation of the elect. But we must also realize that implied in this covenant is the mission of the Spirit as well. It's not just the Son who is appointed to accomplish redemption; the Spirit is also appointed, though not to fulfil the law and make atonement but instead to apply that salvific work to God's elect, uniting them to Christ so that they receive and enjoy all the riches Christ has purchased for them.[9]

Certainly, then, this covenant of redemption is the fountain from which flows all the blessings of redemption that follow. "If there had been no eternal counsel of peace [i.e., covenant of redemption] between the Father and the Son," writes Berkhof, "there could have been no agreement between the triune God and sinful men." Therefore, the covenant of redemption "makes the covenant of grace possible."[10] It provides the very means by which God's grace is

---

6. John Owen, *The Mystery of the Gospel*, The Works of John Owen (Edinburgh: Banner of Truth, 1991), 12:497; cf. *An Exposition of the Epistle to the Hebrews*, in *Works*, 18:87–88. Owen clarifies, however, that there is but one will in God, corresponding to the one nature in God who is triune in person.

7. John Owen, *The Mystery of the Gospel*, Works, 12:497. Owen argues that biblical support is found in Hebrews 10:7 and Psalm 40:7–8. In *Death of Death*, Works, 10:170, he also appeals to Isaiah 49:6–12.

8. Berkhof, *Systematic Theology*, 266. It naturally follows, from both of these points, that Paul would consider Christ as the new head and representative.

9. See J. V. Fesko, *The Trinity and the Covenant of Redemption* (Fearn, Ross-shire, Scotland: Mentor, 2016), 319–44.

10. "The counsel of redemption is the eternal prototype of the historical covenant of grace. . . . The former is eternal, that is, from eternity, and the latter, temporal in the sense that it is realized in time. The former is a compact between the Father and the Son as the Surety and

established and executed in time.[11] Think of it this way. Having been chosen by God in eternity and having been entrusted to the Son by the Father in the covenant of redemption in eternity, the Son was able to become incarnate and redeem us by his blood on the cross, and the Holy Spirit was then able to apply that redemption to us starting at the moment of our new birth.

The Covenant of Creation (i.e., Covenant of Works) and the Protoevangelium

As we saw in Questions 2–3, in the beginning, God not only created Adam, but established a covenant with him, which theologians have called the covenant of creation or works.[12] Though the word "covenant" is not used, a covenantal structure is evident:[13] (a) God sets in place certain stipulations: Adam was to work the garden (Gen. 2:15); (b) Adam was allowed to eat of any tree except the tree of the knowledge of good and evil (2:16–17); (c) there is a penalty for breaking this stipulation, namely, death (2:17);[14] and (d) implied in the threatened penalty is the reward for obedience, namely, eternal life and communion with God.[15]

As with other covenants, God sets the terms and conditions of this first covenant with Adam, and they are gracious indeed.[16] Furthermore, we learn from Paul in Romans 5 that as Adam enters into this temporary, probationary period of testing, he does so as mankind's federal head and representative. The fate of his offspring, therefore, depends upon whether he chooses life or death.

Head of the elect, while the latter is a compact between the triune God and the elect sinner in the Surety" (Berkhof, *Systematic Theology*, 270).

11. Ibid. Horton adds, "the elect were chosen in Christ from all eternity in the covenant of redemption" (Michael Horton, *Pilgrim Theology: Core Doctrines for Christian Disciples* [Grand Rapids: Zondervan, 2011], 245).

12. For a more detailed defence than can be provided here, see Peter J. Gentry and Stephen J. Wellum, *God's Kingdom through God's Covenants: A Concise Biblical Theology* (Wheaton, IL: Crossway, 2015), 69–92.

13. Though the translation and interpretation are debated, Hosea 6:7 may assume a covenant of creation/works when it says: "But like Adam they transgressed the covenant; there they dealt faithlessly with me." See Byron G. Curtis, "Hosea 6:7 and Covenant-Breaking like/at Adam," in *The Law Is Not of Faith: Essays on Works and Grace in the Mosaic Covenant*, eds. Bryan D. Estelle, J. V. Fesko, and David VanDrunen (Phillipsburg, NJ: P&R, 2009), 170–209.

14. The text certainly has physical death in view. Surely it cannot be limited to physical death, lest man not be viewed as a whole being. Spiritual death and eternal death are consequences of Adam's disobedience as well. This is implied when Adam and Eve must leave the garden, no longer able to dwell with God and enjoy communion with God. There is a spiritual, as well as physical, consequence.

15. It is also safe to assume that Adam would not have merely continued in his current state should he have obeyed, but would have experienced eternal life in a much more blessed state than before, though we are not told what that would have involved exactly. Perhaps it would have involved the impossibility of sinning and the highest state of eternal communion with God. See Berkhof, *Systematic Theology*, 216.

16. Berkhof, *Systematic Theology*, 213.

In Genesis 3, of course, Adam sins, thereby breaking the covenant, severing communion with his loving Creator. As a result, Adam is cursed (3:17), and the first couple is cast out of the garden, barred from the tree of life (Gen. 3:22, 24), no longer able to enjoy the communion with God they once had. Though God would have been just to leave Adam in his sin and condemnation, he chose to be gracious. Right away, in Genesis 3:15, there is good news: An offspring will come from the woman, one who will crush the head of the serpent. As the storyline progresses, we learn that this offspring is Christ, the Messiah, who conquers Satan on the cross by taking the penalty for our sin, the only power Satan truly has over us, thereby removing our condemnation.

This gospel promise in Genesis 3:15 is the starting point for all covenants that follow. Covenant theology has labeled this starting point the "covenant of grace."[17] Others, such as progressive covenantalists, would rather not use the phrase "covenant of grace" due, in part, to the diverse ways Scripture speaks of the many covenants in the Bible (covenants with Noah, Abraham, Moses, David, and Jesus [i.e., new covenant]). In order to preserve the conditional and unconditional aspects of each covenant, as well as the ways the new covenant brings to fulfillment all previous covenants, progressive covenantalists would rather refer to a "plurality of covenants" (Gal. 4:24; Eph. 2:12; Heb. 8:7–13). This phrase, says Gentry and Wellum, "allows us to speak properly of the *continuity* of God's plan across time, now fulfilled in the new covenant, and it also helps us avoid flattening the relationships between the covenants and downplaying the *discontinuity* or significant progression between them."[18]

Regardless how one chooses to interpret the covenants (that is the subject of another book), covenant theologians and progressive covenantal theologians both agree that Genesis 3:15 is the first gospel promise, pointing forward to the arrival of the serpent-crusher, Jesus Christ.[19] He arrives as the second Adam, the one who will obey where Adam disobeyed, even laying down his life in order to make atonement for our sin. By his blood the new covenant is established, granting righteousness, forgiveness, and eternal life to all those who trust in him as Savior and Lord.

---

17. E.g., Michael Horton, *Introducing Covenant Theology* (Grand Rapids: Baker, 2007), 104–7.
18. Gentry and Wellum, *God's Kingdom through God's Covenants*, 251. Personally, my view aligns with progressive covenantalism.
19. There are, of course, other positions, such as classic, revised, and progressive dispensationalism, but they will frame this opening narrative differently, especially as it relates to the other "dispensations" they see in the Bible. While there are a diversity of representatives, see the work of Craig A. Blaising and Darrell L. Bock, *Progressive Dispensationalism: An Up-to-date Handbook of Contemporary Dispensational Thought* (Wheaton, IL: Victor Books, 1993), 106–78.

Redemption Accomplished by the Son (Historia Salutis)

As we have seen in Question 6, "salvation" in Scripture can be used in a variety of ways. Sometimes it is used very broadly, including both the work of Christ accomplished in his life, death, and resurrection (the history of salvation or the *historia salutis*), as well as the application of that work by the Holy Spirit (order of salvation or *ordo salutis*).[20] First, let's focus on the former.

In a variety of ways, both the Law and the Prophets foretold a day when the Messiah would come (Luke 24:27; Rom. 1:1–4). At the proper time, God the Father fulfilled the covenant of redemption and the promise made in the protoevangelium (Gen. 3:15) by sending his Son to become incarnate (John 1:1–3; Phil. 2:6–8). Though God had previously spoken by his prophets, in these last days, says the author of Hebrews, he has spoken to us by his Son, who is the "radiance of the glory of God and the exact imprint of his nature" (1:3). As God incarnate, fully God yet fully man, he (a) lived a perfect life in obedience to the Law on our behalf (the active obedience of Christ), successfully doing that which our first father, Adam, failed to do, and (b) died a sacrificial, substitutionary, atoning death on our behalf, taking upon himself the due penalty for our sin, the very wrath of God (the passive obedience of Christ).[21] By his blood, a new and better covenant was established (Matt. 26:28; 1 Cor. 11:25; Heb. 7–10; 12:24), just as God promised through his prophets (Isa. 53; Jer. 31:31).

In Romans 5:12–21 Paul assumes that Adam is our covenant head, our federal representative. As such, Adam's decision resulted in the condemnation of mankind. However, since Christ, too, is the new Adam figure, representing God's people, his obedience to the law and his death under the law countered Adam's disobedience, resulting in justification and eternal life for all those united to Christ. "Since Christ met the condition of the covenant of works," notes Berkhof, "man can now reap the fruit of the original agreement by faith in Jesus Christ."[22] Understood within the framework of original sin, we can also say that while Adam's guilt was imputed to his physical offspring, Christ's righteousness is imputed to his spiritual offspring. While Adam represented the old humanity, Christ represents the new humanity.[23]

It now remains to be seen how the good news concerning our Savior is utilized by the Spirit to create life, faith, and sanctifying works of obedience within those he causes to be born again.

---

20. On this broad use, see Michael Horton, *Pilgrim Theology: Core Doctrines for Christian Disciples* (Grand Rapids: Zondervan, 2011), 245–46.
21. I explain in Question 25 that "active" and "passive" do not strictly refer to "Law" and "cross," for even in his ministry Christ suffers and even at the cross Christ obeys.
22. Berkhof, *Systematic Theology*, 214.
23. Ibid., 447.

Redemption Applied by the Spirit (Ordo Salutis)

What the Son accomplished, the Spirit applies. While Christ's work during the incarnation is referred to as "redemption accomplished," the Spirit's work to apply what Christ has accomplished is labeled "redemption applied." Those whom the Father has chosen, the Son has purchased by his own blood on the cross and the Spirit then unites to Christ. This actual union starts when the elect are efficaciously called to their Savior, regenerated by the Spirit, only to then repent and trust in Christ. Of course, the Spirit's work doesn't stop there; he also justifies, adopts, and sanctifies God's elect. This salvation process brought about in the hearts of God's elect by the Spirit is called the "order of salvation." As we will see, this process pictures the logical order of salvation.

The key question before us now is: How then should the order of salvation be structured? This is a question that the rest of this book will answer. By looking at how we have outlined and structured this book, one can see the order we have chosen to follow. In short, the biblical order is as follows: Effectual calling and regeneration, conversion (faith and repentance), justification, adoption, sanctification (which includes perseverance), and glorification (see Table 2).[24] The umbrella category that undergirds the entire order of salvation is union with Christ (see Questions 8–9), though we will show throughout the book how each step relates to union.

If we could concisely summarize this order we might put it like this: God effectually summons (calls) his elect, causing them to be born again, resulting in faith and repentance (conversion). It is through faith in Christ alone that one is then justified, which proves to be the legal basis of one's union with Christ. Accepted by God, one is adopted into his family and made a fellow heir with Christ, and this new identity leads to the progressive, sanctifying work of the Spirit, whereby the believer is kept by the Spirit, who makes the believer holy, and by God's grace the believer perseveres until that final day when he is glorified.

There is much still to be said as to what each of these steps entails in full. Yet, it is apparent that (1) each aspect of salvation has a biblical location in the order of salvation and (2) each step in this order leads to the next. Older theologians, like William Perkins, called this order of salvation the "golden chain" of salvation because each "link" is bound to the one before and after so that one is left with an unbreakable chain. [25]

---

24. If we were to go back even farther, perhaps we could place election before regeneration. But typically, the order of salvation refers to the *application* of redemption in time, rather than the planning of redemption before time.

25. William Perkins, *Golden Chain*, in vol. 6 of *The Works of Williams Perkins*, ed. Joel R. Beeke and Derek W. H. Thomas (Grand Rapids: Reformation Heritage Books, forthcoming).

Table 3
Order of Salvation
(*Ordo Salutis*)

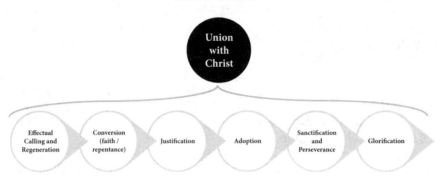

However, not all have been sympathetic to an order of salvation, arguing that Paul, in Romans 8:28–30, does not intend to structure a precise salvation sequence.[26] While it is true that we do not want to overanalyze the order of salvation where Scripture gives no instruction or where no inference can be drawn—forcing the apostle Paul to fit the systematic methods of our own day—nevertheless, we should not go to the opposite extreme by dismissing the order of salvation altogether.[27] Even Paul in Romans 8:28–30, while not giving us every specific detail of the order of salvation, is not leaving salvation unordered. One dare not say that each aspect Paul lists is relative so that being glorified can precede being justified or that being justified can precede being predestined.[28] No, Paul intentionally places predestination before calling and calling before justification and justification before glorification. These categories are not interchangeable but distinguishable, and each follows (either logically and/or chronologically) as a result of what comes before.

The same is true in other passages. In John 3:3–5 Jesus is straightforward with Nicodemus, telling him that unless one is born again he cannot enter the kingdom of God. Now here is an order as well: regeneration precedes entrance into God's kingdom, both of which have to do with the application of

26. G. C. Berkouwer, *Faith and Justification*, trans. Lewis B. Smedes (Grand Rapids: Eerdmans, 1954), 25–36. A similar argument was also made by John Wesley in the eighteenth century. Others who are critical include Karl Barth, *Church Dogmatics*, eds. G. W. Bromily and T. F. Torrance, vol. 4 (Edinburgh: T&T Clark, 1952), pt. 2:499–511; Otto Weber, *Foundations of Dogmatics*, trans. Darrell L. Guder, vol. 2 (Grand Rapids: Eerdmans, 1981), 336–38.
27. Herman N. Ridderbos, *Paul: An Outline of His Theology*, trans. J. R. de Witt (Grand Rapids: Eerdmans, 1975), 206; Anthony A. Hoekema, *Saved by Grace* (Grand Rapids: Eerdmans, 1989), 13–14.
28. Ferguson, *The Holy Spirit*, 100.

salvation. To reverse this order would undermine the condition Jesus has set in place.[29] Or consider the letter of 1 John, specifically passages like 5:1 where the grammatical structure demonstrates that regeneration precedes and produces faith. For John, a "cause and effect relationship exists between God's regenerating activity and saving faith."[30] Or we could turn to the opening chapter of John's gospel where faith is said to precede adoption: "But to all who did receive him [faith], who believed in his name [faith again], he gave the right to become children of God [adoption]" (John 1:12).[31]

Therefore, not only is it impossible for a theologian to think theologically without assuming an order of salvation, but an order of salvation is biblically justified. It's also pedagogically useful.[32] An order rightly distinguishes between different types of causes, properly structuring the relationship of each component in salvation. For example, consider the following types of order:

Table 4

Examples of Types of Order		
Causal Order	**Instrumental Order**	**Chronological Order**
Regeneration prior to faith	Faith prior to justification[31]	Justification prior to glorification

If, as some suggest, we are to do away with an order of salvation, then tragically we lose the ability to distinguish between each step in the order of salvation. The consequence of abandoning the order of salvation is a subtle discarding of theological precision and construction altogether. Yet, there is an important place for ordering doctrine, whether it be temporal, causal, or instrumental. Nevertheless, as Ferguson warns, one must guard against forming an order of salvation that is so mechanical that one displaces Christ

---

29. John Murray, *Redemption Accomplished and Applied* (Grand Rapids: Eerdmans, 1955), 80.
30. Robert L. Reymond, *A New Systematic Theology of the Christian Faith*, 2nd rev. ed. (Nashville: Thomas Nelson, 1998), 709.
31. Murray, *Redemption Accomplished and Applied*, 81.
32. Frame, *Salvation Belongs to the Lord*, 183.
33. Faith is the instrument through which justification occurs; therefore, it is not uncommon for theologians to place faith prior to justification in the order of salvation, usually under conversion. I am not saying, however, that faith is the ground of justification. See Questions 21–26. On faith being presupposed in justification, see Murray, *Redemption Accomplished and Applied*, 85.

from his central role in soteriology.[34] As Questions 8–9 will argue, it is crucial to structure the order of salvation within the category of union with Christ.

How Great Is Our Salvation

As we conclude, we must not fail to realize how the order of salvation should change our lives on a practical level.

First, the doctrine of salvation should lead us to worship God, our great Redeemer. Studying *soteriology* should always lead to *doxology*. The apostle Paul demonstrates such a point beautifully in his letters to the churches. For example, Paul writes to the Galatians, "Grace to you and peace from God our Father and the Lord Jesus Christ, who gave himself for our sins to deliver us from the present evil age, according to the will of our God and Father, to whom be the glory forever and ever. Amen" (Gal. 1:3–5). Notice, Paul begins by exalting God for how he has saved us. But he does not stop there. Such a great salvation leads him to praise, worship, and to give God all glory for what he has done. How easy it is for us to take salvation for granted. But Paul reminds us that our hearts should be overflowing in praise and admiration for God who has delivered us through his Son, Christ Jesus. Therefore, when we contemplate our salvation, we cannot resist the urge to worship God, both publicly and privately.

Second, the doctrine of salvation grounds our future hope, even in the midst of life's trials. As we saw, salvation is not only a past and present reality but a future one as well. However, we may not always feel the reality of our salvation as we wish we would. The reason for this is that there is an already/not yet dimension to our salvation. Yes, we have been saved, but we still await the final consummation of our salvation. In the meantime, we live in the in-between, where we not only experience sin, temptation, suffering, but death itself. Nevertheless, the eschatological nature of our salvation should lead us, even in the midst of our current suffering, to trust in God. He is our future hope and in him rests our full confidence and assurance. As Paul promised those in Philippi, "And I am sure of this, that he who began a good work in you will bring it to completion at the day of Jesus Christ" (Phil. 1:6). With such a great promise, we press on, running the race before us with endurance, looking to Jesus, the founder and perfector of our faith (Heb. 12:1–2).

Summary

The triune God has planned salvation before the foundation of the world. In the covenant of redemption the Father appointed his Son to be our Mediator, and this is a mission the Son voluntarily fulfilled when he accomplished redemption as the incarnate God-man. Though Adam failed to uphold the covenant of creation, Christ, the second and last Adam, has perfectly

---

34. Ferguson, *Holy Spirit*, 99.

obeyed the law and offered up himself on our behalf as an atoning sacrifice for the forgiveness of sins. The Holy Spirit was then sent to apply the work accomplished by the Son of God's elect. The Spirit's application of redemption has been labeled the order of salvation, and this order is seen throughout the New Testament. The Spirit effectually calls and regenerates, grants faith and repentance, justifies, adopts, sanctifies, and preserves God's elect so that they reach glorification.

REFLECTION QUESTIONS

1. Study Romans 8:28–30. What is Paul's train of thought?

2. How important is it that we properly order each stage in the salvation process?

3. Do you find the order of salvation pedagogically helpful as you seek to understand what God is doing to bring you to glory?

4. When you reflect on the many "links" in the "golden chain," do you get a sense for just how much God has done to save you?

5. How does the order of salvation preserve balance so that we are not lazy in the present or lacking confidence in the future?

What Does It Mean to Be United with Christ? (Part 1)

If Christ has died for us, why then do we need the Spirit to unite us to Christ? Sixteenth-century reformer John Calvin answered such a question this way: "We must understand that as long as Christ remains outside of us, and we are separated from him, all that he has suffered and done for the salvation of the human race remains useless and of no value for us. . . . All that he possesses is nothing to us until we grow into one body with him."[1] Calvin was right; our actual union with Christ is absolutely essential. Union with Christ is the central truth of our salvation, for it is "not simply a phase of the application of redemption; it underlies every aspect of redemption."[2] Union with Christ is the "dominant motif and architectonic principle of the order of salvation."[3] Rather than placing union with Christ at a particular point in the order of salvation, union with Christ serves as an umbrella category within which the entire order of salvation finds its beginning, fulfillment, and end goal (John 6:56; 15:4–7; Rom. 8:10; et al.).[4] The Spirit's goal at each stage in our salvation is for the elect to be found *in Christ* (1 Cor. 12:12–13). As John Owen insightfully explains, union "is the cause of all other graces that we are

---

1. John Calvin, *Institutes of the Christian Religion*, ed. John T. McNeil, trans. Ford Lewis Battles, LCC, vols. 20–21 (Philadelphia: Westminster John Knox, 1960), 3.1.1.
2. John Murray, *Redemption Accomplished and Applied* (Grand Rapids: Eerdmans,1955), 165 (cf. 170).
3. Sinclair Ferguson, *The Holy Spirit* (Downers Grove, IL: InterVarsity Press, 1997), 100.
4. Also see 1 Corinthians 15:22; 2 Corinthians 5:17; 12:2; 13:5; Galatians 2:20; 3:28; Ephesians 1:4, 2:10; 3:17; Philippians 3:9; Colossians 1:27; 1 Thessalonians 4:16; 1 John 4:13. There is a potential danger in placing union at a specific point in the order of salvation. For example, if placed after conversion, one might think that union is man's doing. But this would reverse the biblical order. Union flows to us from Christ through the Spirit; we do not create union but it is a gift.

made partakers of; they are all communicated unto us by virtue of our union with Christ. Hence is our adoption, our justification, our sanctification, our fruitfulness, our perseverance, our resurrection, our glory."[5] Therefore, the goal of the order of salvation is for the sinner to directly participate in Christ's benefits through the power of the Spirit (Eph. 1:3).[6]

Union-with-Christ Language in Scripture

In the Pauline letters alone the phrase *in Christ* is used seventy-three times.[7] While we cannot engage in an in-depth analysis here, nevertheless certain uses of this phrase especially deserve our attention in this chapter.

To begin with, Scripture speaks of God saving his people *in Christ*. For example, Paul affirms that we are justified by God's grace through the redemption that is in Christ Jesus (Rom. 3:24; cf. Eph. 2:13). Later in Romans he also states that while the wages of sin is death, "the free gift of God is eternal life in Christ Jesus our Lord" (Rom. 6:23; cf. 1 Cor. 1:4). Similarly, Paul writes to the Corinthians that it is "in Christ" that "God was reconciling the world to himself, not counting their trespasses against them" (2 Cor. 5:19). Furthermore, God "has blessed us in Christ with every spiritual blessing in the heavenly places" (Eph. 1:3). Even though we were dead in our trespasses, God, because of his great love with which he loved us, "made us alive together with Christ" and "raised us up with him and seated us with him in the heavenly places in Christ Jesus, so that in the coming ages he might show the immeasurable riches of his grace in kindness toward us in Christ Jesus" (Eph. 2:4–7; cf. 2 Tim. 1:9). As those who have been seated with Christ, we are called God's "workmanship, created in Christ Jesus for good works, which God prepared beforehand, that we should walk in them" (Eph. 2:10; cf. 5:28–32). Paul can speak of those in Christ as new creations, since the "old has passed away" and the "new has come" (2 Cor. 5:17; cf. Rom. 6:4; 1 Cor. 15:22).

Scripture also speaks of the believer placing his/her faith "in Christ," being justified in Christ, and receiving a new status in Christ. Sinners, says Paul, "are justified by his [God's] grace as a gift, through the redemption that is in Christ Jesus" (Rom. 3:24; cf. Gal. 2:17). As a result, there is "now no condemnation for those who are in Christ Jesus" (Rom. 8:1). In Christ we have "redemption, the forgiveness of our sins" (Col. 1:14; cf. 2:11–12). As those who have been justified, we are to consider ourselves "dead to sin and alive to God in Christ Jesus" (Rom. 6:11).

---

5. John Owen, *An Exposition of the Epistle to the Hebrews*, vol. 21, The Works of John Owen (Edinburgh: Banner of Truth, 1991), 150.

6. Ferguson, *Holy Spirit*, 101–2 (cf. 103–13).

7. In Greek: *en Christō* (ἐν Χριστῷ). On the various uses, see Constantine R. Campbell, *Paul and Union with Christ* (Grand Rapids: Zondervan, 2012), 141–91.

Union with Christ language, however, is not limited to the exact phrase "in Christ" (*en Christō*). Other phrases are used as well, including

- *into* Christ (*eis Christon*; Rom. 6:3; 11:36; 16:5; et al.)[8]
- *with* Christ (*sun Christō*; Rom. 6:4–8; 8:17, 29, 32; et al.)[9]
- *through* Christ (*dia Christou*; Rom. 1:3–5, 8; 2:16; et al.)[10]

Additionally, certain metaphors powerfully convey the image of being united to Christ:

- body of Christ (Rom. 12:4–5; 1 Cor. 6:15; 10:16–17; et al.)[11]
- temple and building (1 Cor. 3:9, 16–17; 6:19–20; 9:13; et al.)[12]
- marriage (Rom. 7:1–4; 1 Cor. 6:15–17; 2 Cor. 11:2–3; Eph. 5:22–32)
- new clothing (Rom. 13:12–14; 1 Cor. 15:51–54; 2 Cor. 5:1–4; et al.)[13]

Each of these metaphors conveys an important aspect of union with Christ. Campbell captures the meaning of each metaphor:

- *The metaphor of the body of Christ* depicts the church as an organic being as each member partakes in Christ and is joined one to another. The metaphor implies union by its very nature.
- *The metaphors of temple and building* convey the corporate nature of the church, with the temple depicting the dwelling of God by his Spirit among his people, and the building denoting a structure incorporated into Christ, its foundation.
- *The metaphor of marriage* profoundly depicts the church's spiritual union with Christ as a personal and exclusive bond as he saves, prepares, and cares for her, while she submits to his headship.
- *The metaphor of clothing* depicts the reality of conversion to Christ as well as its attendant ethical expectations; the believer *has* put on

---

8. 1 Corinthians 8:6, 12; 2 Corinthians 1:21; 2:8; Galatians 2:16; 3:24, 27; Ephesians 4:15; 5:32; Philippians 1:29; Colossians 1:16–17, 20; 2:5; Philemon 6.

9. 2 Corinthians 13:4; Galatians 2:19; Ephesians 2:5; Colossians 2:12, 13, 20; 3:1, 3, 4; Philippians 1:23; 3:10, 21; 1 Thessalonians 4:14, 17; 5:10.

10. Romans 3:22; 5:1–2, 8–9, 11, 17, 21; 7:4, 25; 15:30; 16:27; 1 Corinthians 8:6; 15:57; 2 Corinthians 1:5, 20; 3:4; 5:18; 10:1; Galatians 1:1, 12; 2:16; 6:14; Ephesians 1:5; 2:17–18; Philippians 1:11; 3:9; Colossians 1:16–17, 19–20; 3:17; 1 Thessalonians 5:9; Titus 3:6. Not only are there biblical texts where we are said to be *in Christ*, there are other texts where Christ is said to be *in us* (John 6:56; 15:4–5, Rom. 8:10; 2 Cor. 13:5; Gal. 2:20; Eph. 3:17; Col. 1:27; 1 John 4:13).

11. 1 Corinthians 11:29; 12:12–27; Ephesians 1:22–23; 2:14–16; 4:4, 11–13, 15–16, 23, 29–30; Colossians 1:18, 24; 2:19; 3:15.

12. 2 Corinthians 5:1; 6:16; Ephesians 2:21–22; 2 Thessalonians 2:4; 1 Timothy 3:15.

13. Galatians 3:26–27; Ephesians 4:20–24; 6:10; Colossians 3:9–10, 12.

Christ and *is to* put on Christ. It is a symbol for union with Christ that entails conformity to Christ.[14]

Union-with-Christ language is not limited to the apostle Paul's writings but is used by Jesus as well. In John 6:56, for example, Jesus makes the shocking statement, "Whoever feeds on my flesh and drinks my blood abides in me, and I in him." Jesus is not speaking of literally eating his flesh and drinking his blood but is using this vivid imagery to speak of a spiritual reality (e.g., 6:35), namely, believing and trusting in Christ, particularly in his atoning death for life everlasting (cf. 6:54). In John 15 Jesus again returns to the theme of union when he says, "Abide in me, and I in you" (15:4). Using the analogy of a vine and its fruit (an analogy similar to Paul's "body of Christ"), Jesus goes on to say that we, as branches, cannot bear fruit by ourselves but must remain in Christ, the vine. If we abide in Christ and Christ abides in us, then we will bear much fruit (15:4–5).

One of the most intimate prayers of Jesus is in John 17 as he prepares to undergo his crucifixion. There Jesus prays to his Father for those who will one day believe in him. He prays that "just as you, Father, are in me, and I in you, that they also may be in us, so that the world may believe that you have sent me. The glory that you have given me I have given to them, that they may be one even as we are one, I in them and you in me, that they may become perfectly one, so that the world may know that you sent me and loved them even as you loved me" (17:20–23; cf. v. 26). Jesus speaks of a profound relationship—a mutual indwelling—between himself and believers. So deep and so intense is this indwelling that Jesus actually prays that he would be "in them."

So far we have seen that union-with-Christ language is legion in Scripture. But how are we to put these passages together, specifically in relation to the Spirit's application of salvation? In order to answer such a question we need to examine (1) the source, (2) the basis, and (3) the realization of union with Christ. We will explore the first two in this chapter and the third in the next chapter.

The Source of Union with Christ

Was our union with Christ planned or orchestrated by God before the foundation of the world? The answer is "yes." God's election in eternity past is the source or root of our union with Christ. As Paul explains, God has blessed us "in Christ with every spiritual blessing in the heavenly places" (Eph. 1:3). God "chose us in him [Christ] before the foundation of the world" (Eph. 1:4). It was in love that God "predestined us for adoption through Jesus Christ, according to the purpose of his will" (Eph. 1:5; cf. 1:11). God chose us in Christ so that "we should be holy and blameless before him" (Eph. 1:4). God chose us to be united to Christ not because we were holy and blameless but

---

14. Campbell, *Paul and Union with Christ*, 323 (emphasis added).

so that we would be holy and blameless before him. What Paul demonstrates in Ephesians 1:4 is that the purpose of our election is for us to be united to Christ. Practically, this means that union with Christ was not an afterthought in God's mind but was his intent and purpose from the very start. Christ is always to be conceived of in relation to his people, and likewise his people in relation to their Savior.[15]

Likewise, Paul writes to Timothy that God "saved us and called us to a holy calling, not because of our works but because of his own purpose and grace, which he gave us in Christ Jesus before the ages began, and which now has been manifested through the appearing of our Savior Christ Jesus, who abolished death and brought life and immortality to light through the gospel" (2 Tim. 1:8–10). Once again Paul connects our election to our union with Christ. Before the foundation of the world, God the Father gave his elect to Christ.

Such a truth is reiterated by Jesus himself during his incarnation. Jesus, giving us a window into the Trinitarian nature of our redemption, says, "All that the Father gives me will come to me, and whoever comes to me I will never cast out" (John 6:37). Jesus is clear that his mission is to do the will of the Father, not losing any of those whom the Father has given to him (6:38–39). Those whom the Father has given to him, Christ will raise up on the last day (6:40). What we see from Jesus himself is that God, before time began, gave his elect to his Son.

Last, the connection between union with Christ and election is again evident in Romans 8:29–30: "For those whom he foreknew he also predestined to be conformed to the image of his Son, in order that he might be the first-born among many brothers. And those whom he predestined he also called, and those whom he called he also justified, and those whom he justified he also glorified." Notice, predestination is brought about so that God's elect will be "conformed to the image of his Son." We cannot divorce or abstract election from our union with Christ. The latter finds its source in the former.[16]

The Basis of Union with Christ

If election is the source of our union with Christ, it follows that the work of Christ is its basis. Before the foundation of the world God chose us in Christ, and then at the proper time the Father sent his Son to take on human flesh, live a perfect life in obedience to the Law (i.e., active obedience), suffer and then die in our place, absorbing the due penalty for our sin (i.e., passive obedience), and rise for our justification, accomplishing and securing our redemption (Matt. 20:28; 26:26–29; John 6:51; 11:50; et al.).[17] Christ did this all

---

15. Anthony A. Hoekema, *Saved by Grace* (Grand Rapids: Eerdmans, 1989), 57.
16. Robert Letham, *Union with Christ: In Scripture, History, and Theology* (Phillipsburg, NJ: P&R, 2011), 65–66; idem, *The Work of Christ* (Downers Grove, IL: InterVarsity Press, 1993), 55–56.
17. Romans 3:24–25; 4:25; 5:8, 12–21, 32; 6:25; 8:32; 1 Corinthians 15:3, 20–23; 2 Corinthians 5:14–15, 21; 1 Timothy 2:6; Hebrews 9:28; 1 Peter 2:21–24; 3:18.

on our behalf and *in our stead.*[18] It is on the basis of Christ's redemptive work that the Spirit then applies the work of Christ to us.

That Jesus came to give his life on our behalf, as an atoning sacrifice for our sin, is evident throughout the New Testament. For example, Jesus himself says in John 10:11, "I am the good shepherd. The good shepherd lays down his life for the sheep." In 1 John we read that the one who was without sin "appeared in order to take away sins" (3:5). We did not love God, but "he loved us and sent his Son to be the propitiation for our sins" (4:10). The "Father has sent his Son to be the Savior of the world" (4:14). And in Romans 3 we read that God put forward his Son, Christ Jesus, as a "propitiation by his blood, to be received by faith" (Rom. 3:25). Propitiation by the blood of Christ is the very basis on which our faith in Christ is built (Heb. 2:17; 1 John 2:2; 4:10).[19] Without this propitiating work of Christ, our actual union with Christ is impossible. It is only because Christ gave himself up as a perfect sacrifice on our behalf, paying the penalty for our sin, that the Spirit can then apply the redemptive work Christ has accomplished to us. In other words, it is because Christ came to die for us that the Spirit is then able to unite us to Jesus. Enmity has been removed; the wrath we deserve has been satisfied by Christ. A way has been made to be reconciled to God, and that way is Christ. In him not only do we have our sins forgiven but we are the recipients of the eternal life Christ gives to those who trust in him (cf. 1 John 5:11–12). Christ's death, therefore, is the basis of our union.[20] As Paul says to the Ephesians, "In him we have redemption through his blood, the forgiveness of our trespasses, according to the riches of his grace" (Eph. 1:7; cf. 1:11). Though we were once far off, in Christ Jesus we have been brought near by his blood (Eph. 2:13; cf. Rom. 8:32; Col. 1:20).

Moreover, during the incarnation of Christ, God thought of us as being *in Christ*, even though we did not yet exist. Christ acted as our representative, our federal head. Then, upon faith in Christ, his actions were counted to us as if we did them ourselves. Our union with Christ is legally enacted through imputation. As the Heidelberg Catechism (1563) says, "God, without any merit of my own, out of pure grace, grants me the benefits of the perfect expiation of Christ, imputing to me his righteousness and holiness as if I had never committed a single sin or had ever been sinful, having fulfilled myself all the obedience which Christ has carried out for me, if only I accept such favor with a trusting heart" (Q. 60). Union with Christ has a strong *legal* aspect that cannot be denied and must be given priority

---

18. Letham, *Union with Christ*, 61; Leon Morris, *The Apostolic Preaching of the Cross* (London: Tyndale Press, 1955), 125–85.
19. Calvin, *Institutes*, 2.12.3; also see 3.1.1.
20. Letham, *Union with Christ*, 41.

in relation to our ongoing transformation.[21] As we will see in Questions 21 and 22, the righteousness of Christ, which he earned for us, is imputed to us who believe. We did not yet exist nor were we present in any way, yet since Christ was our legal and covenantal representative, all that he did for us is now counted to us upon faith. God looks at us and sees the satisfying and finished work of his Son. It's on that basis that we are now being transformed inwardly into the image of his Son.

Several texts demonstrate such representation. Paul says in Romans 5:19, "For as by the one man's disobedience the many were made sinners, so by the one man's obedience the many will be made righteous" (cf. 1 Cor. 1:30; Phil. 3:9). Or consider 2 Corinthians 5:21, "For our sake he [God] made him [Christ] to be sin who knew no sin, so that in him [Christ] we might become the righteousness of God." We are "in him [Christ]" because God made Christ to be sin on our behalf. Theologians have called this the "Great Exchange."[22] Christ took our sin (cf. Isa. 53:6; 1 Peter 2:24) and in return we have received the righteousness of Christ. We will return to this great exchange in depth in Question 23.

In sum, Christ has earned for us all the blessings of salvation we so desperately need and as a result we belong to Christ and are now united to Christ (Rom. 5:17). As we will soon discover, it is because Christ has won our salvation through his life, death, and resurrection that the Holy Spirit can then cause us to be born again, thereby uniting us to Christ, bestowing upon us all the blessings that are ours in Christ Jesus (Rom. 6:4–11; Eph. 1:3–14; 2:5–6; 1 Peter 1:3–5).

Summary

Union with Christ is not one step or stage in the order of salvation, but rather is the umbrella category that undergirds and underlies every aspect of salvation. The Spirit's goal at each stage in salvation is for God's elect to be found in Christ. Furthermore, while the source of union with Christ is divine election in eternity past, the basis of this union is the work of Christ in his life, death, and resurrection.

REFLECTION QUESTIONS

1. If Christ died for us, why do we still need the Spirit to unite us to Christ?

2. What does Jesus have to say in John's gospel about being united to him? How does his teaching change the way you view your relationship to him as Savior?

---

21. See Letham, *Union with Christ*, 57–60.
22. Jerry Bridges and Bob Bevington, *The Great Exchange* (Wheaton, IL: Crossway, 2007).

3. What are some of the different metaphors Scripture uses to refer to union with Christ, and what do these metaphors convey?

4. In Ephesians 1:4 Paul teaches that our union with Christ finds its source in the electing choice of God before the foundation of the world. How might Paul's teaching change the way we understand our identity in Christ even before time began?

5. In light of passages like Romans 3:25, would our actual union with Christ even be possible apart from Christ being the propitiation for our sins?

What Does It Mean to Be United with Christ? (Part 2)

So far we have seen that the *source* of our union with Christ is to be found in God's election and the *basis* of our union with Christ is to be found in the work of Christ in his life, death, and resurrection. In this chapter we will learn that our *actual* union with Christ occurs when the Holy Spirit unites us to Christ. Again, don't miss the Trinitarian nature of our salvation. God the Father chose us in Christ before the foundation of the world (Eph. 1:4–5, 11); God the Son was then sent by the Father to die on our behalf (Eph. 1:7–10); and finally the Father and the Son sent the Holy Spirit to apply the benefits of Christ's work to us so that we would actually be united with Christ (Eph. 1:13–14).

What then does our actual union with Christ look like? Anthony Hoekema lists eight ways Scripture speaks of our union with Christ, demonstrating that the entire salvation process (i.e., order of salvation) flows out of our initial union with Christ.[1]

1. We are initially united with Christ in effectual calling and regeneration.[2]

2. We appropriate and continue to live out this union through faith.

3. We are justified in union with Christ.

4. We are sanctified through union with Christ.

---

1. Anthony A. Hoekema, *Saved by Grace* (Grand Rapids: Eerdmans, 1989), 59–64.
2. I have tweaked Hoekema's wording on this first point so as to include effectual calling along with regeneration.

5. We persevere in the life of faith in union with Christ.

6. We are even said to die in Christ.

7. We shall be raised with Christ.

8. We shall be eternally glorified with Christ.

Let's build off of Hoekema's discussion, elaborating upon it at points, as we look at each of these eight points in turn.

1. 'We Are Initially United with Christ in Effectual Calling and Regeneration (the New Birth)'

Though the sinner is spiritually dead, the Father effectually draws his elect *to his Son* (John 6:44, 65; 2 Tim. 1:9) and by the power of the Spirit makes sinners who are dead in their trespasses alive together *with Christ* (Eph. 2:5, 10; cf. Rom. 6:11). As a result, we are a new creation in Christ Jesus (see Questions 12–17).[3]

As Paul can say, "But God, being rich in mercy, because of the great love with which he loved us, even when we were dead in our trespasses, made us alive together with Christ—by grace you have been saved" (Eph. 2:4–5). Paul does not merely say God made us alive but that he made us alive "together with Christ." In verse 10 Paul again hints at our union with Christ through regeneration when he says we were "created in Christ Jesus." Paul is utilizing the language of Genesis 1 to show how the Spirit takes a sinner and makes him into a new creation (cf. 2 Cor. 5:17). God, in his sovereignty, created spiritual life where there was only death, and in doing so he unites us to Christ (Rom. 8:2; 1 Cor. 15:22; Col. 2:11, 13).[4] Therefore, God's election of us in Christ results in God's re-creation of us in Christ.[5]

2. 'We Appropriate and Continue to Live Out This Union Through Faith'

The Spirit brings us into union with Christ through our new birth, but this union is enjoyed through faith. As Paul says in Galatians 3:26, it is in

---

3. John M. Frame, *Salvation Belongs to the Lord, A Theology of Lordship* (Phillipsburg, NJ: P&R, 2006), 186.

4. John Piper, *Finally Alive* (Fearn, Ross-shire, Scotland: Christian Focus, 2009), 32–33, 37.

5. Hoekema, *Saved by Grace*, 60. One might wonder how we can be united to Christ at this point if we are passive in regeneration (i.e., monergism). Berkhof answers, "While the union is effected when the sinner is renewed by the operation of the Holy Spirit, he does not become cognizant of it and does not actively cultivate it until the conscious operation of faith begins. Then he becomes aware of the fact that he has no righteousness of his own, and that the righteousness by which he appears just in the sight of God is imputed to him" (Louis Berkhof, *Systematic Theology* [Grand Rapids: Eerdmans, 1996], 452).

Christ Jesus that we "are all sons of God, through faith." Similarly, Paul says in Ephesians 1:13, "In him you also, when you heard the word of truth, the gospel of your salvation, and believed in him, were sealed with the promised Holy Spirit." And to the Colossians Paul writes that we have been buried with Christ in baptism, "in which you were also raised with him through faith in the powerful working of God, who raised him from the dead" (Col. 2:12).

Moreover, Paul speaks of justification through faith as well. "We ourselves are Jews by birth and not Gentile sinners; yet we know that a person is not justified by works of the law but through faith in Jesus Christ, so we also have believed in Christ Jesus, in order to be justified by faith in Christ and not by works of the law, because by works of the law no one will be justified" (Gal. 2:15–16). Paul's letter to the Romans parallels his letter to the Galatians: "Therefore, since we have been justified by faith, we have peace with God through our Lord Jesus Christ. Through him we have also obtained access by faith into this grace in which we stand, and we rejoice in hope of the glory of God" (Rom. 5:1–2).

However, not only is union with Christ appropriated by faith, but it is lived out through faith as well. For example, Paul says in Galatians 2:20, "I have been crucified with Christ. It is no longer I who live, but Christ who lives in me. And the life I now live in the flesh I live by faith in the Son of God, who loved me and gave himself for me." No longer are we slaves to sin, but now Christ lives within us. Nevertheless, this only happens "by faith in the Son of God."

Paul reiterates our union with Christ through faith to the Ephesians as well. Paul prays that believers would be strengthened with power through the Spirit "so that Christ may dwell in your hearts through faith" (Eph. 3:16–17). It is through faith that Christ permanently dwells in us. Even Paul's instructions to Timothy are revealing. The Scriptures are able "to make you wise for salvation through faith in Christ Jesus" (2 Tim. 3:15).

3. 'We Are Justified in Union with Christ'

As Questions 22 and 24–25 will make clear, justification occurs when God declares us righteous, imputing or crediting the righteousness of Christ to our account. We stand "not guilty" before God, clothed in the perfect righteousness of Christ, having all our sins forgiven (Zech. 3). Yet we cannot divorce justification from union with Christ. Paul writes in 1 Corinthians 1:30–31, "And because of him you are in Christ Jesus, who became to us wisdom from God, righteousness and sanctification and redemption, so that, as it is written, 'Let the one who boasts, boast in the Lord.'" Christ has become our righteousness, and therefore we are "in Christ Jesus." Similarly, Paul writes in 2 Corinthians 5:21, "For our sake he made him to be sin who knew no sin, so that in him we might become the righteousness of God." God made Christ to be sin, though he never sinned, so that "in him" we become the righteousness of God. In other words, it is in Christ that God counts or reckons us perfectly righteous. Luther highlights how, exactly, this imputed righteousness is tied to our union with Christ when he writes, "Through faith in Christ, therefore, Christ's righteousness becomes our righteousness and all that he has becomes ours; rather, he himself becomes ours."[6]

Paul's point is made especially clear in Philippians 3:8–9, where he says that he has suffered the loss of all things in order that he may gain Christ and be found in him, "not having a righteousness of my own that comes from the law, but that which comes through faith in Christ, the righteousness from God that depends on faith" (cf. Rom. 1:17; 3:22). How is it that a sinner is to be "found in him [Christ]"? One is not found in Christ by possessing a righteousness of his own "from the law." Rather, one is found to be in Christ by possessing a righteousness "which comes through faith in Christ." It is this righteousness that is from God and it depends on faith, not on works (cf. Gal. 2:16). As Paul clarifies in Romans 3:24, we are justified by grace as a gift and it is "through the redemption that is in Christ Jesus." By his grace, God in Christ has forgiven our sins (Eph. 4:32; Col. 1:14), and since we have been justified by faith we are at peace with God through our Lord Jesus Christ (Rom. 5:1), no longer condemned (Rom. 8:1). Due to the abundance of God's grace and the free gift of righteousness, we now "reign in life through the one man Jesus Christ" (Rom. 5:17).[7]

Given the priority Paul gives to the forensic (judicial) nature of our justification in these texts (see also Question 22), it is misguided to say that union with Christ involves a relational aspect of salvation, but not a legal one.[8] Quite the contrary, union with Christ not only involves relational categories, but legal ones as well; the two are not in conflict with one another. To be even more specific, *it is the legal that undergirds and grounds the relational.*[9] The transformative aspect of our union with Christ is based upon, grounded in, and dependent upon the forensic or legal aspect of our union with Christ. To put the matter plainly, justification is the very foundation of sanctification, not vice versa (Rom. 5:16; 8:1–17; Gal. 3:14).[10] As Fesko points out, while one might say, "I am sanctified because I am justified," one should not conclude,

6. Martin Luther, "Two Kinds of Righteousness," in *Luther's Works*, ed. Harold J. Grimm (Philadelphia: Fortress, 1957; reprint, 1971), 31:297.

7. Paul speaks of our union with Christ in relation to other categories as well: eternal life and salvation (Rom. 5:8–9, 21; 6:23; Eph. 1:11; 1 Thess. 5:9), reconciliation (Rom. 5:11; 2 Cor. 5:18–19; Col. 1:19–20), and the gift of grace (Rom. 1:3–5; 1 Cor. 1:4, 30). Also consider how Paul connects union with Christ and the Holy Spirit (Rom. 8:2; Eph. 2:17–18; Titus 3:6).

8. For a response to such a view, see J. V. Fesko, *Justification: Understanding the Classic Reformed Doctrine* (Phillipsburg, NJ: P&R, 2008), 274.

9. A. A. Hodge, *Outlines of Theology* (1860; Edinburgh: Banner of Truth, 1991), 484; Geerhardus Vos, "The Alleged Legalism in Paul's Doctrine of Justification," in *Redemptive History and Biblical Interpretation*, ed. Richard B. Gaffin Jr. (Phillipsburg, NJ: P&R, 1980), 384; Fesko, *Justification*, 276.

10. Berkhof, *Systematic Theology*, 452; Michael Horton, *Covenant and Salvation: Union with Christ* (Louisville, Westminster John Knox, 2005), chaps. 9–10; Fesko, *Justification*, 276.

"I am justified because I am sanctified."[11] There is a cause and effect, the cause being our justification, and the effect being our good works in sanctification, as well as the fellowship we have with Christ.[12]

The priority of the forensic to the relational or mystical aspects in our union with Christ properly corresponds to our former union with Adam. In Adam we inherited guilt and corruption, and we argued in Question 3 that the former is the cause of the latter (i.e., immediate imputation). Correspondingly, in Christ we inherit righteousness and also new life. This new life starts with regeneration but also characterizes sanctification. Yet, this new life in sanctification can only be imparted to us because it is based upon our new legal identity as those declared "righteous" in Christ. The imputation of Christ's righteousness secures our new status, and on that basis all the benefits of Christ's resurrection life are now imparted to us. It is this latter reality that can be called the ongoing work of the Spirit. The Spirit, says Horton, "takes what belongs properly to Christ and makes it our own (Jn 16:14), working within us so that we bear the fruit of the Spirit (Jn 15:1–11; cf. Gal 5:22–26)."[13]

Practically (and pastorally) speaking, this means that our imitation of Christ must always be established upon our right standing in Christ. The *indicative* of the gospel, in other words, always grounds the *imperatives* of the Christian life.[14] "Every subjective blessing that we experience *within* us," explains Horton, "is the result of Christ's objective work *for* us, outside of us, in history. We are not declared righteous legally nor caused to abide in Christ forensically because we bear the fruit of the Spirit, but vice versa."[15]

Therefore, it is not that we reject the actual righteousness of sanctification; rather, this actual righteousness is based upon Christ's imputed righteousness.[16] Waving the banner of the Reformation cause, Luther famously said that the imputed righteousness of Christ "is the basis, the cause, the source of all our own actual righteousness."[17] We should not abandon either form of righteousness, but we must be careful always to keep them in their proper relation to one another. To quote Geerhardus Vos, "The mystical is based on the forensic, not the forensic on the mystical."[18]

---

11. J. V. Fesko, *Beyond Calvin: Union with Christ and Justification in Early Modern Reformed Theology (1517–1700)* (Göttingen: Vandenhoeck & Ruprecht, 2012), 29–30.
12. John Calvin, *Institutes of the Christian Religion* 3.3, ed. John T. McNeil, trans. Ford Lewis Battles, Library of Christian Classics, vols. 20–21 (Philadelphia: Westminster, 1960), 3.11.1.
13. Michael Horton, *Pilgrim Theology: Core Doctrines for Christian Disciples* (Grand Rapids: Zondervan, 2011), 273.
14. Ibid.
15. Ibid., 276.
16. Ibid., 273.
17. Luther, "Two Kinds of Righteousness," 31:298. Calvin said the same: *Institutes* 3.1.1; 3.2.24; 3.20.1; 4.15.16.
18. Geerhardus Vos, "The Alleged Legalism in Paul's Doctrine of Justification," in *Redemptive History and Biblical Interpretation*, ed. Richard B. Gaffin Jr. (Phillipsburg, NJ: P&R, 1980), 384.

4. 'We Are Sanctified through Union with Christ'

In 1 Corinthians 1:30 Paul not only says that Christ is our righteousness, but he also says that Christ is our sanctification. Paul opens his letter to the Corinthians addressing them as those who are "sanctified in Christ Jesus" (1 Cor. 1:2). As seen already, Christians are those who have been created in Christ Jesus for good works (Eph. 2:10). As we have received Christ Jesus the Lord, so are we to "walk in him, rooted and built up in him and established in the faith, just as you were taught, abounding in thanksgiving" (Col. 2:6–7; cf. 1 Cor. 15:58). Rather than being tossed around by every wind of doctrine, human cunning, or deceitful scheme, we are to be those who speak the truth in love, growing up "in every way into him who is the head, into Christ" (Eph. 4:15). Indeed, this was Paul's mission in life: "that I may know him and the power of his resurrection, and may share his sufferings, becoming like him in his death" (Phil. 3:10; cf. 2 Cor. 1:5).[19] The point is clear: Our sanctification is through union with our Savior.

5. 'We Persevere in the Life of Faith in Union with Christ'

If our sanctification is in Christ, so also is our perseverance, for these are two sides of the same coin. Those who are in Christ can never be snatched out of Christ's hand (John 10:27–28). Those in Christ belong to Christ. They are his sheep and in him they possess eternal life so that they will never perish (Rom. 5:8–9, 21; 6:23; 8:32; Eph. 1:11; 1 Thess. 5:9). Paul knew this personal assurance well: "For I am sure that neither death nor life, nor angels nor rulers, nor things present nor things to come, nor powers, nor height nor depth, nor anything else in all creation, will be able to separate us from the love of God in Christ Jesus our Lord" (Rom. 8:38–39; cf. Phil. 4:7, 19). Nothing in this life, not even the devil himself, can rip us away from Christ (see Questions 34–35).

Scripture, however, does not merely teach God's preservation of the believer but exhorts believers to press on, to persevere in the faith as well, something that can only be accomplished by abiding in Christ (John 15:4–5; 1 John 2–4), for apart from him we can bear no fruit (Gal. 5:22). Paul modeled such perseverance in his own ministry. He writes to the Philippians that though he, out of all people, had reason to place confidence in the flesh (Phil. 3:5–7), whatever gain he had, he counted as loss for the sake of Christ. "Indeed, I count everything as loss because of the surpassing worth of knowing Christ Jesus my Lord" (Phil. 3:8). For Christ's sake Paul suffered the loss of all things and counted them as rubbish so that he "may gain Christ and be found in him," not by means of a righteousness that comes from the law, but by means of a righteousness that comes from God, "that which comes through faith in Christ" (Phil. 3:9). Paul's aim in all this is to know Christ, the "power of his resurrection," even share in

---

19. Other texts that connect union with Christ and sanctification include 1 Corinthians 1:4–5; 2 Corinthians 2:14; Ephesians 1:3, 15; 6:10; Philippians 2:5; 4:7, 19; Colossians 1:4; 2:20; 1 Thessalonians 4:1.

his sufferings, "becoming like him in his death, that by any means possible I may attain the resurrection from the dead" (Phil. 3:10–11; cf. 1:29; Rom. 8:17).

Paul confesses that he has not obtained this nor is he already perfect. Rather, he presses on to make it his own, and he can do so because "Christ Jesus has made me his own" (Phil. 3:12). Paul forgets what lies behind and strains forward to what lies ahead. "I press on toward the goal for the prize of the upward call of God in Christ Jesus" (Phil. 3:14). Paul admonishes every Christian to do the same, imitating his example (Phil. 3:16, 17). Paul concludes this word of encouragement to the Philippians by reminding them that their citizenship is in heaven, and "from it we await a Savior, the Lord Jesus Christ, who will transform our lowly body to be like his glorious body, by the power that enables him even to subject all things to himself" (Phil. 3:20–21).[20]

6. 'We Are Said to Die in Christ'
"For if we live, we live to the Lord, and if we die, we die to the Lord. So then, whether we live or whether we die, we are the Lord's" (Rom. 14:8). Previously we learned that the love of God for us in Christ is so strong that nothing can separate us from him. Here we discover that even when we physically die we continue to belong to Christ (1 Cor. 15:18). So unbreakable is our identity in Christ that even in death we are said to be in Christ (cf. Rev. 14:13). No wonder, then, Paul can say with great confidence that to live is Christ and to die is gain (Phil. 1:21). Death is gain because to die is to "depart and be with Christ," which is "far better" (Phil. 1:23).

7. 'We Shall Be Raised with Christ'
When we think of our union with Christ, typically our attention is drawn to our union in his death on the cross, which has massive implications for our salvation (Rom. 6:3–8; 7:4; Gal. 3:27–29; 6:14; Col. 3:1–3). However, Paul also thought of our union in relationship to Christ's resurrection. Yes, we are already raised with Christ spiritually (Col. 3:1; Eph. 2:6), no longer being dead in our trespasses and sins. But it is also true that one day we will receive a resurrected body (see Question 40). How is this possible? It is possible because Christ himself rose from the grave. Since he represented us in his death, it is also true that he represented us in his resurrection. Paul explains, "For as in Adam all die, so also in Christ shall all be made alive. But each in his own order: Christ the firstfruits, then at his coming those who belong to Christ" (1 Cor. 15:22–23; cf. Phil. 3:21; Col. 3:4; 1 Thess. 4:14–17; 5:10). A day is coming when all those in Christ will be resurrected bodily from the dead. In that light, we must conclude that union with Christ is not limited to the spiritual, but has physical implications as well.

---

20. Other texts that connect union with Christ and perseverance include Colossians 1:28; 2 Timothy 2:10; 3:12.

8. 'We Shall Be Eternally Glorified with Christ'

One day Christ who is our life will appear. When that day comes, says Paul, we "will appear with him in glory" (Col. 3:4). Similarly, Paul says to the Thessalonians, "For the Lord himself will descend from heaven with a cry of command, with the voice of an archangel, and with the sound of the trumpet of God. And the dead *in Christ* will rise first. Then we who are alive, who are left, will be caught up together with them in the clouds to meet the Lord in the air, and so we will always be with the Lord" (1 Thess. 4:16–17). When Christ returns, the dead "in Christ" will rise. From that point on we will be with the Lord forever in our resurrected state, worshipping him in a new heavens and earth. Our union with Christ, though first actualized in regeneration, will be eternally enjoyed in glorification.

Summary

While the source of union with Christ is divine election in eternity past, and while the basis of union with Christ is the work of Christ in his life, death, and resurrection, we are actually united with Christ in space and time when the Spirit applies the work of Christ to us. Union with Christ is first realized in effectual calling and regeneration, but then we appropriate our union through faith and are justified in union with Christ, which is the forensic ground of our union. Furthermore, we are also sanctified through union with Christ and said to persevere to the end in union with Christ. Finally, Scripture speaks of our death, future bodily resurrection, and glorification as occurring in and with Christ.

REFLECTION QUESTIONS

1. What aspect of union with Christ do you believe is most neglected by Christians today?

2. At what stage in the order of salvation does the Spirit first unite us to Christ?

3. What is the relationship between union with Christ and justification?

4. In regard to union with Christ and sanctification, what are some practical ways you can know Christ more deeply and personally?

5. Is union with Christ merely a past reality, or does union with Christ have implications for future resurrection and glorification?

PART 3

Election, Calling, and New Birth

Is God's Electing Choice Conditioned upon Us? (Part 1)

For those hearing it for the very first time, the doctrine of election can be shocking. Sometimes even Christians who have read their Bible for years have never meditated on God's sovereign choice to elect certain individuals to salvation in eternity.[1] All too often when a believer first hears the words "predestination" or "election" he immediately objects, "That is not in the Bible!" Such an initial reaction is telling, exposing our natural allergy to divine sovereignty. Yet, election is everywhere taught in the Bible and without embarrassment.[2] It cannot be denied that election is a *biblical* doctrine. Even Christians who strongly disagree with one another on the exact meaning of election have acknowledged this much.

Where the debate comes into focus, however, is in how exactly Scripture defines election. Does God, before the foundation of the world, elect certain persons to salvation on the basis of foreseen faith, or does God elect certain persons to salvation according to his sovereign good pleasure alone? In other words, is election conditional or unconditional?

These two views have been debated throughout church history with Arminians and Wesleyans on one side (conditional election) and Calvinists on the other (unconditional election). Space does not permit a historical treatment of these two traditions,[3] nor can we enter into a critique of Arminianism

---

1. I can say this from firsthand experience, as there was a time in my life when I had never thought through the issue, though I had read my Bible for many years.
2. E.g., Acts 13:48; Romans 8:28–30; 9:11–13; Ephesians 1:4–12; 1 Thessalonians 1:4–5; 2 Thessalonians 2:13; 1 Timothy 5:21; 2 Timothy 1:9; 1 Peter 1:1; 2:9; Revelation 13:7–18; 17:8.
3. However, see Shawn Wright's book in this series: *40 Questions about Calvinism*. It should also be qualified that unconditional election is not limited to the Reformed tradition but has been historically affirmed by churches in Lutheran, Anglican, and Baptist denominations as well.

(that has been accomplished by others).[4] Rather, we will simply look at the most important biblical passages relating to election. In doing so, we will discover that Scripture is clear on the matter: God elects certain individual persons to salvation *unconditionally*.

Predestined (Romans 8:28–30)

Perhaps more than any other biblical author, the apostle Paul spells out what is involved in divine election. Consider Romans 8:28–30:

> And we know that for those who love God all things work together for good, for those who are called according to his purpose. For those whom he foreknew he also predestined to be conformed to the image of his Son, in order that he might be the firstborn among many brothers. And those whom he predestined he also called, and those whom he called he also justified, and those whom he justified he also glorified.

Several observations deserve our attention:

1. Paul is speaking about salvation. Foreknew, predestined, called, justified, and glorified all refer to salvation—past, present, and future. It will not suffice to argue that Paul is merely speaking of temporal blessings in the life of a believer.[5]

2. Paul's chain of salvation is referring to the same group of people throughout and this chain of salvation is unbreakable. Those whom God foreknew he also predestined. And those whom he predestined he called. Those whom he called he justified. And those whom he justified he will glorify. Those foreknown and predestined are the same ones God calls, justifies, and glorifies. Certainly Scripture never teaches that God justifies and glorifies everyone. Therefore, it must be the case that God does not foreknow and predestine everyone, but only some. Additionally, do not miss the unbreakable nature of Paul's chain of salvation. Those predestined *will* be called, justified, and glorified. Paul does not say that God seeks to predestine, call, and justify everyone but unfortunately not all believe. Rather, Paul has in mind only the elect. If Paul did not, then he could not say that all those who are predestined, called,

---

4. Arminianism is by no means monolithic. While Arminians agree with one another that election is conditional, nevertheless, there are a variety of approaches under that umbrella. E.g., compare Jack Cottrell's view with Clark Pinnock's view in *Perspectives on Election: Five Views*, ed. Chad Owen Brand (Nashville: B&H, 2006), chapters 3 and 9. Also see Roger E. Olson, *Arminian Theology* (Downers Grove, IL: InterVarsity Press, 2006), 179–99. For a response, see Robert A. Peterson and Michael D. Williams, *Why I Am Not an Arminian* (Downers Grove, IL: InterVarsity Press, 2004), 42–43.

5. E.g., J. Kenneth Grider, *Wesleyan-Holiness Theology* (Kansas City, MO: Beacon Hill, 1994), 250, who argues Paul is speaking of temporal predestination.

and justified are also glorified. Paul has in view an order of salvation that is effectual. God's election results in an effectual call. And God's effectual call always results in justification. And those whom God justifies he will certainly glorify. There is no conditionality in these verses. God works salvation all the way through, from beginning to end.

3. *The believer's hope in suffering is grounded in predestination.* As Paul says in verse 28, "And we know that for those who love God all things work together for good, for those who are called according to his purpose." What a remarkable assurance this promise is for the Christian undergoing suffering in this life. God promises that for those who have been effectually called all things (yes, even evil things) will work together for good. However, the question must be asked, "How is it that the Christian can know that God will work all things together for good?" Christians can rest confidently that God will work all things for good since God has already predestined them for eternal life before the foundation of the world (v. 28).[6]

4. *Predestination in Romans 8:29–30 is unconditional.* Some will argue that when Paul refers to those whom God "foreknew" he is referring to foreknowledge (i.e., God's factual knowledge ahead of time as to who would and would not believe). It is on the basis of this foreknowledge (of foreseen faith) that God then elects. For example, Arminian theologian Jack Cottrell says, "Through his foreknowledge God sees who will believe upon Jesus Christ . . . then even before the creation of the world he predestines these believers to share the glory of the risen Christ."[7] In such a view, the ultimate basis upon which a person is chosen is to be found within himself, for God's election is finally determined on whether or not *the sinner* will believe.

Such a view misses the mark. To begin with, it turns election into mere confirmation. We make the final decision and God simply sees ahead of time and confirms our choice. Additionally, this view reads a certain understanding of foreknowledge into Paul's use of "foreknew." While foreknew can at times mean knowing facts ahead of time, in Romans 8:29 and in a host of other passages, it does not. While it is always true that God knows all things ahead of time, foreknew in Romans 8:29 refers to God foreloving certain persons in a saving way.[8] In other words, Paul speaks of God foreknowing *persons*, not facts. Before the foundation of the world, God set his saving love on us and thought of us in relationship to him.

Consider other texts where "foreknew" is used. Paul writes to the Corinthians, "But if anyone loves God, he is known by God" (1 Cor. 8:3). Paul

---

6. Peterson and Williams, *Why I Am Not an Arminian*, 54.

7. Jack Cottrell, "Conditional Election," in *Grace Unlimited*, ed. Clark Pinnock (Eugene, OR: Wipf and Stock, 1999), 62.

8. S. M. Baugh, "The Meaning of Foreknowledge," in *Still Sovereign: Contemporary Perspectives on Election, Foreknowledge, and Grace*, eds. Thomas R. Schreiner and Bruce A. Ware (Grand Rapids: Baker, 2000), 194.

is not referring to God knowing facts about us, but God knowing us personally, in a saving way. Or consider Galatians 4:8–9, "Formerly, when you did not know God, you were enslaved to those that by nature are not gods. But now that you have come to know God, or rather to be known by God, how can you turn back again to the weak and worthless elementary principles of the world, whose slaves you want to be once more?" Paul is not speaking of knowing facts about God but of coming to know God as a person in a saving way. Jesus, in John 10:14–15, also proves this point: "I am the good shepherd. I know my own and my own know me, just as the Father knows me and I know the Father; and I lay down my life for the sheep." Jesus knowing his elect is compared to the Father knowing his Son and the Son knowing his Father. Jesus is not referring to his factual knowledge of the Father, but knowing the Father as a person. Similarly, when he speaks of knowing his elect he is referring to knowing them in a saving, personal relationship. The same point is reiterated by looking to Jesus in Matthew 7:21–23. There Jesus says that not everyone who calls him "Lord" will enter the kingdom of heaven, but only those who do the will of the Father. Though they may even prophesy, cast out demons, and do many mighty works in the name of Jesus, he will say, "I never knew you; depart from me, you workers of lawlessness." Again, Jesus is not speaking of his factual knowledge but of not knowing these people in a saving relationship.[9]

5. *Nowhere in Romans 8:28–30 do we get the impression that Paul is only speaking of predestination of groups or classes of people rather than specific individuals.* Paul has in mind individuals, "those who love God," "those who are called according to his purpose," etc. These same individuals have the Spirit who "helps us in our weakness," "intercedes for us," and "searches hearts" (Rom. 8:26–27).

God Has Mercy on Whomever He Wills (Romans 9:6–24)

One of the most powerful texts supporting unconditional election is Romans 9:6–24. The context of Romans 9 concerns the salvation of Israel. Paul explains that he has "great sorrow and unceasing anguish" in his heart, wishing himself accursed and cut off from Christ if it could mean the salvation of his brothers, "my kinsmen according to the flesh" (Rom. 9:3). Israel had it all: "the adoption, the glory, the covenants, the giving of the law, the worship, and the promises," as well as "the patriarchs" and from their race "Christ who is God over all" (Rom. 9:5–6). In light of Israel's disobedience and even rejection of Christ, the question naturally arises, "Has God's Word failed?" Paul answers with an emphatic "no." Why? "For not all who are descended from Israel belong to Israel" (Rom. 9:6b). Being a physical offspring of Abraham did not make one a true child of Abraham, for it is not the "children of the

---

9. Many other passages make this point: Genesis 4:1; 18:19; Hosea 13:5; Amos 3:2; Luke 1:34; 1 Peter 1:20.

flesh who are children of God, but the children of the promise are counted as offspring" (Rom. 9:8).

On what basis can Paul make such a shocking assertion? Paul turns to the story of Abraham and Sarah, through whom God promised a son, Isaac. It was through Isaac and Rebecca that God brought forth Jacob and Esau. Notice, however, what Paul says concerning the birth of these two sons:

> And not only so, but also when Rebekah had conceived children by one man, our forefather Isaac, though they were not yet born and had done nothing either good or bad—in order that God's purpose of election might continue, not because of works but because of him who calls—she was told, "The older will serve the younger." As it is written, "Jacob I loved, but Esau I hated" (Rom. 9:10–13).

God chose Jacob and rejected Esau. God loved Jacob and hated Esau. Why is this choice so surprising? It is surprising for several reasons. First, Esau was the oldest, the firstborn, not Jacob. But God chose the second born, Jacob, to fulfill his "purpose in election" (Rom. 9:11). As the text says, "The older will serve the younger." Second, God's choice is not based on anything foreseen in Jacob or Esau. Not at all. Rather, God's choice is according to his good purpose, made before Jacob and Esau were born and "had done nothing either good or bad—in order that God's purpose of election might continue, not because of works but because of him who calls." God's choice was not based on anything Jacob or Esau did but was purely due to God who calls. Should God's choice be conditioned on Jacob and Esau, even in the slightest, his purpose in election would not stand.

Advocates of conditional election will protest at this point, arguing that this is unfair and arbitrary. How can God be just if he chooses one for salvation and rejects the other for damnation not based on anything within them but purely because of the purpose of his will? Ironically, such an objection is very similar to the one Paul encountered and sought to answer in the very next verse: "What shall we say then? Is there injustice on God's part? By no means! For he says to Moses, 'I will have mercy on whom I have mercy, and I will have compassion on whom I have compassion'" (Rom. 9:14–15). Paul does not entertain such an objection. God is sovereign and there is no injustice on his part. He can choose whomever he wills. If advocates of conditional election are correct, there would be no better place for Paul to clarify the meaning of election. If it is true that election is based on God foreseeing our human response, Paul could have quickly qualified himself. But notice, Paul's reaction is just the opposite, arguing that God is not unjust. This is exactly the response one would expect if election is unconditional. In other words, rather than backpedaling, qualifying that election is based on man's faith, Paul instead reinforces divine sovereignty ("I will have mercy on whom I have mercy") and defends God's determination of who will be saved without consideration of anything they have done, good or bad.

The verses that follow are astounding, in every way exalting the sovereign choice of God rather than man's free will. Paul writes,

> What shall we say then? Is there injustice on God's part? By no means! For he says to Moses, "I will have mercy on whom I have mercy, and I will have compassion on whom I have compassion." So then it depends not on human will or exertion, but on God, who has mercy. For the Scripture says to Pharaoh, "For this very purpose I have raised you up, that I might show my power in you, and that my name might be proclaimed in all the earth." So then he has mercy on whomever he wills, and he hardens whomever he wills (Rom. 9:14–18).

There can be no way around it. God, not man, is the determining agent in salvation. God is free to elect whomever he wills, and such a choice is not based on our will, but on God's.

To make such a point, Paul turns to the story of Pharaoh. In order to put on full display his sovereignty, power, glory, and supremacy in delivering his chosen people, God raises up Pharaoh, hardening his heart. Just as God was free to love Jacob and hate Esau (see Rom. 9:11), so also is God free to harden the heart of Pharaoh in order to display his glory in saving Israel. As Paul says, "So then it depends not on human will or exertion, but on God, who has mercy. . . . So then he has mercy on whomever he wills, and he hardens whomever he wills" (Rom. 9:16, 18).

Again, some will object, "Foul! God is unfair! How can he still hold sinners responsible if he has decided beforehand that they will or will not be saved?" Yet again, Paul anticipated the objection, which is what one would expect if he is expounding the unconditional nature of election.

> You will say to me then, "Why does he still find fault? For who can resist his will?" But who are you, O man, to answer back to God? Will what is molded say to its molder, "Why have you made me like this?" Has the potter no right over the clay, to make out of the same lump one vessel for honorable use and another for dishonorable use? What if God, desiring to show his wrath and to make known his power, has endured with much patience vessels of wrath prepared for destruction, in order to make known the riches of his glory for vessels of mercy, which he has prepared beforehand for

> glory—even us whom he has called, not from the Jews only
> but also from the Gentiles? (Rom. 9:19–24).

If conditional election were true, then Paul would have easily responded, "God is not absolutely in control, as your protest misunderstands me to teach. Instead, God grants us free will and makes his choice based upon our response to the gospel."[10] But Paul does not respond this way. Instead, he confronts us: "But who are you, O man, to answer back to God? Will what is molded say to its molder, 'Why have you made me like this?'"

Using the imagery of a potter and his clay, Paul argues that God is like the potter, having complete control and freedom to use his clay as he pleases. The clay never has the right to question the potter ("Why have you made me like this?"). After all, the clay is clay. On the other hand, God is the potter. He is perfectly just "to make out of the same lump one vessel for honorable use and another for dishonorable use." In doing the latter he displays his mercy and glory. In doing the former, he displays his wrath and power. In other words, God, desiring to show his wrath and make known his power, has endured with much patience "vessels of wrath prepared for destruction." Why? In order "to make known the riches of his glory for vessels of mercy, which he has prepared beforehand for glory." God determines the fate of every single individual. He is the potter, making out of the same lump of clay some vessels for glory and others for destruction.

So far we have seen that in no way is election in Romans 9 conditional. However, some will also object that Paul has in mind not individual election but corporate election. In other words, Paul is not referring to the eternal destiny of individual persons but merely to classes or groups (Jew and Gentile). In response, Paul cannot be identifying "objects of his wrath" and "objects of his mercy" as referring to two classes, Jews and Gentiles. Note how Paul argues that the "objects of his mercy" includes "*both* Jews and Gentiles."[11] Furthermore, it is unnecessary to choose between individual and corporate categories. God chooses individuals to salvation (e.g., Jacob and Esau), but these individuals are part of and make up God's people, the church.[12] Jews and Gentiles are elected to be part of God's chosen people (Rom. 9:24–29). He has a remnant who will be saved (Rom. 9:27).[13]

---

10. Peterson and Williams, *Why I Am Not an Arminian*, 62.
11. Ibid., 63. Emphasis added.
12. See Thomas R. Schreiner, "Does Romans 9 Teach Individual Election unto Salvation?" in *Still Sovereign*, 89–106.
13. Neither can it be objected that Romans 9 has in view an election for temporal service rather than eternal salvation. For consider the language Paul uses: "Jacob I loved, but Esau I hated"; "I will have mercy on whom I have mercy"; "one vessel for honored use and another for dishonorable use"; "God, desiring to show his wrath"; "vessels of wrath prepared for destruction"; "prepared beforehand for glory."

Summary

In Romans 9 the apostle Paul teaches that election is unconditional. God's choice is not based upon his foreknowledge (foreseeing our faith). Rather, God's electing choice is due to his mercy and good pleasure alone. For that reason, he alone receives all the glory and credit for our salvation, leaving us not to boast in ourselves but only in God our Savior.

REFLECTION QUESTIONS

1. Read Romans 9. How does Paul's appeal to Jacob and Esau demonstrate that he must have in mind unconditional election?

2. Do you find yourself naturally objecting to Paul's argument in Romans 9, and if so, how does Paul respond to objections to God's justice?

3. If election is unconditional, is there any basis left on which man can boast?

4. How does God's hardening of Pharaoh's heart exalt God's power in the end?

5. How does unconditional election ensure that God is the one who receives all glory and honor in our salvation?

Is God's Electing Choice Conditioned upon Us? (Part 2)

Few passages in the Bible so strongly support unconditional election as Romans 9 does. As we saw in the last chapter, Paul believes God's electing choice is in no way based upon the will of man, not even in part. Unconditional election, however, does not rest on just one text. It is one of those doctrines that is taught across the New Testament. In this chapter, then, we will explore the contours of unconditional election further, seeking to understand its importance to the New Testament authors. We will then turn to the doctrine of reprobation to comprehend how, exactly, God relates to the non-elect as well. Finally, we will discover that election is not a cold, abstract doctrine but one that has many pastoral and practical implications for the Christian life.

Chosen by God (Ephesians 1:4–5, 11)

Next to Romans 9, Ephesians 1 proves to be one of the most pivotal passages for unconditional election.

> Blessed be the God and Father of our Lord Jesus Christ, who has blessed us in Christ with every spiritual blessing in the heavenly places, even as he chose us in him before the foundation of the world, that we should be holy and blameless before him. In love he predestined us for adoption as sons through Jesus Christ, according to the purpose of his will, to the praise of his glorious grace, with which he has blessed us in the Beloved. . . . In him we have obtained an inheritance, having been predestined according to the purpose of him who works all things according to the counsel of his will, so that we who were the first to hope in Christ might be to the praise of his glory (Eph. 1:3–6, 11).

According to Paul, before the "foundation of the world" God chose or elected certain persons to salvation. Notice, like Romans 9, in Ephesians 1 God's choice occurred before anyone was born, before anyone had done anything good or bad. Does Paul, in Ephesians 1, condition election on something in us? Absolutely not. God chose us not only before the foundation of the world but "according to the purpose of his will." God's sovereign will is the determining factor in our election, not our will. Paul reiterates such a point in verse 11: "In him we have obtained an inheritance, having been predestined according to the purpose of him who works all things according to the counsel of his will." God is in control of all things, causing everything to work according to his sovereign plan. Included in "all things" is election. God predestines and brings his elect to salvation not according to anything in them, but according to the counsel of his will.

It is often objected that such a God who chooses some and not others cannot be a God of love. Nothing could be further from the truth. In Ephesians 1:4–5 we read that God chose us out of *love* ("In love he predestined us"). Love is behind God's electing choice. But notice, Paul's mention of divine love once again highlights the unconditional nature of election. Paul teaches that election is not because of something in us (e.g., faith), but purely because of the purpose of his divine love for us. So not only is the basis for election God's sovereign will, but it is God's gracious love as well.

Additionally, in verse 6 we read that not only has God predestined us out of his love for us, but he has done so "to the praise of his glorious grace." Peterson and Williams summarize Paul's message well: "Predestination finally rests on God's sovereign mercy, free grace, loving choice, gracious will."[1] Again, it's not man's will or choice that is the basis, purpose, or *telos* of election, but God's glorious grace. Should we condition election on man's willful choice (something foreign to Ephesians 1), then God would be robbed of such praise.

Moreover, the type of election Paul has in mind always results in salvation. We are chosen before the foundation of the world so that "we should be holy and blameless before him" (Eph. 1:4). Out of love God predestined us "for adoption as sons through Jesus Christ" (Eph. 1:5). In Christ we have obtained an inheritance, "having been predestined according to the purpose of him who works all things according to the counsel of his will, so that we who were the first to hope in Christ might be to the praise of his glory" (Eph. 1:11–12).[2] No wonder Paul can say that God has "blessed us in Christ with every spiritual blessing in the heavenly places" (Eph. 1:3).

---

1. Robert A. Peterson and Michael D. Williams, *Why I Am Not an Arminian* (Downers Grove, IL: InterVarsity Press, 2004), 57.
2. It might be objected that in Ephesians 1:11 the plural is used, rather than the singular, demonstrating that election refers to classes of people rather than individual persons.

What Ephesians 1 demonstrates so well is that predestination is a fountain, out of which flow all the blessings of salvation, blessings which are guaranteed ahead of time. In other words, when God elects sinners, not on the basis of anything in them but only according to the good pleasure of his will, he guarantees that this election will result in salvation. For that reason, it is unbiblical to argue that election must refer to service and not salvation. Paul is referring to spiritual matters of eternal significance. Hence, Paul can say that predestination results in spiritual blessings in the heavenly places (Eph. 1:3), redemption through the blood of Christ (Eph. 1:7), the forgiveness of our trespasses (Eph. 1:7), an eternal inheritance (Eph. 1:11, 14), and the gospel of our salvation (Eph. 1:13). Ephesians 1 shows us that our redemption, adoption, sanctification, and reception of eternal life are all the result of election.

Another reason that election is to salvation and not merely service is the fact that we are predestined *in Christ* (Eph. 1:3–5, 11). Paul is referring to union with Christ when he says God chose us "in him" (Eph. 1:4, 11). Of course, we are chosen in Christ before the creation of the world (Eph. 1:4), but our actual union with Christ awaits that moment when we are effectually called. Nonetheless, before time God had already planned our union with Christ, which means that God not only elected us, but his election of us included the means by which we would be saved.[3]

Reprobation

Looking at election with the apostle Paul's help has revealed its unconditional nature. But what should we make of those who are not elected by God in eternity? In theology, the term "predestination" is a category that includes both election and reprobation. Not only does God choose some for salvation, but he passes over others resulting in their condemnation (i.e., reprobation). As already demonstrated in Romans 9, out of the same lump of clay God makes some vessels for honorable use and others for dishonorable use. Pharaoh is a case in point. God raised him up and hardened his heart to make known his divine power. Therefore, says Paul, God has mercy on whomever he wills, and he hardens the heart of whomever he wills (Rom. 9:19). While his elect obtain salvation, the rest are hardened (Rom. 11:7). Or consider 1 Peter 2:8 where we read that unbelievers stumble because they disobey the word "as they were destined to do."

However, Ephesians was written to the church, so of course Paul uses plural pronouns. As noted with Romans 9, it is a false dichotomy to choose between election being individual or corporate. It is both. God elects individuals, but these individuals make up his church (Eph. 1:12–13). See ibid., 59.

3. Other passages supporting unconditional election include: Genesis 12:1–3; 15:1–6; 17:7; 25:23; 28:15; Deuteronomy 4:37; 7:6–8; 10:14–15; 14:2; Joshua 24:2–3; Mark 13:20–27; John 6:35–45; 10:26–30; 15:14–19; 17:2–24; Acts 13:48; 18:9–10; 2 Thessalonians 2:13; Revelation 13:8; 17:8.

In Matthew 11:25–26 we discover that Jesus himself taught reprobation. "At that time Jesus declared, 'I thank you, Father, Lord of heaven and earth, that you have hidden these things from the wise and understanding and revealed them to little children; yes, Father, for such was your gracious will.'" Notice, Jesus says that the Father has hidden saving truth from "the wise" while revealing it to "little children" (cf. Matt. 13:10–17). Apparently Jesus not only believed in an election to salvation but a reprobation unto condemnation.

Yet, we should not think that reprobation works in the same way as election. They are not, says Horton, "two sides of the same coin."[4] The Reformed theologians who wrote the Canons of Dort explain how they detest the view that says "that in the same manner in which the election is the fountain and cause of faith and good works, reprobation is the cause of unbelief and impiety."[5] God has an *asymmetrical* relationship to election and reprobation. How so? The basis of God's choice to elect certain individuals is his mercy and his mercy *alone*. Election, in other words, is unconditional. Not so with reprobation. Reprobation is based upon God's righteous judgment upon the sinner *as a sinner*. God reprobates individuals on the basis that they did not repent of their sins but instead rejected Christ.[6] On this basis, God is absolutely just to punish them for all eternity. So while election is unconditional, reprobation is conditional. Reprobation, to stress the point, is based on the sinner's wicked choice, whereas election is not based upon man's choice at all.[7] If election was based on man's choice, then there would be no election at all, for as Scripture says, all are enslaved to sin and would never reject their sin and follow Christ (see Questions 4–5). Therefore, reprobation is deserved; election is not. Reprobation is to receive the wages for one's sins, while election means receiving the wages of our Savior's obedience, the *gift* of eternal life (Rom. 6:23; cf. Rom. 11:5; 2 Thess. 2:13; 1 John 5:11). Both reprobation and election are ordained by God (Deut. 32:39; Isa. 45:5–7; Eph. 1:11), yet both are carried out for very different reasons.[8]

This asymmetrical distinction is important because it protects the holy character of God. Evil is ordained by God and good is ordained by God; God is in sovereign and meticulous control of both having decreed both (Gen. 50:20; Dan. 4:34–37; Matt. 10:29–30; Acts 2:22–23; 4:27–28; 17:26). Yet, evil cannot extend from God or his decree in the same way and by the same means as good does. While good has a direct and immediate correlation to God,

---

4. Michael Horton, *Pilgrim Theology: Core Doctrines for Christian Disciples* (Grand Rapids: Zondervan, 2011), 252.
5. Canons of Dort, ch. 5, conclusion, in *Psalter Hymnal: Doctrinal Standards of the Christian Reformed Church* (Grand Rapids: Board of Publications of the Christian Reformed Church, 1976), 115.
6. Bruce A. Ware, "Divine Election to Salvation," in *Perspectives on Election: Five Views*, ed. Chad Owen Brand (Nashville: B&H, 2006), 54.
7. Ibid.
8. Ibid.

evil does not and cannot.[9] Certainly this is made clear in the narratives surrounding both Job (God granting permission to Satan to do evil to Job though God did not commit that evil himself) and Joseph (God ordaining the wicked actions of Joseph's brothers but not committing those evil acts himself). Sin and evil's *indirect* relation to God must be preserved lest we make God the author of sin and evil. Likewise in reprobation. It is key that God reprobate *sinners,* and that his reprobation be based upon their *sin,* lest God be charged with injustice and made the author of sin himself. God "did not predestinate some unto sin," asserts Berkhof, "as He did others unto holiness."[10]

In the end, it is true, as seen in the passages above, that even in the reprobation of the non-elect God is glorified. Though this may seem counterintuitive to our culture today, God is glorified in the execution of his *justice,* not just in the distribution of his *mercy.* At the same time, we should not think that God enjoys or desires reprobation in the way he does election; he is saddened to see sinners perish (Ezek. 18:32).[11] For that reason, among others, we cannot conclude that God's act of reprobation is identical to his act of election. While it is true that God is the one who reprobates individuals in eternity, we must remember that he does so on the basis of what they deserve as sinners.[12]

Unconditional Election and the Christian Life

There are several practical implications the doctrine of election has for the Christian life. First and foremost, the doctrine of election is meant to bring us to our knees in worship and praise of our sovereign, merciful, and gracious God. As Paul explains in Ephesians 1:5–6, God predestined us according to

---

9. Ibid., 54–55.
10. Louis Berkhof, *Systematic Theology* (Edinburgh: Banner of Truth, 2003), 117. Horton makes this point using the contrast of "hardening." "God is not active in hardening hearts in the same way that he is active in softening hearts. Scripture does speak of God hardening hearts (Ex 7:3; Jos 11:20; Isa 63:17; Jn 12:40; Ro 9:18; 11:7; 2Co 3:14). Yet it also speaks of sinners *hardening their own hearts* (Ex 8:15; Ps 95:8; Mt 19:8; Heb 3:8, 13). However, no passage speaks of sinners *softening their own hearts* and regenerating themselves. Human beings are alone responsible for their hardness of heart, but God alone softens and in fact re-creates the hearts of his elect (1 Ki 8:58; Ps 51:10; Isa 57:15; Jer 31:31–34; Eze 11:19; 36:26; 2Co 3:3; 4:6; Heb 10:16). In short, God has only to leave us to our own devices in the case of reprobation, but it requires the greatest works of the triune God to save the elect, including the death of the Father's only begotten Son" (*Pilgrim Theology,* 252).
11. Here it is key to invoke the distinction between God's will of decree and his moral will. According to the former, God wills the reprobation of the non-elect. Yet, according to the latter, he does not "desire" the death of the wicked. God can do both simultaneously and it is not a contradiction. As to why, see John Piper's chapter, "Are There Two Wills in God?" in *Still Sovereign: Contemporary Perspectives on Election, Foreknowledge, and Grace,* eds. Thomas R. Schreiner and Bruce A. Ware (Grand Rapids: Baker, 2000), 107–32.
12. Assumed in this discussion is my infralapsarian position. Space does not allow us to explore the debate between infra- and supralapsarianism, but see the views of Ware and Reymond in *Perspectives on Election,* 1–58, 150–94.

the purpose of his will "to the praise of his glorious grace." We have been predestined so that we might live "for the praise of his glory" (Eph. 1:12). Election gives us every reason to give thanks. Paul writes to the Thessalonians, "We give thanks to God always for all of you. . . . For we know, brothers loved by God, that he has chosen you" (1 Thess. 1:2, 4). And again Paul states, "But we ought always to give thanks to God for you, brothers beloved by the Lord, because God chose you as the firstfruits to be saved, through sanctification by the Spirit and belief in the truth" (2 Thess. 2:13). Salvation is of the Lord. Our election is his doing, not ours. The reason we are not spending an eternity in hell is because God was gracious and merciful, electing us for glory though we deserved otherwise. Appropriately, we have every reason to give thanks.

Additionally, not only should election lead us to worship and praise God, but it should motivate us to evangelize the lost. It is common to object that if we affirm unconditional election then we will undercut any motive to reach the lost. But such an objection is unbiblical. We must not forget that right after Paul exalts God's sovereign choice in Romans 9, he turns in Romans 10 to exhort believers to take the gospel to those who have not heard. In other words, exaltation leads to exhortation, and in Acts 18:10, right after many Corinthians heard the gospel from Paul and believed, God tells Paul, "Do not be afraid, but go on speaking and do not be silent, for I am with you, and no one will attack you to harm you, for I have many in this city who are my people." Shouldn't Paul pack his bags and return home to relax in safety since God already has elected many in this city? Actually, God says quite the opposite: I have many in this city who are my people, so keep preaching the gospel! Paul knew this truth well and that is why he says in 2 Timothy 2:10, "Therefore I endure everything for the sake of the elect, that they also may obtain the salvation that is in Christ Jesus with eternal glory." As believers, we are privileged to be the means by which the gospel goes to the nations. What great confidence we have knowing that God has his elect and when they hear the gospel they will believe.

Finally, election is a doctrine that is meant to give us great assurance and comfort. Paul says that "all things work together for good" (Rom. 8:28). How do we know this is true? Paul explains, "For those whom he foreknew he also predestined to be conformed to the image of his Son, in order that he might be the firstborn among many brothers" (Rom. 8:29). Because God has predestined us, we will be conformed to the image of Christ. Though trials and tribulation will come, God promises that he will work all things (including evil things) for good. What he has begun before the foundation of the world, he will bring to completion. How soothing it is to know that God always has our eternal good in mind and our salvation is secure in Christ.[13]

---

13. At the end of our treatment of election, space does not permit us to answer all objections to unconditional election. For a treatment and response to the most common objections, see Ware, "Divine Election to Salvation," 25–42.

Summary

God's electing choice before the foundation of the world of some individuals to salvation is not based on foreseen faith or merit, but rather is unconditional, based solely on his good pleasure and sovereign will. Unconditional election is a display of God's great mercy, grace, and love, for while God would have been perfectly just to pass over sinners, out of his great love and mercy he chose instead to elect certain sinners to eternal life. It is because election is not based on anything in us, even in the slightest, that such a doctrine is designed to move us to humility, thanksgiving, and worship as we stand in awe that though we deserve eternal condemnation, God would be so loving, so gracious, and so merciful as to set us apart for salvation instead. Additionally, unconditional election is the very basis and impetus for evangelism and missions. It is because God has his elect in every nation that we, as his ambassadors, can preach the gospel to all, confident that God will call his elect to salvation. Finally, unconditional election provides the believer with assurance, for the God who has predestined us also promises that he will work all things together for good.

REFLECTION QUESTIONS

1. According to the apostle Paul, why is it that the doctrine of election should result in praise, worship, and adoration for God?

2. Does the doctrine of election provide you with great comfort and assurance as a believer? If no, why not?

3. In light of Romans 9, do you believe God is fair and just in passing over some sinners while choosing others?

4. In what ways is the doctrine of election an encouragement to evangelize?

5. Does the doctrine of election make you feel as though God personally loves you?

What Is the Difference between the Gospel Call and the Effectual Call?

Scripture paints a very bleak picture of mankind. While popular culture tends to think of mankind as basically good, the Bible says the exact opposite: Each and every one of us is guilty and corrupt, deserving only eternal condemnation and divine wrath. How astonishing it is, then, when we read in that same Bible that despite what we deserve God has graciously sent his Son so that anyone who trusts in him might receive eternal life (John 3:16). God's grace, though, doesn't end with Jesus's death. It continues even after Jesus rose and ascended to the right hand of the Father. With the coming of the Holy Spirit at Pentecost (Acts 2), God has commanded his disciples to share this good news about Jesus with the whole world (Matt. 28:19). It is a gospel to be proclaimed to all people, regardless of class, race, or age. Theologians call this indiscriminate proclamation of the good news about Jesus the "gospel call" to salvation.

And yet, while God has a gospel call that is sent out to all people everywhere without exception, he also has an "effectual call" (or "effective call") whereby he calls only his elect and does so without fail. Notice, in contrast to the gospel call, the effectual call is particular in its scope. Additionally, while the gospel call can be rejected (and is rejected quite often!), the effectual call—as its name reveals—is always successful. We could even say—though sometimes misunderstanding surrounds this word—that it is "irresistible" (hence the label: irresistible grace).[1]

In this chapter we will focus our attention on the gospel call, and in the next two chapters we will turn our attention to God's effectual call.

---

1. "Irresistible" may be misinterpreted to mean that God drags us kicking and screaming. But as we will see in Question 18, God renews our will so that we now desire to come to him. While the word "irresistible" does capture the monergistic nature of calling, a better word is "effectual."

The Scriptural Affirmation of the Gospel Call

The gospel call can be defined as a *public offering of redemption and salvation in the Lord Jesus Christ and an invitation and command to repent and trust in Christ for the forgiveness of sins and the hope of eternal life.*[2] Notice, first of all, that the gospel call is an invitation for all people. Appropriately, the gospel call is also titled the general or universal call, for the gospel is to be preached to people everywhere without discrimination.

Scripture affirms the gospel call both in the Old and New Testaments. For example, God proclaims in Isaiah 45:22, "Turn to me and be saved, all the ends of the earth! For I am God, and there is no other." And again in Isaiah 55:1, "Come, everyone who thirsts, come to the waters; and he who has no money, come, buy and eat! Come, buy wine and milk without money and without price." Using imagery similar to that in Isaiah, Jesus tells the Samaritan woman in John 4:10 that if we ask for a drink he will give us living water. Speaking figuratively of spiritual salvation, Jesus promises that the water he gives will not leave one thirsty but will "become in him a spring of water welling up to eternal life" (John 4:14). The invitation of Jesus in John 4 parallels Revelation 22:17: "The Spirit and the Bride say, 'Come.' And let the one who hears say, 'Come.' And let the one who is thirsty come; let the one who desires take the water of life without price."

Jesus extends the same invitation when he welcomes sinners to eat his flesh, since he is the bread of life (John 6:35–56). In doing so they will live since "everyone who calls on the name of the Lord shall be saved" (Joel 2:32; cf. Acts 2:21). All people are invited to call upon the name of the Lord for salvation. As John 3:16 famously says, "For God so loved the world, that he gave his only Son, that whoever believes in him should not perish but have eternal life" (cf. John 6:40; 11:26; 12:46).[3] As ambassadors, trusted with this gospel, we do not know who will believe since God has not revealed to us the identity of his elect. Our job is simple: Preach the gospel without reservation.

The gospel call is not only issued as an *invitation*, but also as a *command*. Jesus says in Matthew 4:17, "Repent, for the kingdom of heaven is at hand." Or consider the apostle Paul: "The times of ignorance God overlooked, but now he *commands* all people everywhere to repent, because he has fixed a day on which he will judge the world in righteousness by a man whom he has appointed; and of this he has given assurance to all by raising him from the dead" (Acts 17:30). A day of judgment is coming, so God commands all

---

2. For similar definitions, see Louis Berkhof, *Systematic Theology* (Edinburgh: Banner of Truth, 2003), 459–61; Anthony Hoekema, *Saved by Grace* (Grand Rapids: Eerdmans, 1989), 68. For a fuller treatment of effectual calling, see Matthew Barrett, *Salvation by Grace: The Case for Effectual Calling and Regeneration* (Phillipsburg, NJ: P&R, 2013), 69-124. The major points and some wording in this chapter and the next are indebted to my research there.

3. To see how Jesus uses the gospel call in his parables, see Matthew 22:1–14 and Luke 14:16–24.

people to repent lest they perish in their sins. This command demonstrates that it is the *duty* of every sinner to repent and believe. In other words, it is man's duty to repent, regardless of whether or not he has the ability to do so (which, as Question 5 demonstrated, the sinner does not).

We also see the *universality* of the gospel call in Acts 10. The promise of forgiveness for those who trust in Christ is not only for Jews but for Gentiles, as the story of Cornelius demonstrates (Acts 10:42–43). Paul understood the universality of the gospel call as well. Building off of Isaiah 28:16, in Romans 9:33 Paul argues that salvation has come to the Gentiles (cf. Rom. 10:11–13; 1 Peter 2:6). One cannot avoid the universality of this gospel call in 1 John 4:15 either: "Whoever confesses that Jesus is the Son of God, God abides in him, and he in God." These passages, and so many others, are lucid: God offers his gospel freely to both Jew and Gentile alike, and salvation is promised to all who trust in Christ.

The Well-Meant Offer of the Gospel

Lest we forget, it is important to remember that this gospel call is a reflection of God's gracious character. The free offer of the gospel to all people reflects God's desire for the salvation of sinners in every nation. Despite our sin, our God is a patient God, "not wishing that any should perish, but that all should reach repentance" (2 Peter 2:9). He is a God who "desires all people to be saved and to come to the knowledge of the truth" (1 Tim. 2:4).[4] God's *desire* for the salvation of the nations is manifested through his gospel invitation to sinners everywhere without discrimination, an invitation that he issues throughout redemptive history (e.g., Ezek. 18:23; 33:11; Matt. 23:37; 2 Cor. 5:20).

The fruit of God's *genuine desire* for all people to repent and turn to Christ is visibly manifested in the universal proclamation of the gospel (Num. 23:19; Ps. 81:13–16; Prov. 1:24; Isa. 1:18–20; Ezek. 18:23, 32; 33:11; Matt. 21:37; 2 Tim. 2:13). In other words, the gospel call is a *bona fide* calling that is seriously given.

However, some will protest that it is inconsistent to affirm a *bona fide* offer and simultaneously believe that God chooses to make his grace effectual only in his elect (see Questions 13–14). Isn't this gospel call disingenuous, then?

Such an objection misses the mark and proves to be inconsistent for a number of reasons. First, the gospel offer is genuine, since it is the very means God uses to convert sinners. It is through the proclamation of the gospel that the Spirit works within the hearts of dead sinners to bring them to spiritual life (see Questions 16–17). So we cannot divorce the gospel call from the effectual call, although it is important to distinguish between the two.

---

4. However, as John Piper has so thoroughly demonstrated, God's desire for all to repent is reflective of his will of disposition (not his decretive will). Space does not permit a defense of God's will of disposition and decretive will, but see John Piper, "Are There Two Wills in God?" in *Still Sovereign: Contemporary Perspectives on Election, Foreknowledge, and Grace*, eds. Thomas R. Schreiner and Bruce A. Ware (Grand Rapids: Baker, 2000), 107–32.

Second, when God offers his gospel, he never makes a promise he doesn't keep. Many assume that if God offers his gospel to all he must equally seek to save all. But such a promise is never made. The offer of the gospel is not a promise that God will save everyone, but a promise that eternal life will be given on the condition of faith and repentance. Let us be clear: God never promises that he will grant faith and repentance to everyone.

Third, the sincerity of the free offer of the gospel does not depend on whether or not man is spiritually able to fulfill it. Some object that if sinners lack spiritual ability to repent and believe, it is impossible for the gospel offer to be genuine. Some even go so far as to say that God would be deceptive to offer his gospel when he knows man is unable to fulfill its conditions. But as the Dutch Reformed theologian Wilhelmus à Brakel argued, the "fact that man is not able to repent and believe is not God's fault, but man is to be blamed."[5] God is in no way required to lower his conditions of the gospel (i.e., faith and repentance) because man is unable to fulfill them. Additionally, to take the objection one more step back, God is not required to grant his saving grace to anyone in the first place, for we are sinners deserving only judgment. Should God decide to fulfill the conditions of the gospel for any sinner it is but an act of pure grace. After all, what makes grace so amazing is that it is totally undeserved.[6]

The Resistibility of the Gospel Call

One last point deserves mention. Unlike the effectual call, the gospel call can and is resisted. The Old Testament is characterized by this constant theme: Many within Israel rejected Yahweh and instead went after foreign idols. Consider the following Old Testament passages where many in Israel reject Yahweh:

> If you turn at my reproof, behold, I will pour out my spirit to you; I will make my words known to you. Because I have called and you refused to listen, have stretched out my hand and no one has heeded, because you have ignored all my counsel and would have none of my reproof (Prov. 1:23–25).

> When Israel was a child, I loved him, and out of Egypt I called my son. The more they were called, the more they went away; they kept sacrificing to the Baals and burning offerings to idols (Hos. 11:1–2).

---

5. Wilhelmus à Brakel, *The Christian's Reasonable Service*, ed. Joel R. Beeke, trans. Bartel Elshout (Grand Rapids: Reformation Heritage, 1993), 2:207 (cf. 2:208).
6. I have limited myself to three points, but for others see Herman Bavinck, *Reformed Dogmatics*, ed. John Bolt, trans. John Vriend (Grand Rapids: 2008), 4:37; Francis Turretin, *Institutes of Elenctic Theology*, 3 vols., ed. James T. Dennison, Jr., trans. George M. Giger (Phillipsburg, NJ: P&R, 1992–97), 2:510.

They did not keep God's covenant, but refused to walk according to his law (Ps. 78:10).

But my people did not listen to my voice; Israel would not submit to me. So I gave them over to their stubborn hearts, to follow their own counsels. Oh, that my people would listen to me, that Israel would walk in my ways! (Ps. 81:11–13).

For he is our God, and we are the people of his pasture, and the sheep of his hand. Today, if you hear his voice, do not harden your hearts, as at Meribah, as on the day at Massah in the wilderness (Ps. 95:7–8).

What more was there to do for my vineyard, that I have not done in it? When I looked for it to yield grapes, why did it yield wild grapes? (Isa. 5:4; cf. 65:12; 66:4).

Yet they did not listen or incline their ear, but stiffened their neck, that they might not hear and receive instruction (Jer. 17:23; cf. 7:13, 16; 35:17).

They have turned to me their back and not their face. And though I have taught them persistently, they have not listened to receive instruction (Jer. 32:33).

In these passages, it is plain that not all within Israel were truly Israel. In other words, though every Hebrew was a member of national Israel, not every Hebrew was inwardly regenerated by the Spirit.[7] Though Yahweh called those within the nation of Israel to repent and trust in him, they refused. Eventually, their resistance climaxed when Jesus himself preached repentance in order to enter into the kingdom of God, and instead of turning to the Messiah they crucified him. Jesus came to his own with the good news of salvation, but his own did not recognize him (Acts 13:27). Out of great sadness, Jesus cried out, "O Jerusalem, Jerusalem, the city that kills the prophets and stones those who are sent to it! How often would I have gathered your children together as a hen gathers her brood under her wings, and you would not!" (Matt. 23:37; cf. Luke 13:34). And even after Christ rose from the dead and ascended into heaven, many Jews continued to resist the gospel message. In Acts 7, for example, Stephen is martyred for his faith in Christ. Stephen charges his executioners of being just like their fathers who persecuted the prophets. "You stiff-necked

---

7. John Frame, *The Doctrine of God* (Phillipsburg, NJ: P&R, 2002), 317–34.

people, uncircumcised in heart and ears, you always resist the Holy Spirit. As your fathers did, so do you" (Acts 7:51; cf. Heb. 3:8–13).

Why is it so important to emphasize the biblical affirmation of the gospel call? It is important because it is sometimes thought that those who believe the Bible distinguishes between a gospel call and an effectual call deny that grace is resistible. However, this is a caricature. God's grace can be resisted *in the gospel call.* That said, God's grace cannot be resisted *when he so chooses to effectually call his elect.* The key point is this: God's intention, purpose, and design are the difference. The Puritan theologian John Owen said it best, "Where any work of grace is not effectual, God never intended it should be so, nor did he put forth that power of grace which was necessary to make it so."[8]

Summary

The gospel call is an offering of salvation in Christ and an invitation to re-pent and trust in Christ for the forgiveness of sins and the hope of eternal life. The gospel call is a real invitation, sometimes in the form of a command, and it is meant for all people, Jew and Gentile alike. The gospel call is also a well-meant offer of salvation. Some object that the well-meant offer of the gospel is disingenuous if God chooses to effectually call only his elect. However, the gospel call is not disingenuous, for (1) it is the very means God uses to con-vert sinners; (2) God never makes a promise in the gospel call he doesn't keep; and (3) the sincerity of the gospel call does not depend on whether or not man is spiritually able to fulfill it. Finally, while God does have a call that is effectual and cannot be resisted, the gospel call can be resisted by sinners.

REFLECTION QUESTIONS

1. In what ways does the gospel call to all nations provide impetus for mis-sions and evangelism?

2. Does the universal and unprejudiced nature of the gospel call change how you share the gospel with people of different race and class?

3. In what way is the gospel call a means to salvation for those who believe?

4. How does God's love for the lost, as exemplified in the gospel call, impact the way you share the gospel with unbelievers?

5. Do you believe the gospel call is a well-meant offer of salvation?

---

8. John Owen, *A Discourse Concerning the Holy Spirit,* The Works of John Owen (Edinburgh: Banner of Truth, 1991), 3:318. Also see Turretin, *Institutes,* 2:547–48.

Does God's Call Ever Fail? (Part 1)

Why is it that when the gospel is preached some repent and believe while others remain obstinate in unbelief?[1] Perhaps this strikes against our natural instincts, but Scripture teaches that the reason anyone believes is because God has chosen to effectually call his elect, putting on display his sovereign mercy and grace. As we saw in Question 12, God has two calls: a gospel call and an effectual call. While the gospel goes out to all people, inviting and commanding them to repent and believe, it is in the effectual call that God irresistibly, invincibly, and unfailingly calls his elect through the gospel so that they are made alive (i.e., regeneration or new birth) and consequently repent and trust in Jesus (i.e., conversion).[2] In this chapter and the next, then, we will explore where in Scripture we see this irresistibly sweet summons that so beautifully results in being united to Christ.

All That the Father Gives Me Will Come to Me (John 6:36–40; 8:47; 10:26)

One of the strongest passages in support of effectual calling is John 6:35–64. In John 6:22–34 Jesus encounters a group of Jews who refuse to believe in him. The exclusivity of Jesus's teaching is obvious as he instructs the crowd that they must labor for food that endures to eternal life, not food that perishes. Only Jesus himself, the Son of Man, however, can give this food to others (6:27). In response, his listeners ask, "What must we do, to be doing the works of God?" (John 6:28). Jesus responds, "This is the work of God, that you believe in him whom he [the Father] has sent" (6:29).

---

1. The major points and some wording in this chapter and the next are indebted to my previous book, Matthew Barrett, *Salvation by Grace: The Case for Effectual Calling and Regeneration* (Phillipsburg, NJ: P&R, 2013), 69-124.
2. John M. Frame, *Salvation Belongs to the Lord* (Phillipsburg, NJ: P&R, 2006), 185; John Piper, *Finally Alive* (Fearn, Ross-shire, Scotland: Christian Focus, 2009), 84.

The unbelief of his listeners is revealed in their response. They do not believe but instead demand a sign. Only if they see a sign will they believe that Jesus is from the Father. "So they said to him, 'Then what sign do you do, that we may see and believe you? What work do you perform? Our fathers ate the manna in the wilderness; as it is written, 'He gave them bread from heaven to eat'" (6:30–31). Jesus responds, "Truly, truly, I say to you, it was not Moses who gave you the bread from heaven, but my Father gives you the true bread from heaven. For the bread of God is he who comes down from heaven and gives life to the world" (6:32–33). When the Jews ask for this bread, Jesus replies, "I am the bread of life; whoever comes to me shall not hunger, and whoever believes in me shall never thirst" (6:35; cf. Isa. 49:10; 55:1; Rev. 7:16). What does Jesus mean? Answer: God had performed the sign the crowd was seeking by sending Jesus, who is himself the true bread from heaven. Nevertheless, while believing would result in eternal life, the crowd remains obstinate due to the hardness of their hearts.[3]

Jesus, however, is completely aware that the people do not believe in him.

> But I said to you that you have seen me and yet do not be-
> lieve. All that the Father gives me will come to me, and who-
> ever comes to me I will never cast out. For I have come down
> from heaven, not to do my own will but the will of him who
> sent me. And this is the will of him who sent me, that I should
> lose nothing of all that he has given me, but raise it up on the
> last day. For this is the will of my Father, that everyone who
> looks on the Son and believes in him should have eternal life,
> and I will raise him up on the last day (John 6:36–40).

Jesus performs the same signs in front of the crowd, and yet some believe and others do not. How can this be? Both believers and unbelievers hear the same message, witness the same miracles, and yet some fall on their knees in worship while others want to crucify Jesus.

What is the root cause behind belief and unbelief? We might answer, "Man's free will." But Jesus does not give such an answer. Jesus does not explain belief and unbelief by drawing our attention to the reality that some refuse him while others choose him. Though he extends the promise of eternal life to all people (6:35–37, 40, 47, 51), Jesus never affirms that everyone has the ability to believe.

But doesn't the promise of life assume man's ability to turn to Jesus ("*ought* implies *can*")? How can Jesus extend eternal life if his listeners are

---

3. Bruce A. Ware, "Effectual Calling and Grace," in *Still Sovereign: Contemporary Perspectives on Election, Foreknowledge, and Grace*, eds. Thomas R. Schreiner and Bruce A. Ware (Grand Rapids: Baker, 2000), 212.

not spiritually able to take hold of it by faith? For some, the reason some believe while others do not is because man possesses the ability to cooperate with Jesus. What Jesus says in John 6:36–40, however, completely devastates such an assumption.[4] While there may be much "ought," there is no "can" in the words of Jesus. Rather, Jesus affirms an unembarrassed, unapologetic "cannot"! Jesus demonstrates, observes Ridderbos, the "powerlessness of the natural person ('no one') to come to the salvation disclosed in Christ unless the Father who sent him 'draws' that person."[5]

In order to understand Jesus, we must pay attention to verse 37: "All that the Father gives me will come to me, and whoever comes to me I will never cast out." For several reasons, Jesus's words in this verse have divine predestination in mind.[6] First, as D. A. Carson observes, when Jesus says "I will never cast out," he "implies the 'casting out' of something or someone already 'in'. The strong litotes in 6:37f., therefore, does not mean 'I will certainly receive the one who comes', but 'I will certainly preserve, keep in, the one who comes'; while the identity of the 'one who comes' is established by the preceding clause" (cf. John 2:15; 9:34; 10:4; 12:31).[7] Jesus has promised that he will never "cast out" those given to him by the Father. The assumption, therefore, is that there is an elect people, a determined number of chosen ones, who are already "in." They are not "in" because of anything in them but because the Father chose them. And since the Father chose them, he will in turn give them to his Son. Notice, the Father does not give everyone to his Son, but only those whom he has chosen. Only these will come to Jesus when he calls.

Second, in John 6:38 those that the Father gives to the Son will certainly, and without fail, come to Jesus. "All that the Father gives me will come to me," says Jesus. There is no room for conditionality; the coming of sinners to the Son is guaranteed by the Father.

Third, not only is it true that those given to Jesus will inevitably come, but so also is it true that those who inevitably come will be secure and fortified in the arms of Christ.[8] "All that the Father gives me," says Jesus, "will come to me, and whoever comes to me *I will never cast out*" (emphasis added).

To recap, Jesus is affirming that the Father has a specific people he is giving to his Son, those given to the Son will inevitably come, and finally those who belong to the Son he will keep, ensuring their final salvation. From start to finish, from the Father to the Son, there is no failure to bring about

---

4. Ibid.; Loraine Boettner, *The Reformed Doctrine of Predestination* (Philadelphia: P&R, 1963), 178.
5. Herman Ridderbos, *The Gospel of John*, trans. John Vriend (Grand Rapids: Eerdmans, 1997), 232.
6. Andreas J. Köstenberger, *John*, BECNT (Grand Rapids: Baker Academic, 2004), 211.
7. D. A. Carson, *Divine Sovereignty and Human Responsibility* (Eugene, OR: Wipf and Stock, 1994), 184.
8. Ibid.

the salvation of the elect. "Jesus is repudiating any idea that the Father has sent the Son forth on a mission which could fail because of the unbelief of the people."[9]

What does all of this mean then for those Jews who rejected Jesus and would not believe? What is the reason, in other words, for why they do not come to Jesus? Some would argue it is because they have determined by their own free will not to come and therefore they do not belong to Jesus. Shocking as it may be, Jesus affirms the exact opposite. The reason they do not come is because they have not been given to the Son by the Father.[10] Carson states the issue precisely: "You have not been given to the Son by the Father for life and therefore you will not have life but will continue in your unbelief."[11]

If Jesus is not clear enough in John 6:37, he is especially lucid in John 10:26: "But you do not believe *because you are not among my sheep*" (emphasis added). We should not turn this the other way around: "You are not part of my flock because you do not believe." That is not what Jesus says. He does not condition being part of the flock on man's free will to believe. Rather, if someone does not believe it is because they have not been chosen by the Father and given to the Son. Stated in the reverse, the reason he is not part of his flock is because he has not been handed to Jesus by the Father.

Jesus reiterates such a teaching in John 8:47: "Whoever is of God hears the words of God. *The reason why you do not hear them is that you are not of God*" (emphasis added). According to Jesus, the reason one does not hear and believe in the Son is because one does not belong to God in the first place. Whether or not someone believes in Jesus depends upon whether or not the Father has chosen him and then given him to his Son for salvation. If the Father has chosen not to give a person to his Son, then that person will not believe. God's sovereign choice, in other words, is the determining factor, not man's free will.[12]

No One Can Come to Me Unless the Father Who Sent Me Draws Him (John 6:41–51)

As the narrative of John 6:41–51 continues, we discover that effectual calling is again taught by Jesus in his response to the Jews. In verse 44 Jesus

---

9. Ibid.
10. Ridderbos, *John*, 233.
11. Carson, *Divine Sovereignty and Human Responsibility*, 184.
12. As Boice and Ryken state, "If they fail to believe, it is because God has withheld that special, efficacious grace that he was under no obligation to bestow" (James Montgomery Boice and Philip Graham Ryken, *The Doctrines of Grace: Rediscovering the Evangelical Gospel* [Wheaton, IL: Crossway, 2002], 159). Also see Ware, "Effectual Calling and Grace," 214; D. A. Carson, *The Gospel according to John*, PNTC (Grand Rapids: Eerdmans, 1991), 290; Thomas R. Schreiner and Ardel B. Caneday, *The Race Set Before Us* (Downers Grove, IL: InterVarsity Press, 2001), 128–29. Additionally, it is essential to note that coming to Jesus and believing Jesus are one and the same. In John 6:35–37 Jesus equates the two when he asserts that those who come to Jesus will not hunger and those who believe will not thirst.

is clear that no one can come to him unless the Father has already given him over to the Son (cf. 6:65). In other words, the reason a sinner believes is because the Father gives him to Jesus. Unless the Father gives the sinner to Jesus the sinner will not believe. Therefore, it cannot be denied that in 6:44 Jesus is simultaneously affirming both an effectual call and man's spiritual inability to come to Jesus. Every sinner "ought" to come to Jesus, but no sinner is able to come to Jesus unless the Father draws him.[13]

Additionally, it is essential to realize that in John 6:44 the drawing of the Father *necessarily* results in elect sinners coming to Jesus. "No one can come to me unless the Father who sent me draws him [*elkusē auton*]. And I will raise him up on the last day."[14] It is not the case that the drawing here is meant to merely make it possible for sinners to come to Christ should they so choose to do so. Rather, the drawing identified by Jesus is one that is effectual, irresistible, and unfailing.[15] All those drawn *will* and *do* believe.

Some will object, arguing that such a drawing is resistible. But such an interpretation neglects to recognize that Jesus not only says "no one can come to me," yet another affirmation of spiritual inability, but also says "I will raise him up on the last day." All those drawn are resurrected on the last day, indicating that this drawing is an effectual one, resulting in final salvation. All people, then, are not in view, but only those chosen by the Father.[16]

In summary, the drawing Jesus refers to in John 6:44 is an indomitable and insuperable summons. The word "summons" is especially helpful for, as Frame notes, it captures the efficacy of the Father's call. While one might

---

13. Leon Morris, *John*, NICNT (Reprint, Grand Rapids: Eerdmans, 1971), 372.
14. Additionally, consider how *helkō* (ἕλκω), which is used in John 6:44, is also used in James 2:6, "But you have dishonored the poor man. Are not the rich the ones who oppress you, and the ones who drag [*helkousin*; ἕλκουσιν] you into court?" Also, consider Acts 16:19, "But when her owners saw that their hope of gain was gone, they seized Paul and Silas and dragged [*helkusan*; εἵλκυσαν] them into the marketplace before the rulers." R. C. Sproul observes that to substitute "woo" in the place of "drag" in these passages would not be appropriate: "Once forcibly seized, they could not be enticed or wooed. The text clearly indicates they were *compelled* to come before the authorities" (*What Is Reformed Theology?* [Grand Rapids: Baker, 1997], 154).
15. William Hendriksen, *Exposition of the Gospel according to John*, NTC (Grand Rapids: Baker, 2002), 1:238.
16. Carson, *John*, 293. Some will object, arguing that if John 6:44 is referring to an effectual call then universalism follows since in John 12:32 Jesus says he will draw all men to himself. But this neglects to read the passage in context. Jesus is referring to all people without distinction, not all without exception. This becomes evident when we read that just prior to Jesus saying this both Jews *and* Greeks come to him, the latter seeking Jesus out. As Carson and Schreiner explain, Jesus has in mind all *types* and *kinds* of people (cf. Joel 2:28–29), not all people without exception (Carson, *John*, 293, 444; idem, *Divine Sovereignty and Human Responsibility*, 185–86; Thomas R. Schreiner, "Does Scripture Teach Prevenient Grace in the Wesleyan Sense?" in *Still Sovereign*, 241–42).

reject an invitation, one cannot resist a summons.[17] A summons comes with all the authority and power of the King. When God, our gracious, loving, and all-powerful King, summons, he never fails to accomplish that which he has intended. And yet, says Carson, when the Father "compels belief, it is not by the savage constraint of a rapist, but by the wonderful wooing of a lover."[18]

You Gave Them to Me (John 12:37–40; 17:24)

Two final passages deserve our attention. First, John 12:37–40 is an extraordinary passage, highlighting God's sovereignty in salvation. Previously, Jesus had performed incredible miracles, and yet people disbelieved. Why? John gives an answer:

> Though he had done so many signs before them, they still did not believe in him, so that the word spoken by the prophet Isaiah might be fulfilled: "Lord, who has believed what he heard from us, and to whom has the arm of the Lord been revealed?" Therefore they could not believe. For again Isaiah said, "He has blinded their eyes and hardened their heart, lest they see with their eyes, and understand with their heart, and turn, and I would heal them."

The reason they do not believe, says John (quoting from Isa. 58:1 and then 6:10), is because God "has blinded their eyes and hardened their heart" so that they won't believe.[19] Michaels explains, "Not only has God not 'drawn' these people or 'given' them faith, but he has 'blinded their eyes and hardened their hearts' to make sure they would *not* repent and be healed!"[20] John's words remind us of Paul's in Romans 9:18: "So then he has mercy on whomever he wills, and he hardens whomever he wills."

Second, consider John 17 where Jesus, the great high priest, prays to his Father, asking him to "give eternal life to all whom you have given him [the Son]" (17:2). In verse six Jesus says he has manifested the Father's name to "the people whom you gave me out of the world" (17:6). Jesus only escalates the predestinarian pitch of his prayer when he then prays, "Yours they were, and you gave them to me, and they have kept your word" (17:6). Who exactly is Jesus referring to? The answer is in verse 9: "I am not praying for the world but for those whom you have given me, for they are yours." In other words, Jesus is praying specifically and only for the disciples. Furthermore, those whom the Father has

---

17. Frame, *Salvation Belongs to the Lord*, 184.
18. Carson, *John*, 293.
19. Andreas J. Köstenberger, *A Theology of John's Gospel and Letters* (Grand Rapids: Zondervan, 2009), 459–60.
20. Michaels, *John*, 710.

given to the Son will receive eternal life. So Jesus has in mind salvation, not merely Christian service on this earth. As their high priest, he is interceding on their behalf, ensuring that they will remain faithful to the very end.[21]

In John 17:20 we see the particularity, efficacy, and determinism of divine grace on display. Jesus prays not for the whole world but for elect future believers, and in doing so he intercedes on their behalf, guaranteeing that they will believe. Though they have not yet heard the gospel, when they do hear they will believe for they have been given to the Son by the Father and the Son has interceded on their behalf for the sake of their salvation (cf. John 10:14–18).

Summary

Perhaps nowhere in all of the New Testament is effectual calling taught with such boldness as it is by Jesus in the gospel of John. Jesus teaches repeatedly that those whom the Father has chosen to give to him will, without fail, come to him (John 6:36). Jesus also affirms the sinner's inability to come to Jesus when he says that no one "can come to me unless the Father who sent me draws him" (John 6:44; cf. 6:65). And as he teaches in John 10:26, the reason sinners do not believe is because they are not part of God's flock (cf. 8:47). Therefore, if a sinner is to come to Jesus, he must be invincibly drawn by the Father. In short, Jesus does not make man's free will the deciding factor, but God's sovereign choice.

REFLECTION QUESTIONS

1. Are there specific examples in the four Gospels or the book of Acts where Jesus calls a sinner to himself in an effectual manner?

2. What does the effectual call in John 6 tell us about the relationship between the Father and the Son in accomplishing salvation?

3. Does Jesus's affirmation of effectual calling change your perception of Jesus's mission in coming to save sinners?

4. How does Jesus's high priestly prayer change the way you pray for the lost throughout the world?

5. If the reason for why some believe and others do not is to be found in God's sovereign choice and calling rather than in man's free will, should believers ever be prideful that they are saved while others are not?

---

21. Jesus does not limit his intercessory prayer to his disciples. Instead, he also mediates on behalf of future believers. "I do not ask for these only, but also for those who will believe in me through their word" (17:20). See Carson, *Divine Sovereignty and Human Responsibility*, 187.

Does God's Call Ever Fail? (Part 2)

Previously we discovered that effectual calling is a doctrine Jesus himself taught. John 6, in particular, proved to be a key passage, demonstrating that God's call is both particular (i.e., he calls his elect) and effective (i.e., he never fails to draw his elect). It should not surprise us, then, that the effectual call is taught by the apostle Paul as well. While his use of the effectual call is consistent with Jesus, it is important that we explore his thought on this topic for it sheds further light on what this calling entails.

The Golden Chain of Salvation (Romans 8:28)

The apostle Paul's writings are dripping with direct and indirect references to effectual calling (e.g., Rom. 1:6–7; 8:30; 11:29; 1 Cor. 1:2, 9, 24, 26; 7:18; 2 Thess. 2:13–14; 1 Peter 1:3, 14–15; 2:9–10, 21; 2 Peter 1:3–10). When Paul mentions calling in his letters he is not, as some assume, referring to a general, universal invitation either to be rejected or accepted. Paul's language of calling "is performative," accomplishing exactly what is demanded.[1] For example, consider Romans 8:28–30:

> And we know that for those who love God all things work together for good, for those who are called according to his purpose. For those whom he foreknew he also predestined to be conformed to the image of his Son, in order that he might be the firstborn among many brothers. And those whom he predestined he also called, and those whom he called he also justified, and those whom he justified he also glorified.

---

1. Thomas R. Schreiner, *Paul: Apostle of God's Glory in Christ* (Downers Grove, IL: InterVarsity Press, 2001), 241.

Paul has in mind the same group of people throughout the passage. Those whom God predestined he also called. And those whom he called he then justified.[2] If Paul has in mind the same exact group of people throughout this "golden chain" of salvation—which it appears that he does—then it follows that this golden chain of salvation is unbreakable, for one step in the chain necessarily and irreversibly leads to the next. Those whom God has predestined he will certainly call and those called will indeed be justified, and those justified will without fail be glorified.

For our purposes, the verb "called" (*ekalesen*) is especially important. This verb, says Douglas Moo, "denotes God's effectual summoning into relationship with him."[3] John Murray agrees: "Determinate efficacy characterizes the call because it is given in accordance with eternal purpose."[4] Moo and Murray must be right because it is not true that in the gospel call all those called are justified and glorified. Quite the contrary, many who receive the gospel call disbelieve and are condemned.[5] Furthermore, if Paul had meant to refer to the gospel call he would have said that only some of those called were justified and glorified. But Paul says the exact opposite, positively affirming that all those whom God calls he justifies and glorifies. Since the calling Paul references immutably and unfailingly results in justification and glorification, he must be referring to the effectual call.

Additionally, do not miss Paul's mention of divine providence in Romans 8. Not only does Paul affirm that those called are justified and glorified (8:30), he says in verse 28 that those called can rest assured that God has a purpose and that all things will work together for good. Hence, Paul can say that the elect are "called according to his purpose." In no way could Paul have said this of all those who hear the gospel call, for the gospel call goes out to elect and non-elect alike. In other words, it is not true of all those who receive the gospel call that all things will work together for good. For many who hear the gospel call, all things will *not* work together for good since they will be condemned on the last day and spend an eternity in hell (e.g., Matt. 7:23). Once again, therefore, we are reminded that Paul has the effectual call in view, a calling that works, bringing believers to Christ, preserving them to the very end through every trial and tribulation.

Finally, we cannot fail to observe what Romans 8:28–30 means for the order of salvation. In Romans 5:1, Paul argues that justification is by faith. In Romans 8:30, Paul states that all those God calls are justified. What are we to conclude by comparing these two texts? To begin with, it is safe to conclude that we have yet

---

2. Douglas Moo, *The Epistle to the Romans*, NICNT (Grand Rapids: Eerdmans, 1996), 535.
3. Ibid.
4. John Murray, *The Epistle to the Romans*, NICNT (Grand Rapids: Eerdmans, 1959), 1:315.
5. Bruce A. Ware, "Effectual Calling and Grace," in *Still Sovereign: Contemporary Perspectives on Election, Foreknowledge, and Grace*, eds. Thomas R. Schreiner and Bruce A. Ware (Grand Rapids: Baker, 2000), 226.

another reason to believe the effectual call is in view in Romans 8:30. It cannot be said of all those who hear the gospel call that they all have faith that justifies. But in Romans 8:30, it is the case that all those called have faith in Christ for Paul says all those called are in fact justified.[6] Additionally, it is no coincidence that Paul puts calling before justification, just as it is no coincidence that he places justification before glorification. In other words, there is an order here that is unavoidable and meaningful. God's effectual call results in justification (which includes faith), not vice versa. It is God's effectual call that produces the faith that justifies.[7] Therefore, when we construct a biblical order of salvation, it is imperative that calling precede faith. In doing so, we stay true to passages like Romans 8:30 and highlight, as the apostle Paul does, the sovereignty of God in calling his elect to himself. Effectual calling is not something we contribute to; instead it is attributed to God alone.[8]

Those Who Are Called (1 Corinthians 1:9, 18–31)

Many other Pauline passages mention the effectual call (Rom. 1:6–7; 9:22–23; Gal. 1:15; Eph. 4:1–6; Col 3:15; 1 Tim. 6:12), but by far one of the most important is found in 1 Corinthians 1. Paul opens this letter by referring to himself as one who has been "called by the will of God to be an apostle of Christ Jesus" (1:1) and to believers as those who are "called to be saints together with all those who in every place call upon the name of our Lord Jesus Christ" (1:2). Paul praises God for these Corinthian Christians "because of the grace of God that was given you in Christ Jesus" (1:4), a grace that enriched them in all speech and knowledge.

Furthermore, God has not only given grace, but he promises he "will sustain you to the end, guiltless in the day of our Lord Jesus Christ" (1:8). Notice, God will keep his elect to the very end, putting on display his faithfulness. "God is faithful, by whom you were called into the fellowship of his Son, Jesus Christ our Lord" (1:9). Once again, Paul makes mention of the believer's calling. However, Paul does not have in mind a general, gospel call but an effectual call. How do we know this? Paul is clear in 1:9 that all those whom God calls have fellowship with Christ, and this cannot be said of those who reject the gospel call. In other words, Paul is referring to a calling that unites the sinner to Christ, granting the sinner a fellowship reserved and kept only for those whom the Father has elected in eternity.[9]

But Paul's strongest affirmation of the effectual call in 1 Corinthians comes in 1:18–31. While Paul's proclamation of the gospel of Christ (the word of the

---

6. Schreiner, *Paul*, 241.
7. Ibid.
8. Murray, *Romans*, 1:321.
9. Paul's use of "call" to refer to the effectual call in 1:9 is similar to his use of "call" in Romans 1:7; 9:23–24; 1 Corinthians 1:26; Galatians 1:15; and Ephesians 4:1, 4.

cross) is foolishness to those who disbelieve and perish (1:18, 23, 25), this same gospel is the wisdom and power of God to those who are saved (1:18, 21, 24; cf. Rom. 1:16). The same gospel is in view, the same message of the cross is preached, but some hear and view Christ as folly while others hear and accept the gospel as the power of life. As Paul explains in 2 Corinthians 2:15–16, to the former the gospel is an aroma of death, but to the latter it is the fragrance of Christ, the aroma of eternal life. "The gospel, or aroma, is the same! The difference is in those smelling the fragrance and not in the fragrance itself."[10]

So far we have seen that the gospel stays the same. What is it, you might ask, that accounts for the reality that some reject the gospel while others accept the gospel? Paul gives us an answer in 1 Corinthians 1:23–24, "but we preach Christ crucified, a stumbling block to Jews and folly to Gentiles, but to those who are called, both Jews and Greeks, Christ the power of God and the wisdom of God." Paul is contrasting two groups: the "called ones" and the much larger group of Jews and Gentiles. For the latter group, the gospel is a stumbling block and folly. But for the former (the "called ones"), Christ is the power and wisdom of God. Paul's contrast between these two groups rules out any notion that he is only referring to a general, gospel call.[11] "It makes no sense," observes Ware, "to contrast Jews and Greeks generally with those Jews and Greeks who are called (as 1:23–24 does) if the difference between believing Jews and Greeks and disbelieving Jews and Greeks is in their respective choices only." Instead, the contrast "is made between those called from disbelieving Jews and Greeks and, by implication, those not called, making up the general class of Jews and Greeks who regard the gospel as weakness and folly."[12] If Paul had intended to teach the gospel call in this passage, we would not be able to explain why it is that some believe while others do not. However, if Paul has in mind the effectual call, then the contrast he sets before us makes perfect sense. The reason that some believe while others do not is not because of the wisdom of man, but because of God's calling.

That Paul has an irresistible, invincible call in view is also made evident in his assertion that "the called" ones actually believe as a consequence of being called in the first place. Again, the contrast is apparent: unlike those who are not called and consequently see the cross as foolishness, the called ones (including both Jews and Greeks) see Christ as the power and wisdom of God.[13]

Additionally, 1 Corinthians 1:26–31 cannot support any view that sees man's free will as the determining factor to the success of God's call. The called ones are not called and chosen due to any wisdom or power within

---

10. Ware, "Effectual Calling and Grace," 220n32.
11. Schreiner, *Paul*, 241.
12. "The point is that Jews and Greeks generally reject the gospel. But God intervenes, and toward some of these otherwise disbelieving Jews and Gentiles, he extends his saving call. This cannot be a call to all; it must be a call to some" (Ware, "Effectual Calling and Grace," 222).
13. Leon Morris, *1 Corinthians*, TNTC (Downers Grove, IL: InterVarsity Press, 2008), 52.

themselves. As Paul explains, God has intentionally chosen those who are weak, lowly, and despised. Why? So that "no human being might boast in the presence of God" (1:29). Now, if it were true that Jews and Gentiles were called and regenerated due to their choice to believe, then it would be impossible for Paul to preclude boasting. Every man who believes would then have something to boast about "in the presence of God" (1:29). To the contrary, it is "because of him you are in Christ Jesus" and therefore if anyone is to boast he is to "boast in the Lord" (1:31). Again, Ware helpfully summarizes Paul for us when he says, "The basis for boasting in the Lord is not that he made our salvation possible but that he saved us by his calling (1:24, 26) and his choosing (1:27–28, 30). Therefore any and all human basis for boasting is eliminated (1:29), and all honor and glory is owing solely to him (1:31)!"[14]

Called to a Holy Calling (1 Timothy 6:12; 2 Timothy 1:8–10)

While many other Pauline passages could be examined, two final passages deserve our attention. In 1 Timothy 6:12 we read, "Fight the good fight of the faith. Take hold of the eternal life to which you were called and about which you made the good confession in the presence of many witnesses" (1 Tim. 6:12). Similarly, in his second letter Paul exhorts Timothy saying,

> Therefore do not be ashamed of the testimony about our Lord, nor of me his prisoner, but share in suffering for the gospel by the power of God, who saved us and called us to a holy calling, not because of our works but because of his own purpose and grace, which he gave us in Christ Jesus before the ages began, and which now has been manifested through the appearing of our Savior Christ Jesus, who abolished death and brought life and immortality to light through the gospel (2 Tim. 1:8–10).

In 1 Timothy 6:12 calling is in the passive voice (also see Gal. 5:13; Eph. 4:1, 4) and refers to a summons to salvation that results in eternal life, something not true of all those who hear the gospel call.[15] Likewise, in 2 Timothy 1:8–10 calling is salvific, according to God's purpose and grace, which God gave us in Christ Jesus before all time. Especially important is Paul's mention of works. Paul says that we have been called "not because of our works but because of his own purpose and grace." In other words, our calling is not dependent upon anything in us, even our own choosing. Rather, God's calling is deemed successful because of his "own purpose and grace." Any type of synergism

---

14. Ware, "Effectual Calling and Grace," 224.
15. Philip H. Towner, *The Letters to Timothy and Titus*, NICNT (Grand Rapids: Baker, 2006), 411.

that conditions the efficacy of God's special call on man's will is inconsistent with 2 Timothy 1:8–10.[16] Additionally, the grace and purpose Paul refers to in our calling is rooted in election ("which God gave us in Christ Jesus before all time.").[17] Calling, therefore, is just like election, unconditional in nature, not based on anything in us (not even our faith), but instead it is based on God's good purpose and grace.

To conclude, while many other texts from the New Testament epistles could be examined, the passages we have studied in this chapter clearly and strongly support the doctrine of effectual calling.[18]

Election and Effectual Calling

A key characteristic of holistic theological thinking is connecting the dots between one doctrine and another. In that light, having seen the biblical support for effectual calling, it is crucial to see that effectual calling is inseparably connected to unconditional election, and vice versa. The New Testament draws this connection everywhere (John 6:29, 37, 44, 63–64; 15:16, 19; Acts 13:48; Rom. 9:6–24; Eph. 1:4–13; 2 Thess. 2:13–15; 2 Tim. 1:9; 1 Peter 1:2; 2 Peter 1:10). Just as God's election is both (1) particular (only some are chosen) and (2) unconditional, it also must be the case that God's effectual call is particular and unconditional.

God does not effectually call all people, but only those whom he has chosen to salvation. God does not condition his call upon something man does (e.g., faith), but it is his call (much like his sovereign, electing choice) that results in faith. Indeed, it must be. If God has chosen his elect not on the basis of anything they would do (given their depravity and inability), then it follows that the Father would call his elect to his Son effectually. If our inability and enslavement is to be overcome, he must call us invincibly. His calling cannot be conditioned upon anything we would do, as we saw in our exposition of Romans 9. To conclude, unconditional election and effectual calling entail one another. One cannot exist without the other. In Scripture the two always go together.[19]

---

16. Concerning Paul's words about calling according to God's "own purpose and grace," Towner states, "This line emphasizes that God is the initiator of the salvation plan; it does not arise from any human decision or source (the force of the specification 'his *own*' is to strengthen the contrast)" (ibid., 469).

17. William D. Mounce, *Pastoral Epistles*, WBC, vol. 46 (Nashville: Thomas Nelson, 2000), 482.

18. For further study, see 1 Corinthians 7:15; Galatians 5:13; Ephesians 4:4; Colossians 3:15; 1 Thessalonians 4:7; Jude 1:1–2; 1 Peter 1:3, 14–15; 2:9–10, 21; 2 Peter 1:3–10.

19. For a more extensive treatment of this point, see Bruce A. Ware, "Divine Election to Salvation," in *Perspectives on Election: Five Views*, ed. Chad Owen Brand (Nashville: B&H, 2006), 15–25; Matthew Barrett, *Salvation by Grace: The Case for Effectual Calling and Regeneration* (Phillipsburg, NJ: P&R, 2014), 69–124.

Summary

While God has a gospel call for all people, he also has an effectual call that is only for his elect. Unlike the gospel call, which can be resisted, when God calls his elect he does so effectually, irresistibly, and unfailingly. Therefore, the success of God's special call is not dependent upon anything in man or upon anything man does. God's effectual call is according to his good purpose and grace alone, thereby ensuring that God receives all the glory in our salvation.

REFLECTION QUESTIONS

1. How does the doctrine of effectual calling ensure that it is God who receives all the glory in our salvation?

2. Can you think of examples in Scripture where God's effectual call is made especially visible?

3. What passage in this chapter do you believe lends the greatest support to the doctrine of effectual calling?

4. How does an effectual call give you greater assurance that God will bring about the salvation of his elect throughout the world?

5. If God's effectual call is grounded in election and accomplished in time, what confidence can we then have in our sanctification that God will finish what he has started?

What Does It Mean to Be Born Again?

The twentieth-century theologian John Murray once asked, "How can a person who is dead in trespasses and sins, whose mind is at enmity against God, and who cannot do that which is well-pleasing to God answer a call to the fellowship of Christ?"[1] Some will answer, "Man must exercise his free will. Man must be the decider. Man must choose whether or not he will cooperate with God's grace."

Such an answer not only speaks volumes about our natural tendency to elevate human autonomy but reveals an inconsistency with what Scripture says. As we discovered in Questions 4–5, it is impossible for any sinner to respond positively to the gospel call to salvation. Every man is dead in his trespasses, enslaved to sin, unable and unwilling to do that which is pleasing in God's sight (John 6:44; Rom. 8:8).[2] The sinner can in no way answer the gospel call of God, but God must apply his call effectually, regenerating the dead sinner so that he is made alive and born again. "God's call," says Murray, "since it is effectual, carries with it the operative grace whereby the person called is enabled to answer the call and to embrace Jesus Christ as he is freely offered in the gospel. God's grace reaches down to the lowest depths of our need and meets all the exigencies of the moral and spiritual impossibility which inheres in our depravity and inability. And that grace is the grace of regeneration."[3] It is the aim of this chapter to define this grace of regeneration, also called the new birth.

---

1. John Murray, *Redemption Accomplished and Applied* (Grand Rapids: Eerdmans, 1955), 95.
2. Robert L. Reymond, *A New Systematic Theology of the Christian Faith*, 2nd rev. ed. (Nashville: Thomas Nelson, 1998), 450.
3. Murray, *Redemption Accomplished and Applied*, 96.

Regeneration Defined

It makes good biblical sense to follow our affirmation of effectual calling (see Questions 13–14) with the doctrine of regeneration.[4] God effectually calls his elect to himself and, in doing so, makes them alive in Christ (Rom. 8:7–8; Eph. 2:1, 5; Col. 2:13). But if one searches the Scriptures for the word "regeneration" (*palingenesia*), one will undoubtedly be disappointed as the term is only used in Matthew 19:28 and Titus 3:5. Even in these two texts, it is only in Titus 3:5 that the word is actually used to refer to that first, initial transformation from death to new life.[5]

In the history of the church the term "regeneration" has been used in different ways. For example, some of the Reformers used the word broadly to refer to the Christian's entire renewal, encompassing not only conversion but sanctification as well.[6] Since the Reformation, however, theologians have also used the term in a more narrow sense, to refer to that first, initial implantation of new life or to what is commonly called the "new birth." While the term "regeneration" may not be used abundantly in Scripture, nevertheless, the concept of regeneration in this narrow sense pervades Scripture at every turn (John 1:12–13; 3:3–8; Gal. 6:15; Eph. 2:5–6, 10; 4:22–24; Col. 2:11–14; Titus 3:5; James 1:18; 1 Peter 1:3–5; 1 John 2:29; 3:9; 4:7; 5:1, 4). Although we will explore individual texts in the next two chapters, it is essential in this chapter simply to define regeneration as well as its parameters.[7]

We can define regeneration as the "work of the Holy Spirit to unite the elect sinner to Christ by breathing new life into that dead and depraved sinner so as to raise him from spiritual death to spiritual life, removing his heart of stone and giving him a heart of flesh, so that he is washed, born from above and now able to repent and trust in Christ as a new creation. Regeneration is the act of God alone, and therefore it is monergistic in nature, accomplished by the sovereign work of the Spirit apart from and unconditioned upon man's

---

4. Are effectual calling and regeneration distinct steps in the order of salvation? This question falls outside the parameters of this introductory book. However, it should be noted that while I think it is helpful to distinguish between the two—since Scripture does the same in the variety of language it uses (called, born again)—nevertheless, the two should be viewed as synonymous. For my reasons why, see appendix 1 in *Reclaiming Monergism: The Case for Sovereign Grace in Effectual Calling and Regeneration* (Phillipsburg, NJ: P&R, 2013).

5. In Matthew 19:28, the term is used to refer to the renewal of the entire universe.

6. John Calvin, *Institutes of the Christian Religion* 3.3, ed. John T. McNeil, trans. Ford Lewis Battles, LCC, vols. 20–21 (Philadelphia: Westminster, 1960). The Reformers taught the narrow understanding of regeneration as a concept, they just didn't use the term itself in the narrow sense very often. One should not mistakenly think that the Reformers, because they used different vocabulary, rejected the *concept* of regeneration defined in this chapter.

7. The major points and some wording of this chapter are indebted to my previous book, *Salvation by Grace: The Case for Effectual Calling and Regeneration* (Phillipsburg, NJ: P&R, 2013), 125-206.

will to believe. In short, man's faith does not cause or bring about regeneration, but regeneration causes or brings about man's faith."[8]

Regeneration Explained

With the above definition in mind, let's start by explaining what regeneration is not.

1. Regeneration is neither a subtraction from nor an addition to the substance of man's nature.

2. Regeneration is not partial, limited to just one faculty in the human person, but impacts the entire person.

3. Regeneration is a transformation of the sinner's human nature, but it is not an entire transformation resulting in perfectionism, as if the sinner is now incapable of sinning.

On the other hand, we can positively define regeneration by the following four points:

1. Regeneration is a change that occurs instantaneously.

2. Regeneration is a change in the very core of man's nature.

3. Regeneration is an immediate change, one that occurs below consciousness.

4. Regeneration is a supernatural change accomplished by the Holy Spirit through the Word.

Each of the above four points deserves our attention in order to flesh out this definition.[9] First, *regeneration is a change that occurs instantaneously.* Unlike sanctification, which is a progressive, moral transformation over the period of our entire life, regeneration occurs only once and it is instantaneous. In other words, the new birth is a snapshot action—a momentary or punctiliar change that moves the sinner from spiritual death to spiritual life (Acts 16:14; Eph. 2:5).

---

8. This definition is used throughout my book, *Salvation by Grace*. For similar definitions, see Louis Berkhof, *Systematic Theology* (Edinburgh: Banner of Truth, 2003), 469; Murray, *Redemption Accomplished and Applied*, 96; Anthony A. Hoekema, *Saved by Grace* (Grand Rapids: Eerdmans, 1989), 94.

9. Similar points can be found in Charles Hodge, *Systematic Theology* (Grand Rapids: Eerdmans, 1970), 2:675–89; Berkhof, *Systematic Theology*, 468–69; Hoekema, *Saved by Grace*, 102–4.

Second, *regeneration is a change at the very core of man's nature.* And this is fitting given the effects of total depravity (see Question 4). As its name suggests, total depravity is pervasive; sin penetrates to the very center of man. Regeneration must likewise be pervasive, penetrating the very essence of man's heart and nature (Ezek. 36:26).[10] Additionally, just as total depravity impacts every single aspect of man's being, so also does regeneration. No part of man is left untouched by the Holy Spirit. The sinner's mind, will, affections, etc. are all changed by the Spirit. So not only is regeneration intensive in its impact but extensive as well, the entire and total person being made alive in Christ.[11]

Third, *regeneration is an immediate change, one that occurs below consciousness.* As Questions 16–17 will explore in more depth, the new birth is not a conscious synergism whereby the sinner cooperates with God. Man is dead in his sins; therefore what is required is a supernatural, subconscious act of the Spirit that results in the sinner consciously exercising faith and repentance. Regeneration is God's awakening work to bring the sinner from death to life, resulting in the sinner consciously repenting of his sin and trusting in Jesus Christ.[12]

This means that *regeneration is an immediate change.* The new birth is not a mere moral persuasion by the Word, as if God merely seeks to convince sinners to exercise their free will to believe upon hearing the gospel preached. We should not think that the grace that converts us to God "is nothing but a gentle persuasion."[13] Instead, God's special grace is "an entirely *supernatural* work, one that is at the same time *most powerful* and most pleasing, a marvelous, hidden, and inexpressible work, which is not lesser than or inferior in power to that of creation or of raising the dead."[14]

The Dutch Reformed theologian Herman Bavinck helpfully explains the importance of the immediate nature of regeneration: "God's Spirit itself *directly* enters the human heart and with infallible certainty brings about regeneration without in any way being dependent on the human will."[15] While this is a topic that we will address in the next two chapters, it is essential to note here that regeneration does not involve the cooperation of man's will with

---

10. Loraine Boettner, *The Reformed Doctrine of Predestination* (Phillipsburg, NJ: P&R, 1932), 165.
11. Herman Bavinck, *Reformed Dogmatics*, ed. John Bolt, trans. John Vriend (Grand Rapids: Baker, 2008), 4:91–92 (cf. 4:124).
12. John Stott, *Baptism and Fullness*, 3rd ed. (Downers Grove, IL: InterVarsity Press, 2006), 84.
13. This was the belief of the (Arminian) Remonstrants whose views were rejected by the Synod of Dort (1618–1619). See "The Canons of Dort (1618–1619)," in James Dennison Jr., ed., *Reformed Confessions of the Sixteenth Century and Seventeenth Centuries in English Translation, Volume 4, 1600–1693* (Grand Rapids: Reformation Heritage, 2014), Canons 3–4, Rejection of Errors, Par. 7. Cf. Hoekema, *Saved by Grace*, 102; Peter Toon, *Born Again: A Biblical and Theological Study of Regeneration* (Grand Rapids: Baker, 1987), 118–20, 162–65, 171–73, 177–80.
14. "The Canons of Dort (1618–1619)," Canons of Dort, 3–4 article 12 (emphasis added).
15. Bavinck, *Reformed Dogmatics*, 4:81 (emphasis added; cf. 3:580).

God. Rather, regeneration is a direct operation of God upon the dead heart. No human volition is involved. As an immediate act, regeneration can also be called a monergistic act, meaning that God acts alone to awaken the sinner from death to new life.

However, the immediate nature of regeneration in no way is meant to preclude the biblical reference to the word as instrumental in the Spirit's work of new birth (1 Peter 1:23; James 1:18). As Bavinck observes, the immediate nature of regeneration is meant to affirm that "the Holy Spirit, though employing the word, himself with his grace entered into the heart of humans and there effected regeneration without being dependent on their will and consent."[16] For example, consider the analogy used by Charles Hodge, who compares the immediate nature of regeneration to a man who is blind and is miraculously made to see. Notice, the natural light is essential to the faculty of seeing for the first time. However, the light in no way creates the blind man's sight. Rather, that is the supernatural work of God who by his great power and will grants the blind man the ability to see. The same can be said of the immediate nature of regeneration. The word of God is essential. However, the word in itself regenerates no one. It is the supernatural, omnipotent work of the Spirit to breathe new life into a dead corpse that is the cause of spiritual life when there was only death. The Spirit uses the word to accomplish this miracle, but he does so directly, without the sinner's cooperation or consent.[17]

Fourth, *regeneration is a supernatural change accomplished by the Holy Spirit through the word*. As hinted at already, it is the Spirit who breathes spiritual life into the dead sinner but he does so in conjunction with the word (i.e., the gospel). The efficient cause of the new birth is the Spirit, and the instrumental cause is the "word of God" (1 Peter 1:23) or the "word of truth" (James 1:18; cf. John 15:3; 2 Thess. 2:14).[18] Two texts on regeneration highlight the instrumentality of the word in the new birth.[19] In James 1:18 we read, "Of his own will he brought us forth by the word of truth, that we should be a kind of firstfruits of his creatures." And Peter says, "Having purified your souls by your obedience to the truth for a sincere brotherly love, love one another earnestly from a pure heart, since you have been born again, not of perishable seed but of imperishable, through the living and abiding word of God" (1 Peter 1:22–23).

The word of God is absolutely necessary for the salvation of sinners. But the word must be paired with the Spirit if it is to be effectively applied to elect sinners. As Calvin explains, every unbeliever, due to common grace, has the

---

16. Ibid., 3:580. Also see Herman Bavinck, *Saved by Grace: The Holy Spirit's Work in Calling and Regeneration* (Grand Rapids: Reformation Heritage, 2008), 34.
17. Hodge, *Systematic Theology*, 2:703; 3:31.
18. Sinclair B. Ferguson, *The Holy Spirit* (Downers Grove, IL: InterVarsity Press, 1996), 53, 125.
19. In these texts "the word" is the gospel itself, verbally proclaimed. This gospel would be inscripturated, however, in the written Word as well.

God-given gift of a mind, so that he can, for example, successfully work in the liberal arts. However, when it comes to God "the greatest geniuses [e.g., Plato, Aristotle] are blinder than moles."[20] Even the smartest men and women hear the Word of God, but without the inner working of the Spirit, applying the word in the heart, they are left in total darkness. As Calvin observes, "The mind of man is blind until it is illuminated by the Spirit of God [and] the will is enslaved to evil, and wholly carried and hurried to evil, until corrected by the same Spirit."[21]

So word and Spirit cannot be divorced from one another. It is by his word and Spirit that God illuminates the mind of the sinner and forms his heart so that he loves and desires Christ and is made a new creation.[22] Or to use theological vocabulary, it is through the gospel call that God effectually calls and regenerates his elect.[23] As Paul says in 2 Thessalonians 2:14, "To this *he called you through our gospel*, so that you may obtain the glory of our Lord Jesus Christ." What then sets the gospel call apart from the effectual call? In the effectual call the Spirit comes alongside the word and makes it real in the hearts of God's elect, bringing about new spiritual life where there was a black hole of sin and death.

Summary

Regeneration is the work of the Holy Spirit to unite the elect sinner to Christ by breathing new life into that dead and depraved sinner so as to raise him from spiritual death to spiritual life, removing his heart of stone and giving him a heart of flesh, so that he is washed, born from above and now able to repent and trust in Christ as a new creation. Regeneration is the act of God alone, and therefore it is monergistic in nature, accomplished by the sovereign work of the Spirit apart from and unconditioned upon man's will to believe. In short, man's faith does not cause regeneration, but regeneration causes man's faith.[24]

---

20. Calvin, *Institutes*, 2.2.18. Cf. Anthony N. S. Lane, "Anthropology," in *The Calvin Handbook*, ed. Herman J. Selderhuis (Grand Rapids: Eerdmans, 2008), 282.
21. John Calvin, *Ecclesiae Reformandae Ratio*, quoted in Lane, "Anthropology," 283. Also see Calvin, *Institutes* 2.2.20.
22. Calvin, *Institutes* 2.5.5.
23. On the instrumentality of the word not undermining the sovereignty of the Spirit, see Ferguson, *The Holy Spirit*, 125; Francis Turretin, *Institutes of Elenctic Theology*, 3 vols., ed. James T. Dennison Jr., trans. George Musgrave Giger (Phillipsburg, NJ: P&R Publishing, 1992–97), 2:431; "The Westminster Confession of Faith (1646)," in *Reformed Confessions of the Sixteenth Century and Seventeenth Centuries in English Translation, Volume 4, 1600–1693*, question 67.
24. Again, this paragraph is taken from Matthew Barrett, *Salvation by Grace*.

REFLECTION QUESTIONS

1. What are some misguided views of the new birth that you see communicated in different Christian and evangelical circles today?

2. Explain how the subconscious nature of regeneration is evident in a biblical text like John 3:8.

3. How do the examples of Lydia and Saul (Paul) in Acts demonstrate the instantaneous and immediate nature of regeneration?

4. Have you witnessed an unbeliever trust in Christ recently? If so, in what ways has the Spirit's work of new birth changed various aspects of that person's life (e.g., mind, will, affections, etc.)?

5. What could be some of the negative consequences if we separate word and Spirit in the new birth?

Is the New Birth Something We Bring About? (Part 1)

Is the new birth something that God does entirely, or is it something we participate in and bring about ourselves? In other words, are we passive or active in the new birth? Does the Spirit work supernaturally to raise us spiritually from the dead, or do we cooperate with the Spirit, either resisting or accepting his efforts to bring about the new birth? These questions and others characterize what has been called "monergism-synergism" debate. Those in the Calvinist tradition have argued that God works monergistically in the new birth. He is the sole actor, bringing us from death to new life, and we are completely passive, dead in our trespasses and sins. However, those in the Arminian tradition have argued for synergism. God works synergistically in the new birth, meaning that God and man cooperate with one another. Man is not passive, but active, cooperating with or resisting God's effort to bring about the new birth.

For the latter view (synergism) the new birth always comes subsequent to faith and repentance in the order of salvation.[1] The new birth, in other words, is conditioned upon man's will to believe. However, for the former view (monergism) the new birth always precedes faith and repentance. Man can in no way repent and believe until God has raised him from death to new life. Of course, when we talk about the new birth preceding conversion (faith and repentance), we are not speaking *chronologically*, as if these events took place at different periods in time. In our experience, everything seems to happen all at once. Rather, we are speaking *logically*, referring to the causal order of things.

---

1. For an in-depth presentation of various types of synergistic views, see Matthew Barrett, *Salvation by Grace: The Case for Effectual Calling and Regeneration* (Phillipsburg, NJ: P&R, 2013), chapter 5. The major points and wording in this chapter and the next are indebted to my treatment in that publication.

To use an analogy, consider a light switch. When someone walks into a room and turns on the light switch, what comes first, the turning on of the light switch or the appearance of light in the room? In our experience, they both happen simultaneously. However, what if we rephrase the question and ask: Which event *causes* the other? Does the appearance of light in the room turn on the light switch, or does turning on the light switch cause light to appear in the room? The answer is obvious: It is the turning on of the light switch that causes or brings about light in the room. The same applies when we speak of the ordering between the new birth and conversion. In time, both seem to happen simultaneously in our own experience. However, does one cause or bring about the other? Is it our will to believe and cooperate with the Spirit that brings about our new birth, or is it God's work in the new birth that brings about our faith and repentance?

In this chapter and the next it will become apparent that the overwhelming testimony of Scripture is in favor of monergism. Man is dead in his trespasses and sins, but God has made him alive in Christ Jesus. In other words, it is God's supernatural, effectual, and irresistible work in the new birth that causes or brings about conversion (faith and repentance), not vice versa.

The New Birth According to Jesus (John 3:3–8)

The fundamental issue with Israel in the Old Testament was their lack of a circumcised heart. But God had promised through the prophets that a day was coming when he would give all his people a new heart and put his Spirit within each and every one of them (Ezek. 11:19; 36:26; cf. 37:1–14; Deut. 30:6; Jer. 31:33; 32:39–40). What the Lord declared through the prophets, Jesus reiterates to the Jews of his own day. For example, in John 3 Nicodemus, a ruler of the Jews, comes to Jesus by night and says to him, "Rabbi, we know that you are a teacher come from God, for no one can do these signs that you do unless God is with him" (John 3:2). Jesus gives an answer that is startling to Nicodemus:

> Jesus answered him, "Truly, truly, I say to you, unless one is born again he cannot see the kingdom of God." Nicodemus said to him, "How can a man be born when he is old? Can he enter a second time into his mother's womb and be born?" Jesus answered, "Truly, truly, I say to you, unless one is born of water and the Spirit, he cannot enter the kingdom of God. That which is born of the flesh is flesh, and that which is born of the Spirit is spirit. Do not marvel that I said to you, 'You must be born again.' The wind blows where it wishes, and you hear its sound, but you do not know where it comes from or where it goes. So it is with everyone who is born of the Spirit (John 3:3–8).

Previously, in John 2, we learn that though Jesus performed miracles, many who watched did not believe. Jesus, therefore, did not entrust himself to them as he knew what was within them—namely, unbelief and wickedness (2:25). Jesus recognized that the fundamental problem was not only what was within man (unbelief), but what was not within man (a new heart or spirit). In other words, the problem, says Jesus, is that there is a lack of regeneration by the Holy Spirit.[2]

Therefore, when Jesus responds to Nicodemus he pinpoints the central issue. Unless you are born again by the Spirit you will never believe in who I say that I am, nor enter my Father's kingdom.[3] So Nicodemus has his curiosity answered, though not in the way he anticipated, especially as a religious leader.

But what does Jesus mean by the phrase "born again," which can also be translated "born from above"?[4] Perplexed and confused, Nicodemus misunderstood Jesus, believing he was referring to being physically born a second time (3:4). However, Jesus is not referring to a second birth from the flesh but one from heaven, from the Spirit (3:5–6).[5] The emphasis on "water" and "Spirit" (3:5) is an important one. Water does not refer to physical birth, which would contradict Jesus's very point that this new birth is from the Spirit not from the flesh. Nor does it refer to water baptism, since nowhere else does John use the phrase in such a way.[6] Instead, water should be interpreted symbolically. Jesus is using water to picture the Spirit's work in cleansing the sinner. Water represents the spiritual washing that occurs in the new birth.[7]

Such an interpretation of water becomes all the more clear when we consider how Jesus's language appears to echo Yahweh's promise in Ezekiel 36:25–27: "I will sprinkle clean water on you, and you shall be clean from all your uncleannesses, and from all your idols I will cleanse you. And I will give you a new heart, and a new spirit I will put within you. And I will remove the heart of stone from your flesh and give you a heart of flesh. And I will put my Spirit within you, and cause you to walk in my statutes and be careful to obey my rules." Ferguson explains that water and Spirit "refers to the two-fold work of the Spirit in regeneration: he [God] simultaneously gives new life and cleanses

---

2. Andreas J. Köstenberger, *John*, BECNT (Grand Rapids: Baker Academic, 2004), 117; Leon Morris, *John*, NICNT (Reprint, Grand Rapids: Eerdmans, 1971), 183.

3. In John 3:3 Jesus says unless a man is born again he cannot "see" the kingdom of God. And in 3:5 Jesus answers that a man cannot "enter" the kingdom of God. Seeing and entering are therefore synonymous.

4. Literally, top to bottom. See Köstenberger, *John*, 123.

5. John's use of flesh (*sarx*) in John 3 is not the same as Paul's use of flesh. For Paul flesh refers to the sinful, enslaved, corrupt nature. But in John 3, John is referring to flesh as physical flesh. Therefore, the contrast is not between sinful flesh and spiritual new life. Instead, the contrast is between physical birth and spiritual birth (new life).

6. D. A. Carson, *The Gospel according to John*, PNTC (Grand Rapids: Eerdmans, 1991), 191; Thomas R. Schreiner, *New Testament Theology: Magnifying God in Christ* (Grand Rapids: Baker, 2008), 462–63; Köstenberger, *John*, 123–24.

7. John Murray, *Redemption Accomplished and Applied* (Grand Rapids: Eerdmans, 1955), 98.

the heart."[8] So water and Spirit are used in tandem, referring to the reality of being cleansed, purified, renewed, and washed by the Spirit in regeneration.[9]

Furthermore, the role of the Spirit should not be missed. In verse 6 Jesus states that he who is born of the Spirit is spirit. Stated otherwise, sinners regenerated by the Holy Spirit are made spiritual.[10] By "Spirit" Jesus is referring to the Holy Spirit (John 3:8; cf. John 1:13; 1 John 2:29; 3:9; 4:7; 5:1, 4, 18), conveying that regeneration is a divine work, supernatural in nature. Once again, the Old Testament promises are in view. Yahweh covenanted with Israel, but they were unfaithful, rejecting his law and going after foreign gods (Judg. 2:11–15). While the nation of Israel was chosen by God, nevertheless, not all within Israel were regenerate (cf. Rom. 9:6). God, therefore, made a new covenant (Jer. 31:33), promising to give his people a new heart and a new spirit (Ezek. 11:19–20). And not only did he promise to put a new heart or spirit within, but the Lord promised to put his Spirit within as well, causing his people to walk according to his ways (Ezek. 36:27).[11]

The key question for our purposes, however, is whether or not the new birth described in John 3 is monergistic in nature. In other words, does the Spirit work effectually on a passive sinner to bring about new life? Our answer comes in verses 7 and 8 where any type of cooperation (i.e., synergism) with God in the new birth is precluded by the imagery of "birth" itself. Human birth is unilateral in every way. No infant has a say in being born nor does he do anything to be born. Being born is not conditioned upon the infant's will to accept it or reject it. Instead, the infant is passive. Likewise, the same applies in spiritual birth. The sinner is completely passive. He does not will to be born. God alone acts to bring about life. The sinner plays no part whatsoever. Carson explains, "Jesus's reply is not framed in terms of what Nicodemus must do to see the kingdom, but in terms of what must happen to him. The point is made both by the nature of the demanded transformation (a man neither begets nor bears himself) and by the passive mood of the verb."[12]

---

8. Sinclair Ferguson, *The Holy Spirit* (Downers Grove, IL: InterVarsity Press, 1996), 122. Schreiner also observes that "both 'water and Spirit' follow a single preposition (*ex*), indicating that water and Spirit refer not to two different notions but rather to the same spiritual reality" (*New Testament Theology*, 462–63).

9. Schreiner, *New Testament Theology*, 462–63. John's gospel often uses water and Spirit interchangeably. For example, see John 7:37–39.

10. Murray, *Redemption Accomplished and Applied*, 104.

11. The Spirit is not mentioned in Jeremiah 31 as it is in Ezekiel 36. Nonetheless the promise is consistent with what the Lord says through Ezekiel. See Schreiner, *New Testament Theology*, 435. Also consider Joel 2:28–32, where like Jeremiah 31, Ezekiel 11 and 36, the Lord also promises that this new age will be accompanied by the Spirit who brings salvation.

12. D. A. Carson, *Divine Sovereignty and Human Responsibility* (Eugene, OR: Wipf and Stock, 1994), 180. Also see Anthony A. Hoekema, *Saved by Grace* (Grand Rapids: Eerdmans, 1989), 97; Edwin H. Palmer, *The Person and Ministry of the Holy Spirit* (Grand Rapids:

Not only does the imagery of birth display God's sovereignty and man's passivity, but so also does the imagery of the wind. Jesus's reference to the wind highlights the power of the Holy Spirit in bringing about the new birth. Previously we saw with the reference to water that the Spirit is the divine agent who effects regeneration (John 3:5).[13] To begin with, it is crucial to observe the presence of the passive voice in John 3:3–8. As Hamilton explains, "This new birth is not something that people do to or for themselves. Each time the verb *gennaō* appears in John 3:3–8 it is passive (3:3, 4 [2x], 5, 6 [2x], 7, 8). John 1:13 ('born of God') provides clear warrant for seeing these as divine passives. God causes people to experience the new birth from above by the Spirit."[14] Hamilton presses the point further, "The need for new birth is connected to another clear feature in this passage: the stress on human inability to experience God's kingdom apart from this new birth. The word *dunamai* appears five times in 3:2–5 and again in verse 9. The new birth is brought about by God, and without it people are unable to see/enter the kingdom of God."[15] In other words, by using the divine passive Jesus places emphasis on the sovereignty of the Spirit.

Additionally, the omnipotence of the Spirit is seen once more in the comparison Jesus makes between wind and Spirit. Jesus states, "Do not marvel that I said to you, 'You [plural] must be born again.' The wind [spirit] blows where it wishes, and you hear its sound, but you do not know where it comes from or where it goes. So it is with everyone who is born of the Spirit." The word for Spirit (*pneuma*) in the Greek language is also the word for wind and vice versa. The parallel between the two is apparent in John 3:8. When Jesus refers to the wind he is referring to the Spirit.[16] When Jesus says the wind blows wherever it wishes, he is talking about the Spirit, who moves wherever he pleases. The Spirit is not subordinated to man's will, controlled by the sinner's choice. Rather, the Spirit blows wherever the Father pleases, bringing new life where there was only death.[17]

To summarize, man does not cooperate with God in the new birth, but rather he is passive. God works alone and unilaterally to bring about the new birth. The new birth is mysterious indeed, for we only see the effects of the Spirit (faith and repentance). Yet, behind what we visibly see is the Spirit at

---

Baker, 1974), 82–83; J. I. Packer, "Regeneration," in *EDT* (Grand Rapids: Baker, 2001), 925; idem, "Call, Calling," in ibid., 184.

13. Hoekema, *Saved by Grace*, 97–98.

14. James M. Hamilton, Jr., *God's Indwelling Presence: The Holy Spirit in the Old and New Testaments*, NACSBT, vol. 1. (Nashville: B&H, 2006), 130.

15. Ibid.

16. Herman Ridderbos, *The Gospel according to John*, trans. J. Vriend (Grand Rapids: Eerdmans, 1997), 129.

17. Murray, *Redemption Accomplished and Applied*, 99. Also see John M. Frame, *Salvation Belongs to the Lord* (Phillipsburg, NJ: P&R, 2006), 186.

work, creating a new creature in Christ. And it is only in bringing about this new birth that the effects of the Spirit are seen, namely, repentance and faith in Jesus. Therefore, the new birth is in no way contingent upon the sinner's will to believe, but rather the sinner's will to believe is conditioned upon the Spirit's sovereign choice to bring about the new birth.[18]

The New Birth in 1 John

If Jesus, in John's gospel, taught that the new birth is not something we bring about, but rather is the sovereign work of the Spirit (John 3:3–8), then it is no surprise when we discover that John taught the same in his first epistle. For John, the new birth always precedes any and every act of faith on man's part.[19]

In 1 John 5:1 we read: "Everyone who believes that Jesus is the Christ *has been* born of God, and everyone who loves the Father loves whoever has been born of him."[20] "Believes" in the phrase "Everyone who believes" (or "Everyone believing") refers to ongoing faith, for it is a present active participle in the nominative case.[21] But notice, when John says all those believing "*have been* born of him," "have been born" refers to an action that has already taken place in the past (it is completed) and has ongoing effects in the present, for it is a perfect passive indicative.[22] In other words, 1 John 5:1 assumes that regeneration (the action in the perfect passive indicative) precedes and causes faith (the action in the present active participle).[23] As John Stott explains, "The combination of the present tense (believes) and perfect tense [has been born] is important. It shows clearly that believing is the consequence, not the cause, of the new birth. Our present, continuing activity of believing is the result, and therefore, the evidence, of our past experience of new birth by which we became and remain God's children."[24] Therefore, man's faith is

---

18. Schreiner, *New Testament Theology*, 463.
19. Space only allows us to look at a few passages, but also consult 1 John 2:29; 3:9; 4:7; 5:18.
20. Piper calls 1 John 5:1 "the clearest text in the New Testament on the relationship between faith and the new birth" (John Piper, *Finally Alive* [Fearn, Ross-shire, Scotland: Christian Focus, 2009], 118; also see 138–39).
21. On the use of the participle, see Daniel B. Wallace, *Greek Grammar: Beyond the Basics, An Exegetical Syntax of the New Testament* (Grand Rapids: Zondervan, 1996), 613–55.
22. Ibid., 572–73; M. Zerwick, *Biblical Greek Illustrated by Examples* (Rome: Pontificii Instituti Biblici, 1963), 96; William D. Mounce, *Basics of Biblical Greek: Grammar* (Grand Rapids: Zondervan, 2003), 225. Additionally, John is not using the perfect tense randomly or without intention. The perfect tense, says Moulton, is "the most important, exegetically, of all the Greek Tenses" and as Wallace observes, "when it is used, there is usually a deliberate choice on the part of the writer" (J. H. Moulton, *A Grammar of New Testament Greek* [Edinburgh: T&T Clark, 1908], 1:140).
23. See Bruce A. Ware, "Divine Election to Salvation," in *Perspectives on Election: Five Views*, ed. Chad Owen Brand (Nashville: B&H, 2006), 20.
24. John Stott, *The Letters of John* (Grand Rapids: Eerdmans, 1988), 175. Cf. Peterson and Williams, *Why I Am Not an Arminian*, 189; Hoekema, *Saved by Grace*, 100–1.

always the result of the Spirit's regenerating work, never the cause. As Robert Yarbrough states, "In Johannine theology, spiritual rebirth seems to precede and ultimately create faith: those who believe do so not so much as the result of human volition as of prior divine intention."[25]

Likewise, the same applies to love. As 1 John 5:1 says, "everyone who loves the Father loves whoever has been born of him" (1 John 5:1). Again, one's love for the Father does not precede the new birth, but it is the new birth that precedes and creates a love for the Father. As God promised in Deuteronomy 30:6, "And the LORD your God will circumcise your heart and the heart of your offspring, *so that you will love* the Lord your God with all your heart and with all your soul, that you may live" (Deut. 30:6, emphasis added). No sinner can love the Lord unless the Lord first causes him to be born again.

Three verses later John also says, "For everyone who has been born of God overcomes the world. And this is the victory that has overcome the world— our faith" (1 John 5:4). According to John, faith is what overcomes the world. But overcoming the world, and by implication our faith, is the result of being born of God. In other words, the reason we can have faith that overcomes the world is because God has caused us to be born again. We know that this faith is a saving faith because John says in the next verse that the only one who can overcome the world is the one who believes that Jesus is the Son of God (1 John 5:5). As we saw in 1 John 5:1, belief or faith in Jesus as the Son of God is always the result of the new birth, not its cause.

Summary

According to Scripture, the sinner is absolutely passive in regeneration, spiritually dead, and in desperate need of new life. As Jesus demonstrated in John 3:3–8, it is the Holy Spirit, who, like the wind, moves wherever he pleases, to bring about new birth. The new birth does not involve man's cooperation, but is entirely the work of God, a reality evident in the analogy of birth itself.

REFLECTION QUESTIONS

1. How does Scripture's use of various images (e.g., water, wind, birth) high-light the sovereignty of the Spirit in the new birth?

2. How does the sovereignty of the Spirit in John 3 change your perception toward how evangelicals today use "born again" language?

3. If the new birth is a synergistic process, does God still receive all the glory and credit?

---

25. Robert W. Yarbrough, *1–3 John*, BECNT (Grand Rapids: Baker, 2008), 270.

4. How are Old Testament promises in passages like Jeremiah 31 and Ezekiel 36 fulfilled in the new covenant?

5. How does the reality of the new birth impact what it means to enter into the kingdom of God?

Is the New Birth Something We Bring About? (Part 2)

In the previous chapter we saw from Jesus himself that the new birth is something God alone brings about, without and apart from the sinner's cooperation. In this chapter we will see further support from Jesus's apostles, specifically Peter and Paul.[1] Each of these authors likewise teaches that God works efficaciously by the power of the Spirit to bring his elect from death to new life.

Caused to Be Born Again (1 Peter 1:3–5)

Much like James, Peter uses language when describing the new birth that lifts up our eyes away from ourselves to instead marvel at the great sovereignty of God in regeneration.

> Blessed be the God and Father of our Lord Jesus Christ! *According to his great mercy, he has caused us to be born again* [*anagennēsas*] to a living hope through the resurrection of Jesus Christ from the dead, to an inheritance that is imperishable, undefiled, and unfading, kept in heaven for you, who by God's power are being guarded through faith for a salvation ready to be revealed in the last time (1 Peter 1:3–5, emphasis added).

Notice, first of all, why God is to be praised. According to Peter, God is to be praised because he has caused us to be regenerated or born again. In verse 23 of the same chapter, Peter will use new birth language once again, claiming that his readers "have been born again, not of perishable seed but of

---

1. Space is limited, so we've restricted ourselves to Paul and Peter, but also see James 1:18.

imperishable, through the living and abiding word of God." In both verses we hear the same message, namely, it is God the Father who takes the initiative in bringing about the new birth.

Second, when God causes us to be born again, he does so according to his "great mercy." The very definition of mercy precludes even the slightest human contribution. Moreover, as we saw in Questions 3–5, the sinner prior to the new birth is dead in his sin, deserving only divine wrath and condemnation. God, however, has had great mercy, causing those dead in sin to be made alive in Christ Jesus (see Eph. 2:4–5). Therefore, like John 3:5–6, in 1 Peter 1:3–5 human contribution, even if it be the slightest cooperation of the will, is not a possibility. As Schreiner asserts, "The focus therefore is on God's initiative in producing new life. No one takes any credit for being born. It is something that happens to us."[2]

Third, when Peter describes God's work in the new birth, he uses the language of causation: "According to his great mercy, he has caused us to be born again." The miracle of the new birth is not a combined effort. Rather, God must cause the sinner to be born again. While some may not like the language of causation out of fear that it attributes too much power to God, Peter never avoids it but uses it without apology, once again drawing our attention to God's power at work in our new birth.

Fourth, God caused us to be born again through the resurrection of Jesus Christ from the dead. Christ not only died for our sins but was raised so that we would be born again. The very God who raised Christ from the dead also raises us spiritually from death to new life, giving us a living hope and an imperishable inheritance. In summary, 1 Peter 1:3–5 highlights the resurrection power of God, causing his elect to be born again not on the basis of anything they have done but only on the basis of his great mercy and grace.

Made Alive with Christ (Ephesians 2:1–7; Colossians 2:11–14)

Peter is not the only one who draws the connection between resurrection and regeneration; the apostle Paul does as well.[3] For example, consider Paul's words in Ephesians 2:1–7:

> And you were dead in the trespasses and sins in which you once walked, following the course of this world, following the prince of the power of the air, the spirit that is now at work in the sons of disobedience—among whom we all once lived in the passions of our flesh, carrying out the desires of the body

---

2. Schreiner, *1, 2 Peter, Jude*, NAC, vol. 37 (Nashville: B&H, 2003), 61. Also see L. A. Goppelt, *Commentary on 1 Peter* (Grand Rapids: Eerdmans, 1993), 81–83.

3. I have restricted our discussion to Ephesians 2:1–7 and Colossians 2:11–14, but also see 2 Corinthians 4:3–6.

and the mind, and were by nature children of wrath, like the rest of mankind. But God, being rich in mercy, because of the great love with which he loved us, even when we were dead in our trespasses, made us alive [*sunezōopoiēsen*] together with Christ—by grace you have been saved—and raised us up with him and seated us with him in the heavenly places in Christ Jesus, so that in the coming ages he might show the immeasurable riches of his grace in kindness toward us in Christ Jesus.

Ephesians 2 is one of the most powerful portrayals of what actually happens when a sinner is born again. As Paul explains, we are dead, spiritually lifeless, due to our sinfulness. We are not injured, but able to cooperate with God. Rather, we are six feet under, rotting away in the grave. But God, being rich in mercy and because of his great love for us, makes us alive, resurrecting us from the dead, breathing spiritual life into our dead, dry bones. Human cooperation (synergism) is nowhere to be found in this text, as if God's resurrection power and initiative is conditioned upon man's willful permission. Instead, Paul's resurrection language demonstrates that it is God, and God alone, who resurrects sinners from spiritual death to spiritual life, and therefore he alone deserves the glory and credit.

And notice, spiritual resurrection is immediate, instantaneous, and unilateral. One minute the sinner is dead and the next moment alive (Eph. 2:10).[4] Our spiritual resurrection (or regeneration) is, says Paul, much like the physical resurrection of Christ. Though Christ was dead in the tomb, God made him alive by his great power (Eph. 1:19–20).[5] Similarly, consider the story of Lazarus. Lazarus stunk, being dead four days. But at the very command of Christ, "Lazarus, come out" (John 11:43), he instantly and immediately sat up and walked out of the tomb! So is our regeneration by the Spirit.[6] Our faith does not precede our resurrection, but our spiritual resurrection necessarily and absolutely precedes and causes faith.[7]

Additionally, when we are "made alive," our spiritual resurrection is not only comparable to the resurrection of Christ, but we are made alive with Christ, meaning that the new life we have now received is found in him and

---

4. Ibid., 59–60.

5. Frank Thielman, *Ephesians*, BECNT (Grand Rapids: Baker, 2010), 134; T. G. Allen, "Exaltation and Solidarity with Christ: Ephesians 1.20 and 2.6," *JSNT* 28 (1986): 103–20.

6. Loraine Boettner, *The Reformed Doctrine of Predestination* (Philadelphia: P&R, 1963), 166; John Piper, *Finally Alive* (Fearn, Ross-shire, Scotland: Christian Focus, 2009), 68, 79, 84; Sinclair Ferguson, *The Christian Life: A Doctrinal Introduction* (Edinburgh: Banner of Truth, 1981), 34–35.

7. Robert L. Reymond, *A New Systematic Theology of the Christian Faith*, 2nd ed. (Nashville: Thomas Nelson, 1998), 709.

with him (see Eph. 2:5). We have been seated with Christ in the heavenly places (2:6). In the age to come we will know the "immeasurable riches of his grace in kindness toward us in Christ Jesus" (2:7).[8] Our new birth, therefore, is the fruit of the resurrection of Jesus. We see the reality of our spiritual resurrection more clearly when we compare it to what we looked like previously. Our spiritual life is set in contrast to our deadness in trespasses and sins, our bondage to the world ("following the course of this world"; 2:2), Satan ("following the prince of the power of the air"; 2:2), and the flesh ("once lived in the passions of our flesh, carrying out the desires of the body and the mind," 2:3). Like the rest of the world, we were "by nature children of wrath" (2:3). As O'Brien observes, being made alive or regenerated not only results in repentance and forgiveness in Christ but it also means that we have been liberated from these "tyrannical forces" (the world, Satan, the flesh).[9] As Paul exclaims in Colossians 2:13, "And you, who were dead in your trespasses and the uncircumcision of your flesh, God made alive together with him, having forgiven us all our trespasses" (cf. Rom. 6:11).

Before we move on, however, it is essential to observe that Paul says it is "by grace you have been saved" (2:5)—and surely regeneration is included in this grand scheme of salvation in Paul's mind.[10] A theme that runs throughout the Pauline epistles is the contrast between grace and works. Grace, for Paul, stands in opposition to human merit or any contribution whatsoever by man, even if it be small (Eph. 2:8–10). We can define grace as God's favor towards sinners in spite of what they deserve (Rom. 3:21–26; 4:4; 5:15).

Notice that "save" is often used to refer to an eschatological reality, specifically to deliverance from divine judgment and wrath on the last day.[11] Thielman observes the diversity of the term. In some passages Paul can "describe it [saved] as an ongoing event in the present (1 Cor. 1:18; 15:2; 2 Cor. 2:15) and say, 'Now is the day of salvation' (2 Cor. 6:2; cf. Isa. 39:8; Best 1998:602)." But Paul "normally refers to it as something believers will experience in the future, presumably at the final day (1 Thess. 2:16; 1 Cor. 3:15; 5:5; 10:33; Rom. 5:9–10; 9:27; 10:9; 11:26)."[12] Interestingly, however, Ephesians 2 is the exception to the rule. As O'Brien argues, "saved" refers specifically to what "has already been accomplished and experienced." It describes a "rescue from death, wrath, and bondage and a transfer into the new dominion with its manifold blessings. The periphrastic perfect construction draws attention to the resulting state of salvation."[13] Or as Thielman says, Paul is referring

---

8. Peter T. O'Brien, *The Letter to the Ephesians*, PNTC (Grand Rapids: Eerdmans, 1999), 167; idem, *The Holy Spirit* (Downers Grove, IL: InterVarsity Press, 1996), 119.
9. O'Brien, *Ephesians*, 167.
10. Ibid., 168.
11. Ibid., 169.
12. Thielman, *Ephesians*, 135.
13. O'Brien, *Ephesians*, 169. Also see Thielman, *Ephesians*, 135.

to salvation as something that is "emphatically present for believers," even though the "use of the perfect tense in Eph. 2:5, 8 for salvation is unusual."[14]

In summary, while Paul does lift our heads upward in verse 7 to the eschatological consequences of our salvation (we are seated with Christ in the age to come), in verses 5 and 6 being saved by grace is referring to a present reality, one that includes being made alive together with Christ by divine grace. The conclusion we must draw from the text is that being regenerated or made alive in Christ is not a work that is attributed to man's own effort or willful cooperation. Instead, it is by grace, and by grace alone, that we have been made alive. It is God's prerogative, and it is his power that resurrects the sinner from death to life.[15]

Paul uses the language of being made alive with Christ once again in Colossians 2:11–14. Drawing upon the Old Testament, Paul writes:

> In him [Christ] also you were circumcised with a circumcision made without [human] hands, by putting off the body of the flesh by the circumcision of Christ, having been buried with him in baptism, in which you were also raised with him through faith in the powerful working of God, who raised him from the dead. And you, who were dead in your trespasses and the uncircumcision of your flesh, God made alive together with him, having forgiven us all our trespasses, by canceling the record of debt that stood against us with its legal demands. This he set aside, nailing it to the cross.

Speaking through Moses, Jeremiah, and Ezekiel, Yahweh promised that he would circumcise the heart of his people (see Question 15; cf. Deut. 10:16; 30:6; Jer. 4:4; Ezek. 44:7). Through the redemptive work of Christ and the advent of the Holy Spirit, that new covenant promise has now become a reality. Therefore, says Paul, in Christ the believer has been circumcised, but this circumcision is not one made with hands; rather it is spiritual (i.e., a circumcision of the heart).[16]

The metaphor of circumcision itself, much like the metaphor of birth, indicates that regeneration is a work accomplished by God alone, without

---

14. Thielman, *Ephesians*, 135.
15. Thomas Schreiner, *Paul: Apostle of God's Glory in Christ* (Downers Grove, IL: InterVarsity Press, 2001), 246.
16. Douglas J. Moo, *The Letters to the Colossians and to Philemon*, PNTC (Grand Rapids: Eerdmans, 2008), 197. Also see T. K. Abbott, *A Critical and Exegetical Commentary on the Epistles to the Ephesians and to the Colossians*, ICC (Edinburgh: T&T Clark, 1979), 250; Richard R. Melick, Jr., *Philippians, Colossians, Philemon*, NAC, vol. 32 (Nashville: B&H, 1991), 257; N. T. Wright, *The Epistles of Paul to the Colossians and to Philemon*, TNTC (Downers Grove, IL: InterVarsity Press, 1986), 105.

our participation. It is a miracle that happens to us, not one we bring about. We are not able to circumcise our own hearts, but God must be the one to circumcise our hearts for us. Only then can we trust in Christ. And as a consequence of having a circumcised heart, says Moo, "No longer are we dominated by those 'powers' of the old era, sin, death, and the flesh; we are now ruled by righteousness, life, grace, and the Spirit (see esp. Rom. 5:12–8:17; 12:1–2; Gal. 1:4; 5:14–6:2)."[17]

Paul does not limit himself to the metaphor of circumcision. Instead, he moves on to the imagery of resurrection from the dead. So not only are we in Christ due to our spiritual circumcision, but we have been buried with Christ in baptism and raised with Christ through faith "in the powerful working of God, who raised him from the dead" (Col. 2:12). Paul then takes us directly to the doctrine of regeneration: "And you, who were dead in your trespasses and the uncircumcision of your flesh, God made alive [*sunezōopoiēsen*] together with him, having forgiven us of all our trespasses" (Col. 2:13). Like Ephesians 2, Paul once again uses death and resurrection language to describe our new birth. Specifically, Paul draws a parallel (see 2:12–13) between raising Jesus from the dead and raising sinners from the dead spiritually. Paul titles this spiritual resurrection of the sinner the "powerful work of God." Paul is right, for what could illustrate and demonstrate God's power more than raising the dead to life?[18] The giving of this new life is an "act of pure grace" and, as O'Brien points out, is in no way conditioned on man.[19]

The Washing of Regeneration (Titus 3:3–7)

In Ephesians 2 and Colossians 2, Paul very clearly affirms the total depravity and spiritual inability of man by describing each and every one of us as dead in our trespasses and sins. Paul continues to emphasize man's bondage and slavery to sin in Titus 3:3–7.

> For we ourselves were once foolish, disobedient, led astray, slaves to various passions and pleasures, passing our days in malice and envy, hated by others and hating one another. But when the goodness and loving kindness of God our Savior appeared, he saved us, not because of works done by us in righteousness, but according to his own mercy, by the washing of regeneration [*loutrou palingenesias*] and renewal of the Holy Spirit, whom he poured out on us richly through

---

17. Moo, *The Letters to the Colossians and to Philemon*, 201. Likewise, see F. F. Bruce, *The Epistles to the Colossians, to Philemon, and to the Ephesians*, NICNT (Grand Rapids: Eerdmans, 1989), 108.

18. Peter T. O'Brien, *Colossians, Philemon*, WBC, vol. 44 (Waco, TX: Word, 1982), 122.

19. Ibid., 123. Also see Melick, *Philippians, Colossians, Philemon*, 262.

> Jesus Christ our Savior, so that being justified by his grace
> we might become heirs according to the hope of eternal life.

Foolish, disobedient, led astray, slaves to various passions and pleasures, passing our days in malice and envy, hated by others and hating one another—each of these phrases and the way Paul piles one phrase on top of another only serve to reveal man's total spiritual inability. Any type of cooperation on man's part with divine grace is precluded for man is dead in his sins, enslaved to the pleasures of the flesh (cf. Titus 2:12; 1 Tim. 6:9).

But Christ (God our Savior) appeared and according to his mercy, and not because of our works, he saved us (Titus 3:5). How? By "the washing of regeneration and renewal of the Holy Spirit, whom he poured out on us richly through Jesus Christ our Savior" (Titus 3:5–6). Notice, first of all, that the salvation Paul speaks of is unconditional in nature. As Knight recognizes, Paul's two prepositional phrases provide the basis for God's redemption of sinners, the first of which dismisses any "contribution on our part" and the second of which is an "equally strong affirmation that salvation is solely based on God's mercy."[20] The Holy Spirit applies the mercy of God by washing (regenerating) the sinner clean. The Spirit's purpose, therefore, is to make effective Christ's redeeming work by purifying a people unto God (cf. Titus 2:14), and he does exactly this through the miracle of regeneration.[21] Works-righteousness or works-plus-faith is eliminated (cf. Rom. 3:21–28; 4:2–6; 9:11; Gal. 2:16; Eph. 2:8–9; Phil. 3:9; 2 Tim. 1:9).[22]

Second, the unconditional nature of our salvation cannot be bypassed or avoided by claiming, as some do, that though salvation is by faith alone and not works, nevertheless, there remains room for man to cooperate with the Spirit in order to bring about the washing of regeneration. Such an argument fails to take seriously the point Paul is making, namely, that man is a slave to sin and he can in no way whatsoever contribute to the Spirit's work of new birth. The washing of regeneration is the Spirit's work on a filthy, corrupt, dead sinner. This becomes even more apparent when we identify the similarity between Titus 3:3–7 and 1 Corinthians 6:11. Paul begins with a long list of sins to which man is enslaved and then says, "But you were washed, you were sanctified, you were justified in the name of the Lord Jesus Christ and by the Spirit of our God." So not only does Paul appeal once again to man's passivity and depravity—man was walking according to the flesh, not the Spirit—but

---

20. George W. Knight III, *The Pastoral Epistles: A Commentary on the Greek Text*, NIGTC (Grand Rapids: Eerdmans, 1992), 340.
21. William D. Mounce, *Pastoral Epistles*, WBC, vol. 46 (Nashville: Thomas Nelson, 2000), 448.
22. Knight, *The Pastoral Epistles*, 341; Mounce, *Pastoral Epistles*, 447. Also see Philip H. Towner, *The Letters to Timothy and Titus*, NICNT (Grand Rapids: Baker, 2006), 779–80; Thomas D. Lea and Hayne P. Griffin, *1, 2 Timothy, Titus*, NAC, vol. 34 (Nashville: B&H, 1992), 322.

Paul also uses the language of being "washed" to refer to the Spirit's work of renewal and cleansing that occurs in regeneration. Paul is once again emphasizing the power of the Spirit to wash the sinner, causing him to walk in newness of life (cf. Ezek. 36:26–27).[23] Surely Paul would have agreed with Jesus who, also connecting regeneration to the work of the Spirit, said in John 3 that the Spirit blows wherever he wills.[24] The only difference is that in Titus 3 Paul has shifted the metaphor from birth (John 3:5), or resurrection from the dead (Eph. 2:5; Col. 2:13), or circumcision (Col. 2:14–15), to the washing of the dirty, stained sinner. Nonetheless, the meaning remains the same.

Theological Conclusion

In light of the many biblical texts we've examined in the last two chapters, what theological conclusions can we draw? I limit myself to two. (1) Regeneration is monergistic. It's not a cooperation between God and man (i.e., synergism), one in which the success of God's regenerate action ultimately is conditioned upon man's decision. Rather, the sinner is spiritually dead and therefore totally passive. God must raise him to new life, and this is something God alone can do. (2) Since regeneration is monergistic and man is passive, regeneration always precedes faith in the order of salvation. Man's response (faith and repentance) is only possible because God has breathed new life into his spiritually dead corpse.

Summary

Nowhere in Scripture is regeneration conditioned upon man's will. Rather, God is the sovereign actor and decider, creating spiritual life by the power of his will. The biblical authors use different metaphors to convey this truth. Not only is the imagery of birth utilized, but also the imagery of death and resurrection. Regeneration is a spiritual resurrection from the grave, one that is immediate, instantaneous, unilateral, and monergistic in nature.

REFLECTION QUESTIONS

1. Whereas Jesus used the imagery of birth, what imagery do Peter and Paul use to teach what takes place in regeneration?

2. How does "resurrection" language convey divine sovereignty in regeneration?

---

23. Paul may very well have in mind Ezekiel 36:25–27 (also assumed by Jesus in John 3:5). Knight, *The Pastoral Epistles*, 343–44; John Murray, *Redemption Accomplished and Applied* (Grand Rapids: Eerdmans, 1955), 100; Towner, *The Letters to Timothy and Titus*, 774.
24. Anthony A. Hoekema, *Saved by Grace* (Grand Rapids: Eerdmans, 1989), 99.

3. How do the examples of Paul (Acts 9:1–18) and Lydia (Acts 16:14) highlight the monergistic nature of new birth?

4. How does the truth that regeneration precedes faith change the way we describe what takes place when a sinner believes in Jesus for the first time?

5. In what ways does God's sovereignty in regeneration lead you to worship and praise your Savior?

Does God Coerce Our Free Will?

As seen in Questions 12–14, we learned that God not only has a gospel call that goes out to all people but an effectual call that is reserved for his elect. The latter is often objected to, however, because such a calling is effectual. In other words, when God calls his elect to himself he does so without fail. But doesn't an effectual call result in God coercing our free will? After all, we are passive and God must do everything. How is our will not violated since we cannot resist such a calling? These objections are answered when we consider the nature of God's renewing work in regeneration, as well as the type of freedom man possesses.

From Bondage to Liberation

In Question 4 we learned that though man's slavery to sin is necessitated by his corrupt nature, nevertheless, such a slavery is a willful slavery because sin is what he most wants to do (i.e., freedom of inclination).[1] Such a conception of the will must be brought into consideration when we seek to understand divine grace as well. Remember, prior to God's effectual call and the Spirit's work of regeneration, man's will is enslaved, in bondage to sin (e.g., Eph. 2:1–3). Consequently, the will is passive, not active, toward God.

Therefore, when God so chooses to effectually call and regenerate his elect, man in no way cooperates, for he is spiritually dead. It is only as a consequence of regeneration that the will becomes spiritually active. As Paul explains, while we were dead in sin, now we have been "made alive to God in

---

1. The classic defense of freedom of inclination is Jonathan Edwards, *Freedom of the Will* (New Haven, CT: Yale University Press, 1957). Also see works by Martin Luther and John Calvin in the bibliography. For a much fuller treatment of free will, of which this chapter is indebted to, see Matthew Barrett, *Salvation by Grace: The Case for Effectual Calling and Regeneration* (Phillipsburg, NJ: P&R, 2013), chapter 4.

Christ Jesus" (Rom. 6:11). We used to be in bondage, enslaved to sin, but having died with Christ we have been "set free from sin" (Rom. 6:7, 18, 22).

How strange it is, then, to refer to such a supernatural work of God as *coercion*. It is not coercion that is at play, but liberation! We must understand that, when God liberates our will in regeneration, the liberation that takes place is a liberation from the bondage to sin. Therefore, not only are we freed *from* sin's grip, but we are freed *to* trust in Jesus Christ.[2]

The Renewal and Reorientation of the Will

Additionally, in regeneration the will is *reoriented* by God so that one will repent of his sins and trust in Christ, both of which could not happen prior to being regenerated due to his enslavement to sin. As seen in Question 4, prior to regeneration the will is in every way impacted by the fall (e.g., John 8:34; Eph. 2:1–3). Sin has pervaded every aspect of man, so much so that even his will is distorted. Yes, the faculty of his will exists, but due to the effects of sin, his will is bent and forever inclined towards ungodliness. What he needs is the miracle of new birth, which always precedes any spiritual activity on man's part. In other words, the active will of man is always the *effect* of God previously *causing* the sinner to be born again (see Question 15–17). For that reason, many of the Puritans argued that God's grace, in bringing about the new birth, "does not wrench or force the will; it regenerates and reforms the will in order that it might freely choose to believe."[3] He reorients and reforms the will so that whereas before the sinner hated Christ, now he wants to choose Christ. To put the point colloquially: The sinner is given a renewed "wanter."

Hence, coming to Christ may be effectual, determined by God, but such a coming is exactly what the regenerated sinner now wants to do. As Welty explains:

> Since freedom from coercion means having the freedom to do what you want to do, then yes, if you do something even though you did not want to do it, that would be coercion. But at no stage in the Calvinistic pre-conversion/conversion/ postconversion story is the sinner forced to *do* anything he does not *want* to do. Rather, God (mysteriously, no doubt) changes our wants. We go from wanting our idols and sins to wanting God and righteousness. But wants are not actions. So regeneration does not produce any actions that go against

---

2. See John Calvin, *Institutes of the Christian Religion*, ed. John T. McNeil, trans. Ford Lewis Battles, LCC, vols. 20–21 (Philadelphia: Westminster John Knox, 1960), 3.19.1–9; Anthony A. Hoekema, *Created in God's Image* (Grand Rapids: Eerdmans, 1986), 237–43.

3. Richard Muller, "Grace, Election, and Contingent Choice: Arminius's Gambit and the Reformed Response," in vol. 2 of *The Grace of God, the Bondage of the Will*, eds. Thomas R. Schreiner and Bruce A. Ware (Grand Rapids: Baker, 1995), 277.

our wills. Instead, regeneration is a matter of God's *renewing* the will so that the whole person delights in God and is inclined to find Him wholly attractive, to prefer Him above all else. And with that renewed will, we choose in accordance with it, and we choose Christ. . . . It is never a matter of God's making someone act *contrary to* his will.[4]

"Renewing the will" is a key phrase. God reorients, reforms, and renews the will so that it now wants what it previous despised. Whereas before the sinner delighted in sin, now God has worked upon the will in regeneration in such a way that the sinner now delights in Christ. Whereas before he was inclined only to sin, God has so renewed the will that he now is inclined to Christ. What the sinner previously found repulsive, he now, because of the reformation and renewal that has taken place, sees as attractive. Therefore, being regenerated by the Holy Spirit, the sinner now chooses Christ as that which he most desires, as that which he cherishes above all else. He does not act contrary to his will (as in coercion), but he acts in accordance with his regenerated will.

Divine Necessity

Such a reorientation, reform, and renewal of the will is not inconsistent with divine necessity. Notice, prior to regeneration man is enslaved to sin. Therefore, necessity is involved in every way, and yet he still chooses that which he most wants and desires, namely, sin. In other words, while he is necessitated by sin, sinning is what he most wants to do and so he acts in accordance with his will. Similarly, in effectual calling and regeneration the sinner is under a divine necessity or determinism. God calls his elect and he does so invincibly. And yet, such a divine determinism does not mean that the sinner is coerced. He may be necessitated to choose Christ, but such a divinely determined choice is absolutely consistent with what man now *wants* to do—namely, choose Christ. So though God does indeed act effectually to call and regenerate the sinner, having been regenerated he now chooses Christ as that which he wants and desires more than anything else.[5] He does not come to Christ kicking and screaming, but joyfully, willingly, and gladly.

In the history of the church, many have used theological language that acutely captures such a reality. For example, the Westminster Confession says God effectually calls his elect by his Word and Spirit and he accomplishes this "by enlightening their minds . . . taking away their heart of stone . . . renewing

---

4. Greg Welty, "Election and Calling: A Biblical Theological Study," in *Calvinism: A Southern Baptist Dialogue*, eds. E. Ray Clendenen and Brad J. Waggoner (Nashville: B&H, 2008), 241.
5. Heinrich Heppe, *Reformed Dogmatics*, ed. Ernst Bizer, trans. G. T. Thomson (Eugene, OR: Wipf & Stock, 1950), 520.

their wills . . . and effectually drawing them to Jesus; yet so as they come most freely, being made willing by his grace."[6] Or consider the Synod of Dort's affirmation that "this divine grace of regeneration does not act in people as if they were blocks and stones; nor does it abolish the will and its properties or coerce a reluctant will by force, but spiritually revives, heals, reforms, and—in a manner at once pleasing and powerful—bends it back."[7]

Correcting Caricatures

To conclude, some have preferred the label "effectual grace" in contrast to "irresistible grace" simply because the latter is sometimes misunderstood, as if God is coercing the sinner against his will.[8] As Carson explains, "The expression [irresistible grace] is misleading, because it suggests what the theologians themselves usually seek to avoid, viz. the idea that the inevitability of the coming-to-Jesus by those given to Jesus means they do so *against* their will, squealing and kicking as it were."[9] J. Gresham Machen helpfully corrects such a caricature:

> The Biblical doctrine of the grace of God does not mean, as caricatures of it sometimes represent it as meaning, that a man is saved against his will. No, it means that a man's will itself is renewed. His act of faith by which he is united to the Lord Jesus Christ is his own act. He performs that gladly, and is sure that he never was so free as when he performs it. Yet he is enabled to perform it simply by the gracious, sovereign act of the Spirit of God.[10]

Yes, God's grace works effectually, for he renews, reforms, heals, and reorients the will, and always does so successfully. But though he does so in such a way that the sinner comes to Christ inevitably, nevertheless it is because he has renewed the will effectually that the sinner comes to Christ most willingly. Packer, quoting Westminster (10.1), explains such a mystery, "Grace is irresistible, not because it drags sinners to Christ against their will, but because

---

6. "The Westminster Confession of Faith (1646)," in *Reformed Confessions of the Sixteenth Century and Seventeenth Centuries in English Translation, Volume 4, 1600–1693*, ed. James T. Dennison Jr. (Grand Rapids: Reformation Heritage, 2014), chapter 12.

7. "The Canons of Dort (1618–1619)," in *Reformed Confessions of the Sixteenth Century and Seventeenth Centuries in English Translation, Volume 4, 1600–1693*, Canons 3/4.

8. Michael Horton, *Covenant and Salvation* (Louisville: Westminster John Knox, 2007), 216–42.

9. D. A. Carson, *Divine Sovereignty and Human Responsibility* (Eugene, OR: Wipf and Stock, 1994), 185.

10. J. Gresham Machen, *The Christian View of Man* (Edinburgh: Banner of Truth, 1984), 244.

it changes men's hearts so that they 'come most freely, being made willing by his grace.'"[11]

Summary

In effectual calling and regeneration, God does not coerce the will or do violence to the will, but rather renews, reorients, and reforms the will, liberating the will from bondage to sin. Free will, both before and after regeneration, is best understood as a freedom of inclination. Prior to regeneration man is enslaved to sin, and yet his bondage is a most willful and voluntary one as sin is what he most wants to do. However, when God works to effectually call and regenerate the dead and depraved sinner, his will is renewed, reoriented, and reformed. The sinner is now enabled to willfully repent and receive Christ by faith. Repentance and faith *will* follow God's effectual call and regenerative work. And yet, responding in repentance and faith is exactly what the sinner most desires and therefore he does so freely.

REFLECTION QUESTIONS

1. What is the common, popular view of "free will," and is it biblical?

2. Define and explain what is meant by "freedom of inclination"?

3. Is freedom of inclination compatible with divine sovereignty?

4. Is the human will in bondage to sin and is this bondage voluntary and willful?

5. How does God work in regeneration to renew and reorient the will?

---

11. J. I. Packer, *A Quest for Godliness: The Puritan Vision of the Christian Life* (Wheaton, IL: Crossway, 1990), 295.

PART 4

Conversion, Justification, and Adoption

What Is Saving Faith?

Faith and repentance are two essential ingredients that make up the evangelical doctrine of conversion. Conversion occurs when we hear the gospel, repent of our sins, and trust in Christ alone for salvation. As we will learn, these two components (faith and repentance) are gracious gifts from God (see Question 21), gifts that God not only extends but works within us. Conversion, therefore, is ultimately a supernatural and sovereign work of God, leaving us no room to boast in ourselves.

Conversion and the Order of Salvation

At the start, several general points should be made about conversion. First, conversion naturally follows regeneration in the order of salvation (see Questions 16–17). The new life God has created now takes form. The dead have been spiritually resurrected, and as their eyes open it is Christ whom they see. This new spiritual ability to see the Savior cannot but result in a turning away from sin (repentance) and a turning to Christ (faith). Or to use theological language: While regeneration occurs in the *subconscious* (since it is God's monergistic work on a spiritually dead sinner), conversion involves the *conscious* life of the person, whereby the sinner willfully and mindfully repudiates sin and embraces Jesus as Savior.[1] The new life God has planted within must sprout into the open air, receiving spiritual sunlight (the Son of light!). We can say with Berkhof, then, that a "conversion that is not rooted in regeneration is no true conversion."[2]

Second, like regeneration, conversion is a one-time event. It is not like sanctification, which is a drawn-out, lifelong process (see Questions 32–33). Rather, conversion occurs at the start of the Christian life and is never repeated. It's not as if a sinner is converted, sins, loses his salvation, and then must be converted

---

1. Louis Berkhof, *Systematic Theology* (Edinburgh: Banner of Truth, 2003), 484.
2. Ibid., 485.

all over again. No, those whom God predestines, calls, regenerates, and converts, he also sanctifies and glorifies (Rom. 8:28–30). All those truly born again will persevere to the end (see Questions 36–37). So conversion is not repeatable, but occurs at the genesis of the Christian life, and since it is grounded in the new birth it naturally results in perseverance unto glory.[3]

With these two broader points in mind, in this chapter we will explore the contours of saving faith, and in the next chapter we will turn our attention to repentance.

Defining Faith

What is saving faith exactly? Is it mere knowledge about Christ? Or is it much more, including one's assent and trust? In Scripture, saving faith includes all three: knowledge (*notitia*), assent (*assensus*), and trust (*fiducia*). "We cannot be said to believe or to trust in a thing or person of which we have no knowledge," said B. B. Warfield, and "equally we cannot be said to believe that which we distrust too much to commit ourselves to it."[4] Let's look briefly at each of these key components of faith.

Knowledge

Today, unfortunately, it is common to view knowledge as the enemy of faith, as if faith must be a *blind* trust in something or someone unknown. In such a view, it is not the object of one's faith that matters, nor whether one's knowledge is true, or whether the object of one's knowledge is true, but only whether one's faith is genuine. Ignorance, in other words, is irrelevant for it is replaced by sincerity.[5] It matters not what or who you believe in, nor whether your knowledge is accurate and trustworthy, but only the authenticity of your belief is relevant.

In Scripture, however, knowledge matters, so much so that without a proper understanding of the gospel one cannot be saved. As Paul rhetorically asks in Romans 10:14, "How then will they call on him in whom they have not believed? And how are they to believe in him of whom they have never heard? And how are they to hear without someone preaching?" It is absolutely necessary that the sinner have knowledge of the gospel, of who Christ, is and what he has accomplished in his life, death, and resurrection.

The apostle Paul teaches that believing what is false always leads to unrighteousness and condemnation (2 Thess. 2:11–12). On the other hand, believing

---

3. As we will see in Questions 36–37, this does not mean that those converted will never fall into sin, but it does mean that they cannot fall away from God's converting grace.
4. Benjamin B. Warfield, "On Faith in Its Psychological Aspects," in *Biblical and Theological Studies* (Philadelphia: P&R, 1952), 402–3.
5. For a critique of such a view, see Robert L. Reymond, *A New Systematic Theology of the Christian Faith*, 2nd ed. (Nashville: Thomas Nelson, 1998), 727.

what is true is essential if one is to be redeemed (2 Thess. 2:10; 2 Tim. 2:25).[6] The author of Hebrews says that faith involves the "conviction of things not seen," and "conviction" certainly assumes a certainty in regard to knowledge.

Yet, we would be mistaken to then assume that knowledge alone is sufficient for salvation. Knowledge of the gospel is *necessary* for saving faith, but it is not *sufficient* in and of itself. Such a point is made evident by the ministry of Jesus. Even though the most religious Jewish leaders listened to Jesus and understood his claims to deity, nevertheless, many disbelieved and instead sought his death (e.g., John 5:18; 8:39–59).[7] As Stephen says in Acts, they are like their forefathers who received special revelation from God himself, but chose instead to reject God's prophets (e.g., Acts 7:51–53). So mere knowledge isn't enough.

Furthermore, if mere knowledge were sufficient for saving faith, then even the demons would be saved. But notice what James says: "You believe that God is one; you do well. Even the demons believe—and shudder!" (2:19). Apparently, mere knowledge of who God is and what his Son has done is not sufficient. Even the demons possess such knowledge. Something more is needed.

Assent

Not only do we need an understanding of the gospel, but assent or approval as well.[8] In other words, not only must one possess knowledge, but one must believe that this knowledge is true. Faith involves a "conviction" (Heb. 11:1), and conviction not only assumes the intellect (i.e., knowledge) but *intellectual assent*.

One of the major problems with the religious leaders in Jesus's day was this: Though they had knowledge (they heard Jesus teach), they did not agree, approve, or assent to what Jesus said. For instance, consider John 5:18. Though Jesus, through his teaching and miracles, taught that God was his Father, the Jews did not believe this was true. Instead, they sought to kill him because he was "calling God his own Father, making himself equal with God." So though they had knowledge (i.e., Jesus claimed to be equal with God), they refused to approve such a claim and give their assent.[9] Therefore, knowledge must be accompanied by assent or approval.[10]

---

6. Many biblical texts are clear on this matter (John 8:24; 11:42; 14:11; 16:27; 20:31; Rom. 10:9; 1 Thess. 4:14; Heb. 11:6; 1 John 5:1, 4). In these texts each propositional truth is preceded by πιστεύω ὅτι (*pisteuō hoti*; "believe that"). Such a grammatical construction emphasizes that knowledge is involved in the content of saving faith.
7. To qualify, we might question how well the religious leaders actually understood Jesus, since so often they seem to misunderstand him entirely.
8. The word "conviction" could also be used.
9. Also see John 8:48–59.
10. Many contemporary examples could also be given. A Christian may witness to a Mormon, and the Mormon may understand the truth claims the Christian is making (and even how those claims differ from his own). Yet, this knowledge or understanding does not mean faith is present, for the Mormon will disagree, refusing to assent to this knowledge.

And yet, knowledge *and* assent, though necessary, are still not sufficient. It is not enough to merely know and approve of the truth (e.g., Acts 26:27–28). One outstanding example is Nicodemus, a ruler of the Jews, who came to Jesus at night and said, "Rabbi, we know that you are a teacher come from God, for no one can do these signs that you do unless God is with him" (John 3:2). Here we have assent. Nicodemus and others like him agreed that Jesus was from God and that God was truly with him. Did this then mean that Nicodemus had saving faith? Not at all. In fact, Jesus says just the opposite, telling Nicodemus that he must be born again to enter the kingdom of God (John 3:4–14). Therefore, while knowledge and assent are necessary aspects of saving faith, by themselves they are insufficient. Again, something more is needed.

Trust

Not only is knowledge and assent (conviction) necessary, but so also is dependence on and trust in Jesus. In other words, not only must a person hear the gospel and approve of it, but he must also trust in Jesus who is proclaimed in that gospel. It's not enough to believe in him; one must believe *on him* as a person as well.[11] As the Heidelberg Catechism so famously says, faith "is not only a certain knowledge whereby I hold for true all that God has revealed to us in His Word, but also a hearty trust which the Holy Ghost works in me by the gospel" (Q. 21). The sinner must place his faith in Jesus alone to save him. In doing so, one transitions from being a mere spectator of the gospel to entering into a saving relationship with Christ and commitment to him as Savior and Lord.[12]

It follows that saving faith must include sincere dependence on and trust in Jesus alone for eternal life and the forgiveness of sins.[13] Such dependence and trust involves the heart of a person. The "seat of faith" is not located in one's intellect, feelings, or will, though all of these have their own role in regards to faith; rather, the seat of faith is "only in the heart," for it is the heart that is the "central organ of man's spiritual being, out of which are the issues of life."[14] And because the seat of faith is the heart, it follows that faith involves, in matters of eternal life, safety, security, assurance, gratitude, and joy.[15]

That trust in and dependence on Jesus are essential for salvation is apparent throughout the Bible. For example, Jesus repeatedly proclaims that a sinner must believe in him if he is not to perish but instead inherit eternal life. Jesus says in John 3:16 and 18, "For God so loved the world, that he gave

---

11. Murray, *Redemption*, 112.
12. Wayne Grudem, *Systematic Theology* (Grand Rapids: Zondervan, 1994), 710.
13. Berkhof writes how *fiducia* "consists in a personal trust in Christ as Saviour and Lord, including a surrender of the soul as guilty and defiled to Christ, and a reception and appropriation of Christ as the source of pardon and of spiritual life" (*Systematic Theology*, 505).
14. Ibid.
15. Ibid.

his only Son, that whoever believes in him should not perish but have eternal life. . . . Whoever believes in him is not condemned, but whoever does not believe is condemned already, because he has not believed in the name of the only Son of God." Or consider the words of Jesus in John 5:24: "Truly, truly, I say to you, whoever hears my word and believes him who sent me has eternal life. He does not come into judgment, but has passed from death to life." John begins his gospel saying the same, "But all who did receive him [Jesus], who believed in his name, he gave the right to become children of God" (1:12).[16] John even ends his gospel on the same note, explaining that he has written about the signs of Jesus "so that you may believe that Jesus is the Christ, the Son of God, and that by believing you may have life in his name" (20:31).

Unfortunately, for many today "belief" and "faith" are words that fail to reflect the biblical meaning. In the twenty-first century the word "believe" is used to say that one believes something is true. One does not necessarily mean, however, that such belief also includes personal dependence, reliance, or even commitment.[17] In Scripture, however, "believe" and "faith" are used to convey not only knowledge and assent, but trust as well. When Jesus says that "whoever believes in him should not perish but have eternal life," he does not mean mere assent or agreement, but also refers to trust and dependence in him for salvation. Such trust is personal, relying upon Jesus to fulfill his promise to forgive sin and grant eternal life.[18]

Moreover, we know that believing in Jesus means more than mere knowledge and assent, for Scripture describes belief as *coming* to Jesus for salvation (John 6:37; 7:37; Matt. 11:28–30; Heb. 7:25). Faith means turning away from ourselves and to Christ instead. Other images in Scripture also picture faith as trust and dependence. Faith is described as *eating* Christ (John 6:51), *drinking* Christ (John 4:14), and *abiding* in Christ (John 15:5). Berkhof is on the right track to conclude that faith must be a "certain conviction, wrought in the heart by the Holy Spirit, as to the truth of the gospel, and a hearty reliance (trust) on the promises of God in Christ."[19]

Faith: A Deep-Rooted Assurance

The author of Hebrews defines faith beautifully: "Now faith is the assurance of things hoped for, the conviction of things not seen" (Heb. 11:1). We have seen that saving faith involves not only knowledge and assent, but also trust. But here we see another component to trust, namely, faith as *assurance*.[20] In and through faith comes a guarantee that the sinner will one day

---

16. Belief here is not merely cognitive understanding or comprehension, but reception of Christ and his teaching (see John 1:12).
17. Ibid.
18. Leon Morris, *The Gospel According to John*, NICNT (Grand Rapids: Eerdmans, 1971), 336.
19. Berkhof, *Systematic Theology*, 503.
20. See the works of Joel Beeke in the bibliography for a more in depth treatment on assurance.

receive and possess the salvation promised to him.[21] Faith is a knowledge of and trust in God's promised mercy. As Calvin said so well, faith is a "firm and certain knowledge of God's benevolence towards us, founded upon the truth of the freely given promise in Christ, both revealed to our minds and sealed upon our hearts through the Holy Spirit."[22] Or as the Heidelberg Catechism explains, faith is "a deep-rooted assurance, created in me by the Holy Spirit through the gospel, that . . . not only others, but I too, have had my sins forgiven, have been made forever right with God, and have been granted salvation" (Q. 21). Therefore, by trusting in who Christ is and what he has done, the believer finds that he is not left drowning in doubt, but instead his salvation rests upon a firm confidence that cannot be shaken.[23]

The Object and Ground of Faith

It should be obvious by now that the *object* of our faith is Jesus Christ. Or if we desire to use "gospel categories," we could also say that the object of our faith is the gospel of Jesus Christ. This much is apparent throughout the book of Acts. It is the gospel of Jesus Christ that is proclaimed as the hope of salvation for lost and condemned sinners. Christ is the center of the apostolic message. So when the Philippian jailer asks Paul and Silas what he must do to be saved, they respond, "Believe *in the Lord Jesus,* and you will be saved, you and your household" (Acts 16:31, emphasis added). We then read that Paul and Silas "spoke the word of the Lord to him and to all who were in his house," explaining who Christ is, what he has done, and what this means for their salvation (16:32).

If Jesus is the object of our faith, then the *ground* of our faith is the truthfulness and faithfulness of God, who not only makes a gospel promise but keeps it.[24] That God is faithful to fulfill his saving promises is proven to be the case by the fact that the Father sent his Son to die on the cross for the salvation of his people. The faithfulness of the triune God is proven once more when the Father and Son send the Spirit to apply the work of Christ won for God's elect. The order of salvation, therefore, bears witness to the veracity of God, as well as his faithfulness to bring about the great work of salvation he planned in eternity. On that basis, our faith is grounded in the very character of God. It is because he is a true and faithful God that we can place our faith in him, trusting in his gospel promises.

---

21. Anthony A. Hoekema, *Saved by Grace* (Grand Rapids: Eerdmans, 1989), 139.
22. John Calvin, *Institutes of the Christian Religion,* ed. John T. McNeil, trans. Ford Lewis Battles, LCC, vols. 20–21 (Philadelphia: Westminster John Knox, 1960), 3.2.7.
23. This should not be taken to mean, however, that the believer never struggles with doubt. See "The Westminster Confession of Faith (1646)," in *Reformed Confessions of the Sixteenth Century and Seventeenth Centuries in English Translation, Volume 4, 1600–1693,* ed. James T. Dennison Jr. (Grand Rapids: Reformation Heritage, 2014), 18.1–4.
24. On this point, see Berkhof, *Systematic Theology,* 506.

Summary

Saving faith involves three essential components: knowledge, assent, and trust. The sinner who truly believes in Christ is one who not only knows who Christ is and what he has done, not only agrees to and assents to the facts of the gospel, but depends upon and trusts in Christ alone for the forgiveness of sins and the hope of eternal life. Moreover, trust and dependence involve a deep-rooted assurance that one's sins are forgiven, he/she has been made right with God, and he/she has received salvation by grace alone. Therefore, faith involves a firm confidence that cannot be broken. Finally, the object of saving faith is Jesus Christ, or more specifically the gospel of Jesus Christ, while the ground of saving faith is the truthfulness and faithfulness of God.

REFLECTION QUESTIONS

1. How does Scripture define saving faith?

2. What are some of the most common misconceptions about faith you have encountered?

3. Are "knowledge" and "assent" sufficient, or must faith also involve "trust" and "dependence"?

4. What does it mean for faith to be a "deep-rooted assurance," and what comfort does this bring you in your Christian life?

5. What does it mean for faith to be a "conviction of things not seen"?

What Is True Repentance?

One of the most profound definitions of repentance can be found in The Westminster Confession of Faith:

> By it [repentance], a sinner, out of the sight and sense not only of the danger, but also of the filthiness and odiousness of his sins, as contrary to the holy nature, and righteous law of God; and upon the apprehension of His mercy in Christ to such as are penitent, so grieves for, and hates his sins, as to turn from them all unto God, purposing and endeavouring to walk with Him in all the ways of his commandments (15.2).

As seen in this classic confessional statement, and as we will explore in this chapter, repentance is a sorrow for one's sin *and* a commitment to reject sin and instead trust Christ. Sorrow and remorse for sin, though essential, are not enough to constitute repentance. Rather, sorrow for sin must be accompanied by a decisive resolve to reject, forsake, renounce, and abandon sin. What is required, therefore, is not merely grief over one's sin. Even unbelievers may grieve over their actions because they fear punishment. For true repentance to take place there must be more, namely, a turning away from sin and a resolve or commitment to reject sin (Job 42:5–6; Isa. 55:7; Ezek. 33:11; Jer. 8:6; Joel 2:12–13).[1] In short, there must be a change of heart and mind that results in a change of life.[2]

---

1. Such a turning can be seen even in the word "repentance" itself. In the New Testament the term refers to a "turn about" or a "changing of one's mind."
2. "It is not only modifying a few convictions here and there, but realizing that your whole interpretation of reality—God, yourself, your relation to God and the world—is misguided" (Michael Horton, *Pilgrim Theology: Core Doctrines for Christian Disciples* [Grand Rapids: Zondervan, 2011], 263).

Turning from Sin to God

For example, consider Peter and Judas: two of Christ's disciples, and two men who sinned greatly against Christ. Peter denied Christ three times. Judas betrayed Christ, handing him over to be arrested. But notice the difference between these two men after the fact. Peter went outside and wept bitterly. Yet after Jesus rose from the dead, Peter was restored to his Savior, being instructed to feed the sheep Christ would entrust to him (Matt. 26:75; John 21:15–17). Judas was also filled with regret after his sin. After realizing he had betrayed his master and handed him over to be condemned, the text says he "changed his mind," but it was too late (Matt. 27:3). Returning the thirty pieces of silver, the blood price for Christ, Judas told the chief priests and elders, "I have sinned by betraying innocent blood" (Matt. 27:4). After throwing the silver back into the temple, Judas hanged himself. Two men, two sinners, two betrayers of Christ, and yet one is restored and the other condemned (Matt. 27:3; Acts 1:25). Peter's repentance resulted in forgiveness and redemption, while Judas' sorrow led to condemnation and death. Peter's repentance was genuine and sincere, as he sought the forgiveness that only Jesus could give (John 21:7–17). Judas, though regretting his decision, never sought a repentance that led to forgiveness. He was overcome with remorse, but his sorrow was not a "godly grief" that produces a repentance leading "to salvation without regret" (2 Cor. 7:10).[3] When Judas "hanged himself," St. Augustine observes, "he did not atone for the guilt of his detestable betrayal but rather increased it, since he despaired of God's mercy and in a fit of self-destructive remorse left himself no chance of a saving repentance."[4]

A similar case is Esau who sold his birthright to his brother Jacob for a hot meal (Gen. 27:34–38). Listen to how the author of Hebrews interprets this tragic story: "For you know that afterward, when he [Esau] desired to inherit the blessing, he was rejected, for he found no chance to repent, though he sought it with tears" (Heb. 12:17). Esau was grieved and full of sorrow, particularly over the consequences and outcome of his choice. And yet, though he wept, his weeping never led to true repentance. So grief is insufficient in and of itself. Grief and sorrow are necessary, but they must be accompanied by a decision, a resolve, a commitment in one's heart to turn from sin and walk in obedience to God. As Paul says to the Corinthians, "I rejoice, not because you were grieved, but because you were grieved into repenting. . . . For godly grief

---

3. Besides Judas, also consider Hymenaeus and Alexander in 1 Timothy 1:19–20 whom Paul says "made shipwreck of their faith" and were "handed over to Satan that they may learn not to blaspheme." In 2 Timothy 2:17–18 Paul again mentions Hymenaeus but also Philetus, both of whom "swerved from the truth." Later, in 4:10, Paul says Demas fell "in love with this present world" and has "deserted me." In these cases and others John's words ring true: "They went out from us, but they were not of us; for if they had been of us, they would have continued with us" (1 John 2:19). Jesus's parable of the sower assumes this unfortunate reality (Matt. 13:20–21). Cf. Louis Berkhof, *Systematic Theology* (Grand Rapids: Eerdmans, 1996), 483.

4. Saint Augustine, *City of God* (New York: Penguin, 1972), 1.17.

produces a repentance that leads to salvation without regret, whereas worldly grief produces death" (2 Cor. 7:9).

The difference, then, between Judas and Peter, or Esau and Jacob, is the difference between legal repentance and evangelical repentance.[5] Legal repentance is merely a fear of judgment and punishment. Evangelical repentance is a conviction of sin that leads to the gospel, where forgiveness is to be found.[6] While legal repentance ends with damnation, evangelical repentance leads the sinner out of the gates of hell and into the court of God's kingdom.

Three Aspects of Repentance

Since faith and repentance are inseparable (as we will see), it should not be surprising that repentance shares many of the same characteristics as faith (see Question 19). Three particular aspects of repentance can be identified.

First, repentance involves *knowledge* (or *intellect*). It is when the sinner is confronted with the holiness, justice, wrath, and majesty of God that he is convicted of sin and led to repentance by the Spirit. In other words, the sinner knows that he is a sinner and a very wretched one at that. Such was the case with Isaiah who experienced the holiness of God and fittingly cried out, "Woe is me! For I am lost; for I am a man of unclean lips, and I dwell in the midst of a people of unclean lips, for my eyes have seen the King, the LORD of hosts!" (Isa. 6:5).

Second, repentance involves the sinner's *affections and emotions*. Genuine, sincere repentance not only means one acknowledges that he is in the wrong, but it also means that there is tremendous grief and sorrow for one's sin (2 Cor. 7:10), and not just sorrow because of the result or consequence of one's sin (as was the case with Esau and Judas).[7] The sinner is grieved for violating God's moral law, knowing that he has displeased the Lord.[8]

Third, like faith, repentance involves the *human will*. As faith is a turning to Christ, repentance is a willful turning away from sin. Such a turning away from sin and to Christ *results* in a life of obedience, as one bears the fruit that comes from genuine repentance in sanctification (see Question 32). In other words, repentance, if genuine, has an effect and that effect is a transformed life (e.g., Matt. 16:24). As the Heidelberg Catechism explains, repentance is

---

5. Michael Horton, *Pilgrim Theology: Core Doctrines for Christian Disciples* (Grand Rapids: Zondervan, 2011), 264.
6. To qualify, true repentance does involve fear, but it is a fear that results in turning to God. As Calvin explains, repentance is "the true turning of our life to God, a turning that arises from a pure and honest fear of him" (John Calvin, *Institutes of the Christian Religion*, ed. John T. McNeil, trans. Ford Lewis Battles, LCC, vols. 20–21 [Philadelphia: Westminster John Knox, 1960], 3.3.5).
7. Anthony A. Hoekema, *Saved by Grace* (Grand Rapids: Eerdmans, 1989), 127.
8. Grief, however, can take on different external manifestations. For some, it involves loud cries and tears, but for others an internal quietness. Either expression can be genuine signs of a disrupted heart.

"the dying-away of the old self, and the coming-to-life of the new" (Q. 88). To repent is to be "genuinely sorry for sin, to hate it more and more, and to run away from it" (Q. 89). John Calvin, as well as John Owen after him, described repentance as the "mortification of the flesh and the vivification of the spirit."[9] To repent is to pick up one's cross, crucify sin, and follow Jesus.

The point in mentioning these three components is to emphasize that the whole person must be involved. It will be all too apparent to God that mere acknowledgement of sin (without authentic conviction or sorrow) does not come from the heart. On the other hand, superficial emotional outburst that lacks knowledge of one's guilt before a holy God will fall short as well. Neither should one think that the participation of one's "will" must mean that repentance is a "new obedience," as if repentance is the condition for being born again.[10] This approach can lead to doubt and anxiety, as the repentant never knows whether his "new obedience" is good enough. One struggles "to the point of despair," Horton laments, "over whether the quality and degree of their repentance is adequate for them to be forgiven, as if repentance were the ground of forgiveness and the former could be measured by the intensity of emotion, resolve, and victory over specific sins."[11] We must remember instead that the ground of our right standing with God is "nothing but the blood of Jesus," to quote the old hymn. Far from turning repentance into a "new obedience," true repentance accompanied by faith rests assured because it rests in Christ. The soul that turns from this world and to its Savior now has peace with God, for he/she has been reconciled by the blood of its Savior (Rom. 5:1, 10–11). For this reason, the New Testament constantly connects repentance to the gospel (Luke 24:46–47; Acts 2:37–38; 5:31; 20:21; Heb. 6:1).

Model Repentance (Psalm 51)

Everything we've said about repentance is modeled by king David in Psalm 51. It is hard to think of a greater saint and yet a greater sinner than David. What distinguished David from Saul was that David was characterized by true repentance. After committing adultery and then murder, David cried out to God with a broken, contrite heart. Listen to David's repentant heart before God after being convicted of his sin by Nathan the prophet:

> Have mercy on me, O God,
>   according to your steadfast love;
> according to your abundant mercy
>   blot out my transgressions.

9. Calvin, *Institutes of the Christian Religion*, 3.3.8; cf. John Owen, *Overcoming Sin and Temptation* (Wheaton, IL: Crossway, 2006).
10. Horton, *Pilgrim Theology*, 265.
11. Ibid.

Wash me thoroughly from my iniquity,
and cleanse me from my sin!

For I know my transgressions,
and my sin is ever before me.
Against you, you only, have I sinned
and done what is evil in your sight,
so that you may be justified in your words
and blameless in your judgment.
Behold, I was brought forth in iniquity,
and in sin did my mother conceive me.
Behold, you delight in truth in the inward being,
and you teach me wisdom in the secret heart.

Purge me with hyssop, and I shall be clean;
wash me, and I shall be whiter than snow.
Let me hear joy and gladness;
let the bones that you have broken rejoice.
Hide your face from my sins,
and blot out all my iniquities.
Create in me a clean heart, O God,
and renew a right spirit within me.
Cast me not away from your presence,
and take not your Holy Spirit from me.
Restore to me the joy of your salvation,
and uphold me with a willing spirit (Ps. 51:1–12).

Notice that the components of true repentance described above are present in David's prayer:

- David acknowledges that he has transgressed God's law and therefore stands guilty before God (51:2, 3).
- David knows he has wronged his neighbor, but he correctly sees that sin is first and foremost an affront and offense against God, our Maker and Lord (51:4).
- David not only confesses his evil actions, but his corrupt condition (51:5).
- David does not look to his own works, but to God's mercy, grace, and love in order to receive forgiveness and cleansing (51:1, 2, 7, 9, 10, 12).
- David's repentance does not result in despair (like Judas and Esau), but instead David throws himself upon the mercy of God, asking God for a clean heart (51:10).
- David's repentance is clothed in faith. His cries of repentance are characterized by trust in the God who can forgive him, cleanse him, and restore salvation to him (51:7–12; cf. 13, 17, 18–19).

Horton is right to label this type of repentance a "paradigm shift" since this "change of mind is not just intellectual, but shakes the whole person to the very foundations."[12] It is this type of repentance that is present at conversion, but it is also this type of repentance that continues on into sanctification, characterizing the authentic Christian.[13]

Faith and Repentance Are Inseparable

Faith and repentance cannot be divorced from one another. They are two sides of the same coin. John Murray eloquently explains how the "faith that is unto salvation is a penitent faith and the repentance that is unto life is a believing repentance. . . . Faith is faith in Christ for salvation from sin. But if faith is directed to salvation from sin, there must be hatred of sin and the desire to be saved from it. Such hatred of sin involves repentance." Murray concludes, "Again, if we remember that repentance is turning from sin unto God, the turning to God implies faith in the mercy of God as revealed in Christ. It is impossible to disentangle faith and repentance. Saving faith is permeated with repentance and repentance is permeated with faith."[14] Faith and repentance are intertwined; you cannot have one apart from the other. Furthermore, faith and repentance seem to occur simultaneously.[15] In other words, it is impossible to hang onto one's sin and at the same time embrace Christ. The former keeps one from doing the latter. It is only by turning from one's sin in repentance that one truly trusts in Christ for salvation.

Some, however, have tried to argue that one can have true, saving faith and at the same time not truly repent for sin. Such a view is couched in the language of accepting Christ as Savior but not as Lord.[16] In such a view, what is necessary is that one assent to the facts of the gospel. Only later will repentance come when the Christian submits to Christ as Lord resulting in a changed life. But the New Testament teaches no such view. Instead, Scripture teaches that a sinner, if he is to be converted, must not only trust in Christ but truly repent of his sins. In the Old Testament the prophet Isaiah declares, "Seek the LORD while he may be found; call upon him while he is near; let the wicked forsake his way, and the unrighteous man his thoughts; let him return to the LORD, that he may have compassion on him, and to our God, for he will

---

12. Ibid., 263.
13. On repentance in sanctification, see John Murray, *Redemption Accomplished and Applied* (Grand Rapids: Eerdmans, 1955), 116.
14. Ibid., 140.
15. Theologians disagree as to which one comes first or has priority over the other. Calvin, for example, argued that repentance follows faith (*Institutes* 3.3.1).
16. Lewis Sperry Chafer, *Systematic Theology* (Wheaton, IL: Victor, 1988), 3:372–87; Zane C. Hodges, *The Gospel Under Siege* (Dallas: Redención Viva, 1981). For a refutation of this view, see John MacArthur, *The Gospel According to Jesus* (Grand Rapids: Zondervan, 1988, rev. ed. 1994).

abundantly pardon" (Isa. 55:6–7). Here we see very plainly that repentance is absolutely necessary if the sinner is going to be pardoned by God. He must forsake his sinful, wicked ways and abandon his unrighteous thoughts. Only then will the Lord pardon his iniquities. Also, notice that after Isaiah requires repentance of the sinner, faith is inseparably linked as well. Not only must the sinner forsake his way, but he must return to the Lord, trusting in the Lord to have compassion and forgive his sins (cf. Acts 20:21; Heb. 6:1).

But is it not true, one might object, that there are passages in the New Testament where only faith is mentioned? Indeed, there are (e.g., John 3:16; Acts 16:31; Rom. 10:9; Eph. 2:8–9). Yet, there are also passages where only repentance is mentioned (e.g., Luke 24:46–47, Acts 2:37–38; 3:19; 5:31; 17:30; Rom. 2:4; 2 Cor. 7:10). The assumption of the New Testament authors, in other words, is that repentance always comes with faith in Christ. In mentioning one the other is always implied. After all, how can one turn *from* sin without turning *to* Christ? For example, such an assumption is apparent in a passage like Luke 24:46–47: "Thus, it is written, that the Christ should suffer and on the third day rise from the dead, and that repentance and forgiveness of sins should be proclaimed in his name to all nations, beginning from Jerusalem" (cf. Matt. 3:2, 8; 4:17; Acts 2:37–38). Jesus only names "repentance," but of course faith is implied in the phrase "forgiveness of sins." Certainly a sinner must not only repent but trust in Christ to receive forgiveness. Likewise, we can say the same of passages where faith is explicitly mentioned and repentance is implied.

Additionally, as was seen in Luke 24:46–47, it is paramount to acknowledge that Scripture absolutely requires repentance for salvation. For instance, when Peter gives his Pentecost sermon and the people respond by asking what must they do, Peter's response is straight forward: Repent! If one repents he will receive the forgiveness of sins and the gift of the Holy Spirit (Acts 2:37–38). Shortly thereafter, Peter heals a lame beggar. When Peter addresses those looking on, he tells them about Christ, whom they killed but God raised from the dead, to which the apostles now bear witness (Acts 3:14–16). What does Peter tell his listeners next? "Repent therefore, and turn again, that your sins may be blotted out" (Acts 3:19). So, repentance is required for salvation. Without it there can be no forgiveness of sins.

Moreover, the very reason God exalted Christ at his right hand as ruler and Savior was "to give repentance to Israel and forgiveness of sins" (Acts 5:31). Or as Paul says in Acts 17:30, "The times of ignorance God overlooked, but now he commands all people everywhere to repent, because he has fixed a day on which he will judge the world in righteousness by a man whom he has appointed." Therefore, if the sinner does not repent, he will face divine judgment on the last day. Nonetheless, in this time in between the first and second coming of Christ, God has shown enormous kindness, forbearance, and patience, though such kindness "is meant to lead you to repentance" (Rom. 2:4; cf. 2 Peter 3:9). If there is no repentance, says Paul, then the sinner is storing up wrath for the day of wrath when God's righteous judgment will be revealed (Rom. 2:5). But if the sinner has a "godly grief," then this godly grief will produce repentance, which leads "to salvation without regret" (2 Cor. 7:10).[17]

Finally, there is a grave danger ahead of us should we travel down the path where no repentance is required for conversion. Think about the preaching of the gospel, for example. Should we neglect to preach repentance to sinners (contrary to Peter's example in Acts 2:38), then we have failed to preach the whole gospel (or at least its full implications).[18] How potentially disastrous this might be, for many could fall under the false assurance that they have been saved without forsaking their sin. However, Christ demands our entire self and he does so at the very start (i.e., conversion). Should we refuse to make Christ our Lord, it is all too clear that we never really made him Savior in the first place. We cannot choose to have part of Christ. No, Christ demands unqualified Lordship over us.

Summary

Repentance is a sorrow for one's sin as well as a commitment to reject sin and instead follow and obey Christ. Repentance involves knowledge of one's sinfulness, grief and sorrow for one's sin, and a willful abandonment of sin and a turning to Christ instead. Faith and repentance are inseparable, and Scripture nowhere teaches that a person can have faith without repenting of sin. Conversion always includes both faith and repentance.

REFLECTION QUESTIONS

1. Do people today understand the gravity of their sin before a holy God, and if not, what implication does this have for conversion?

2. Why is it that grief over sin by itself is insufficient for repentance?

3. Can you think of examples, both in the Old Testament and New Testament, of true versus false repentance?

4. What signs of repentance can you identify in your own life?

5. In the past, when you have been convicted of sin and turned to Christ, what was the outcome or result?

---

17. It is no wonder then why Jesus exposed the sin of his listeners (Luke 18:18–30; 19:1–10; John 4:16; 3:1–21), requiring a turning away from sin if they were to follow him. Also, preaching repentance characterized Paul's gospel ministry (Acts 26:17–18).
18. D. Chamberlain, *The Meaning of Repentance* (Philadelphia: Westminster, 1943), 80. For a more extensive treatment of this point, see Wayne Grudem, *"Free Grace" Theology: 5 Ways It Diminishes the Gospel* (Wheaton, IL: Crossway, 2016).

Are Faith and Repentance Gifts of God's Grace?

A re faith and repentance something the sinner does by his own free will, or are they gifts from God?[1] Protestants in the heritage of the sixteenth-century Reformation have argued that faith and repentance, while no doubt involving the will of man, are first and foremost the work of God, the fruit and result of effectual calling and regeneration. Yet, unlike regeneration where man is totally passive, in conversion man is active, playing a role, for *he* must repent of his sin and believe in Christ. However, in Scripture repentance and faith are not merely gifts from God but they are gifts that God works effectually within his elect.[2] Consider the analogy of a blind man who is healed by God. The blind man must not only be given the power to see, but God himself must open the blind man's eyes if he is going to see. In other words, God produces not only the will to believe but the act of believing itself.[3] "Without regeneration it is morally and spiritually impossible for a person to believe in Christ," says Murray, "but when a person is regenerated it is morally and spiritually impossible for that person not to

---

1. For a much fuller treatment of faith and repentance, of which this chapter is indebted to, see Matthew Barrett, *Salvation by Grace: The Case for Effectual Calling and Regeneration* (Phillipsburg, NJ: P&R, 2013), chapter 4.

2. As Francis Turretin writes, "God is said to give not only the power of believing, but the belief (*to pisteuein*) or the act itself (Phil. 1:29)" (*Institutes of Elenctic Theology*, 3 vols., ed. James T. Dennison Jr., trans. George Musgrave Giger [Phillipsburg, NJ: P&R Publishing, 1992–97], 2:523 [cf. 552]).

3. As John Owen explains, "The Scripture says not that God gives us ability or power to believe only—namely, such a power as we may make use of if we will, or do otherwise; but faith, repentance, and conversion themselves are said to be the work and effect of God" (*A Discourse Concerning the Holy Spirit*, in The Works of John Owen [Edinburgh: Banner of Truth, 1991], 3:320 [cf. 3:323–24]).

believe."[4] Now that the sinner has been given a new heart, that heart must beat according to its nature, and the first beat is belief in its Savior.[5]

Faith: An Effectual Gift from God

In Acts 13:48 Paul and Barnabas have been commissioned by the Holy Spirit, and upon arriving in Antioch in Pisidia Paul is invited to speak on the Sabbath day. Paul works his way through the story of the Old Testament, demonstrating that God had promised a Savior to Israel, one who would be an offspring of David, saving God's people from their sins (Acts 13:18–27). And of course this Savior spoken of in the law and the prophets is Jesus Christ, to whom Paul is a witness. Though Israel did not recognize him, putting him to death on a cross though no guilt was to be found in him, God has raised him from the dead (13:30–33), so that "forgiveness of sins is proclaimed to you" (13:38) in the name of Jesus, and "everyone who believes is freed from everything from which you could not be freed by the law of Moses" (13:39).

Paul receives an invitation to return, and on the next Sabbath the whole city is listening. But many Jews, filled with jealousy, revile Paul. In response Paul makes an astonishing proclamation. "It was necessary that the word of God be spoken first to you. Since you thrust it aside and judge yourselves unworthy of eternal life, behold, we are turning to the Gentiles" (Acts 13:46). Suddenly, the Gentiles break out in rejoicing and gladness:

> And when the Gentiles heard this, they began rejoicing and glorifying the word of the Lord, *and as many as were appointed to eternal life believed.* And the word of the Lord was spreading throughout the whole region. But the Jews incited the devout women of high standing and the leading men of the city, stirred up persecution against Paul and Barnabas, and drove them out of their district (Acts 13:48–50, emphasis added).

Why is it that the Jews reject the gospel while the Gentiles accept it? We might expect the text to say that it is because of the will of man. God did his best to persuade them to believe, but only those who exercised their will to believe were saved. But that is not what Luke says. Instead, Luke records that the reason the Gentiles believed, while the Jews reviled Paul and his message, was because "as many as were appointed to eternal life believed" (13:48). Note, the text does *not* say "as many as believed were appointed to eternal

---

4. John Murray, *Redemption Accomplished and Applied* (Grand Rapids: Eerdmans, 1955), 106.
5. "Regeneration is the renewing of the heart and mind, and the renewed heart and mind must act according to their nature" (ibid.).

life." Rather, Luke explains that it is God's election or appointment (ordina-
tion; cf. Acts 15:2; 22:10; 28:23; Matt. 28:16–17; Luke 7:8; Rom. 13:1; 1 Cor.
16:15–16) that determined who would and would not believe.[6] God, not man,
determines who will and will not believe in Christ and until God regenerates
the sinful heart of man, he will not respond in faith and repentance (cf. Acts
2:37; 16:14; 18:10).[7] Yes, we are the ones who repent and believe, but we do so
only because God has previously appointed us to eternal life and has, at the
appointed time, moved us to repent and trust in his Son.

Our second passage is Ephesians 2:8–10: "For by grace you have been
saved through faith. And this is not your own doing; it is the gift of God,
not a result of works, so that no one may boast. For we are his workmanship,
created in Christ Jesus for good works, which God prepared beforehand,
that we should walk in them." Or as the NASB translates verse 8, "For by
grace you have been saved through faith; and that not of yourselves, it is the
gift of God." The phrases "*this* is not your own doing" and "*it* is the *gift* of
God" are controversial. Some will protest that "this" and "it" in the Greek
do not refer to faith as the gift Paul has in mind, for "faith" is feminine
while "that" is a neuter pronoun. If Paul meant to say faith is a gift he would
have placed the pronoun in the feminine. Likewise with "grace," which is
also feminine in gender. Yet, most Calvinists acknowledge this grammatical
construction. Take Calvin himself who says, "His [Paul's] meaning is, not
that faith is the gift of God, but that salvation is given to us by God, or, that
we obtain it by the gift of God."[8]

Nevertheless, we still must ask ourselves, what in verse 2:8 is the antecedent of "that" ("this," in the ESV)? Paul is referring to the gift of salvation in
its totality.[9] As Schreiner comments, "Paul wanted to communicate that everything said in Ephesians 2:8 is God's gift. That is, if he had used the mascu-
line or feminine form of the pronoun, some might have concluded that some

6. Darrell L. Bock, *Acts*, BECNT (Grand Rapids: Baker Academic, 2007), 465; C. K. Barrett,
    A Critical and Exegetical Commentary on The Acts of the Apostles 1–14, ICC (Edinburgh:
    T&T Clark, 1994), 658; Richard N. Longenecker, *The Acts of the Apostles*, EBC, vol. 9
    (Grand Rapids: Zondervan, 1981), 430; Bruce A. Ware, "Divine Election to Salvation," in
    Perspectives on Election: Five Views, ed. Chad Owen Brand (Nashville: B&H, 2006), 9.

7. David Peterson, *The Acts of the Apostles*, PNTC (Grand Rapids: Eerdmans, 2009), 399.

8. John Calvin, *Commentaries on the Epistles of Paul to the Galatians and Ephesians*, trans.
    William Pringle (Grand Rapids: Eerdmans, 1948), 228–29. Or as Schreiner reiterates, the
    demonstrative pronoun *this (touto)* is neuter and "thus cannot be the specific antecedent to
    grace or *faith* since the words *grace (charis)* and *faith (pisteōs)* are both feminine. Nor can it
    refer specifically back to *saved*, for the participle *saved (sesōmenoi)* is masculine" (Thomas
    R. Schreiner, *Paul: Apostle of God's Glory in Christ* [Downers Grove, IL: InterVarsity Press,
    2001], 246–47).

9. Samuel C. Storms, *Chosen for Life: The Case for Divine Election* (Wheaton, IL: Crossway,
    2007), 71. Also see Clinton E. Arnold, *Ephesians*, ZECNT (Grand Rapids: Zondervan,
    2010), 139.

of the elements contained in this verse were not part of God's gift. By using the neuter he emphasizes that the whole is God's gift."[10] Therefore, every aspect of salvation is by grace alone (*sola gratia*). "From beginning to end, from its inception to its consummation, salvation is a gift of God to his elect."[11] But what should we make of "faith" then? Sam Storms answers: "That faith by which we come into experiential possession of what God in grace has provided is as much a gift as any and every other aspect of salvation. One can no more deny that faith is wrapped up in God's gift to us than he can deny it of God's grace."[12] In other words, "gift" does refer to salvation in total, but salvation is by grace alone and as Paul asserts in 2:8, it is "by grace you have been saved through faith." Salvation is "not your own doing" but is a "gift of God." It follows that faith is also by grace alone, a gift from God.[13]

Faith, therefore, does not originate in the sinner. Nor is faith made effectual by the sinner. Faith is not, as Thielman recognizes, a synergism that brings about God's grace. "In Paul's thinking, faith is not something that people offer to God and with which God's grace then cooperates to save them. Rather, faith is aligned with grace, and both faith and grace stand over against anything that human beings can offer God: it is neither a work deserving payment nor a ground for boasting (Rom. 4:2–5, 16)."[14] Thielman's last phrase, "it is neither . . . a ground for boasting," is crucial. For Paul, all boasting is excluded. Any type of work that includes human effort is precluded by Paul's emphasis on grace. Salvation "is not based on human performance or on any effort to win God's approval."[15]

Previously, Paul went to great lengths to highlight that man is dead in sin (Eph 2:1–3). So how then could human effort, even if it be little, be included? As O'Brien states, "It was impossible for the readers to turn to their previous behaviour as the basis for achieving salvation."[16] Boasting is excluded since man is "in no position to claim even the slightest credit for their acceptance with God (note Paul's argument in Rom. 4:1–8). . . . Men and women have nothing which they can bring as their own to the living God."[17] If faith is not a gift from God but the product of our own determination, it is difficult to see

---

10. Schreiner, *Paul*, 246.
11. Storms, *Chosen for Life*, 71.
12. Ibid.
13. "The point being made, then, is that the response of faith does not come from any human source but is God's gift. . . . God's magnificent rescue from death, wrath, and bondage is all of grace. It neither originates in nor is effected by the readers. Instead, it is God's own gift, a point which Paul goes out of his way to emphasize by changing the normal word order and contrasting 'God's' with 'yours'" (Peter T. O'Brien, *Ephesians*, PNTC [Grand Rapids: Eerdmans, 1999], 175–76).
14. Frank Thielman, *Ephesians*, BECNT (Grand Rapids: Baker, 2010), 143.
15. O'Brien, *Ephesians*, 177.
16. Ibid.
17. Ibid., 177–78.

how we have avoided coming to God with something of our own. If we insist that faith is a gift that man can reject or, even if it is accepted, a work of man primarily, then boasting has not been excluded (Eph. 2:9–10).[18]

Our third passage is Philippians 1:29–30: "For it has been *granted* to you that for the sake of Christ you should not only *believe* in him but also suffer for his sake, engaged in the same conflict that you saw I had and now hear that I still have" (emphasis added). According to Paul, God, in his sovereignty, bestows suffering. But not only is suffering a gift, Paul also says belief (faith) in Christ is a gift as well.[19] The wording is essential, however, for Paul specifically says "it [belief] has been granted." "Granted" (*echaristhē*) means to give freely and graciously. In fact, it is the same word from which *grace* is derived.[20] It does not mean, as our English language assumes so often, reluctance or mere permission on God's part.[21] Rather, God grants belief or faith in Christ to those whom he has chosen. Faith or belief in Christ is from God, not something the sinner produces. And if God does not grant it, belief will not result. Philippians 1:29–30 demonstrates that faith is not something we do by our own free will, but rather it is something that God produces in us.

Our fourth and final passage is 2 Peter 1:1: "Simeon Peter, a servant and apostle of Jesus Christ, To those who have obtained a faith of equal standing with ours by the righteousness of our God and Savior Jesus Christ." Is it by man's will that faith is obtained? At first glance, that might appear to be the case. Actually, Peter assumes just the opposite. When Peter refers to obtaining faith, he is speaking of a gift that we receive from God and by God's choice. "What is of paramount importance here," says Storms, "is the word translated 'have obtained' or 'have received.' It is related to a verb that means 'to obtain by lot' (see Luke 1:9; John 19:24; Acts 1:17). Thus, faith is removed from the realm of human free will and placed in its proper perspective as having originated in the sovereign and altogether gracious will of God."[22] We do not want to deny that faith is an act of believing on the sinner's part (*fides qua creditor*). Indeed, it is. However, we must qualify that faith is ultimately a divine work, not a human work. "Faith is something merely passive," observes Calvin, "bringing nothing of ours to the recovering of God's favor but receiving from Christ that which we lack."[23] Therefore, as J. I. Packer observes,

---

18. For example, Wesley explicitly rejected Calvin's thesis that in salvation God is everything and man is nothing and instead argued that "man is the sole determinative factor in the decision of his own justification" (William R. Cannon, *The Theology of John Wesley: With Special Reference to the Doctrine of Justification* [New York: University Press of America, 1974], 117).
19. Moisés Silva, *Philippians*, 2nd ed., BECNT (Grand Rapids: Baker Academic, 2005), 84.
20. Schreiner, *Paul*, 247.
21. Storms, *Chosen for Life*, 71.
22. Ibid., 72.
23. John Calvin, *Institutes of the Christian Religion*, ed. John T. McNeil, trans. Ford Lewis Battles, LCC, vols. 20–21 (Philadelphia: Westminster, 1960), 3.13.5. Also see Herman

those who turn faith primarily into a human work make "man's salvation dependent ultimately on man himself, saving faith being viewed throughout as man's own work and, because his own, not God's in him."[24] Rather, as we have seen in these four texts, saving faith is sovereignly granted to the sinner and effectually applied within him.

Repentance According to Scripture

Like faith, so also is repentance a gift granted to us by the Father and effectually applied by the Spirit.[25] Consider three essential biblical texts.

First, Paul writes in 2 Timothy 2:24–26, "And the Lord's servant must not be quarrelsome but kind to everyone, able to teach, patiently enduring evil, correcting his opponents with gentleness. God may perhaps *grant them repentance* leading to a knowledge of the truth, and they may come to their senses and escape from the snare of the devil, after being captured by him to do his will" (emphasis added). Paul has in mind unbelievers when he is referring to his "opponents," namely those who oppose the Lord's servant (2:24). These opponents are in "the snare of the devil" and therefore are in desperate need of repentance and a knowledge of the truth (2:25). As those enslaved to Satan they are unable to repent nor do they want to repent, but instead love sin and do the bidding of their father, the devil (Eph. 2:1–5). In order for the sinner to be liberated from this slavery to the devil, God must be the one to grant the sinner repentance, lest he be left in his sinful captivity.[26] Since God must be the one to grant the sinner repentance—for the sinner cannot repent of himself (see Questions 4–5)—repentance is not universally given but a gift made effectual only for the elect. "Were repentance something God gives to all, Paul would hardly have said that 'perhaps' God may grant repentance. Clearly he envisions the real possibility that God may *not* so grant."[27] God does not give a merely enabling grace to all people so that they can decide for themselves whether or not they will repent and believe, making God's grace ultimately dependent upon man's will. Such a line of thought contradicts

---

Bavinck, *Reformed Dogmatics*, ed. John Bolt, trans. John Vriend (Grand Rapids: Baker, 2008), 4:125; Francis Turretin, *Institutes of Elenctic Theology*, 3 vols., ed. James T. Dennison, Jr., trans. George M. Giger (Phillipsburg, NJ: P&R, 1992–97), 2:523.

24. J. I. Packer, *A Quest for Godliness: The Puritan Vision of the Christian Life* (Wheaton, IL: Crossway, 1990), 128. Packer has the Arminian view in mind.

25. Herman Bavinck writes, "True repentance according to Scripture, does not arise from the natural 'man' but from the new life that was planted in a person by regeneration." Therefore, "Faith and repentance both arise from regeneration" (*Reformed Dogmatics*, 4:163, 152).

26. "If a person is to repent, he or she must be enabled by God to do so. He must be 'granted' repentance as a gift. Whether or not a person repents, says Paul, is ultimately up to God. It rests with him and his sovereign good pleasure to give or to withhold that which leads to 'a knowledge of the truth.' That God does not bestow this gift universally is self-evident" (Storms, *Chosen for Life*, 72–73). Likewise, see Schreiner, *Paul*, 247–48.

27. Storms, *Chosen for Life*, 72–73.

2 Timothy 2:24–26 where it is not man, but God himself who determines whether he will grant repentance.[28]

Our second and third biblical texts are Acts 5:31 and 11:18. In Acts 5:31 Peter says, "God exalted him [Jesus] at his right hand as Leader and Savior, to give repentance to Israel and forgiveness of sins." And then in Acts 11:18 we learn that God not only has granted repentance to the Jews but to the Gentiles as well. "When they [the Jewish believers] heard these things [how the Gentiles believed the gospel] they fell silent. And they glorified God, saying, 'Then to the Gentiles also God has granted repentance that leads to life.'" Notice, seeing and hearing of how the Gentiles have believed in Christ does not lead Peter and the Jews to conclude that these Gentiles exercised their free will. Instead, all credit is given to God. In his sovereignty, God granted repentance to these Gentiles. The gift of repentance is God's prerogative. As Storms argues, "Peter would not need to have drawn such a conclusion if repentance were a universal gift that all receive. . . . If everyone, even those who persist in unbelief, are granted repentance, Peter could not and would not have reasoned as he did."[29] In other words, God does not seek to grant repentance to all people, relying upon man's decision to accept his gift or not. Rather, God alone determines to whom he will grant repentance and his choice is not in any way contingent or conditioned upon man's cooperation (cf. Acts 2:47).

Summary

Scripture teaches that faith and repentance are first and foremost the work of God, the fruit and result of effectual calling and regeneration. Yes, unlike regeneration where man is totally passive, in conversion man is active, playing a role, for *he* must repent of his sin and believe in Christ. However, in Scripture repentance and faith are not merely gifts offered by God but they are gifts that God works effectually within his elect.

REFLECTION QUESTIONS

1. Where in Scripture do the biblical authors describe faith and repentance as gifts from God?

2. How should a biblical understanding of faith and repentance as effectual gifts from God change the way we speak of our conversion experience?

3. How does the effectual nature of faith and repentance eliminate our inclination to boast before God?

---

28. Ibid.
29. Ibid.

4. Looking back on the moment you first believed, in what ways do you see God at work in bringing you to faith in Christ?

5. Do evangelicals today tend to speak of regeneration as something God does as opposed to faith as something we do?

Is Justification a Legal Declaration or a Moral Transformation?

What is justification? How do we gain right standing before God? And is our justification a legal declaration or a moral transformation?

Such questions as these bring us to the doctrine which the Protestant Reformers believed was at the very center of the Christian faith.[1] The Reformers affirmed that justification by faith alone is the doctrine on which the church stands or falls. John Calvin claimed it is "the main hinge on which religion turns" and the "principal article of the whole doctrine of salvation and the foundation of all religion."[2]

Given its importance, it's not surprising that justification has proved to be the dividing line between Protestant Christians and all other religious groups. Such a doctrine distinguishes Protestant Christianity, for the gospel we proclaim is not one based upon good works—not even good works initiated by the Spirit's help and God's grace—but rather is by grace *alone*, through faith *alone*, in Christ *alone*.

The Great Divide

One of the most longstanding debates between Protestants and Roman Catholics is whether justification is an instantaneous, declarative, judicial act of God, or whether (as with Rome) justification is an ongoing process of moral renewal and transformation (think sanctification). *The Catechism of the Catholic Church* defines the Roman Catholic position: "justification is not only the remission of sins, but also the sanctification and renewal of the

---

1. Space in this chapter does not permit us to respond to the New Perspective on Paul, but see works in the bibliography by Schreiner, Piper, Waters, Fesko, and Westerholm.
2. John Calvin, *Institutes of the Christian Religion*, ed. John T. McNeil, trans. Ford Lewis Battles, LCC, vols. 20–21 (Philadelphia: Westminster, 1960), 3.6.1; 3.2.1 (cf. 3.11.1).

interior man."[3] This process of justification is one in which the person actually becomes intrinsically righteous.

Martin Luther, John Calvin, Thomas Cranmer, and many other Reformers of the sixteenth-century rejected Rome's view as unbiblical. The whole counsel of Scripture, they argued, indicates that justification should not be confused with sanctification. Calvin, for example, defined justification as "the acceptance with which God receives us into his favor as righteous," consisting "in the remission of sins and the imputation of Christ's righteousness."[4] Justification occurs at a specific moment in time when the sinner trusts in Christ alone. God declares the sinner "not guilty," and his judicial verdict is not based on the righteousness of the believer (not even in the slightest) but rather on the righteousness of another, namely Christ, in whom the believer has placed his trust. Christ's righteousness is imputed to the one whose faith rests in Jesus alone.

It would be difficult to overemphasize the fact that this instantaneous act of God is a *legal* (judicial, forensic) act, one that occurs when God declares us to be righteous in his sight, forgiving our sins and counting the righteousness of Christ as that which belongs to us.[5] A great exchange has taken place, as we will see in Question 23. Our sins have been transferred to Christ and Christ has paid the penalty for those sins at Calvary by satisfying the wrath of God. In exchange, God has imputed to our account the perfect obedience and righteousness of Christ, so that we not only stand before God forgiven but righteous. With this marvelous exchange in mind, we could say that the legal declaration God makes in justification means that the believer has a new status in Christ and likewise a new identity.

Only as a result of God's declaration do good works follow, for they are the fruit and result of justification, not its cause. "Although both [justification and sanctification] are inseparable gifts of union with Christ through faith," says Horton, "justification is a verdict that declares sinners to be righteous even while they are inherently unrighteous, simply on the basis of Christ's righteousness imputed to them." Indeed, this is what led Luther to conclude that we are simultaneously righteous and a sinner. Horton adds, "Where Rome teaches that one is finally justified by being sanctified, the Reformed conviction is that one is being sanctified because one has already been justified. Rather than working toward the verdict of divine vindication, the believer leaves the court justified in the joy that bears the fruit of faith: namely, good works."[6]

Today the divide between Protestants and Roman Catholics remains. In the sixteenth century, Rome responded to the Reformers and made their

---

3. *The Catechism of the Catholic Church* (New York: USCCB, 1995), 492. Notice, the Catechism is quoting the Council of Trent (1574).
4. Calvin, *Institutes* 3.11.2.
5. "Forensic" means having to do with a legal event or proceeding.
6. Michael Horton, "Traditional Reformed View," in *Justification: Five Views*, eds. James K. Beilby and Paul R. Eddy (Downers Grove, IL: InterVarsity Press, 2001), 85–86, 87.

stance conspicuous at the Council of Trent. Since Trent there has been dialogue over justification, particularly in light of Vatican II and certain ecumenical movements.[7] Nevertheless, Trent's statements remain in effect and, as we saw above with the *Catechism of the Catholic Church,* Rome continues to teach that justification involves the inner renewal and sanctification of man, simultaneously denying that justification is on the basis of Christ's work *alone* and by faith *alone.* Justification continues to be, for Rome, the *process* of being *made intrinsically* righteous.

Of course, Rome is not the only one who continues to oppose the Protestant position. Today the historic Protestant doctrine of justification is challenged by a host of groups, such as Protestant Liberalism, Neo-Orthodoxy, the New Perspective on Paul, the "evangelical catholic" and New Finnish view(s), Radical Orthodoxy, Liberation theology, and many, many others.[8] It would take us too far astray to interact with each of these here, but I mention them merely to emphasize the importance of defining and defending a biblical view of justification in our own day.

"Justify" in Scripture

To begin, it is essential that we consider some of the most important reasons our right standing before God consists of a judicial declaration by God.[9] First is the biblical meaning of the word "justify" itself. Both in Hebrew and in Greek "to justify" is forensic in nature, conveying the imagery of a courtroom. The Hebrew verb *hitsdik,* as well as the piel form *tsiddek,* refer to a judicial declaration.[10] The accused party is declared to be right in the eyes of the law and in accordance with the law (e.g., Exod. 23:7; Deut. 25:1; Prov. 17:15; Isa. 5:23; Jer. 3:11).[11] Likewise, the same is true with the Greek word *dikaioō,* "to declare just" or "declare righteous" (as opposed to "make righteous"). It is not an infused habit that this word intends to convey but rather a forensic vindication.[12] Its lexical meaning is "to be cleared in court."[13]

---

7. E.g., *Joint Declaration on the Doctrine of Justification: The Lutheran World Federation and the Roman Catholic Church* (Grand Rapids: Eerdmans, 2000).
8. For a treatment of each of these and others, see Michael Horton, *Covenant and Salvation: Union with Christ* (Louisville: Westminster John Knox, 2007). Out of all of these, the New Perspective on Paul may be the most influential. For a summary and assessment, see Thomas Schreiner, *40 Questions about Christians and Biblical Law* (Grand Rapids: Kregel, 2010), 35–40.
9. On the forensic nature of justification in the Old Testament, see Deuteronomy 25:1; Job 27:5; Proverbs 17:15; Isaiah 5:23.
10. Horton, "Traditional Reformed View," 91-92.
11. Ibid., 92.
12. Ibid.
13. Walter Bauer, *BDAG*, 3rd rev. ed. (Chicago: University of Chicago Press, 2001), 246–50. Unfortunately, the Latin Vulgate confuses matters, using the word *iustificare,* which means "to make righteous." The impression is given that justification must be a drawn-out event,

Consider texts where the term or concept appears. For example, in Luke 18:10–14 Jesus compares two men, one a Pharisee and the other a tax collector. While the Pharisee thanked God he was not a sinner like the tax collector, appealing to his good works ("I fast twice a week; I give tithes of all that I get."), the tax collector beat his breast, crying out, "God, be merciful to me, a sinner!" Jesus concludes that the tax collector, not the Pharisee, went down to his house "justified" (*dedikaiōmenos* from *dikaioō*). Justified, in Luke 18:14, means that the tax collector was declared righteous before God. His sins were forgiven and he was justified from the condemnation due for his sins. He received mercy.

Paul's letters especially highlight the judicial nature of justification, as seen in how Paul compares justification to condemnation. Condemnation is the opposite of declaring or pronouncing the sinner righteous. As Paul writes to the Roman Christians, "Who shall bring any charge against God's elect? It is God who justifies. Who is to condemn? Christ Jesus is the one who died—more than that, who was raised—who is at the right hand of God, who indeed is interceding for us" (Rom. 8:33–34). Conceivably, the charge that could be brought against the sinner is that he is guilty before God, the judge, and therefore condemned. However, God has justified his elect, and he has done so on the basis of Christ's perfect life and atoning death by which he made intercession before the throne of God. Again, justification in Romans 8:33–34 is the opposite of condemnation and therefore is not the process of making one righteous, but rather declaring one righteous in status.[14]

The forensic nature of justification is explicit in Romans 4:5 as well. "And to the one who does not work but believes in him who justifies the ungodly, his faith is counted as righteousness" (Rom. 4:5). The word "counted" (sometimes translated "credited") is a judicial word, meaning to declare someone righteous (as opposed to make someone righteous). According to Paul, the one justified by God is not the one who performs good works of the law, but is the one who believes, and consequently his faith is counted or credited as righteousness.[15]

First Corinthians 4:4 also adds support. Paul says that it is a "very small thing" to be "judged by you or by any human court" (4:3). Rather, Paul is far more concerned about God's judgment. Will he be "acquitted" before God (4:4)? That word "acquitted" (from the root *dikaioō*) refers to justification. On the last day, everyone will stand before God, the judge, and either be acquitted

---

a process even, involving the inner renewal of one's moral nature, much like sanctification. See Alister E. McGrath, *Iustitia Dei: A History of the Christian Doctrine of Justification* (Cambridge: Cambridge University Press, 1986), 11–14; Michael Horton, *Pilgrim Theology: Core Doctrines for Christian Disciples* (Grand Rapids: Zondervan, 2011), 291.

14. Anthony A. Hoekema, *Saved by Grace* (Grand Rapids: Eerdmans, 1989), 154. Other texts where condemnation is used in a judicial sense include John 3:17–18; Romans 5:16–17; 8:1, 33–34.

15. Also see Luke 7:29; Romans 5:1; 10:4, 10.

or condemned. If one is acquitted before God, it is not because he/she has been made righteous but rather because he/she has been declared righteous by God.

In numerous other places Paul asserts that the ungodly are *not* justified by works of the law (Rom. 3:20, 28; 4:2; Gal. 2:16; 3:11; 5:4), and each time "justify" has a forensic meaning (that is: to declare righteous). The setting is that of a courtroom. God is judge and as judge he will determine whether those who trusted in their works are justified in his sight.[16] Paul's answer is clear: No one who trusts in his works will be justified, for all fall short of the law's perfect standard. No one can perfectly keep the law. The verdict will be "not righteous" and "guilty" every time.

By contrast, those who do not trust in their works but trust in the works of another, namely, Christ Jesus receive a very different verdict: righteous (Rom. 3:24, 26–30; 5:1, 9; Gal. 2:16–17; 3:8, 24; Titus 3:7). Again, the context is a legal one. The judge will once again pronounce his verdict. This time, however, the ungodly person is announced righteous, though not because he has obeyed the law (he hasn't!). Instead, he is declared "righteous" because the righteousness of Christ has been reckoned to his account. He now has a righteous status before the judge, and one that results in his justification. God is just, then, to justify the ungodly (Rom. 4:5) because the basis of their justification is the perfect obedience of Jesus.[17]

To summarize, Justification is not a change in our moral nature, nor a process that spans the Christian life whereby one is inwardly transformed until he is inherently righteous. No, justification is an instantaneous act of God whereby he judicially declares the sinner just. While regeneration and sanctification have to do with the change that takes place in our moral nature, justification has to do with the legal change in our *status* before God. While the former is God's act (particularly the Spirit's act) "within us," the latter is God's judgment "with respect to us."[18] Consider John Murray's analogy of a surgeon and a judge. Regeneration is like surgery. The surgeon goes within us, removing the cancer inside. In contrast, justification is equivalent to a verdict in a courtroom. The judge proclaims a verdict and his verdict concerns our judicial status, namely, whether we are innocent or guilty.[19]

The Contrast Between Condemnation and Justification

Another reason justification should be defined as a judicial, forensic declaration has to do with the way Scripture contrasts justification with condemnation (Deut. 25:1; Prov. 17:15; John 3:17–18; Rom. 4:6–7; 8:1, 33–34; 2 Cor.

---

16. Schreiner, *40 Questions about Christians and Biblical Law*, 118.
17. Other texts that support a forensic reading include Romans 2:13; 8:29–30; 1 Corinthians 6:11; 1 Timothy 3:16. Some have appealed to Romans 6:7 to support a transformative, rather than forensic, view. For a response, see ibid., 119.
18. John Murray, *Redemption Accomplished and Applied* (Grand Rapids: Eerdmans, 1955), 121.
19. Ibid.

5:19). Condemnation has to do with guilt, the law, and one's judicial status before a holy God. Its contrast with justification is yet another indication that our right standing is a judicial matter with God.

Scripture unquestionably teaches that God is absolutely holy and therefore will not tolerate sin and wickedness lest his holiness and justice be compromised. "You who are of purer eyes than to see evil and cannot look at wrong" (Hab. 1:13a). Unsurprisingly, the wrath of God is directed against sin (Rom. 1–2). As was demonstrated in Question 3, each and every person is by nature an object of divine wrath. Paul's words are sobering: "And you were dead in the trespasses and sins in which you once walked, following the course of this world, following the prince of the power of the air, the spirit that is now at work in the sons of disobedience—among whom we all once lived in the passions of our flesh, carrying out the desires of the body and the mind, and were by nature children of wrath, like the rest of mankind" (Eph. 2:1–3).

When we commit sin and are disobedient to the law of God, the wrath of God is our just reward (Eph. 5:6). We are alienated from God due to our sinfulness (Col. 1:21). We are cursed (Gal. 3:10) and our rejection of God's Son only provokes divine wrath even further. As Jesus declared, "Whoever believes in the Son has eternal life; whoever does not obey the Son shall not see life, but the wrath of God remains on him" (John 3:36). In short, we stand guilty before a holy God, deserving only eternal wrath and condemnation. Christ, and Christ alone, can deliver us from the wrath we deserve (Rom. 5:9), because only he is qualified to be our propitiation (Rom. 3:25; Heb. 2:17; 1 John 2:2; 4:10).

In contrast to our just condemnation before a holy God, justification is God's instantaneous and forensic declaration that the believing sinner is not guilty but righteous, not on the basis of anything he has done, but on the basis of what Christ has done on his behalf in his life, death, and resurrection, so that the righteousness of Christ is credited to the believer for the forgiveness of sins and a righteous standing before God.[20] Such a declaration is not only gracious but judicial and forensic in nature. "There is therefore now no condemnation for those who are in Christ Jesus" (Rom. 8:1). So Paul can ask rhetorically, "Who shall bring any charge against God's elect? It is God who justifies" (8:33). The contrast between condemnation and justification—both of which have to do with legal, judicial standing—could not be more conspicuous.

At the moment of faith in Christ, the sinner undergoes an instantaneous and permanent change of *legal status* in his relation to God. Whereas before he was guilty, now, because of what Christ has done on his behalf, he is

---

20. Vickers defines justification as "the legal declaration from God that a person stands before him forgiven and as one who lives up to the entirety of God's will. It absolutely depends on turning, by faith, away from our own works to receive God's verdict of 'righteous' in Christ as a pure gift" (Brian Vickers, *Justification by Grace through Faith* [Phillipsburg, NJ: P&R, 2013], 2).

declared not guilty. On the basis of Christ's work, God forgives the believing sinner of all his sins. Whereas before the sinner stood condemned before a holy God, in justification the sinner is acquitted, having his sins forgiven and having the righteousness of Christ imputed or credited to his account. Such a full definition deserves to be unpacked in this chapter and those to come.

The Righteousness of God

That justification is a judicial and forensic matter is further supported by the biblical concept of the "righteousness of God." We will spend time addressing the righteousness of God when we look at Romans 3 in Questions 24–25. For now, however, we should note some basic contours.

Divine righteousness can take on two forms: the righteousness *of* God and the righteousness *from* God.[21] The righteousness *of* God describes God's holy character. For sinners, the righteousness *of* God is really bad news. As Paul explains in Romans 3:10, no one is righteous, but all stand guilty and condemned before their Maker who is perfect in holiness. The just punishment for sin is the righteous judgment of God, his eternal and unquenchable wrath which will be unleashed on the Day of Judgment (Rom. 3:4–6; cf. Ps. 51:4). In the first three chapters of Romans, therefore, Paul mostly has in mind the God who *is* righteous and how he judges as the one who is righteous.[22] It is not God's saving righteousness that Paul is speaking about but his judging righteousness.[23]

In Romans 3:19–20 Paul demonstrates how God's righteousness is reflected in the law. Held up to lawbreakers, the law acts as a mirror, exposing our guilt and the judgment we deserve.[24] Paul is on solid footing to then conclude in Romans 3:20 that it is impossible for anyone to be justified in God's sight by his own works. The law, says Paul, cannot justify us; it can only condemn. If our standing before God is to be remedied, we need some good news to counter this very bad news.

That good news comes in Jesus. Why? Because "in Christ" we receive the righteousness that is *from* God (Rom. 1:17; 3:21–26; 4:2–6; 5:19; 10:3; 2 Cor. 5:21; Phil. 3:9). This is not the righteousness which condemns but the righteousness that justifies.[25] How, though, does God justify exactly? Does he turn a "blind eye" to his holy standard? Does he relax his law so that a lower standard is sufficient? No, God does not abandon or relax his law; indeed,

---

21. Horton, *Pilgrim Theology*, 279–302.
22. The exception would be Romans 1:17. See John Murray, *The Epistle to the Romans*, NICNT (Grand Rapids: Eerdmans, 1959), 30.
23. Schreiner, *40 Questions about Christians and Biblical Law*, 124.
24. Horton, *Pilgrim Theology*, 292.
25. For the Old Testament background to the righteousness of God, see Schreiner, *40 Questions about Christians and Biblical Law*, 109–16. Schreiner argues, rightly I believe, that God's saving righteousness shouldn't be equated with covenant faithfulness.

that would violate his just, holy character.[26] Rather, Christ meets the requirements of the law in our place, as our substitute. By means of his perfect life of obedience and his propitiary sacrifice on the cross (Rom. 3:21–25), God not only remains just but becomes the justifier of the one who trusts in Jesus (3:26). Upon faith in Christ alone, the Father imputes the righteousness of his Son to our account. Thanks to the free gift of this righteousness *from* God, we no longer stand condemned in his courtroom. Yes, we are inherently unrighteous, but through Christ we now are credited with the righteousness of our Savior, which we receive not by works of the law but through faith alone.[27] With Paul, the sinner can say: I do not have a righteousness "of my own that comes from the law, but that which comes through faith in Christ, the righteousness from God that depends on faith" (Phil. 3:9). The righteousness God gives as a gift, therefore, supports the judicial nature of justification.[28]

The judicial nature of justification can be supported in many other ways—the fact that justification is not by works but by *faith alone* (Rom. 1:17; 3:22, 26; 4:3, 5, 9, 13; 9:30; 10:4; Gal. 2:16; 3:6, 11; 5:5; Phil. 3:9), the link between "righteousness" and "forgiveness" (Rom. 4:1–8, 25; 8:33), as well as scriptural language for being "counted" (*logizomai*) righteous (Rom. 4:3–6, 8–11, 22–24; 9:8; 2 Cor. 5:10; Gal. 3:6). On this basis, justification in Scripture does not refer to the transformation of the sinner (being *made* righteous) but to a legal declaration of God.

Summary

At the moment of faith in Christ the sinner undergoes an instantaneous and permanent change of *legal status* in his relation to God. Whereas before he was guilty, now, because of what Christ has done on his behalf, he is declared not guilty but righteous. Whereas before the sinner stood condemned before a holy God, in justification the sinner is acquitted, having his sins forgiven and having the righteousness of Christ imputed or credited to his account. In short, justification is not a process by which the sinner is made intrinsically righteous, but an instantaneous, legal declaration on the basis of Christ's imputed righteousness to the sinner's account.

---

26. This is one of the major problems with medieval and Roman Catholic views of justification. Horton explains: "For medieval theologians, righteousness was the goal toward which we were to strive, and grace was likened to a medicinal substance that is infused into our soul, so that we may do what lies within us. Begun in baptism, justification increased with our cooperation, anticipating a future justification according to works. Of course, if it were a strict judgment according to works (condign merit), no one could be saved—even after centuries of purgatorial fires. However, God accepts our earnest attempts to cooperate with grace *as if* they were meritorious (congruent merit). Ironically, this is actually a weak view of God's righteousness and judgment as revealed in the law" (*Pilgrim Theology*, 293).
27. Ibid., 292.
28. On each of these, see Schreiner, *40 Questions about Christians and Biblical Law*, 122–24.

REFLECTION QUESTIONS

1. If justification were a long process in which the sinner is made intrinsically righteous, could the sinner have assurance that he/she is ever right with God?

2. What biblical support might you give to someone who struggles to believe that justification is a legal declaration?

3. How does the biblical language of "condemnation" lend support to the forensic nature of justification in the book of Romans?

4. What is the difference between saying our justification depends in part upon our own righteousness (our own works) and saying that our justification depends entirely upon the righteousness of Christ?

5. How does the legal and forensic notion of justification distinguish Protestants from Roman Catholics?

What Is the Great Exchange?

So far in our exploration of the doctrine of justification we've learned that when God justifies the sinner he forensically or judicially declares that sinner righteous in his sight. But what exactly does that entail? More precisely, how is it that God can declare us "not guilty" but "justified" when we are still actually sinners by nature?

We will answer this question in more depth in the next two chapters where we will look to what Scripture says in particular. In this chapter, however, we merely want to introduce key terms and concepts, offering an initial answer to this important question. In response, we must give two answers: Justification means that (1) our sins have been forgiven, and that (2) the righteousness of Christ has been imputed to our account. Protestants have called this the "great exchange."

Justification Involves the Forgiveness of Sins

When God declares us just in his sight, he is declaring that we no longer have to pay the penalty we deserve for sin. For those who trust in Jesus, that penalty has already been paid. Christ bore the wrath of God on our behalf, taking upon himself the penalty for sin that was ours (Rom. 3:25; Heb. 2:17; 1 John 2:2; 4:10). As a result, "There is therefore now no condemnation for those who are in Christ Jesus" (Rom. 8:1). The guilt that condemned us has been placed on Christ. So who "shall bring any charge against God's elect? It is God who justifies. Who is to condemn? Christ Jesus is the one who died—more than that, who was raised—who is at the right hand of God, who indeed is interceding for us" (Rom. 8:33–34).

When we place our trust in Christ, all of our sins are forgiven. King David, long before the cross of Christ, recognized what a blessing it is to have one's sins forgiven. God, says David, is to be blessed for he "forgives all your iniquity" (Ps. 103:3). He is merciful and gracious, and he "does not deal with us according to our sins, nor repay us according to our iniquities"

(Ps. 103:10). As far "as the east is from the west, so far does he remove our transgressions from us" (Ps. 103:12). Notice, Paul quotes Psalm 32:1–2 when he writes, "And to the one who does not work but believes in him who justifies the ungodly, his faith is counted as righteousness, just as David also speaks of the blessing of the one to whom God counts righteousness apart from works: 'Blessed are those whose lawless deeds are forgiven, and whose sins are covered; blessed is the man against whom the Lord will not count his sin'" (Rom. 4:5–8).[1] Therefore, justification means that all our sins (past, present, and future) are forgiven. God does not count our sin against us.

Justification Involves the Imputation of Christ's Righteousness

But if the forgiveness of our sins is all there is to justification, we have a significant problem. As important and essential as it is to have our sins forgiven, if we *only* have our sins removed we still stand before God empty, without a positive righteousness that gives us favor with God. In other words: The forgiveness of our sins leaves us in an awkward state of neutrality, emptiness, and nakedness. Yes, we are not guilty before God, but we are not yet righteous before God either. Our debt has been cancelled but no funds have been transferred to our account yet.[2] Our dirty robe has been removed, but no clean robe covers our nakedness, presenting us before God as holy.

What we need is a positive righteousness, but such a righteousness must come from a perfect, flawless life of obedience, and we certainly have no such righteousness (hence the need to have our sins forgiven). In other words, what we need is an *alien* righteousness—a righteousness that is not our own, but one that is reckoned to our account. The only way we can be declared righteous is if the perfect merit of Christ is imputed to our account, which leads us to our second point, namely, not only, as Calvin states, does justification consist "in the remission of sins" but also in "the imputation of Christ's righteousness."[3] This "great exchange" (or double imputation) is pictured in the following diagram:

---

1. John Murray, *The Epistle to the Romans*, NICNT (Grand Rapids: Eerdmans, 1968), 123.
2. Michael Horton, *Pilgrim Theology: Core Doctrines for Christian Disciples* (Grand Rapids: Zondervan, 2011), 294.
3. John Calvin, *Institutes of the Christian Religion*, ed. John T. McNeil, trans. Ford Lewis Battles, LCC, vols. 20–21 (Philadelphia: Westminster, 1960), 3.11.2.

Table 5:
The Great Exchange

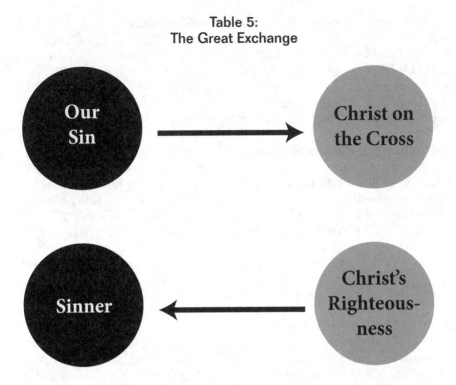

Justification is not only the *non-imputation* of sin but the *imputation* of righteousness.[4] It is insufficient to merely have our sins forgiven; we need the positive merit of Christ reckoned to our account if we are to be declared *just* before a holy God.[5]

To clarify, to impute is to reckon to someone's account. Like "to justify," "to impute" is also a legal, forensic, or judicial concept. In Scripture we see the concept utilized to speak of Adam's sin imputed to his progeny (Rom. 5:12–21), our sin imputed to Christ, our substitute (2 Cor. 5:21), and the righteousness of Christ imputed to sinners (Rom. 3:21–26; 4:2–6; 5:19; 2 Cor. 5:21), which is the sense in which we are referring to imputation here. In other words, justification involves the righteousness of Christ being reckoned to those who trust in Jesus. By living a perfect life and by dying an atoning death, Christ earned or merited

---

4. Contra N. T. Wright, *Romans*, NIB 10 (Nashville: Abingdon, 2003), 492–93; James D. G. Dunn, *Romans 1–8*, WBC 38a (Dallas: Word, 1988), 207. For a helpful critique of Wright's rejection of imputation, see J. V. Fesko, *Justification: Understanding the Classic Reformed Doctrine* (Phillipsburg, NJ: P&R, 2008), 211–63.

5. Fesko, *Justification*, 205.

a perfect righteousness, and this righteousness is credited to all those who place their faith in God's Son (Rom. 4:6; cf. Gen. 15:6). As Paul says in 2 Corinthians 5:21, "For our sake he made him to be sin who knew no sin, so that in him we might become the righteousness of God" (2 Cor. 5:21).

As we will see in the next chapter, imputation is affirmed in the Old Testament and New Testament alike, and it is the Christian's only hope for right standing in the heavenly courtroom before the divine judge.

The Active and Passive Obedience of Christ

If, as we've claimed, imputation is an essential component to justification, then it must also be asked whether Christ's obedience is just as critical to a right understanding of justification. In other words, does the righteousness of Christ include his entire life lived—that is, one of perfect obedience to the law of God—or just his atoning work on the cross whereby he offered himself up as a propitiation for sin?

Theologians have answered this question by appealing to two distinguishable, but inseparable, aspects of the work of Christ: active and passive obedience. Active obedience refers to Christ keeping the law of God perfectly during his ministry on earth.[6] Passive obedience, on the other hand, refers to the suffering of Christ (which reaches a climax on the cross), whereby he acted as our substitute, taking upon himself the penalty for our sin (the wrath of God).[7] To answer our question above, *both* aspects of the righteousness of Christ (active and passive) are essential if Christ's work is to be credited or imputed to the believer.

Thus far we have most definitely seen that the passive obedience of Christ is imputed to our account. As discussed, Christ died as a propitiation, as a substitute in our stead, taking upon himself the wrath of God that was our due penalty. As Paul says, it was for our sake that God made Christ "to be sin who knew no sin" (2 Cor. 5:21). So, the passive obedience of Christ is absolutely part of the righteousness imputed to believers. But what about the active obedience of Christ? Is it also part of the righteousness credited to believers?

The answer must be yes. As already emphasized, it is not enough for us to have our guilt removed and the penalty for our sins cancelled, as essential as that is. We need a positive righteousness added to us so that we can stand before God justified. Such a righteousness is found in Christ alone, who lived the perfect life we could not live.[8]

---

6. Perhaps the best defense of the active obedience to date is Brandon C. Crowe, *The Last Adam: A Theology of the Obedient Life of Jesus in the Gospels* (Grand Rapids: Baker Academic, 2017).

7. Notice how Calvin does not limit passive obedience to the cross: "From the time he took on the form of a servant he began to pay the price of liberation in order to redeem us" (*Institutes*, 2.16.5).

8. Brian Vickers, *Justification by Grace through Faith* (Phillipsburg, NJ: P&R, 2013), 41.

In the context of redemptive history, Christ came as the second, last Adam, obeying where Adam disobeyed.[9] He obeyed the law perfectly, earning a righteousness on our behalf that we so desperately needed in order to be justified.[10] Paul says in Romans 5:19, "For as by the one man's disobedience the many were made sinners, so by the one man's obedience the many will be made righteous." In other words, it was through Adam's disobedience that we were made sinners. However, by Christ living a perfect life of obedience, unstained by sin, we, Adam's children, are now counted righteous. No longer are we guilty in Adam, but now we are justified, declared righteous, in Christ.

Some will object that Romans 5:19 should be restricted to the cross, not applied to Christ's wider obedience. David VanDrunen insightfully explains, however, why such a restriction is too narrow and why the whole of Christ's obedience should not be precluded:

> First is the implausibility of the objectors' own interpretation. Was the crucifixion itself really *one* act of Christ? Insofar as Christ submitted himself to this fate and interacted with his Father and those around him, the crucifixion was a series of actions rather than a single act. Also, if one desires to see the imputation of passive obedience taught in this passage, surely it must be admitted that Christ's passive obedience was no more a single act than his active obedience, since he suffered throughout his life and thereby learned obedience in order to become a perfect high priest (e.g., Heb. 2:10, 17–18; 5:7–10). To see Christ's active obedience in Romans 5:19 involves no more conceptual difficulty than seeing his passive obedience in general or the crucifixion in particular. There must have been some reason for Paul's emphasis on the oneness of Christ's righteousness action other than the isolation of a single discrete event.[11]

---

9. I am assuming, in such a statement, that perfect obedience to the law is necessary. The necessity of perfection stems from the nature of divine justice itself (Exod. 23:7; Nah. 1:3; Deut. 10:17; Prov. 17:15; Pss. 15:1-2; 24:3–4) and consequently from the nature of the divine law (Gen. 1-2; 1 Sam. 15:22; Ps. 40:6-8; Jer. 7:22-23; Hos. 6:6; Mic. 6:6-8; Matt. 19:17–19; Mark 12:33; Luke 10:25–28; Gal. 3:10–12 [Deut. 27:26; Lev. 18:5]; 5:3; Rom. 2:13. See David VanDrunen, "To Obey Is Better Than Sacrifice: A Defense of the Active Obedience of Christ in Light of Recent Criticism," in *By Faith Alone: Answering the Challenges to the Doctrine of Justification*, eds. Gary L. W. Johnson and Guy P. Waters (Wheaton, IL: Crossway, 2006), 134–39.

10. Herman Bavinck, *Reformed Dogmatics*, vol. 3, *Sin and Salvation in Christ*, ed. John Bolt, trans. John Vriend (Grand Rapids: Baker, 2009), 215.

11. VanDrunen, "To Obey Is Better Than Sacrifice," 143–44

VanDrunen goes on to give several contextual reasons from Romans 5 why it is much "more plausible" to follow John Murray's "suggestion that the one act ought to be seen as the whole of Christ's obedience in its 'compact unity.'"[12] But for our purposes it is his conclusion that is especially relevant: It is best to see 5:19 as describing "the cross as the climax of a course of obedience extending throughout his [Christ's] entire earthly life and encompassing his fulfillment of every aspect of the law."[13] Not only does such a conclusion align with the focus and progression of the Gospel narratives—in Luke's Gospel, for example, the cross is "the goal toward which his long course of obedience was pointing" (Luke 9:51 [Isa. 50:7])[14]—but elsewhere Paul practically says this much: "And being found in human form, he humbled himself by becoming obedient to the point of death, even death on a cross" (Phil. 2:8). "Christ's obedience, then, began at the very inception of his human existence, and his death brought it to its dramatic completion."[15] Paul goes so far as to make the exaltation of Christ in Philippians 2:9–11 dependent upon such obedience, the very reason Christ can be exalted as the risen, conquering king.[16]

Therefore, the righteousness we must have is not our own, based on the law, but a righteousness "through faith in Christ, the righteousness from God that depends on faith" (Phil. 3:9). It is Christ who has been made "our righteousness" (1 Cor. 1:30) and on that basis we stand before God justified. In short, Christ had to "fulfill all righteousness" for our sake, not his own (Matt. 3:15). Hence, it was necessary for Christ to be born "under the law" (Gal. 4:4–5) and to learn "obedience through what he suffered" in order to become "the source of eternal salvation" (Heb. 5:8). It was essential that he be "tempted as we are," yet remain "without sin" so that we can "with confidence draw near to the throne of grace" (Heb. 4:15). Paul powerfully captures the type of righteousness we need: "But now the righteousness of God has been manifested apart from the law, although the Law and the Prophets bear witness to it—the righteousness of God through faith in Jesus Christ for all who believe" (Rom. 3:21–22).

---

12. Ibid., 144. See John Murray, *The Epistle to the Romans* (Grand Rapids: Eerdmans, 1959, 1965), 1:200–202.
13. VanDrunen, "To Obey Is Better Than Sacrifice," 145.
14. Ibid.
15. Ibid.
16. "Crucial for the present discussion is that Paul makes the exaltation the consequence of the obedience and the obedience the cause of the exaltation. Paul does this by connecting the conclusion of his description of Christ's obedience in 2:8 and the beginning of his description of Christ's exaltation with the strong causal conjunction διό: Christ 'was obedient unto death, even the death of the cross, *therefore* God exalted him' (AT). God exalted Christ on the basis of his obedience." Ibid., 146. Also see R. Scott Clark, "Do This and Live: Christ's Active Obedience as the Ground of Justification," in *Covenant, Justification, and Pastoral Ministry*, ed. R. Scott Clark (Phillipsburg, NJ: P&R, 2007), 230.

It should be conceded that these terms, active and passive, are somewhat limited (as is all theological language). Surely even Christ's suffering on the cross involved his active obedience, for he is obeying the will of his Father (John 10:18). The active obedience of Christ does not cease when Jesus goes to the cross but in reality is reaching its greatest fulfillment. Furthermore, we do not want to do harm to the unity of Christ's obedience, as if we could somehow separate the active and passive aspects of Christ's work. These categories are not meant to bifurcate the work of Christ but rather distinguish important and different facets of that one work.[17] That said, the categories should be preserved as they help us think through two inter-related, united, yet distinguishable aspects of the righteousness of Christ.

In closing, Fesko reminds us that these two aspects of Christ's obedience parallel Adam's identity in the garden. Adam was created good, not just in a physical sense but in a moral sense as well. He possessed an original, positive righteousness, not merely the "absence of sin."[18] Therefore, his failure to obey God's commandment must be remedied not merely by a pardoning of sin but by the imputing of an alien righteousness, one that is perfect. Hence, it is necessary not only for Christ to pay the penalty for sin but to obey and fulfill the law (Matt. 3:15; 5:17–18; Luke 2:21–22; Gal. 4:4–5). We rejoice with Berkhof that "the ground of justification can be found only in the perfect righteousness of Jesus Christ, which is imputed to the sinner in justification."[19]

Summary

The imputation of Christ's righteousness is absolutely essential to the believer's right standing before a holy God. Not only does justification involve the forgiveness of our sins but the crediting of Christ's obedience to our account. Therefore, not only do we need the passive obedience of Christ, whereby he suffers for us, but the active obedience of Christ, whereby he obeys the law perfectly on our behalf.

---

17. Fesko, *Justification*, 152.
18. Ibid., 150.
19. Louis Berkhof, *Systematic Theology* (Grand Rapids: Eerdmans, 1938; 1993), 523. Also see, Francis Turretin, *Institutes of Elenctic Theology*, vol. 2, trans. George Musgrave Giger, ed. James T. Dennison, Jr. (Phillipsburg, NJ: P&R, 1994), 445; Herman Witsius, *The Economy of the Covenants Between God and Man* (Phillipsburg, NJ: P&R, 1990), 1:190-91; Charles Hodge, *Systematic Theology* (Grand Rapids: Eerdmans, 1995), 2:517; Geerhardus Vos, "The Alleged Legalism in Paul's Doctrine of Justification," in *Redemptive History and Biblical Interpretation: The Shorter Writings of Geerhardus Vos*, ed. Richard B. Gaffin Jr. (Phillipsburg, NJ: P&R, 1980), 398.

REFLECTION QUESTIONS

1. What is the biblical meaning of "to impute"?

2. Is the forgiveness of our sins enough, or do we need something more (i.e., the righteousness of Christ) and why?

3. Why must the righteousness that justifies us before God be an alien righteousness?

4. How does the distinction between Christ's active and passive obedience help us understand the doctrine of imputation?

5. As you think back on your sinful record, is the work of Christ a great comfort and assurance?

Is the Righteousness of Christ Imputed to Believers? (Part 1)

Christians focus a lot of attention on the need for forgiveness. And rightly so. As we've seen, the Bible is clear: Jesus died so that our sins would be forgiven. At the same time, if this is all we say, then we have failed to tell the rest of the story. It's not enough for God to forgive us of our sins. In order for God to declare us just, we need an alien righteousness—that is, the perfect righteousness of Jesus Christ. Only then, when we have the positive merit of Christ reckoned to our account, can God truly declare us just in his sight.

Consider briefly how the transition from the first Adam to the second Adam situates imputation within its proper biblical context. In Question 2 we saw how Scripture teaches that the guilt of Adam's sin is imputed to us, Adam's children. Graciously, God imputes our guilt to Christ, who pays the penalty for our sin on the cross (2 Cor. 5:21). Then, with our guilt being imputed to Christ, the righteousness of Christ is imputed to us upon faith in Christ (e.g., 1 Cor. 1:30; Phil. 3:9).[1] When God looks at us, he sees the righteousness of Christ, credited to us by grace through faith. The righteousness we receive from God is an *alien* righteousness. In other words, we are not justified before God by our own, inherent or merited, righteousness but by the righteousness of God that comes to us through his Son, Jesus Christ (Rom. 3:21–22).[2]

---

1. When we speak of Christ's obedience being reckoned to our account, it is critical to emphasize that this only occurs when the sinner places his faith in Christ alone. Notice how Paul connects imputation and faith in Romans 3:21–22. God imputes to us righteousness (that is, a righteous status), but this righteousness is only given to those who believe in Jesus. Therefore, faith is the *instrumental means* by which we receive the righteousness of Christ, which is always a gift from God, not something merited by good works.
2. For a far more in-depth defense of imputation than can be provided here, see Brian Vickers, *Jesus' Blood and Righteousness: Paul's Theology of Imputation* (Wheaton, IL: Crossway, 2006); John Piper, *Counted Righteous in Christ: Should We Abandon the Imputed*

Notice, there is a threefold imputation at work in our salvation, as illustrated in the following chart:

Table 6
Threefold imputation

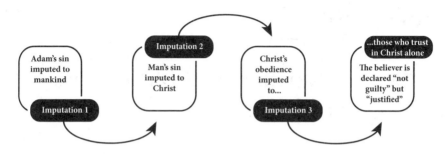

The discerning reader will also notice that we have used the word "imputation" instead of "infusion." That is because we are not talking about an infusion of righteousness into our moral fiber, but the crediting or reckoning of a righteous standing, giving us a new legal status and identity. Theologians refer to this as "forensic righteousness," as opposed to "transformative righteousness." With those distinctions in mind, let's now take a look at the biblical support for such a doctrine.

Imputation in the Old Testament

The concept of imputation is not a New Testament novelty. To see this, perhaps it is helpful to begin our treatment of imputation with the Old Testament, identifying whether or not the concept of imputation is present. While we cannot explore every Old Testament passage that utilizes imputation language and imagery, nevertheless, the following four passages lend tremendous support to the doctrine of imputation. To be clear, no single passage below fleshes out the imputation of Christ's righteousness; that's not the point of this section on the Old Testament (but see the next chapter on the New Testament, which does just that). Rather, our point in what follows is merely to show that the concept of imputation itself is taught in the Old Testament and is central to how God deals with the sin of his people, providing for them a justified standing in his sight.

The Day of Atonement (Leviticus 16)

In the Old Testament Israel faced a huge problem. Though they were to be in covenant with Yahweh, they were covenant-breakers. More precisely, as

---

Righteousness of Christ? (Wheaton, IL: Crossway, 2002); Thomas Schreiner, *Faith Alone: The Doctrine of Justification* (Grand Rapids: Zondervan, 2015).

covenant-breakers they had violated God's law and stood before a holy God as transgressors. This is a major problem because God is holy. He will not tolerate sin nor can sinners be in his presence lest they be consumed by his holy wrath.

Nadab and Abihu, the sons of Aaron, learned this the hard way. In Leviticus 10 they offered "unauthorized fire before the Lord, which God had not commanded them." As a result, "fire came out from before the Lord and consumed them, and they died before the LORD" (10:2). Moses then said to Aaron, "This is what the LORD has said: 'Among those who are near me I will be sanctified, and before all the people I will be glorified'" (10:3).

At the start of Leviticus 16, Aaron's two sons are mentioned again. After their deaths the Lord spoke to Moses in order to instruct Aaron on the proper way to enter into the Holy Place, that is, if Aaron was to avoid being put to death himself (16:1–2). To enter into the most holy place, the very presence of God, something had to be done, given that Aaron was a sinner and the people he represented were sinners too.

Aaron was instructed to enter into the Holy Place with a "bull from the herd for a sin offering and a ram for a burnt offering" (16:3). Aaron was to wear the "holy linen coat," for it and other garments were "holy garments" (16:4). And he was to "bathe his body in water" before putting them on as well (16:4). Next, "two male goats" were to be "taken from the congregation of the people of Israel" (16:5). Why? These two male goats would be "for a sin offering, and one ram for a burnt offering" (16:5).

But notice, offering is not only made for the people, but for Aaron himself, for he, like the people, is sinful and in need of atonement. First, Aaron was to offer up a bull "as a sin offering for himself" in order to "make atonement for himself and for his house" (16:6). Now Aaron was ready to also make an offering for the people as their high priest. God commanded Aaron to take two goats and "set them before the Lord at the entrance of the tent of meeting" (16:7). Why two goats? One goat was to be presented as a "sin offering" but the other goat was to be kept alive. This goat would make atonement by being sent away into the wilderness (16:10). What happens just before the goat is sent away proves critical. The live goat is placed before the Lord and Aaron lays "both his hands on the head of the live goat." With his hands on the goat, Aaron then confesses "over it all the iniquities of the people of Israel, and all their transgressions, all their sins" (16:21). With sins confessed, the goat was then to be sent into the wilderness. In doing so, the goat bears "all their iniquities on itself to a remote area" (16:22). In this symbolic act, the punishment of the people is placed on this scapegoat who suffers death outside the camp, cut off from the people, sent into the wilderness to die.[3]

---

3. Michael Ovey, Andrew Sach, *Pierced for Our Transgressions: Rediscovering the Glory of Penal Substitution* (Wheaton, IL: Crossway, 2007), 50.

Here we have a magnificent picture of imputation. If the people were to be right with God, then their sins had to be dealt with. Graciously, God provided a way for that to happen. God would impute the sins of his people to a goat, and this goat would bear these sins into the wilderness forever, resulting in Israel's guilt being remitted and Israel being purified. The goat acts as the substitute, the one who bears the iniquities of the people. But it is God who mercifully imputes the guilt of his people to this goat, as symbolized when Aaron, the people's priestly mediator, places his hands on the goat. In other words, the sins of the people are transferred to the substitute, reckoned to the substitute, never to be seen again.

Leviticus 16 pictures the Day of Atonement, that is, the day when the high priest would enter into the Most Holy Place but once a year. However, the book of Hebrews tells us that "it is impossible for the blood of bulls and goats to take away sins" (10:4). So as important as the Day of Atonement was, Israel longed for a greater Day of Atonement, one that would not have to be repeated but would take away her sins once for all. The Day of Atonement in Leviticus 16 was a type, pointing forward to the atonement Christ would offer up on behalf of God's people as great high priest. Hebrews 9 makes this very point, explaining how Christ "appeared as high priest" and entered into the tent (though this tent was not made with hands). Yet when he entered in as high priest he "entered once for all into the holy places, not by means of the blood of goats and calves but by means of his own blood, thus securing an eternal redemption" (9:12). The author goes on, "For if the blood of goats and bulls, and the sprinkling of defiled persons with the ashes of a heifer, sanctify for the purification of the flesh, how much more will the blood of Christ, who through the eternal Spirit offered himself without blemish to God, purify our conscience from dead works to serve the living God" (9:13–14).

Hebrews 9:25–28 colorfully draws a parallel between Christ's atonement and the Day of Atonement. Christ, the author explains, did not enter into "holy places made with hands," which were but "copies of the true things" (9:24). Rather, Christ entered into "heaven itself," appearing before the "presence of God on our behalf" (9:24). In this sense, Christ is like Aaron, the priest who enters into the Most Holy Place, into the very presence of the holy God, and he does so representing the people. But unlike Aaron and all priests after Aaron, Jesus did not have to do so repeatedly. As the Son of God himself, he was able to do so just once, making an atonement sufficient for all eternity (9:26). What is so shocking, however, is that while Aaron offered up an animal, Christ offered up himself for atonement. Christ "appeared once for all at the end of the ages to put away sin by the sacrifice of himself" (9:26; cf. 10:12, 14). In short, Christ was "offered once to bear the sins of many" (9:28). Like the Day of Atonement, God imputed to Christ the sins of his people. Just as Aaron laid his hands on the goat in order to transfer the sins of the people, so our sins have been transferred to Christ. As Paul says in 2 Corinthians 5:21, "For our sake he made him to be sin who knew no sin, so that in him we might become the righteousness of God."

The point to take away is a crucial one: In Leviticus 16 we see strong biblical support for the concept of imputation and in such a way that what takes place on the Day of Atonement actually prefigures the imputation of our sins to Christ on the cross. As we've mentioned before, imputation is a "great exchange," our guilt being imputed to Christ, and Christ's righteousness imputed to us. Leviticus 16 lends great reinforcement to the first half of this exchange.

The Suffering Servant (Isaiah 53)

One of the most profound and striking texts on imputation is Isaiah 53. Like Leviticus 16, Isaiah 53 places the categories of substitution and imputation on the table, and it does so by bringing to bear the notion of "penalty."

Isaiah 53 speaks of a suffering servant, one who had "no form or majesty that we should look at him, and no beauty that we should desire him" (53:3). This sufferer is called a "man of sorrows" because he "was despised and rejected by men" and "acquainted with grief" (53:3). This man of sorrows, however, does not suffer for suffering's sake; no, he suffers for the sake of others. He acts as a substitute, one on whom the affliction and transgressions of others is placed. "Surely," says Isaiah, "he has borne our griefs and carried our sorrows; yet we esteemed him stricken, smitten by God, and afflicted" (53:4). This suffering substitute is "smitten by God" for a reason: He bore on himself our sin and took its full penalty. Or as Isaiah puts it, the suffering servant "was pierced for our transgressions; he was crushed for our iniquities" (53:4–5a). The "Lord has laid on him the iniquity of us all" (53:6b). Verse 10 not only says it was "the will of the Lord to crush him" but "his soul" made an "offering for guilt." Here is the concept of imputation once more. We know from the New Testament that this suffering servant is Jesus, the Christ (Acts 8:30–35; 1 Peter 2:22–25). But here in Isaiah 53 we learn early on that the suffering servant has imputed to him our transgressions, our iniquities. Receiving these imputed transgressions, he bears their full penalty and punishment, which is why Isaiah can say the servant is crushed, that is, crushed by God for our sake.

Yet this suffering servant also brought about our right standing: "the righteous one" makes "many to be accounted righteous" (53:11b). "Accounted righteous"—that is transactional language, language that refers to our legal standing before God. It's a major reason why those who are "in Christ Jesus" no longer face condemnation (Rom. 8:1). Here we see the flip side of the imputation coin. On one side, our iniquities are imputed to Christ (Isa. 53:4–10), but on the other side of the coin is the imputation of righteousness, given freely to the sinner so that he is no longer accounted guilty but righteous in God's sight.

Pure Vestments (Zechariah 3 [Isaiah 61:10])

So far, we have seen the first half of imputation, namely, the imputation of our sin to Christ. Now we turn to the second half of that great exchange: the imputation of righteousness to us, the sinner. The second half of imputation has already been hinted at in Isaiah 53:11b ("the righteous one" makes "many to be accounted righteous"); now we will see imputation in full bloom.

One of the most beautiful images of imputation is found in Zechariah 3, the vision in which Joshua, the high priest, is reclothed. To set the scene, the high priest Joshua stands in heaven's courtroom before God, the judge, representing God's people. Yet, there is another standing there as well: Satan. Standing to his right, Satan acts as Joshua's prosecutor, ready and eager to accuse Joshua and expose his condemnation. Satan's case against Joshua is an easy one. Joshua is clothed in "filthy garments," and by "filthy" the text likely means Joshua's garments were covered with disgusting, smelly excrement.

Remember where Joshua is: He stands in God's courtroom! Surely the situation could not be worse. Joshua stands defiled before a holy judge. But before Satan can get an accusing word off his lips, God rebukes Satan, exclaiming that though Joshua is a "brand" in the fire, he is a "brand plucked from the fire" (3:2). God then commands his angel to remove Joshua's filthy garments. What does this removing of Joshua's clothing picture? The removal of Joshua's iniquities. "Behold, I have taken your iniquities away from you" says the Lord (3:4a). But notice, the Lord not only removes Joshua's filthy garments, thereby removing his iniquities; he also reclothes Joshua, but this time with "pure vestments" (3:4b). Imputed to Joshua is a right standing before God, his judge.

What's remarkable, though, is that it is the judge himself who clothes Joshua, and not just Joshua but the people as well since Joshua is their representative before Yahweh. No longer condemned in the heavenly courtroom (Satan's mouth has been shut up!), Joshua has been justified, clothed in the righteousness that God himself provided. Connected to the rest of the storyline of Scripture, we know that here, in Zechariah 3, we have but a shadow of the great gospel exchange to come. On the basis of Christ's life, death, and resurrection, the sinner's filthy garments are removed, resulting in his forgiveness, and he is instead royally clothed in the righteousness of Christ, a garment that meets the approval of the heavenly judge. To return to Isaiah, we too rejoice in the Lord and say that "he has clothed me with the garments of salvation; he has covered me with the robe of righteousness" (61:10a).

Summary

The concept of imputation is not foreign to the Old Testament. Both the imputation of our sins to a substitute and the imputation of righteousness to sinners is present. The Day of Atonement (Lev. 16), the suffering servant (Isa. 53), and the clothing of Joshua (Zech. 3) demonstrate that the imputation of Christ's righteousness mentioned in the New Testament is a concept rooted in the Old Testament.

REFLECTION QUESTIONS

1. What step in the process of atonement in Leviticus 16 symbolizes the imputation of sin?

2. In what ways is Christ like and unlike Aaron, the high priest? Compare Leviticus 16 with Hebrews 9:25–28.

3. What language is used in Isaiah 53 to convey that our sins have been imputed to a substitute, i.e., the suffering servant?

4. In Zechariah 3, why is it that Satan's accusation against Joshua falls short?

5. How does the imagery of "pure vestments" (Zech. 3:4b) parallel the imputations of Christ's righteousness?

Is the Righteousness of Christ Imputed to Believers? (Part 2)

When the reformer Martin Luther was confronted by Paul's phrase "the righteousness of God" in Romans 1, Luther was overwhelmed, losing all hope, for he knew that he could not match up to the perfect standard of God's righteousness.[1] Such a righteousness, thought Luther, would be revealed as God's wrath against all ungodliness and unrighteousness in men. However, Luther's understanding of the gospel completely shifted when he suddenly realized that the righteousness of God Paul spoke of is not always God's punitive justice, whereby he punishes the ungodly.[2] Paul is also referring to the righteousness that is *from* God, namely, the righteous status God graciously and freely gives to condemned sinners. In other words, Paul has in mind the saving righteousness that sinners receive by faith. And this righteousness, Luther realized, was an alien righteousness. It was not a righteousness from within the sinner (i.e., a transformative, infused righteousness) but the perfect, stainless righteousness of Jesus Christ imputed to the sinner's account upon faith (i.e., a forensic righteousness).[3] Luther's heavy conscience was relieved, for he realized that it was not his good works—which could never earn him a righteousness good enough to stand before a perfectly holy God—but the righteousness of Christ that comes through faith alone, that gives him a right standing before God. In this chapter, we transition from the Old Testament to the New Testament in order to focus our attention on the doctrine of imputation. As we do so, we will discover,

---

1. E.g., Martin Luther, "Preface to the Complete Edition of Luther's Latin Writings," *LW* 34:336–337. Luther has in mind Romans 1:17 specifically.
2. I.e., *iustitia distributiva*, or distributive justice.
3. For how the ending phrase used by Paul, "from faith for faith," has been interpreted, see J. V. Fesko, *Justification* (Phillipsburg, NJ: 2008), 196–97.

as Luther did, that the righteousness of Christ is imputed to those who believe, giving them a right legal standing before God.

The Righteousness of God through Faith (Romans 3:21–26)

Romans 3:21 is one of the most important texts in support of imputed righteousness. After affirming that no one is righteous and that no human being will be justified by works of the law, Paul writes, "But now the righteousness of God has been manifested apart from the law, although the Law and the Prophets bear witness to it—the righteousness of God through faith in Jesus Christ for all who believe." What does Paul mean by "the righteousness of God"?[4]

In Romans 3:21, Paul has in mind the righteousness *from* God, one that is given freely to the sinner who trusts in Jesus alone to save him (cf. Phil. 3:9; Rom. 5:17). In other words, Paul is not describing God's righteousness by which he judges and punishes the ungodly for their failure to keep the law (see Rom. 1–2). Nor is he describing a transforming righteousness, one in which the sinner is made inherently righteous by works of the law (as in Roman Catholicism).[5] Rather, he is speaking of a righteousness that is from God, revealed apart from the law, one that is appropriated simply by faith in Christ (Rom. 3:22) and results in the ungodly being declared legally (forensically) righteous. This is the righteousness Paul referred to in Romans 1:17 and will refer to again in Romans 10:1–6. It is the righteousness that is a gift from God. The question we now must answer is this: What exactly is this righteousness that God gives in Romans 3:21?

The answer to this question comes to us in Romans 3:24–25. Paul explains that all have sinned and fallen short of the glory of God and "are justified by his grace as a gift, through the redemption that is in Christ Jesus, whom God put forward as a propitiation by his blood, to be received by faith." The basis of justification is the cross of Christ. God has accomplished redemption, and he has done so by putting forward his own Son, who was a "propitiation by his blood." First, the word "redemption" (*apolutrōseōs*) communicates the notion of buying back a slave and giving him his freedom by paying a ransom.[6] Paul's point is that God, through Jesus Christ, has purchased a people for himself. He ransomed us and the price was the blood of his own Son.[7]

---

4. For three views on how to interpret "the righteousness of God," see Fesko, *Justification*, 195–200.
5. Those who try to interpret righteousness as "transforming" righteousness include Adolf Schlatter, *The Theology of the Apostles: The Development of New Testament Theology*, trans. Andreas J. Köstenberger (Grand Rapids: Baker, 1999), 234–36; Ernst Käsemann, "The Righteousness of God," in *New Testament Questions of Today*, trans. W. J. Montague (Philadelphia: Fortress, 1982), 168–82. For a critique, see Thomans R. Schreiner, *40 Questions about Christians and Biblical Law* (Grand Rapids: Kregel, 2010), 121–28.
6. Anthony A. Hoekema, *Saved by Grace* (Grand Rapids: Eerdmans, 1989), 157.
7. This ransom is not paid to Satan, but to God.

Second, the Greek word here for "propitiation" (ἱλαστήριον; *hilastērion*) is important. There has been debate as to whether this word refers to "expiation" (forgiveness of sins; the washing away of sins) or "propitiation" (satisfaction of God's wrath).[8] C. H. Dodd, for example, argued for expiation and believed that judgment was merely sin's natural consequence.[9] However, others have showed that judgment is the manifestation of God's wrath against sin. Roger Nicole and Leon Morris, for example, have persuasively argued this point exegetically from both the Old Testament and the New Testament, especially demonstrating that texts like Romans 3:25–26 do refer to propitiation after all.[10]

Judging not just from the word itself but also from the context, Paul teaches that God's holy wrath against our sin has been pacified and appeased, and our guilt has been removed through Christ who offered himself up as a substitutionary sacrifice (cf. Rom. 3:25; Heb. 2:17; 1 John 2:2; 4:10). Previously God had passed over former sins, withholding the punishment they deserved, an act that could put his justice in jeopardy. However, God's justice was satisfied at the cross. God, out of his great love for us, gave his one and only Son to shed his blood as an atoning sacrifice on our behalf, satisfying the wrath of God that we deserve. As 1 John 4:10 teaches us, "In this is love, not that we have loved God but that he loved us and sent his Son to be the *propitiation* for our sins" (emphasis added). At the cross, mercy and justice kiss one another. God not only showed himself to be just (since his justice was satisfied by Christ absorbing the full penalty for sin) but to be the justifier of the "one who has faith in Jesus" (Rom. 3:26). It is on the basis of this atonement that the righteousness of Christ is legally reckoned to the believer's account, giving the believer right standing with God.

Counted as Righteousness (Romans 4:2–6)

A second powerful text supporting the doctrine of imputation is Romans 4:2–6 where Paul turns to the example of Abraham.

> For if Abraham was justified by works, he has something to boast about, but not before God. For what does the Scripture say? "Abraham believed God, and it was counted to him as righteousness." Now to the one who works, his wages are not counted as a gift but as his due. And to the one who does not work but believes in him who justifies the ungodly, his faith is counted as righteousness, just as David also speaks of the blessing of the one to whom God counts righteousness apart from works.

---

8. Schreiner, *40 Questions about Christians and Biblical Law*, 126.
9. C. H. Dodd, *The Bible and the Greeks* (London: Hodder & Stoughton, 1935), 82–95.
10. Roger Nicole, "C. H. Dodd and the Doctrine of Propitiation," *WTJ* 17 (1955): 117–57; Leon Morris, *The Apostolic Preaching of the Cross*, 3rd ed. (Grand Rapids: Eerdmans, 1965), 144–213. For a more theological treatment, see J. I. Packer, "What Did the Cross Achieve: The Logic of Penal Substitution," *TynBul* 25 (1974): 3–45.

Notice how Paul uses the word "counted" (ESV), or in some translations "credited" (e.g., NASB), indicating that imputation is most definitely in view.[11] Paul's language is a reminder once again that justification is a forensic matter, whereby the work of justification involves crediting and imputing.[12] But what is it exactly that is credited to the sinner? Some have argued that faith itself is the righteousness in view. After all, Paul says, "his faith is counted as righteousness." However, such a view is misguided for several reasons.

First, the righteousness of justification that Paul is referring to is grounded upon the propitiatory work of Christ, not man's faith.[13] As Vickers explains, "The righteousness in view is not made up of faith but is found in faith's object. Paul does not say that justification is because of faith but by faith. Faith is the means by which we are made right with God through Christ, the object of faith and the foundation of our righteousness."[14] As several Pauline texts demonstrate (e.g., Rom. 3:25–26; 5:1–2; 9:30), faith is the *instrumental means* through which we are justified. It is not the basis or ground of justification. This much is apparent in Paul's affirmation that faith is "counted" as righteousness. Faith is being counted or reckoned not as actual righteousness itself, but for something that it inherently is not, namely, righteousness.[15]

Second, Paul is making a contrast between works and faith, between a righteousness based on doing works of the law and a righteousness that comes through trusting in Jesus alone. If we make faith itself our righteousness, then we have simply turned faith into a work, and certainly this would undermine the contrast Paul is making. Faith, however, is only significant because of its object, namely God. Vickers is helpful: "Faith is what unites us to God's righteousness, so when Paul says that Abraham's faith was counted as righteousness, he means specifically that his faith *in God* was counted as righteousness."[16]

Faith is not the "new covenant version of works," but faith is the means by which a righteous status is reckoned, by grace alone, to the ungodly.[17] To be more specific, according to Paul it is Christ Jesus, whom we have been united to, who is our righteousness (1 Cor. 1:30; cf. 2 Cor. 5:2). In other words, while our sin was reckoned or credited to Christ on the cross, his righteousness was credited to us upon faith. It is in union with Christ, therefore, that we receive

11. The word λογίζομαι (*logizomai*) is used in 4:3, 4, 5, 6, 8, 9, 10, 11, 22, 23, 24. It is also used in the Septuagint (see Num. 18:27; 2 Sam. 19:20) and there it takes on a legal meaning as well. See J. V. Fesko, *Death in Adam, Life in Christ: The Doctrine of Imputation*, Reformed Exegesis and Doctrinal Studies (Ross shire: Scotland, 2016), 199.

12. See Douglas Moo, *The Epistle to the Romans*, NICNT (Grand Rapids: Eerdmans, 1996), 266.

13. Notice how Romans 4:25a parallels Isaiah 53:12 LXX and Romans 4:25b parallels Isaiah 53:11 LXX. See Fesko, *Death in Adam, Life in Christ*, 205–6.

14. Brian Vickers, *Justification by Grace through Faith* (Phillipsburg, NJ: P&R, 2013), 76.

15. Ibid., 96–97.

16. Ibid., 77.

17. Paul's point is reiterated by appealing to David in Romans 4:6–8. Ibid.

his righteousness. As Paul explains in Philippians 3:9, those in Christ do not have a righteousness that is their own, one that comes from the law, "but that which comes through faith in Christ, the righteousness from God that depends on faith" (Phil. 3:9).

The Free Gift of Righteousness (Romans 5:19)

Though his emphasis changes directions from Romans 3 and 4, Paul preaches this good news of imputation in Romans 5:17–19 as well:[18] "For if, because of one man's trespass, death reigned through that one man, much more will those who receive the abundance of grace and the free gift of righteousness reign in life through the one man Jesus Christ. Therefore, as one trespass led to condemnation for all men, so one act of righteousness leads to justification and life for all men. For as by the one man's disobedience the many were made sinners, so by the one man's obedience the many will be made righteous." According to Paul, the righteousness that is imputed or credited to us is not our own; rather, we have freely received a righteousness that is from God, that is, the righteousness of Jesus Christ.[19]

Paul's logic becomes all the more clear when we look at the word "made" in verse 19: "many will be made righteous." This word is commonly used to "designate the place and/or status a thing or person holds or to which a thing or a person is appointed."[20] Though New Testament authors do not use this word as a synonym for "impute," this does not mean that the concept of imputation is absent. Vickers observes that the legal status in 5:18–19 that "one has before God is on the basis of someone else's actions." In other words, people "are recognized in connection to Adam as those who sinned and in connection to Christ as those who fulfilled everything needed to be deemed righteous. The status with which we are appointed is due to the fact that we are counted to have sinned in Adam and counted to have obeyed in Christ."[21] Therefore, though the word "made" is not synonymous with "impute," nevertheless, we should not separate the two.

The case for imputation in Romans 5:19 is only strengthened when we pair that word "made" (*katastathēsontai*) with "righteous" (*dikaioi*). The "word denotes righteous acts or describes a person's character, when he [Paul] pairs it with *made*, which refers to being appointed or placed into a position, then *righteous* is not focused on behavior or character but on our position

---

18. Fesko notes how in "Romans 4 Paul focuses upon imputation at a personal soteriological level, or as it relates to the *ordo salutis*. But here in Romans 5 Paul rises above the terrain and offers a bird's eye view of the *historia salutis*" (*Death in Adam, Life in Christ*, 208).

19. On Paul's shifting emphasis as to what "counts" for righteousness in Romans 4 and 5, see Vickers, *Jesus' Blood and Righteousness: Paul's Theology of Imputation* (Wheaton, IL: Crossway, 2006), 115–22.

20. Ibid., 46–47.

21. Ibid.

before God." Vickers concludes, "We are made to hold the position of those whose acts and behavior are righteous on the basis of Christ's obedience."[22] This righteousness does not come from us but apart from anything we have done. The perfect record of Christ's obedience is credited to us who believe. Again, we cannot ignore the covenantal structure here: In the covenant of works Adam's unrighteous status brought about our condemnation, but in the new covenant Christ's righteous status has brought about our justification. That is Paul's point in Romans 5.

We Might Become the Righteousness of God (2 Corinthians 5:21)

In our last Pauline text, 2 Corinthians 5:21, the apostle writes, "For our sake he made him to be sin who knew no sin, so that in him we might become the righteousness of God." In such a short sentence Paul captures the essence of the great exchange. Our sin is imputed to Christ; Christ's righteousness is reckoned to us. Notice, this is not a transformation that takes place. Christ does not actually become sin or a sinner, which would violate his sinlessness (1 John 3:5). Likewise, justification and imputation do not refer to the moral transformation of the ungodly (that is to mistake justification with sanctification). Instead, Paul refers to a forensic transaction. Acting as their substitute, Christ is *reckoned* as a sinner, and punished in the sinner's place. By contrast, the sinner is *reckoned* righteous. He is given a righteous status, specifically the righteous status of Christ. John Calvin explains why Paul must have imputation in mind:

> How can we become righteous before God? In the same way as Christ became a sinner. For He took, as it were, our person, that He might be the offender in our name and thus might be reckoned a sinner, not because of His own offenses but because of those of others, since He Himself was pure and free from every fault and bore the penalty that was our due and not His own. Now in the same way we are righteous in Him, not because we have satisfied God's judgment by our own works, but because we are judged in relation to Christ's righteousness which we have put on by faith, that it may become our own.[23]

It is hard to improve upon Calvin's words. Paul is referring to a double imputation in this text: Our guilty status has been reckoned to Christ, and

---

22. Ibid., 49.
23. John Calvin, *2 Corinthians and Timothy, Titus and Philemon*, trans. T. A. Smail, ed. David W. Torrance and T. F. Torrance, CNTC 10 (Grand Rapids: Eerdmans, 1960), 78.

his righteous status has been reckoned to us.[24] A glorious exchange has taken place: our sin for his righteousness.[25]

The Righteousness from God that Depends on Faith: Philippians 3:9

One of the clearest passages on imputation is Philippians 3:9. After listing his many credentials as a "Hebrew of Hebrews" and his many zealous works of the law as a Pharisee with the greatest zeal, Paul writes, "But whatever gain I had, I counted as loss for the sake of Christ. . . . For his sake I have suffered the loss of all things and count them as rubbish, in order that I may gain Christ and be found in him, not having a righteousness of my own that comes from the law, but that which comes through faith in Christ, the righteousness from God that depends on faith" (3:7, 8b–9).[26]

Here Paul refers not to the judging righteousness of God (Rom. 1:18–3:20) but to God's saving righteousness—not to the righteousness of God but to the righteousness from God. This righteousness is given to the ungodly *as a gift*. It is not Paul's inherent righteousness, one that comes from works of the law (cf. Rom. 10:1–6), for no one can be justified by works of the law (Rom. 3:20). Instead, it is a righteousness that is external and alien to Paul, and one that cannot be earned by Paul, no matter how great his zeal. Moreover, this righteousness, he says, only comes through faith in Jesus (cf. Rom. 10:6). And this makes sense because if righteousness is a gift from God, then it must depend upon faith alone.

Summary

The New Testament teaches that the righteousness of Christ is imputed or credited to those who believe. The believer's right standing before God is not based on his own inherent righteousness, but on an alien righteousness reckoned to his account.

REFLECTION QUESTIONS

1. What New Testament text lends the greatest support to the doctrine of imputation, and why?

---

24. John Murray, *The Imputation of Adam's Sin* (Philadelphia, NJ: P&R, 1959), 76. Also see D. A. Carson, "Vindication of Imputation: On Fields of Discourse and Semantic Fields," *Justification: What's at Stake in the Current Debates*, eds. Mark Husbands and Daniel J. Treier (Downers Grove, IL: InterVarsity Press, 2009), 69.

25. Other texts that support the doctrine of imputation include 1 Corinthians 1:30 and Romans 9:30–10:4.

26. On whether Paul has in mind faith in Christ or the faithfulness of Christ, see Question 26, footnote 3.

2. Is your assurance of your right standing before God strengthened knowing that an alien righteousness (the righteousness of Christ) has been credited to you?

3. How would your assurance differ if you stood before God on the basis of your own righteousness?

4. How does the doctrine of imputation change your perception of who Christ is and what he has done on your behalf?

5. If imputation is rejected, what negative consequences would follow?

Is Justification by God's Grace Alone, through Faith Alone?

"If anyone says that a sinful man is justified by faith alone . . . let him be anathema."

Rome was not ambiguous. According to the Council of Trent, justification is *not* by faith *alone*. Interestingly, Paul says something very different. While Rome affirms the necessity of good works alongside faith in order to be justified, Paul says "For we hold that one is justified by faith apart from works of the law" (Rom. 3:28). It is no wonder, then, that the Protestant Reformers affirmed the material principle of the Reformation (i.e., faith alone; *sola fide*). Our goal in this chapter is to do the same, demonstrating that justification is by grace alone through faith alone.

Faith: Instrumental Cause

Before we do so, however, it is necessary to introduce certain theological categories into the discussion for precision. Previously we discussed and defended the imputation of Christ's righteousness, and in doing so we distinguished (though we did not divorce) the passive and active righteousness (or obedience) of Christ (see Questions 24–25). We concluded that Christ's obedience (both active and passive) is the *ground* of our justification (Rom. 3:24; 5:9, 19; 8:1; 10:4; 1 Cor. 1:30; 6:11; 2 Cor. 5:21; Phil. 3:9). *Solus Christus,* Christ alone, means that our justification is based upon the redemptive work of Christ *alone* as that which is sufficient for our salvation. Justification is not partly based upon Christ's work and partly on our own; rather, it is entirely based upon what Christ has done on our behalf. Hence the extreme importance of affirming Christ as our substitute and federal head. We do not stand before God's throne claiming, even in the smallest sense, a righteousness of our own; instead, we only lay claim to the righteousness of Christ. The imputation of his righteousness to our account is the reason for our new, justified status.

If Christ's salvific obedience (both active and passive) is the *ground* of our right standing before God, then faith cannot be the ground or basis of justification. Doing so would turn faith itself into a work and undermine the sufficiency of Christ's saving work. So we should be careful how we use the language of faith. For example, when someone asks, "On what basis are you right before God?", it would be imprecise to answer, "On the basis of *my faith.*" Instead, we should say, "It is only on the basis of Christ's work for me," and then follow that up with: "which I receive through faith in him alone." Faith is not the basis but the *instrument* through which we are justified.[1] Or to use theological language: Faith is the "instrumental cause" of justification (Rom. 3:28, 30; Gal. 2:16; 3:8).[2]

With the instrumentality of faith in mind, the central issue before us now is whether justification is through faith *alone.* As we will now see, the answer is a resounding yes according to Scripture, which serves to buttress this concept of faith being "instrumental" (as opposed to the "ground") of our justification.

Not by Works of the Law (Romans 3:21–31)

As he so often does, Paul begins Romans 3 by emphasizing the total depravity of man (3:9–18; cf. Eph. 2:1–3). The sinner, says Paul, is under the law and the whole world is held accountable to God. But is it by works of the law that the sinner is justified? By no means! "For by works of the law no human being will be justified in his [God's] sight, since through the law comes knowledge of sin" (Rom. 3:20). In other words, the law does not justify us but exposes our sinfulness due to our failure to uphold it. The law reveals our condemnation, demonstrating that we stand before a holy God as lawbreakers rather than law-keepers. Through works of the law no person will be justified, for there is no one righteous, no, not one (Rom. 3:10). And there is no one who does good, not even one (Rom. 3:12).

---

1. There are many reasons why it will not work to make faith the basis of justification. Calvin puts his finger on one of them: "If faith in itself justified one by its own virtue, then, seeing that it is always weak and imperfect, it would be only partly effectual and give us only a part of salvation" (John Calvin, *Institutes of the Christian Religion*, ed. John T. McNeil, trans. Ford Lewis Battles, LCC, vols. 20–21 [Philadelphia: Westminster, 1960], 3.11.7).

2. God justifies "not by imputing faith itself, the act of believing, or any other evangelical obedience to them as their righteousness; but by imputing the obedience and satisfaction of Christ unto them." The WCF concludes, "Faith, thus receiving and resting on Christ and his righteousness, is the sole instrument of justification" ("The Westminster Confession of Faith [1646]," in *Reformed Confessions of the Sixteenth Century and Seventeenth Centuries in English Translation, Volume 4, 1600–1693*, ed. James T. Dennison Jr. [Grand Rapids: Reformation Heritage, 2014], 11.1).

However, the bad news in Romans 3 is countered by good news. The righteousness of God, says Paul, has been "manifested apart from the law, although the Law and the Prophets bear witness to it" (3:21). But Paul is more specific still, for it is the "righteousness of God through faith in Jesus Christ for all who believe," Jew and Gentile (Rom. 3:22).[3] While we have sinned and fall short of the glory of God, we are justified by God's grace as a gift, and this occurs through the redemption that is in Christ Jesus. Notice, justification is by grace alone. Justification is not earned or merited. Rather, it is a gift, a gift simply to be received by faith. Furthermore, this gift was made possible precisely because God put his Son forward as a "propitiation by his blood" (Rom. 3:25).[4] But again, Christ and his atoning work on our behalf is to be "received by faith." God has shown himself not only to be just but also the justifier of the "one who has faith in Jesus" (Rom. 3:26). The emphasis is not on our works, but on faith. It is through faith that the sinner is justified before God.

Lest one doubt the emphasis placed on justification by grace alone through faith alone, Paul is especially clear in what he chooses to say next. It is because justification is a gift, received by faith, that no sinner can boast before God. Boasting, in other words, is excluded (Rom. 3:27). On what basis, one might ask, is boasting excluded? Is it excluded by a law of works? "No, but by the law of faith. For we hold that one is justified by faith apart from works of the law" (Rom. 3:27–28). Paul could not be more forthright: justification is *not* by works of the law. Rather, justification is by faith and faith alone. If justification is by works of the law, then man has grounds to boast. If his own good works or merit play a role in his justification (even if this role is minimal), then he has a basis on which to brag. To the contrary, says Paul, boasting is absolutely excluded. Why? It is excluded because there is nothing, not even the smallest good deed, that gives man right standing before God.[5] Rather, the sinner is declared right before God purely because of Christ, who was put forward as a propitiation by his blood. And it is by trusting in Christ, depending upon and receiving his atoning, substitutionary work on the cross, that a sinner is justified.

3. Thomas R. Schreiner, *Romans*, BECNT (Grand Rapids: Baker, 1998), 181–99. When it comes to texts such as Romans 3:22, 26; Galatians 2:16, 20; 3:22; Ephesians 3:12; and Philippians 3:9, there is debate as to whether Paul is using a subjective genitive ("the faithfulness of Christ") or an objective genitive ("faith in Christ"). As assumed throughout this book, I find the arguments for the objective genitive most convincing. For a summary of the debate, see Thomas R. Schreiner, *40 Questions about Christians and Biblical Law* (Grand Rapids: Kregel, 2010), 134–37.

4. Schreiner, *Romans*, 190–99.

5. Douglas J. Moo, *The Epistle to the Romans* NICNT (Grand Rapids: Eerdmans, 1996), 246; Schreiner, *Romans*, 200–8.

Abraham's Faith (Genesis 15:6; Romans 4:3–5)

Not only is Romans 3:21–31 clear in its exclusion of good works as contributing in any way to our justification, but so is Romans 4 with the example of Abraham. Was Abraham justified by works? If so, says Paul, then he has something to boast about. But what does Scripture actually say concerning Abraham? It says that "Abraham believed God, and it was counted to him as righteousness" (Rom. 4:3).

In the context of Genesis 15, God appears to Abraham and makes a covenant with him, promising to give him an heir. Through this heir God will make Abraham into a great nation, giving him as many descendants as the stars in the sky. Did Abraham believe the Lord? The text gives us the answer: "And he believed the LORD, and he counted it to him as righteousness" (Gen. 15:6). The key question for Paul, looking back on this incident, is this: Is Abraham counted righteous because of his works, or by faith? Abraham was counted righteous by God not because of works he performed but because he trusted in *God's promise*.[6] Paul concludes,

> Now to the one who works, his wages are not counted as a gift but as his due. And to the one who does not work but believes in him who justifies the ungodly, his faith is counted as righteousness, just as David also speaks of the blessing of the one to whom God counts righteousness apart from works: "Blessed are those whose lawless deeds are forgiven, and whose sins are covered; blessed is the man against whom the Lord will not count his sin" (Rom. 4:5–8; citing Ps. 32:1–2).

Paul lays before us not only the example of Abraham but David as well. Citing Psalm 32:1–2, David also bears witness to the fact that God counts the ungodly righteous apart from works.

Paul, however, anticipates an objection: Perhaps Abraham was righteous before God because of his obedience in being circumcised. Paul counters by demonstrating that Abraham's faith was counted as righteousness *before* circumcision (Rom. 4:10).[7] "He received the sign of circumcision as a seal of the righteousness that he had by faith while he was still uncircumcised" (Rom. 4:11). As a result, he not only became the father of those who would be circumcised and walk in the faith of their father Abraham, but also of the uncircumcised (Gentiles), that is, all those who believe (Rom. 4:11–12).

---

6. J. V. Fesko, *Justification: Understanding the Classic Reformed Doctrine* (Phillipsburg, NJ: P&R, 2008), 191. Also see Gerhard von Rad, *Genesis*, OTL (Philadelphia: Westminster, 1972), 185.

7. Moo, *Romans*, 268.

Paul does not leave us with Abraham, however, but transitions from Abraham to those in the new covenant. Like Abraham, whose faith was counted to him as righteousness, so also are we counted righteous, not by works, but through faith. As Paul explains, the "words 'it was counted to him' were not written for his sake alone, but for ours also." How so? Paul explains, "It will be counted to us who believe in him who raised from the dead Jesus our Lord, who was delivered up for our trespasses and raised for our justification" (Rom. 4:24–25). Paul concludes, "we have been justified by faith," and therefore we have "peace with God through our Lord Jesus Christ" (Rom. 5:1).

Justified by Faith in Christ (Galatians 2:16; 3:11; 5:4)

Paul's emphasis on justification by faith alone is reiterated in Galatians. In chapter 2, Paul describes how he opposed Peter to his face "because he stood condemned" (Gal. 2:11). Previously Peter ate with Gentile believers, but when "certain men came from James," Peter drew back and separated himself, only eating with Jewish Christians. These "certain men" were part of the "circumcision party," a group of Jews who demanded that the ceremonies of the Mosaic law and covenant, with regard to circumcision, special days, and food, be followed. In this instance, it is likely that these men were advocating that Jewish Christians eat separately from Gentile Christians, thereby following the kosher dietary laws.[8] Peter, fearing these men, succumbed despite his previous fellowship with Gentile believers. Subsequently, these Gentile believers felt as though they were second-class Christians. Unless they were to follow the ceremonial laws of the Jews (including circumcision [Gal. 2:3; 5:2–12; 6:12–15], dietary laws [Gal. 2:12–14], and holidays and festival days [Gal. 4:10]), they were considered lower-ranked members of the church.

However, as Paul's opposition to Peter demonstrates, Peter's actions were in direct conflict with the gospel of justification by faith alone. By treating the Gentile believers in this way, Peter and the others were communicating that in order to really gain right standing before God one had to live like a Jew. Yet, as Paul explains in Galatians 2:4, such a position leads back into slavery. Paul resisted this temptation; to give in was to destroy the "truth of the gospel" (Gal. 2:5). Paul knew their "conduct was not in step with the truth of the gospel" (Gal. 2:14), so he opposed Peter in front of everyone, saying, "If you, though a Jew, live like a Gentile and not like a Jew, how can you force Gentiles to live like Jews?" (Gal. 2:14).

Paul, in light of this background with Peter and the circumcision party, transitions into the doctrine of justification by faith alone. "We ourselves are Jews by birth and not Gentile sinners; yet we know that a person is not justified by works of the law but through faith in Jesus Christ, so we also have believed

---

8. Again, my purpose here is not to interact with the New Perspective on Paul, but see works in bibliography by Piper, Schreiner, and Westerholm.

in Christ Jesus, in order to be justified by faith in Christ and not by works of the law, because by works of the law no one will be justified" (Gal. 2:15–16). Having clearly affirmed that justification is *not* by works, but rather through faith in Jesus Christ, Paul rebukes the "foolish Galatians," asking them if they received the Spirit "by works of the law or by hearing with faith" (Gal. 3:2). "Are you so foolish? Having begun by the Spirit, are you now being perfected by the flesh? Did you suffer so many things in vain—if indeed it was in vain? Does he who supplies the Spirit to you and works miracles among you do so by works of the law, or by hearing with faith—just as Abraham 'believed God, and it was counted to him as righteousness'?" (Gal. 3:3–6).

Next, Paul shows that those who rely on works of the law are not justified before God but are cursed. As Deuteronomy 27:26 says, "Cursed be everyone who does not abide by all things written in the Book of the Law, and do them" (Rom. 3:10). It is surely the case, as Paul makes clear in Romans 3:11–12, that no man can perfectly abide by all things written in the Law, for there is no one who is righteous and no one who does good. Paul then concludes, "it is evident that no one is justified before God by the law, for 'The righteous shall live by faith.' But the law is not of faith, rather 'The one who does them shall live by them'" (Rom. 3:11–12; citing Hab. 2:4 and Lev. 18:5). Nevertheless, Christ redeemed us from the curse of the law, and he did so by becoming a curse for us (Gal. 3:13). Therefore, it is not by works of the law that a sinner is justified, but through faith in Jesus Christ.[9] It is "in Christ Jesus" that the blessing of Abraham comes even to Gentiles, Gentiles who receive the "promised Spirit through faith." Those who are the true children of Abraham are those who place their faith in Jesus.

By Grace You Have Been Saved through Faith (Ephesians 2:8–9)

A third passage that supports justification by faith alone is Ephesians 2:8–9. Much like Romans 3–4, Paul begins Ephesians 2 describing man's total depravity. All of mankind is dead in trespasses and sins, and by nature children of wrath. There is no possible way the sinner can be justified by his own works, for he does not obey the law (indeed, he cannot; Rom. 8:7–8), but instead he carries out his sinful desires. Hence, God's grace is absolutely necessary, not just in part, but in whole.

> And you were dead in the trespasses and sins in which you once walked. . . . But God, being rich in mercy, because of the great love with which he loved us, even when we were dead in our trespasses, made us alive together with Christ— by grace you have been saved—and raised us up with him and seated us with him in the heavenly places in Christ Jesus, so that in the coming ages he might show the immeasurable

---

9. Thomas R. Schreiner, *Galatians*, ZECNT (Grand Rapids: Zondervan, 2010), 166–67.

> riches of his grace in kindness toward us in Christ Jesus. For by grace you have been saved through faith. And this is not your own doing; it is the gift of God, not a result of works, so that no one may boast (Eph. 2:1–2a, 4–9).

Few passages highlight with such clarity the gracious nature of salvation like Ephesians 2. Salvation is not by works, Paul states. True, we were created for good works (Eph. 2:10), but these good works are not the basis of our right standing before God; instead, they are the fruit and result of being born again and declared just before God.

Moreover, Paul makes plain that our salvation is by grace alone through faith alone.[10] Although we fully deserve it, God has delivered us from judgment and condemnation, and he has done so by sending his own Son (John 3:16; 1 Tim. 1:15; 1 John 3:5; 4:10, 14; 5:11–12), making us alive together with Christ (Eph. 2:5). This is not, says Paul, our own doing, "not a result of works, so that no one may boast" (Eph. 2:8–9). Rather, we have been saved by grace through faith (Eph. 2:8). Salvation, in other words, is a gift, given to us by God.[11] Once again, Paul is clear: We are not saved by our works, but by grace through faith in Jesus Christ.

The Righteousness of God That Depends on Faith (Philippians 3:8–9)

That justification is not by works, not even in the slightest, but by faith alone, is again evident in Philippians 3:8–9:

> Indeed, I count everything as loss because of the surpassing worth of knowing Christ Jesus my Lord. For his sake I have suffered the loss of all things and count them as rubbish, in order that I may gain Christ and be found in him, not having a righteousness of my own that comes from the law, but that which comes through faith in Christ, the righteousness from God that depends on faith.

As we've seen in Questions 24–25, justification includes the imputation of the righteousness of Christ. The righteousness of Jesus is credited or reckoned to

---

10. Paul does not use the word justification in Ephesians 2:8–9, but salvation. Most likely, Paul is using the word "salvation" as a broader concept in Ephesians 2 than the word "justification." Nevertheless, salvation surely encompasses justification. So it is safe to conclude that Ephesians 2:8–9, though not mentioning justification specifically, certainly would entail that justification is by grace alone.

11. Frank Thielman, *Ephesians*, BECNT (Grand Rapids: Baker, 2010), 143–46; Peter T. O'Brien, *The Letter to the Ephesians*, PNTC (Grand Rapids: Eerdmans, 1999), 167–69; Clinton E. Arnold, *Ephesians*, ZECNT (Grand Rapids: Zondervan, 2010), 139–40.

those who believe. Therefore, the believer's right standing before God is not on the basis of his own righteousness (not even in part), but rather on the basis of an alien righteousness, namely, that of Jesus Christ. As Paul asserts, the righteousness that gives us right legal standing before God, our Judge and Maker, is not our own righteousness, one that comes from obeying the law; instead, our right legal standing is a righteousness that God gives to us as a free gift. We do not receive this righteousness by meriting it or performing good works, but simply through faith in God's Son. As Paul says, "the righteousness from God" is one that "depends on faith" and "comes through faith in Christ." Once again we see that it is through faith, and faith alone (*sola fide*), that the sinner is justified before God.[12]

Summary

According to Scripture, justification is not through faith plus works, but by grace alone, through faith alone. The righteousness that gives us right legal standing before God is not a righteousness of our own that comes from obeying the law; rather, our right legal standing comes by a righteousness that God gives to us. It is not a righteousness we merit but one we simply receive as a gift through faith in Jesus.

REFLECTION QUESTIONS

1. In Romans 3:21–31, how does Paul view works of the law, and what does this mean for one's doctrine of justification?

2. Read Genesis 15. What key events in the story of Abraham might support justification by faith alone?

3. In light of Paul's letter to the Galatians, how were Peter's actions inconsistent with the gospel that the Gentiles had embraced by faith?

4. What kind of righteousness does Paul claim he possesses in Philippians 3:8–9?

5. Why is it that justification by grace alone through faith alone should move us not to boasting but instead to humility?

---

12. Therefore, it is appropriate to title faith the *instrumental means* of justification, not the basis of justification (which is the work of Christ). See Question 18.

What Does It Mean to Be Adopted as Children of God?

What does it mean in Scripture that those who believe then become children of God? What does it mean in Scripture to be adopted by God? In the most basic sense, adoption occurs when God makes us one of his children, a member of his family. Before we were God's enemies, now we are his sons and daughters, even his heirs (Rom. 8:17; Heb. 6:7; James 2:5). Before we belonged to our father, the devil (John 8:44), but now we have a new Father, who has adopted us into his family through Christ Jesus. Before we were strangers and aliens, but now we are fellow citizens, members of the household of God (Eph. 2:18–19).

Adoption in Scripture

The doctrine of adoption can be found throughout the New Testament gospels and epistles.[1] Perhaps one of the most important passages in Scripture describing our adoption is Galatians 4:1–7, where Paul describes our former slavery to sin and the world. However, when the "fullness of time had come," says Paul "God sent forth his Son, born of woman, born under the law, to redeem those who were under the law, so that we might receive adoption as sons." What blessings come to those who are now sons? Paul answers, "And because you are sons, God has sent the Spirit of his Son into our hearts, crying, 'Abba! Father!' So you are no longer a slave, but a son, and if a son, then an heir through God." Christ has redeemed us from the law, and in turn made us

---

1. For three extensive studies on adoption, see Trevor J. Burke, *Adopted into God's Family: Exploring a Pauline Metaphor*, NSBT 22, ed. D. A. Carson (Downers Grove, IL: InterVarsity Press, 2006); Robert A. Peterson, *Adopted by God: From Wayward Sinners to Cherished Children* (Phillipsburg, NJ: P&R, 2001); David B. Garner, *Sons in the Son: The Riches and Reach of Adoption in Christ* (Phillipsburg, NJ: P&R, 2016).

sons. As sons we possess the Spirit of Christ so that our identity is now one of an heir. Of course, Christ himself is the "heir of all things" (Heb. 1:2; cf. Luke 20:14), but as those who are "in Christ" we too share in his great inheritance. His "inheritance is a public trust" says Horton, and therefore those who are in him "hold all things in common with Christ."[2] For that reason God is unashamed to call us "brothers," for we now belong to his family (Heb. 2:11) and our elder brother is Christ (Heb. 2:17–18).

Paul states something similar in Romans 8:14–17:

> For all who are led by the Spirit of God are sons of God. For you did not receive the spirit of slavery to fall back into fear, but you have received the Spirit of adoption as sons, by whom we cry, "Abba! Father!" The Spirit himself bears witness with our spirit that we are children of God, and if children, then heirs—heirs of God and fellow heirs with Christ, provided we suffer with him in order that we may also be glorified with him.

According to Paul, those adopted not only have the Spirit but have God as their own Father. And if we are sons of the Father, then so also are we heirs with his Son, Christ Jesus, receiving all the benefits he has won for us. What is so shocking about Paul's claim (that we are "heirs") is not merely that we are heirs of these salvific benefits, but that we are heirs of God himself. As Paul himself says, as God's children we are "heirs of God."[3] And much more, for we are "fellow heirs with Christ" as well. As Paul says in Galatians 3:28, if we are "Christ's" then we are "Abraham's offspring, heirs according to promise."

Moreover, we must not miss the role of the Spirit. In both Galatians 4:1–7 and Romans 8:14–17, it is the Holy Spirit who is sent. He is called the "Spirit of adoption" and for good reason too since it is through him that we cry out, "Abba! Father!" The Spirit, says Paul, is the one who bears witness with our spirit that we are God's children. Therefore, he plays a central role in granting God's children assurance. However, it is not as if the Spirit mystically and subjectively "whispers to us 'You are God's son,'" giving us *new* revelation "over and above Scripture." Rather, says Burke, the Spirit's work is "reiterative rather than innovative."[4] He is reminding us and making us aware of what Christ has already done and on that basis who we are in Christ. "God's Spirit is sent into our hearts to let us know we are his adopted sons, for when doubts

---

2. Michael Horton, *Pilgrim Theology: Core Doctrines for Christian Disciples* (Grand Rapids: Zondervan, 2011), 298.

3. Thomas R. Schreiner, *Romans*, BECNT (Grand Rapids: Baker Academic, 1998), 427; Peterson, *Adopted by God*, 161; Burke, *Adopted into God's Family*, 98; C. E. B. Cranfield, *Romans*, vol. 1, ICC (Edinburgh: T&T Clark, 1975), 419.

4. Burke, *Adopted into God's Family*, 150; cf. Sinclair Ferguson, *Children of the Living God* (Edinburgh: Banner of Truth, 1989), 73.

start to creep in, as they invariably do, knowledge of our standing before God is important."[5]

Many other New Testament passages say the same. For example, at the start of John's Gospel we learn that though Christ came to his own people, they rejected him. Yet, "all who did receive him, who believed in his name, he gave the right to become children of God, who were born, not of blood nor of the will of the flesh nor of the will of man, but of God" (John 1:12). By faith in Christ one is adopted as one of God's children. On the other hand, those who disbelieve in Christ remain "children of wrath" (Eph. 2:3), "sons of disobedience" (Eph. 2:2; 5:6), and sons of their "father the devil" (John 8:42–44).

Furthermore, adoption is not limited to Jews but is for Gentiles as well. The true children of Abraham are not those of the flesh but those of the promise (Rom. 9:7–8; Gal. 4:28, 31; Eph. 3:6; 1 Peter 3:6). In the old covenant, says Paul, "We were held captive under the law, imprisoned until the coming faith would be revealed." Paul concludes that "the law was our guardian until Christ came, in order that we might be justified by faith" (Gal. 3:23–24). But now that faith has come, "we are no longer under a guardian, for in Christ Jesus you are all sons of God, through faith" (Gal. 3:25–26). Sonship (adoption), in other words, comes through faith, faith in God's Son Jesus Christ. Therefore, John appropriately describes believers as those who have been given the love of the Father "that we should be called children of God" (1 John 3:1–2; cf. Rom. 8:23; Heb. 2:11–13).

Adoption: Already, Not Yet

While adoption occurs as a result of faith in Jesus Christ, it is crucial to note that Scripture also speaks of our adoption as past, present, and future. First, adoption is not just something that takes place in time upon profession of faith in Christ, but God predestined his elect to adoption before the foundation of the universe. As Paul explains in Ephesians 1:4b–6, "In love he [God] predestined us for adoption as sons through Jesus Christ, according to the purpose of his will, to the praise of his glorious grace, with which he has blessed us in the Beloved." Predestination, in other words, is the *origin* of our adoption as sons.[6] In light of the unconditional nature of God's electing choice (see Questions 10–11), it is also clear that adoption is due to God's grace *alone*. Not only is human merit excluded in election but in adoption too, and therefore it is appropriate to say that we are adopted by grace alone (*sola gratia*). Adoption is just as much a gift from God's free grace as other aspects of salvation. As with election, in adoption man's boasting is excluded.[7]

---

5. Burke, *Adopted into God's Family*, 150.
6. John Murray, "Adoption," in *Collected Writings of John Murray* (Edinburgh: Banner of Truth, 1976), 2:230.
7. Burke, *Adopted into God's Family*, 75.

Pride in ourselves and conceit over what we have done are incompatible with adoption. Instead, the proper response is humility, expressing our gratitude to the Father for making us part of his family.[8]

Additionally, we cannot fail to observe just how warm and relational predestination is, since God chose us *to be sons*. He predestined us to be part of *his family*. Contrary to popular opinion, predestination is not a cold, mean, heartless, and random decision by God, but is inseparably connected to God's familial love. As Paul demonstrates in Ephesians 1:4–6, predestination is joined to the prepositional phrase "in love" for the very purpose of highlighting just how affectionate the Father has been in electing us to be his adopted sons and daughters.[9] How extraordinary it is that though there was nothing in us to love—nothing in our character or record that, as Packer says, "shows us worthy to bear his name"—and though we were in no way "fit for a place in God's family," God set his saving love on us.[10]

Second, while God predestines his elect to adoption, and while adoption becomes a reality in time upon faith in Christ, Scripture speaks of our adoption as a future reality as well. As Paul says in Romans 8:23, "And not only the creation, but we ourselves, who have the firstfruits of the Spirit, groan inwardly as we wait eagerly for adoption as sons, the redemption of our bodies" (cf. Gal. 5:5). Here Paul connects the future resurrection of our bodies to our adoption as sons. So while we already have been adopted by God, we eagerly await the return of Christ and the resurrection of our bodies whereby our adoption will be finally complete (Phil. 3:21). "As Christians we are adopted into God's family, yet we will not experience the consummation of our adoption until the day of the resurrection."[11]

In summary, adoption was planned in eternity past, made a reality in the present, and yet awaits future glory. "The biblical theology of adoption, then, encompasses (1) the Father's love from all eternity, (2) redemption from past enslavement, (3) a status and way of life in the present, and (4) a future expectation of glory."[12]

The Basis of Adoption

So far we have seen that the *origin* of our adoption is to be found in God's electing choice before the foundation of the world (Eph. 1:3–6). That said, the *basis* or *ground* of adoption is the work of Christ. Notice that in Ephesians

---

8. Ibid., 76.
9. Ibid., 76–77.
10. J. I. Packer, *Knowing God* (London: Hodder & Stoughton, 1988), 241.
11. Thomas R. Schreiner and Ardel B. Caneday, *The Race Set Before Us: A Biblical Theology of Perseverance and Assurance* (Downers Grove, IL: InterVarsity Press, 2001), 68.
12. Robert L. Reymond, *A New Systematic Theology of the Christian Faith*, 2nd ed. (Nashville: Thomas Nelson, 1998), 761. Also see Burke, *Adopted into God's Family*, 43–44, 135–37, 177–93.

1:3–6, Paul says God, out of love, predestined us "for adoption as sons through Jesus Christ." Paul says the same in Galatians 4:5; though we were enslaved to the world, God, when the "fullness of time had come," sent his Son, "born under the law, to redeem those who were under the law, so that we might receive adoption as sons." It is because Christ redeemed us who were under the law that we are no longer slaves, but sons and heirs (Gal. 4:6–7). Both of these texts demonstrate that the basis of adoption, like justification, is to be found in the work of Christ.[13] Naturally, then, there is a profoundly Christological nature to our adoption.[14] Not only is our adoption grounded in the work of Christ, but adoption is intimately connected to union with Christ (as seen in Questions 8–9). Adoption and union with Christ are "complementary aspects."[15]

Adoption in the Order of Salvation

The danger in reading specific passages on adoption is to think that adoption and regeneration (the new birth; see Questions 15–17) are synonymous. However, the two concepts, though closely related, are actually distinct for a variety of reasons. First, while regeneration or new birth is a change in our nature (i.e., we are made new creatures), adoption, like justification, is a judicial act.[16] As John Murray clarifies, adoption is "the bestowal of a status, or standing, not the generating within us of a new nature or character." In other words, adoption "concerns a relationship and not the attitude or disposition which enables us to recognize and cultivate that relationship."[17] In regeneration the Spirit renews our nature and disposition; in adoption the Father gives the regenerate the right and privilege to be his son or daughter. Furthermore, the word "regeneration" or "new birth" itself conveys a different meaning than adoption. The difference is clearly seen when we think of how birth and adoption work in a human family. In the former, the mother physically gives birth to a child (i.e., natural generation), while in the latter the child is not physically an offspring but is transferred or brought into the family, not by birth, but through a legal process.

---

13. See Burke, *Adopted into God's Family*, 42; Ferguson, *Children of the Living God*, 30.
14. John Calvin, *Institutes of the Christian Religion*, ed. John T. McNeil, trans. Ford Lewis Battles, LCC, vols. 20–21 (Philadelphia: Westminster, 1960), 2.12.2; Burke, *Adopted into God's Family*, 188.
15. John Murray, *Redemption Accomplished and Applied* (Grand Rapids: Eerdmans, 1955), 170.
16. This does not mean, however, that relational categories are precluded. Rather, the relational is grounded upon the legal. See Michael Horton, "Traditional Reformed View," in *Justification: Five Views*, eds. James K. Beilby and Paul R. Eddy (Downers Grove, IL: InterVarsity Press, 2001), 110.
17. Murray, *Redemption Accomplished and Applied*, 133. Also see Michael Horton, *The Christian Faith* (Grand Rapids: Zondervan, 2011), 645; Raymond, *Systematic Theology*, 761.

Moreover, in the New Testament adoption is not directly connected with the new birth, but rather with saving faith. For example, John opens his gospel saying, "But to all who did receive him, who believed in his name, he gave the right to become children of God, who were born, not of blood nor of the will of the flesh nor of the will of man, but of God" (John 1:12–13). Adoption and the new birth are both mentioned by John, but they are not spoken of interchangeably. Rather they are to be distinguished from one another.[18] Adoption ("the right to become children of God") is connected to belief (faith). All those who believe are given the right to become children of God. And all those who believe and become children of God do so because they have already been born of God, something that is not by "the will of man, but of God." In other words, first we are born again (regeneration), then comes faith (conversion and justification), which is followed by adoption.[19] For example, consider how Paul writes to the Galatians: "Now before faith came, we were held captive under the law, imprisoned until the coming faith would be revealed. So then, the law was our guardian until Christ came, in order that we might be justified by faith. But now that faith has come, we are no longer under a guardian, for in Christ Jesus you are all sons of God, through faith" (Gal. 3:23–26). Because justification by faith has occurred we are no longer captive to the law but rather are sons of God in Christ Jesus. It is through faith and as a result of faith that we are adopted by God. Adoption, therefore, is the result of conversion in the order of salvation.[20]

But what, you might ask, is the relationship between justification and adoption? After all, the two are closely related since it is through faith that one is adopted by God. In response, we must recognize that the two, though closely related, are nevertheless distinct from one another. In regeneration we receive new spiritual life, and in justification we are declared not guilty before God, now having a new status in Christ. Our sins have been forgiven, and now we have a right legal standing before a holy God. However, our salvation takes one giant step further in adoption. Yes, we are *new creatures* (regeneration) with a *new status* (justification), but in adoption we now have a *new*

---

18. There are many good reasons to interpret "children of God" as referring to adoption, not regeneration. See Matthew Barrett, *Salvation by Grace: The Case for Effectual Calling and Regeneration* (Phillipsburg, NJ: P&R, 2013), 163–67.

19. We are referring not to a *chronological* order but to a *logical* order.

20. Some might object by appealing to Galatians 4:6, where we read that because we are sons God has sent his Spirit. The assumption would be that this is a reference to the Spirit's work in regeneration, and therefore must be the result of adoption. However, in Galatians 3:26 Paul directly connects adoption to faith, not regeneration. We should interpret Galatians 4:6 not as the Spirit's work of regeneration, but as the Spirit's subsequent work, whereby he gives the sinner assurance that he is part of the family of God (cf. Rom. 8:15–16). See Wayne Grudem, *Systematic Theology* (Grand Rapids: Zondervan, 1994), 738.

relationship with the Father, and as one of his children we now receive and share all the spiritual blessings to be found in Christ Jesus.[21]

It is accurate to say then that the sinner's adoption is the fruit of justification, its natural result and outcome.[22] As William Ames remarks, "Adoption of its own nature requires and presupposes the reconciliation found in justification. . . . The first fruit of adoption is that Christian liberty by which all believers are freed from the bondage of the law, sin, and the world."[23] Such liberty is equally accompanied by an enormous privilege. Having been clothed with the righteousness of our Savior, we now join his redeemed assembly as children of the King. "In Christ," Horton rejoices, "our rags are exchanged for robes of regal splendor, and we are seated at the same table with Abraham, Isaac, and Jacob."[24] Justified, we join the wedding feast and can rightfully do so since the king has dressed us in his own wedding garments (Matt. 22:1–13; cf. Isa. 61:10–11). Much like the prodigal son, we have a father who has sprinted to us and before we can finish our confession he has placed on us the "best robe" and killed the fattened calf for a celebratory feast (Luke 15:22–23).[25] As those who have been legally adopted, we now, as children, enjoy the riches of our Father's kingdom, and the greatest jewel of all is knowing him.

We must conclude, then, that (1) the legal basis for adoption is justification (much like sanctification and glorification), and (2) adoption itself is both legal and relational in nature, the former grounding the latter. Horton brings this point home: Adoption is "not a goal held out to children who successfully imitate their parents; nor is it the result of an infusion of familial characteristics or genes." Instead, adoption "is a change in legal status that issues in a relationship that is gradually reflected in the child's identity, characteristics, and actions. From the courtroom, with the legal status and inheritance unalterably established, the child moves into the security of a growing and thriving future."[26]

---

21. Reymond, *A New Systematic Theology of the Christian Faith*, 759.
22. This seems to be assumed by the WCF: "All those that are justified, God vouchsafeth, in and for His only Son Jesus Christ, to make partakers of the grace of adoption, by which they are taken into the number, and enjoy the liberties and privileges of the children of God, have His name put upon them, receive the spirit of adoption, have access to the throne of grace with boldness, are enabled to cry, Abba, Father, are pitied, protected, provided for, and chastened by Him as by a Father: yet never cast off, but sealed to the day of redemption; and inherit the promises, as heirs of everlasting salvation" ("The Westminster Confession of Faith [1646]," in *Reformed Confessions of the Sixteenth Century and Seventeenth Centuries in English Translation, Volume 4, 1600–1693*, ed. James T. Dennison Jr. [Grand Rapids: Reformation Heritage, 2014], 12).
23. William Ames, *The Marrow of Theology*, trans. John Dykstra Eusden (1623; Grand Rapids: Baker, repr. 1997), 165. Also see Horton, *The Christian Faith*, 645.
24. Horton, *Pilgrim Theology*, 297.
25. Ibid., 297.
26. Ibid., 300.

What Benefits Do We Receive as Adopted Children?

What benefits do we receive having been adopted by God? There are many! Consider ten benefits that result from being adopted by God.[27]

1. We can now come to the Father directly in prayer (Matt. 6:9).
2. As children of God we now have God as our Father. Whereas before God stood against us as judge, now, having been justified by grace through faith, and then adopted by God into his family, we no longer stand in judgment but are one of his own children. Therefore, we enter into a loving relationship with God as our Father. No longer are we slaves, but sons (Gal. 4:7).
3. God has bestowed upon us the Holy Spirit who gives us assurance that we are his children (Rom. 8:14–16). Moreover, the Spirit comforts us and even empowers us to live the Christian life (Luke 11:13).
4. As his children, our Father takes care of our needs (Matt. 6:32).
5. Because he has adopted us as his own, the Father pours out upon us many good gifts (Matt. 7:11).
6. As children, and as fellow heirs with Christ (Rom. 8:17; Heb. 2:11–13), we have an inheritance that is eternal, imperishable, undefiled, and unfading, kept in heaven for us (1 Peter 1:4; cf. Rev. 2:26–27; 3:21; Heb. 1:14).[28]
7. As his adopted children, we are able to approach our Father asking him to forgive us our sins (Matt. 6:9–12), with confidence that our relationship with our Father will be restored after displeasing him by our sin (1 John 1:9; 3:19–22).
8. Those who are adopted by God are also led, guided, and directed by the Spirit of God in holiness (Rom. 8:14).
9. As children of God, no longer are we punished as unbelievers, but we receive the loving discipline of our heavenly Father who desires to see us walk according to his holy ways (Heb. 12:5–10; cf. Eph. 5:1; Phil. 2:15; 1 Peter 1:14–16; 1 John 3:10).
10. Those adopted by God will not only share in the sufferings of Christ but in his glory (Rom. 8:17).

In conclusion, what greater privilege can a sinner receive than being declared a child of God? Surely adoption reminds us that we have received the highest honor, for though we were sinners, children of Adam, because of what Christ has done, we are now declared children of God, heirs of all the promises of God, including everlasting life.

---

27. Many of these points are indebted to Reymond, *Systematic Theology*, 762; Grudem, *Systematic Theology*, 739–41.
28. Horton, *The Christian Faith*, 644.

Summary

Scripture teaches that though we were enemies, now we are sons, heirs, children of God the Father, members of his household, adopted into his family, receiving all of the saving benefits purchased for us by Christ. There is an already/not yet aspect to our adoption. While our adoption was predestined before the foundation of the world, came to fruition in time and space by the power of the Holy Spirit and through faith, its ultimate fulfillment and consummation awaits the redemption of our bodies. Adoption should not be confused with regeneration and justification but should be distinguished from both in important ways, following conversion in the order of salvation.

REFLECTION QUESTIONS

1. How does the concept of adoption differ from regeneration, justification, and sanctification?

2. What does it mean to be adopted by God, and where in Scripture do we see biblical support for such an idea?

3. What are some of the benefits we receive having been adopted by God? Explain why these are significant.

4. If we have been adopted by God already, what does Scripture mean by referring to adoption as a future reality as well?

5. Does the imagery of adoption give you a fresh appreciation for what God has done to bring you into his family as one of his own children?

PART 5

Sanctification, Perseverance, and Glorification

QUESTION 28

What Is the Difference between Definitive and Progressive Sanctification?

What is holiness? We know what holiness is and looks like by looking at God, who is called "holy" repeatedly in Scripture (e.g., Josh. 24:19; Ps. 99:5, 9; Isa. 54:5; Jer. 51:5; Rev. 4:8; 20:6). God alone is said to be holy (1 Sam. 2:2). No one makes him holy, nor does he become holy (as if he wasn't holy before). In fact, we can go so far as to say that by definition God *is* holy.

Entailed in such a statement are two truths: (1) God is set apart from everything else, transcendent in his glory (Isa. 6:1–5).[1] There is a Creator-creature distinction, God being set apart from his creation, above it and distinct from it. (2) God is perfect in purity (i.e., ethical holiness; cf. Ps. 77:13; Isa. 5:16), and so he stands in stark contrast to stained, corrupt, and guilty sinners. If we are to be holy, therefore, it will have to be God's doing. God does this in two ways: (1) He sets us apart as holy and (2) he makes us holy.[2]

These two ways correspond to definitive and progressive sanctification. Peterson captures both aspects in his definition of holiness: "Holiness means *being set apart for a relationship with the Holy One, to display his character in every sphere of life*."[3] God "desires that the status of holiness which he gives us

---

1. In Isaiah 6, we actually see *both* God's holy transcendence and his holy purity.
2. To qualify, God's holiness is inherent to his being, but our holiness is God-given and derivative. "God's holiness is natural while ours is by grace or derivation from the triune fullness" (Michael Allen, *Justification and the Gospel: Understanding the Contexts and Controversies* [Grand Rapids: Baker Academic, 2013], 46).
3. David Peterson, *Possessed by God: A New Testament Theology of Sanctification and Holiness* (Downers Grove, IL: InterVarsity Press, 1995), 24 (emphasis original).

through the redemptive work of Christ should be expressed in a quality of life reflecting his character and will."[4]

Definitive and Progressive Sanctification

Typically when Christians refer to "sanctification," they have in mind the *lifelong process* of being progressively *made* holy. However, we must not move too quickly to this inner renewal. As Michael Horton explains, "Before we can speak of our being put to holy use and growing in grace, we must see that sanctification is first of all God's act of setting us apart from the world for himself."[5] Horton's point is an important one. Our life is not to be reformed merely for the sake of being a good person; no, the inward reformation and renewal is meant to bring us into line with the identity we already have in our Savior.[6] As those who are already *in Christ*, we are now being made *like Christ*. What we do, therefore, is to conform to who we are. In theological terms, progressive sanctification is grounded upon definitive sanctification, a distinct, definitive, and instantaneous act of God at the start of the Christian life. Since we have been declared holy, we are now to live in a holy way.[7] We are not made holy in order to be set apart, but we are set apart by God as holy so that we might then live in a holy manner. As Peterson says, "Believers are definitively consecrated to God in order to live dedicated and holy lives, to his glory."[8] And as Packer puts it, the "positional holiness of consecration and acceptance underlies the personal transformation that is normally what we have in mind when we speak of sanctification."[9]

This order and distinction is seen throughout Scripture. Horton observes that in "both the Hebrew and the Greek, the root of the verb translated 'to sanctify' is 'to cut.'" "God's act of sanctifying cuts people, places, and things *away* from their ordinary association *for* his own use."[10] Applied to definitive sanctification, we have been set apart by means of the sacrifice of Christ and

---

4. "For those who are genuinely consecrated to God, the goal can be nothing less than blamelessness in word and action (*cf.* Phil. 2:15). God himself is pure and blameless and he desires his children to reflect his character" (ibid., 79).

5. Michael Horton, *Pilgrim Theology: Core Doctrines for Christian Disciples* (Grand Rapids: Zondervan, 2011), 313.

6. Or as Horton puts it: "Whereas most people think that the goal of religion is to get people to become something that they are not, the Scriptures call believers to become more and more what they already are in Christ" (ibid.).

7. "We are holy (definitive sanctification); therefore we are to be holy (progressive sanctification)" (ibid.; cf. Peterson, *Possessed by God*, 27).

8. Peterson, *Possessed by God*, 27. For more on definitive sanctification, see John Murray, "Definitive Sanctification," in *Collected Writings of John Murray*, 4 vols. (Edinburgh: Banner of Truth, 1977), 2:277–84.

9. J. I. Packer, *Keep in Step with the Spirit: Finding Fullness in Our Walk with God*, 2nd ed. (Grand Rapids: Baker, 2005), 87.

10. Horton, *Pilgrim Theology*, 311.

his blood of the new covenant (Heb. 10:29). As the author of Hebrews says, "we have been sanctified through the offering of the body of Jesus Christ once for all" (Heb. 10:10). Our Savior "suffered outside the gate in order to sanctify the people through his own blood" (13:12). Paul has something similar in mind when he writes to the Ephesians that Christ "loved the church and gave himself up for her, that he might sanctify [*hagiasē*] her" (Eph. 5:25–26).

As a result of Christ's sacrifice, sin's death grip on us has been broken. No longer does sin have dominion over those who believe in Jesus. "There is therefore now no condemnation for those who are in Christ Jesus" (Rom. 8:1). We have now been set apart as "saints" (e.g., Rom. 1:7), as "those sanctified in Christ Jesus" (1 Cor. 1:2), in order to serve a new master.[11] Liberated from sin's dominion, we now belong to the dominion of our resurrected king. And yet, though we no longer are citizens of this old dominion, the final reality and fulfillment of our new dominion awaits us. On the one hand, our identity is not defined by this transient, wicked world; yet, this side of glory we continue to live in it.[12] There is, in other words, an already/not yet tension to sanctification. We have been definitively sanctified, but we are in the process of being progressively sanctified. Sin's dominion is broken by the cross of Christ, but we still live in a world in which the annihilation of its existence and ongoing effect within us awaits our Lord's second return. So while the war has been won, reorienting and redefining our citizenship so that we are saints of God, the battle with sin rages on within as we long for our final renewal and glorification.[13] So though we are saints (definitive sanctification), purifying is necessary (progressive sanctification). Holiness is both a divine *gift* and a divine *command* (Rom. 12:1; 2 Cor. 7:1; Eph. 1:4; 2:10; 5:25–26; 1 Peter 1:15–16; 1 Thess. 4:3, 7; 5:23).[14]

Both sides of this sanctification coin are present in Scripture. At the opening of his first letter to the Corinthians, for example, Paul addresses "the church of God that is in Corinth, to *those sanctified* in Christ Jesus" (1:2a; cf. 1:30).[15] Later on in the letter, after strongly asserting that the unrighteous will not inherit the kingdom of God, Paul says, "And such were some of you. But you were washed,

---

11. Also consider: 2 Corinthians 1:1; Ephesians 1:1; Philippians 1:1; Colossians 1:2; 1 Peter 1:1–2. For a discussion of these verses, see ibid.

12. "We no longer belong to this passing evil age, although we still live in it" (ibid., 313).

13. Therefore, we might want to qualify the phrase "progressive sanctification," clarifying that its "progressive" nature does not assume the Christian life is a straight line. Change takes time. We have victories; we have moments of failure. So though the line is on the upward climb, it has ups and downs. See Peterson *Possessed by God*, 125.

14. Packer, *Keep in Step with the Spirit*, 80.

15. Peterson adds insight: "Here the perfect passive participle 'sanctified' should be understood as another way of speaking about *their conversion and incorporation into Christ*. It can hardly refer to their holiness of character or conduct, since Paul spends much time in this letter challenging their values and their behaviour, calling them to holiness in an ethical sense. He does this on the basis that they are already sanctified in a relational sense, but need to express that sanctification in lifestyle" (*Possessed by God*, 41).

you *were sanctified*, you were justified in the name of the Lord Jesus Christ and by the Spirit of our God" (6:11). In both of these passages, the grammar leads us to believe that Paul is using sanctification language to refer to a past event that was instantaneous and once for all (cf. Acts 20:32; 26:18).[16] And yet, this same apostle exhorts the Corinthians countless times to flee sexual immorality since their bodies are temples of the Holy Spirit (e.g., 1 Cor. 5:12–20), which assumes the need for progressive sanctification (e.g., "So glorify God in your body"; 5:20). Perhaps Paul had in mind the words of Jesus who said it was necessary for the Father to prune every branch in Christ (the vine) so that it will bear more fruit (John 15:2). And yet, Jesus went on to say, "Already you are clean because of the word that I have spoken to you" (15:3).

Definitive sanctification, to be clear, is central for the New Testament authors. Whether the concept is explicitly stated or quietly implied (usually by the grammar of the text), definitive sanctification characterizes the New Testament letters at every turn (e.g., Acts 20:32; 26:18; Rom. 15:16; 1 Cor. 1:2, 30; 6:11; Eph. 5:25–27; 1 Thess. 4:7; 2 Thess. 2:13–15; Heb. 10:10, 14; 1 Peter 1:2). In his book, *Possessed by God: A New Testament Theology of Sanctification and Holiness,* New Testament scholar David Peterson explains how the New Testament authors do not always use the verb "to sanctify" (*hagiazein*) to "refer to a process of ethical development." Instead, they highlight "the fact that God claimed them as his own and made them members of his holy people." In other words, "He turned them around and brought them to himself in faith and love."[17]

Peterson also makes the insightful point that if our perseverance and progress in sanctification is rooted in our definitive sanctification (and we believe it is), then there are significant implications for how we should live the Christian life.

> Although God calls upon us to express the fact that we have been sanctified by the way we live, our standing with him does not depend on the degree to which we live up to his expectations. It depends on his grace alone. Those who are bowed down by the pressure of temptation and an awareness of failure need to be reminded of the definitive, sanctifying work of God in Christ, by which he has established us as his holy people. On this basis, they should be urged to press on in hope and grasp again by faith the benefits of Christ's sacrifice. Approaching the exalted Lord with

---

16. "Each aorist passive verb in Greek is preceded by the strong adversative 'but' (*alla*), though English translations rarely make this clear. Paul is offering three different descriptions of the same reality, rather than alluding to a process of being washed, then, sanctified, and then justified" (ibid., 45).

17. Peterson, *Possessed by God*, 46.

boldness, we may always receive mercy and find "grace to help in time of need" (Heb. 4:16).[18]

The Nature of Sanctification

So far we have given our attention to *definitive* sanctification, but what are we to make of *progressive* sanctification? Sanctify means "to make holy."[19] Applied to progressive sanctification, being made holy entails a conscious separation from sin, being set apart and devoted to God and his kingdom (John 17:17; Rom. 6:19, 22; 2 Cor. 7:1; 1 Thess. 4:3, 4, 7–8; 2 Tim. 2:21).[20] It is the lifelong process of being made holy (sanctified) by the Holy Spirit, who delivers us from the corruption of sin and renews our nature into the image of our Savior, Jesus Christ, the true, perfect image of God.[21] We can define progressive sanctification, then, as "that gracious and continuous operation of the Holy Spirit, by which He delivers the justified sinner from the pollution of sin, renews his whole nature in the image of God, and enables him to perform good works."[22] This work of the Spirit, unlike regeneration, involves our active participation as we die daily to sin in order to live in a way that is pleasing and glorifying to God. The goal of this lifelong process is to be conformed into the image of our Savior, Jesus Christ, who is the perfect image of God. In short, sanctification is God making us holy.[23]

Right away, however, clarification is needed. When we refer to sanctification or holiness we do not have in mind mere moral improvement or rectitude. "A man may boast of great moral improvement, and yet be an utter stranger to sanctification," Berkhof warns.[24] The biblical idea of holiness and sanctification is far more; it has in mind moral improvement no doubt but always "in relation to God, for God's sake, and with a view to the service of God."[25]

---

18. Ibid., 48 (cf. 67).
19. From the two Latin words *sanctus* (holy) and *facere* (to make). See Hoekema, *Saved by Grace*, 193.
20. Peterson, *Possessed by God*, 17.
21. Sanctification will then come to completion and culmination in our glorification. See, e.g., 1 Thessalonians 3:13 and 5:23.
22. Louis Berkhof, *Systematic Theology* (Edinburgh: Banner of Truth, 2003), 532.
23. This definition is similar to the Westminster Larger Catechism (Q.75): "Sanctification is a work of God's grace, whereby they whom God hath, before the foundation of the world, chosen to be holy, are in time, through the powerful operation of his Spirit applying the death and resurrection of Christ unto them, renewed in their whole man after the image of God; having the seeds of repentance unto life, and all other saving graces, put into their hearts, and those graces so stirred up, increased, and strengthened, as that they more and more die unto sin, and rise unto newness of life." Also see Anthony A. Hoekema, *Saved by Grace* (Grand Rapids: Eerdmans, 1989), 192.
24. Berkhof, *Systematic Theology*, 532.
25. Ibid.

While we will spend the next few chapters exploring the doctrine of sanctification, notice at the start several components to the nature of God's sanctifying work in us based on our definition above.[26]

First, sanctification is the work of the Spirit and therefore a supernatural and gracious work of God in us. On the surface, it might seem like sanctification is our doing, but as we'll see in Question 30, sanctification is the work of God. Yes, it certainly does involve us; we must kill sin and live for God. Yet, we can only do so because God is the one at work in us (e.g., Gal. 5:22; Eph. 3:16; Col. 1:11; 1 Thess. 5:23; Heb. 13:20–21). The Spirit works in us and through us in order to deliver us from sin's corruption and renew our nature in the image of God. Sanctification, we can conclude, is very much by God's grace. We work *because* he is graciously and powerfully at work in us.

Second, sanctification involves putting off the old man, persistently and regularly killing sin. Sanctification involves putting to death our sinful desires (Rom. 6:5–14; Col. 3:1–4, 7–10). It involves mortifying and removing the corruption and pollution in our nature (Gal. 5:24). Very practically, this means that we, as Christians, not only resist the temptation to sin, but when we identify sinful tendencies within we actively and even aggressively put a stop to them and instead, with the help of the Spirit, cultivate godly inclinations and habits. The stress on the Spirit is key. This is not something we do on our own or in our own strength. As John Owen said, "All other ways of mortification are vain, all helps leave us helpless; it must be done by the Spirit. Men, as the apostle intimates, Romans 9:30–32, may attempt this work on other principles, by means and advantages administered on other accounts, as they always have done, and do: but, saith he, 'This is the work of the Spirit; by him alone is it to be wrought, and by no other power is it to be brought about'"[27]

Third, sanctification involves putting on the new man, conforming ourselves to the Word of God that we might be renewed into the image of Christ. It's not enough to tear down the old man; the new man must be built up in good works (Eph. 4:17–24, 25–32; Col. 3:12–17). Like mortification, vivification too is the work of the Spirit within, conforming us into the likeness of our Savior.

Fourth, sanctification is a lifelong process. As we'll see in Question 33, the Bible does not teach that believers reach a state of perfection or entire sanctification in this life. Scripture everywhere assumes that the Christian has not reached, nor will he reach, a state of sinlessness (Phil. 3:14–15; James 3:2; 1 John 1:8, 10). Rather, being made holy is a progressive path, one that will not reach its finality until glory.

---

26. Similar points can be found in ibid., 532–34. Moving forward, when I use the word "sanctification," I have in mind "progressive sanctification," unless I specify otherwise.
27. *Of the Mortification of Sin in Believers*, in *The Works of John Owen* [Edinburgh: Banner of Truth, 1991], 6:7.

Scripture teaches that the Christian is engaged in warfare against sin this side of heaven (Gal. 5:16–17) and that his/her progress in holiness is progressive rather than instantaneous (Rom. 12:2; Eph. 4:11–16; 1 Peter 2:2; 2 Peter 3:18). To appeal to a human analogy: If regeneration is new birth and glorification is when man is made perfect in all his maturity, then sanctification is that stage in between called "growth."[28] This side of glorification there is always much growing to do. While the Christian has a perfect status (justification), in his moral nature he remains imperfect (sanctification) until the last day (glorification).

With these four points in mind, I close by quoting the Puritan John Owen, who is perhaps most famous for his profound insight into the sanctification of the believer. Owen captures the essence of what we've just described: "Sanctification is an immediate work of the Spirit of God on the souls of believers, purifying and cleansing of their natures from the pollution and uncleanness of sin, renewing in them the image of God, and thereby enabling them, from a spiritual and habitual principle of grace, to yield obedience unto God, according unto the tenor and terms of the new covenant, by virtue of the life and death of Jesus Christ."[29]

Summary

Definitive sanctification takes place at the beginning of the Christian life when God sets us apart, consecrating us for himself, and declares us holy. It's on the basis of this positional holiness that transformation in holiness can take place. Progressive sanctification, on the other hand, is that act whereby the Holy Spirit, by God's grace, delivers us from the corruption or pollution of sin by renewing our nature into the image of God. This work of the Spirit, unlike regeneration, involves our active participation as we die daily to sin in order to live in a way that is pleasing and glorifying to God. The goal of this lifelong process is to be conformed into the image of our Savior, Jesus Christ, who is the perfect image of God. In short, sanctification is God making us holy.

---

28. Berkhof, along this line of thought, says "regeneration is the beginning of sanctification" (*Systematic Theology*, 536).

29. Owen goes on to add: "Hence it follows that our holiness, which is the fruit and effect of this work, the work as terminated in us, as it compriseth the renewed principle or image of God wrought in us, so it consists in a holy obedience unto God by Jesus Christ, according to the terms of the covenant of grace, from the principle of a new nature" (John Owen, *A Discourse Concerning the Holy Spirit*, in *Works*, 3:386). Also see Packer on Owen's description of sanctification in *Keep in Step with the Spirit*, 81.

REFLECTION QUESTIONS

1. What are the major differences between definitive and progressive sanctification?

2. Why is it that our inner transformation in holiness should not be divorced from our positional holiness?

3. What are the key components to progressive sanctification?

4. How does a Godward focus in sanctification guard us from turning sanctification into merely a moral improvement of ourselves?

5. Can we say that sanctification is by grace?

What Is the Difference between Justification and Sanctification?

In Questions 2–3, we learned that original sin consisted of both guilt and corruption (or pollution). This distinction is key to understanding the difference between justification and sanctification. While justification addresses our guilt, sanctification deals with our corruption.

Guilt has to do with our legal status before God. As children of Adam and active lawbreakers, the punishment we deserve is eternal condemnation. In his abundant grace, God transferred our guilt to Christ as he bore our punishment. In return, the perfect righteousness (obedience) of Christ has been imputed to our account upon faith in Christ alone. God, therefore, declared us not guilty but righteous in his sight. And so Paul can say with much excitement: "There is therefore now no condemnation for those who are in Christ Jesus" (Rom. 8:1).[1]

But what about our corruption or pollution? How is it dealt with? How is it removed? After all, says J. I. Packer, not only does Scripture say that our "guilt" needs "to be forgiven," but our "filth" needs "to be cleansed."[2] As children of Adam we inherit our father's corrupt nature. To make matters even worse, we

---

1. It is hard to improve upon Question 60 in The Heidelberg Catechism (in *Reformed Confessions of the Sixteenth Century and Seventeenth Centuries in English Translation, Volume 2, 1552–1566*, ed. James T. Dennison Jr. [Grand Rapids: Reformation Heritage, 2010]):
   Q. How are you righteous before God?
   A. Only by a true faith in Jesus Christ; that is, though my conscience accuse me that I have grievously sinned against all the commandments of God and kept none of them, and am still inclined to all evil, yet God, without any merit of mine, of mere grace, grants and imputes to me the perfect satisfaction, righteousness, and holiness of Christ, as if I had never had nor committed any sin, and myself had accomplished all the obedience which Christ has rendered for me; if only I accept such benefit with a believing heart.
2. J. I. Packer, *Keep in Step with the Spirit: Finding Fullness in Our Walk with God*, 2nd ed. (Grand Rapids: Baker, 2005), 32.

act upon that polluted nature whenever we sin. This is precisely the point where sanctification comes into view. The process of sanctification—which is ignited at regeneration and continues throughout our life—is one in which our nature is being renewed and transformed. While justification is a legal declaration that takes place once-and-for-all, sanctification is a continuous, progressive, and life-long process whereby the Spirit removes the pollution of sin and transforms us into the image of our Savior (Eph. 4:20–24).[3] The goal of sanctification is to be holy as the Lord our God is holy (Lev. 19:2). We approach such a goal whenever we, by faith in Christ and by the strength and power of the Spirit, turn away from sin and obey God.

With those differences in mind, consider the following comparison which highlights the contrast:[4]

Table 7
Key Differences between Justification and Sanctification

Justification	Sanctification
Removes guilt of sin	Removes pollution of sin
Occurs exterior to sinner in God's tribunal	Occurs within and progressively changes the entire person
Declared righteous: sinful record forgiven; righteousness of Christ imputed to sinner's account	*Made righteous:* mortification of sin; vivification unto holiness
Restores sinner to filial rights as child of God, including eternal life	Renews believer into conformity with the image of God in Christ
Instantaneous, once-for-all, completed act (though with ongoing results and benefits)	Life-long, progressive process; completed only at glorification
Believer merely receives and rests upon Christ and his benefits	Believer works but only because God works in him
All believers have same status	Believers differ in holy maturity[4]

---

3. We are following Berkhof's definition: Sanctification is "that gracious and continuous operation of the Holy Spirit, by which He delivers the justified sinner from the pollution of sin, renews his whole nature in the image of God, and enables him to perform good works." Louis Berkhof, *Systematic Theology* (Edinburgh: Banner of Truth, 2003), 532.
4. Some of the wording and phrases in this chart are from: Berkhof, *Systematic Theology,* 513–14; J. V. Fesko, *A Christian's Pocket Guide to Growing in Holiness* (Fearn, Ross-shire, Scotland: Christian Focus, 2012), 5.
5. To qualify, I do not mean that there is a two-class, two-tier Christianity, as one might see in Wesleyanism with entire sanctification or in Keswick circles with victorious living doctrine. Rather, all I mean in this phrase is that on the road to glory, some are farther along in Christian maturity than others, which is very different than justification whereby each Christian has the same, exact status: righteous in Christ.

With this contrast in view, we must be careful to make proper distinctions. Justification may be the *basis* of the Christian life and sanctification (the *terminus a quo*), but it cannot be the *goal* of sanctification (the *terminus ad quem*).[6]

Double Grace and Union with Christ: Sanctification in the Order of Salvation

With such a distinction between justification and sanctification in mind, where shall we place sanctification in the order of salvation (*ordo salutis*)? One will notice that in our "golden chain of salvation" sanctification is placed *after* justification in the order of salvation. That is intentional.

Justification, in other words, is the foundation of sanctification, not vice versa. The *legal* is what grounds the *transformative*, and the *indicative* is what grounds the *imperative* (see Rom. 6:12–14). Or think of it this way: Sanctification always flows out of justification, its cause; justification does not flow out of sanctification. As John Calvin said, "justification of faith is the beginning, foundation, cause, proof, and substance of works righteousness."[7] In that light, it is the gift of a new righteousness standing in Christ (justification) that not only is the ground but the motivation of our faith fueled deeds. As Michael Horton says, "Whereas Rome maintains that God's justifying verdict is a future reward for our faithfulness cooperation, evangelical faith teaches that this verdict is the present gift that motivates our faithful response. We do not work for a secure future, but from a secure present."[8]

Table 8
Order of Salvation (Ordo Salutis)

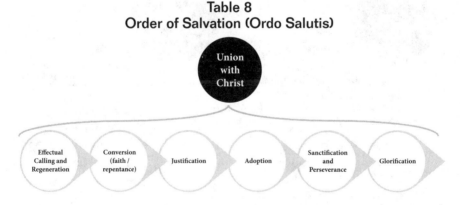

---

6. Michael Horton, *Pilgrim Theology: Core Doctrines for Christian Disciples* (Grand Rapids: Zondervan, 2011), 283.
7. John Calvin, *Institutes of the Christian Religion*, ed. John T. McNeil, trans. Ford Lewis Battles, LCC, vols. 20–21 (Philadelphia: Westminster, 1960), 3.17.9.
8. Horton, *Pilgrim Theology*, 303. Also Packer: "In reality, holiness is the goal of our redemption. As Christ died in order that we may be justified, so we are justified in order that we may be sanctified and made holy" (J. I. Packer, *Rediscovering Holiness: Know the Fullness of Life with God* [Ventura, CA: Regal, 2009], 33).

Should the order between justification and sanctification be reversed, a flood of problems would follow.[9] Due to his struggle with sin and the imperfection of his nature, the believer would never be sure if he had right standing with God. His right standing would also be based upon his own works, rather than upon the work of Christ alone.

So we must carefully distinguish between justification and sanctification, seeing the former as the cause and fountain of the latter.[10] And yet, we cannot divorce the two from each other for they are inseparably connected. Out of our union with Christ is birthed a double grace (as Calvin called it), so that we are not only reconciled to God through the righteousness of Christ (having in heaven now a gracious Father rather than a condemning Judge), but also sanctified by the Spirit of Christ so that our daily life is characterized by an ever-growing cultivation of piety, holiness, blamelessness, and purity.[11] "Christ justifies no one," says Calvin, "whom he does not at the same time sanctify. These benefits are joined together by an everlasting and indissoluble bond."[12]

Table 9
Union, Headship, and Double Grace
Adam vs. Christ

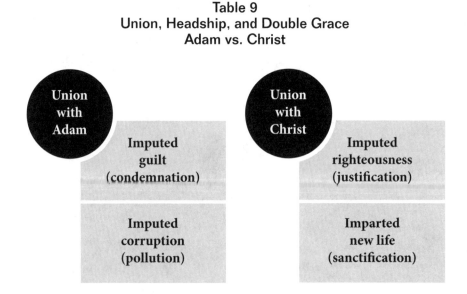

9. I am not talking about a pedagogical order, as if it is wrong to teach on sanctification before teaching on justification in, say, a Sunday school class. Rather, what I am referring to is the placement of the two in the order of salvation.
10. "Justification is the judicial basis for sanctification" (Berkhof, *Systematic Theology*, 536).
11. Calvin, *Institutes* 3.2.1. Also see J. Todd Billings, *Calvin, Participation, and the Gift: The Activity of Believers in Union with Christ* (Oxford: Oxford University Press, 2007), 106–7.
12. Calvin, *Institutes* 3.16.1.

Stemming from union with Christ, this double grace corresponds to the two-fold nature of Christ's covenantal work. Paul portrays Christ as the second Adam in Romans 5. Whereas the headship of the first Adam resulted in the imputation of guilt and corruption due to his failure to obey the covenant of works, the second Adam's new covenant obedience and propitiary death now results in the imputation of a righteous status as well as the impartation of new life. "In Christ we have both justification and new life, an alien righteousness imputed and Christ's own resurrection life imparted." And yet, says Horton, "it is complete justification alone, rather than partial sanctification, that assures us of objective peace with God (Ro 5:1)."[13]

Two Ditches on Each Side of the Road to Holiness: Legalism and Antinomianism

This balance we have just described is key. On the one hand, we avoid the error of Roman Catholics who confuse the two, allowing sanctification to swallow up justification, a move which compromises grace *alone* and faith *alone*. On the other hand, we dare not abstract sanctification from justification. To do so is to view justification as involving divine grace but turns sanctification into the product of manmade effort.[14] In this view, justification has to do with grace but sanctification is only about works. Sanctification does differ from justification in that it involves our active participation, effort, and good works (while justification does not). However, sanctification is by God's grace, too. To be more precise, we work in sanctification only because God works in and through us. Holiness is reached, in the end, only by God's grace. Paul had to sternly remind the Galatians of this very principle (Gal. 3:3).

If we get this balance right, we avoid our doctrine of sanctification falling into one of two ditches on each side of the road: legalism and antinomianism. Both, says Horton, "conspire to persuade us that God is a cosmic tyrant who does not deserve our allegiance."[15] Let's consider each in turn. On one side is legalism. The legalist has removed God's grace from the sanctification process. He is the Pharisee in Luke 18 who prayed self-righteously: "God, I thank you that I am not like other men, extortioners, unjust, adulterers, or even like this tax collector. I fast twice a week; I give tithes of all that I get" (18:11–12).

The Christian legalist fails to imitate Christ as one who is first and foremost united to Christ by grace alone through faith alone. Instead, says Horton, he reduces the Christian life to a "moralistic attempt to live *up to* Christ's example rather than our living *out of* the realities of Christ's saving work."[16] He

---

13. Horton, *Pilgrim Theology*, 293.
14. G. C. Berkouwer, *Studies in Dogmatics: Faith and Sanctification* (Grand Rapids: Eerdmans, 1952), 20–21; Horton, *Pilgrim Theology*, 306.
15. Horton, *Pilgrim Theology*, 142.
16. Ibid., 306. Countering the legalist, Horton writes, "Apart from our union with Christ and especially the imputation of righteousness in that union, sanctification is simply another

is still operating, in other words, as if he is under the law. And he is under the false impression that the law itself has the power to justify and sanctify. Much like the Pharisee in Luke 18, however, the legalist is blind to his own hypocrisy. He cannot see what everyone else can: He is self-righteous. He cannot obey the law perfectly. And he thinks he is not *totally* and *entirely* dependent upon God's grace, not only for his justification but for his sanctification too. Certainly the law plays an irreplaceable role in the Christian life, but the legalist has distorted not only its role but its power as well. This is one ditch on the path to glory, and it can be avoided by reminding ourselves, as Scripture does, that even sanctification is by grace.

On the other side is another ditch, the ditch of antinomianism. The antinomian assumes that divine commands are no longer relevant since he is no longer under law but under grace. But he has forgotten that the law is now written on our heart (Jer. 31:33; Heb. 10:16). Yes, we are no longer condemned by the law, for Christ's perfect obedience has been imputed to our account. By faith in Christ, we now stand before God righteous, not guilty. As Paul says in Ephesians 2:8–9, "For by grace you have been saved through faith. And this is not your own doing; it is the gift of God, not a result of works, so that no one may boast." However, the antinomian forgets to finish Paul's train of thought. In the very next verse Paul adds, "For we are his workmanship, created in Christ Jesus for good works, which God prepared beforehand, that we should walk in them" (2:10). So while we are saved by grace alone through faith alone, such grace and faith always result in good works. Obedience to God's commands, therefore, is absolutely essential to the Christian life of holiness. They are *not* optional, but essential. The indicative of the gospel and justification by grace does not exclude the imperative of sanctification that follows, but is its fountain head. Obedience to God's commands is no longer the basis of our right, legal standing before God, but it is the natural and necessary fruit of justifying faith, as our new heart now loves God and loves neighbor, fulfilling the two greatest commandments (Matt. 22:37–40).[17]

---

religious self-improvement program determined by the powers of this age (the flesh) rather than of the age to come (the Spirit)" (ibid., 310; also see Calvin, *Institutes* 3.19.5).

17. This raises the complicated issue of how to understand the Mosaic Law. Are Christians still under the laws God gave to Israel under Moses (i.e., the Mosaic Law), either in part or in whole, or are Christians no longer under the Law of Moses but instead, as those who are members of the "new covenant" (e.g., Luke 22:20; 1 Cor. 11:25), under the law of Christ? Much could be said but the latter option seems most biblical for a variety of reasons. Schreiner explains, "Strictly speaking, the idea that believers are under the third use of the law is mistaken, for we have seen that the entire [Mosaic] law is abolished for believers." Yet, this doesn't mean, however, that the Mosaic Law is irrelevant for new covenant Christians. Schreiner qualifies himself, saying, "Still, the notion is not entirely wrong since Paul's teaching is filled with exhortations that call upon believers to live in a way that pleases God." This is a key qualification; antinomianism is *not* acceptable even to those who think we are no longer under the Mosaic Law. There are still commands from God that are to

The apostle Paul guards us against both legalism and antinomianism in Romans 6. Paul begins the chapter explaining the great news that we have been united to Christ in his death and resurrection (6:4–5). Our "old self," says Paul, "was crucified with him in order that the body of sin might be brought to nothing, so that we would no longer be enslaved to sin" (6:6). But it's not just the death of Christ that matters here; it's his resurrection too. "Now if we have died with Christ, we believe that we will also live with him. We know that Christ, being raised from the dead, will never die again; death no longer has dominion over him" (6:8–9). If death no longer has dominion over Christ, then those united to Christ also are liberated from this dominion. Or as Paul explains, "For the death he died he died to sin, once for all, but the life he lives he lives to God. So you also must consider yourselves dead to sin and alive to God in Christ Jesus" (6:10–11).

In these verses we witness the *indicative* of the gospel.[18] We have died with Christ and we have risen with Christ. On that basis, then, Paul can issue an *imperative*: "Let not sin therefore reign in your mortal body, to make you obey its passions. Do not present your members to sin as instruments for unrighteousness, but present yourselves to God as those who have been brought from death to life, and your members to God as instruments for righteousness. For sin will have no dominion over you, since you are not under law but under grace" (6:12–14). These words not only issue a sobering reality check, but an "identity" check. If we are in Christ, then our new identity demands a new way of life. As those no longer in Adam but now in Christ, sin has no dominion over us, just as it has no dominion over our covenant head, Christ Jesus. Therefore, we no longer jump at its command; it no longer is our master and lord.

Romans 6 is a tapestry, weaving together the indicative of the gospel with the imperative of holy living. There we discover that our identity in Christ (our union with Jesus) is the basis for Paul's command. It is because we *have* died and risen with Christ that Paul now commands us to live according to

---

be obeyed for those in the new covenant. Moreover, even the principles within the Mosaic Law remain applicable to new covenant believers. "Even though the Old Testament law is not literally binding upon believers, we see principles and patterns and moral norms that still apply to us today since the Old Testament is the word of God" (Thomas R. Schreiner, *40 Questions about Christians and Biblical Law* [Grand Rapids: Kregel, 2010], 99). A similar view is expressed in Thomas R. Schreiner, *The Law and Its Fulfillment: A Pauline Theology of Law* (Grand Rapids: Baker Academic, 1993). Also see Jason C. Meyer, *The End of the Law: Mosaic Covenant in Pauline Theology* (Nashville: B&H, 2009); Douglas J. Moo, *The Epistle to the Romans* (Grand Rapids: Eerdmans, 1996), 415–16; Douglas J. Moo, "The Law of Christ as the Fulfillment of the Law of Moses: A Modified Lutheran View," in *Five Views on Law and Gospel*, ed. Stanley N. Gundry (Grand Rapids: Zondervan, 1999), 319–76.

18. Horton, *Pilgrim Theology*, 308–9. David Peterson, *Possessed by God: A New Testament Theology of Sanctification and Holiness* (Downers Grove, IL: InterVarsity Press, 1995), 97–100, is even more specific, making a case that "definitive sanctification" is in view when Paul describes this indicative.

the ways of Christ. "Practical holiness involves 'putting to death' in our lives what God has already sentenced to death on the cross ('mortification') and living out the new life given to us by the indwelling Christ ('vivification' or 'aspiration')."[19] Legalism and antinomianism compromise Paul's message. Legalism falls short because it ignores the new status we have in Christ as those not under law but under grace (Rom. 6:14). Antinomianism gets ahead of itself, for it hears those words "not under law but under grace" and assumes obedience to divine commands is outdated. In its worse forms, antinomians might even then say that sin is permissible. Paul anticipates this move and counters: "What then? Are we to sin because we are not under law but under grace? By no means!" (6:15). He then explains how we are either slaves to sin or to righteousness. If we obey sin, he warns, then it is clear: We are slaves to sin, and sin leads to death (6:16).

We are not, however, slaves to sin as we once were. We have been set free. Yet it is a freedom to obey. Ironically, true freedom involves a slavery, but it is a slavery to righteousness (6:17–18). "Those who belong to the crucified and resurrected Lord Jesus," says Peterson, "need no longer live as the helpless slaves of sin."[20] Paul, in other words, leaves no room for antinomianism. Our mission, in light of our new identity and new master, is clear: "For just as you once presented your members as slaves to impurity and to lawlessness leading to more lawlessness, so now present your members as slaves to righteousness leading to sanctification" (6:19). Paul concludes, "But now that you have been set free from sin and have become slaves of God, the fruit you get leads to sanctification and its end, eternal life" (6:22).

In the end, Romans 6 clarifies that the ditch on each side of the road is only avoided by a proper understanding of the gospel. As Horton explains, "The antinomian has too narrow a view of the gospel, as if it were mere fire insurance—canceling our debt without actually marrying us to Christ—while the legalist turns the gospel into law."[21] Paul refuses to succumb to either error. Instead, he takes us back to the gospel, pointing us to our union with the crucified and risen Christ, so that we properly understand how our righteous, legal status and our ongoing, moral renewal relate to one another.

Summary

Justification removes our guilt; sanctification removes our pollution. Justification is a forensic, legal declaration concerning our status; sanctification is a transformative, moral renewal in our nature. Justification occurs exterior to the sinner in God's tribunal; sanctification occurs within and progressively changes the entire person. Justification means we are declared

---

19. Peterson, *Possessed by God*, 112–13.
20. Ibid., 100.
21. Horton, *Pilgrim Theology*, 308.

righteous, having our sinful record forgiven and the righteousness of Christ imputed to our account; sanctification means we are made righteous through the mortification of sin and vivification unto holiness. Justification restores us to filial rights as children of God; sanctification renews us into conformity with the image of God in Christ. Justification is instantaneous; sanctification is progressive. In justification we rest upon Christ; in sanctification we work but only because God works in us. In justification all have the same status; in sanctification we differ in our maturity.

REFLECTION QUESTIONS

1. What are some of the main differences between justification and sanctification?

2. What could be a negative consequence of confusing justification and sanctification?

3. Where should we place sanctification in the order of salvation and why?

4. Whose image are we being conformed to in the sanctification process and how does this change our outlook on the Spirit's work within us?

5. Name some of the dangers in both legalism and antinomianism for the Christian life.

QUESTION 30

Who Is the Author of Sanctification?

Who is the author of sanctification? Answering this question is more difficult than one might think. On the one hand, sanctification seems to be *our* doing. Likewise, good works toward others are *our* doing as well. Yet if we stop there, sanctification—at least at first sight—would appear to be our work, accomplished by our own efforts. But that is only half the story. No doubt, there is truth to these statements. We are active, striving to do that which God has commanded us to do. And yet, Scripture tells us that sanctification is the work of God. In other words, though sanctification involves our effort, it has God as its primary author.

Such a mystery should lead us to be very careful when describing sanctification. Some will describe sanctification as a "cooperation" between God and the Christian. That word "cooperation" is used in order to highlight that it is both God and us at work in sanctification. But there is a danger in that term. It might give the impression that sanctification is like a pie divided up into two parts, God's part and our part. In this scheme, God does his work and we do our work. It might also give the impression that each party is equal, ruling out any dependence upon God in the process, failing to recognize that sanctification is a supernatural work.

Such approaches, however, need greater nuance and precision. Yes, sanctification involves God and us, but Scripture emphasizes that God is primary. Though we are at work in the sanctification process, we are absolutely dependent upon God. If he is not at work in us and through us, then even our greatest effort amounts to nothing. John Murray says it well: "It is imperative that we realize our complete dependence upon the Holy Spirit. We must not forget, of course, that our activity is enlisted to the fullest extent in the process of sanctification. But we must not rely upon our own strength of resolution or purpose. It is when we are weak that we are strong. It is by grace that we are being saved as surely as by grace we have been saved."[1] Therefore, to be precise, we work *because* God is at work in us.

Sanctification by God's Triune Grace

Throughout Scripture we see that sanctification is the work of God, accomplished in us and through us, but always by his power and according to his will. Though it may be painful to hear, Hebrews 12 addresses how we, at times, will experience the Father's discipline, and yet this discipline is meant to help us, not harm us. In Hebrews 12:10 the author turns to the illustration of human fathers: "For they disciplined us for a short time as it seemed best to them, but he disciplines us for our good, that we may share his holiness." For our purpose, notice how the author not only says discipline is for the good of the child, but as God's children we are disciplined so that we "may share his holiness." So discipline is a means to holiness. Our heavenly Father (i.e., "the Father of spirits" in 12:9) disciplines us in order to bring about our holiness. Clearly Hebrews 12:10 attributes sanctification, even the means to such sanctification, to God.

It's not just the Father who is the author of our sanctification, but the Son also is said to be its author. Titus 2:11–14 is a tremendous example of how God and man are both at work in sanctification.

> For the grace of God has appeared, bringing salvation for all people, training us to renounce ungodliness and worldly passions, and to live self-controlled, upright, and godly lives in the present age, waiting for our blessed hope, the appearing of the glory of our great God and Savior Jesus Christ, who gave himself for us to redeem us from all lawlessness and to purify for himself a people for his own possession who are zealous for good works.

Paul teaches that we, Christians, are those who:

- renounce ungodliness.
- renounce worldly passions.
- live self-controlled, upright, godly lives in the present age.
- wait for our blessed hope, the appearing of the glory of our great God and Savior Jesus Christ.

Certainly man's responsibility in sanctification cannot be escaped but is essential to transformation.

---

1. John Murray, *Redemption Accomplished and Applied* (Grand Rapids: Eerdmans, 1955), 147.

However, Paul does preface this list by acknowledging that it is the "grace of God" that is "training us" to do all of these things. He then explains how it is our Savior, Jesus Christ, "who gave himself for us to redeem us from all lawlessness and to purify for himself a people for his own possession who are zealous for good works." Part of the mission of Jesus was to sanctify us, even make us passionate to act in godly ways. We are his people, bought with his blood, and his desire is that we reflect his own character.[2]

So far we've seen that the Father and Son author our sanctification, but the Spirit is not left out either. In fact, our sanctification—whether definitive or progressive sanctification (see Question 28)—is attributed to the Spirit more often than not because he is the Trinitarian person who dwells within us (1 Cor. 4:16–17; 6:19), a point to which we shall return. In Romans 15:16, for example, Paul explains how he was sent to be a "minister of Christ Jesus to the Gentiles in the priestly service of the gospel of God, so that the offering of the Gentiles may be acceptable, *sanctified by the Holy Spirit.*" In 2 Thessalonians 2:13 he overflows with thanksgiving to God because "God chose you as the first fruits to be saved, through *sanctification by the Spirit* and belief in the truth." The apostle Peter says something very similar. Opening his first letter he addresses those who are elect exiles "according to the foreknowledge of God the Father, in the *sanctification of the Spirit,* for obedience to Jesus Christ and for sprinkling with his blood" (1 Peter 1:2).

Other passages do not specify a member of the Trinity but enlist the entire Godhead in the authorship of our sanctification. Such is the case in Paul's prayer at the close of his first letter to the Thessalonians: "Now may the God of peace himself *sanctify you completely*, and may your whole spirit and soul and body be kept blameless at the coming of our Lord Jesus Christ. He who calls you is faithful; he will surely do it" (5:23–24).

These passages and many others demonstrate that sanctification is not something we are to accomplish in our own strength, nor is it something we do by ourselves. Rather, it is a gift from God, and it is to be accomplished in his strength and by his power.[3]

Strive for Holiness

It should be clear by now that the triune God is at work to sanctify us. And yet, as mysterious as this may be, we are not passive in this process but active; in fact, we are exhorted in Scripture *to* act. We will see this more thoroughly in Question 36–37, but for now notice how God commands us to act.

In Romans 12:1–2 Paul appeals to his readers to "present your bodies as a living sacrifice, holy and acceptable to God, which is your spiritual act of worship." Paul then gives a command that should result in action. "Do not be

---

2. On the Son's role in sanctification, one might also consider Ephesians 5:25–27.
3. See Anthony A. Hoekema, *Saved by Grace* (Grand Rapids: Eerdmans, 1989), 200.

conformed to this world, but be transformed by the renewal of your mind, that by testing you may discern what is the will of God, what is good and acceptable and perfect." Surely Paul did not believe that God's authorship of sanctification means we sit back, relax, and let go. Rather, Paul calls every believer to action:

- present your bodies
- do not be conformed
- be transformed
- discern what is the will of God

God puts responsibility into the hands of the Christian, commanding him to act, live, and think in a certain way. Therefore, though he is writing in a different context, Paul can say, "Since we have these promises, beloved, let us cleanse ourselves from every defilement of body and spirit, bringing holiness to completion in the fear of God" (2 Cor. 7:1). Holiness is a work in progress, something we must bring to completion.[4]

The author of Hebrews says the same, instructing Christians to vigorously and repeatedly pursue holiness. He not only commands Christians to "strive" for peace with others, but to strive "for the holiness without which no one will see the Lord" (Heb. 12:14). That word "strive" (*diōkete*) conveys the complete opposite of passivity: a man in pursuit of holiness. And this pursuit after holiness doesn't happen once only to result in a victorious life thereafter. No, it is an active and continuous pursuit, one that lasts throughout life.

Work *Because* He Works

We've seen two biblical truths: (1) Sanctification requires our active participation and labor, and yet (2) God is the primary author of our sanctification. The most precise way to describe this relationship and preserve the balance between these two truths is to say that we work *because* God works. While our work in the process of sanctification is essential and necessary, we must not forget that in this work we are totally dependent upon the strength, grace, and power of God himself. As Berkouwer so helpfully explains, "For progress of sanctification never meant working out one's own salvation under one's own auspices; on the contrary, it meant working out one's own salvation with a rising sense of dependence on God's grace."[5]

The duality we are seeking to preserve here is beautifully captured by Paul when he instructs the Philippians to "work out your own salvation with fear and trembling, *for it is God who works in you*, both to will and to work for his

---

4. On this pursuit being a responsibility God gives to each one of his children, see J. C. Ryle, *Holiness* (London: James Clarke, 1956), 19–20.

5. G. C. Berkouwer, *Faith and Sanctification* (Grand Rapids: Eerdmans, 1952), 112.

good pleasure" (Phil. 2:12–13, emphasis added). God is the divine author; he is the one at work in us; he is the one bringing about his will in our lives; and so, on that basis, we pursue holiness. As Hoekema so insightfully explains, "The harder we work, the more sure we may be that God is working in us."[6]

The Indwelling Holy Spirit

Now that we are clear that it is God who is at work in us to sanctify us, it is important to recognize that this sanctifying work is only possible because the Holy Spirit indwells. Throughout the Gospels Jesus refers to the Holy Spirit as a gift through whom the Christian enjoys communion with the triune God (Matt. 12:28; 28:19–20; Mark 13:11; Luke 11:13; 12:12; 24:49; 24:49; John 3:5–8; 14:26; 20:22).[7] But in what way is the Holy Spirit a gift? There are many. But most fundamentally, the Spirit is given to us as a gift by his indwelling presence. According to the New Testament, every new covenant believer is permanently indwelt by the Holy Spirit.[8] To put it colloquially, the Holy Spirit makes his home within us.[9] Packer notes that the Spirit's work is to "mediate Christ's presence to believers—that is, to give them such knowledge of his presence with them as their Savior, Lord, and God."[10] This is the "essence of the Holy Spirit's ministry."[11] To understand the significance of the Spirit's indwelling, let's focus briefly on the Spirit's work in redemptive history.

In the beginning the garden of Eden was designed to be a type of temple, one characterized by God's presence. The sound of the Lord walking through the garden could be heard (Gen. 2:8).[12] As a priestlike figure, Adam's responsibility was to oversee this temple (Gen. 2:8–15)—something he failed to do when the serpent entered into this holy place. Sadly, Adam's failure to guard God's Edenic temple resulted in exile, an exile that would drive Adam away from the presence of God.

Nevertheless, God graciously entered into a covenantal relationship with Israel. In doing so, he would be with his people in a unique way. The tabernacle (and, later on, the temple) would be where the presence of God descended. God redeemed Israel to be a people for himself, set apart, holy to the Lord. However, in the Old Testament the Spirit was typically given only to certain leaders and

---

6. Hoekema, *Salvation by Grace*, 202.
7. David Peterson, *Possessed by God: A New Testament Theology of Sanctification and Holiness* (Downers Grove, IL: InterVarsity Press, 1995), 28.
8. It is not as if some are indwelt by the Spirit while others are not. No, to be a Christian is to be indwelt by the Spirit.
9. For a valuable treatment of the Spirit, see Graham Cole, *He Who Gives Life: The Doctrine of the Holy Spirit*, Foundations of Evangelical Theology (Wheaton, IL: Crossway, 2007).
10. J. I. Packer, *Keep in Step with the Spirit: Finding Fullness in Our Walk with God*, 2nd ed. (Grand Rapids: Baker, 2005), 43.
11. Jesus' presence "should be thought of not in spatial, but rather in relational terms" (ibid., 49).
12. Gregory K. Beale, *The Temple and the Church's Mission: A Biblical Theology of the Dwelling Place of God*, NSBT (Downers Grove, IL: InterVarsity Press, 2004).

for certain tasks (e.g., Exod. 31:3; 35:31; Num. 11:16–17; 27:18; Deut. 24:9; Judg. 14:6; 2 Sam. 16:13; Ps. 51:11; Ezek. 2:2; 3:24). Furthermore, no one could enter into the holy of holies but the high priest on the Day of Atonement (see Lev. 16), and even then he had to approach this holy place with the appropriate sacrifice offered not only for the sins of the people but for his own sins. In that light, Moses longed to see the day when there would be a greater, more permanent, and universal presence of the Spirit. "Would that all the LORD's people were prophets, that the LORD would put his Spirit on them!" (Num. 11:29).[13]

This longing also took the form of prophecy when God promised in Ezekiel 37:26–28, "I will make a covenant of peace with them. It shall be an everlasting covenant with them. And I will set them in their land and multiply them, and will set my sanctuary in their midst forevermore. My dwelling place shall be with them, and I will be their God, and they shall be my people. Then the nations will know that I am the Lord who sanctifies Israel, when my sanctuary is in their midst forevermore." In Joel we are given further specifics: The Holy Spirit will be poured out on God's people (Joel 2:28–29). And in Jeremiah the "new covenant" is explicitly named. What's so "new" about this new covenant? In this new covenant God will put his law within, writing it on the heart (Jer. 31:33). "And no longer shall each one teach his neighbor and each his brother, saying, 'Know the Lord,' for they shall all know me, from the least of them to the greatest, declares the Lord" (Jer. 31:34). Unlike the old covenant, in the new covenant the Spirit will ensure that all of Israel is truly Israel. One of the defining marks will be the permanent indwelling of the Spirit in all God's people.

If we continue reading God's promise in Jeremiah 31, we will notice that God also says he will forgive his people's iniquity and remember their sins no more (31:36). But this requires a better sacrifice and a better Mediator as well as a better covenant. Christ *is* that better sacrifice (Heb. 9–10) and better Mediator (Heb. 7), and he cuts the better covenant by means of his own blood (Heb. 8). He is the *agnus Dei*, the lamb of God, who was slain for the sins of the world (John 1:29). As God incarnate, Jesus is called Immanuel, God with us, because he tabernacled among God's covenant people (Matt. 1:23) in order to save them from their sins (Matt. 1:21). John describes him as the Word who not only was with God but with us: "And the Word became flesh and dwelt among us" (John 1:14a). Indeed, Jesus himself indicates that he is God's new temple (Matt. 26:61). Through his life, death, and resurrection, we can now confidently enter into the very presence of God as those clothed in the righteousness of Christ (2 Cor. 5:21; cf. Zech. 3).

Moreover, not only has Christ ascended to the right hand of his Father where he intercedes for us (Rom. 8:34), but the Father and the Son have sent the Spirit to permanently indwell us (Rom. 8:9, 11; 1 Cor. 3:16; 6:19; Eph. 2:22; 2 Tim. 1:14). For this reason, Scripture can refer to new covenant believers as

---

13. Jesus himself anticipates the fulfilment of such a desire in John 7:39; 14:17.

temples of the Holy Spirit: "Do you not know that you are God's temple and that God's Spirit dwell in you?" (1 Cor. 4:16). How serious it is should we then corrupt God's holy temple with sin: "If anyone destroys God's temple, God will destroy him. For God's temple is holy, and you are that temple" (4:17; cf. 6:19).

According to Paul, indwelling and sanctification go hand in hand. In light of what we are (God's temple) and who indwells us (the Holy Spirit), we pursue holiness, even guarding God's temple from corruption and defilement. Therefore, says Packer, the indwelling of the Spirit results in (1) "personal fellowship with Jesus," (2) "personal transformation of character into Jesus's likeness," (3) and receiving the "Spirit-given certainty of being loved, redeemed, and adopted through Christ into the Father's family" (cf. Rom. 8:17).[14]

Indwelling should also result in being "filled" with the Holy Spirit. While the Holy Spirit indwells every believer at regeneration and conversion—indeed, he must or we do not actually belong to Christ (Rom. 8:9)—Scripture introduces another, even distinct, concept called "filling" and it is something Christians are to pursue.[15] For example, Paul commands the Ephesians not to "get drunk with wine" but to "be filled with the Spirit" (Eph. 5:18). Paul's imperative is all too often neglected when we instead ignore the will of God, are tempted into sin, and consequently grieve and quench the Holy Spirit (Eph. 4:30; 1 Thess. 5:19). Christians need to hear this imperative loud and clear. We are to be those who walk by the Spirit, live by the Spirit, and keep in step with the Spirit (Gal. 5:16, 25). In doing so, we will not be characterized by the works of the flesh but by the fruit of the Spirit (Gal. 5:16–23; cf. Col. 3:12–17).

Yet, the presence of God that we now experience is but a taste of what is to come. One day we will experience the presence of God like never before. According to the book of Revelation, in the new heaven and earth, the holy city, the new Jerusalem (Rev. 21:1–2), God will dwell with his people for all eternity. "Behold, the dwelling place of God is with man. He will dwell with them, and they will be his people, and God himself will be with them as their God" (Rev. 21:3). God dwelling with his people will mean that there will be no more tears of pain and death, for "the former things" will have "passed away" (21:4). All things will be made new by King Jesus (21:5).

Certainly there will be much joy on that day, but the greatest joy of all will be found in enjoying God's presence. In his lifetime, David understood that God's presence is the ultimate goal. "One thing I have asked of the Lord, that will I seek after: that I may dwell in the house of the Lord all the days of my life, to gaze upon the beauty of the Lord and to inquire in his temple" (Ps. 27:4;

---

14. Packer, *Keep in Step with the Spirit*, 43.
15. My purpose here is not to address "spirit baptism," which would take us too far astray. Suffice it to say that "spirit baptism" is distinct from both indwelling and filling. I would make the case, *contra* certain Pentecostal groups, that "spirit baptism" occurs at conversion and is not a subsequent experience that elevates one to a second level of "Christian." See John Stott, *Baptism and Fullness: The Work of the Holy Spirit Today* (Downers Grove, IL: 2006).

cf. 23:6).[16] Yet even now, this side of the new heaven and earth, we experience his presence, for the Spirit is not only *for* us but *within* us. Therefore, the Holy Spirit is the guarantee of that greater presence to come on the last day.

To conclude, the road of sanctification is not one we travel alone. Rather, the Holy Spirit is the gift of the Father and the Son, indwelling us and helping us fight against sin as we are continually and progressively transformed into the image of Christ.

The Holy Spirit, the Church, and the Means of Grace

If it is true that sanctification is not a road to be travelled alone, then one would expect the Holy Spirit to use *means* to conform us into the image of Christ. One of the serious dangers in thinking through our salvation is forgetting the role of the local church. Too often we buy into the mentality that Christianity is just about *me* and my *personal* relationship with Jesus.

A solo Christian or lone-ranger Christian, however, is totally foreign to the Bible. God does not justify the believer only to send him off on the road to sanctification all by himself, involving the church only where he deems fit or useful. Rather, the church plays *the* central role in spiritual growth. If we are to grow in *likeness* to Christ, Scripture says that we must be part of the *body* of Christ. To be a faithful Christian is to be a member of the church, which is the bride of Christ (Rom. 7:1–4; 1 Cor. 6:15–17; 2 Cor. 11:2–3; Eph. 5:22–32) and the body of Christ (Rom. 12:4–5; 1 Cor. 6:15–16; 10:16–17; 11:29; 12: 12–27; Eph. 1:22–23; 2:14–16; 4:4, 11–16; 5:23, 29–30; Col. 1:18, 24; 2:29; 3:15). What sense does it make for a person to become a Christ-follower yet not belong to his body (Rom. 12:5; 1 Cor. 12:12–27)? To be united to Christ is to be united to his body, his bride.[17] In short, the church is the soil in which our sanctification grows, as passages like Hebrews 10:19–25 and Colossians 3:12–17 make clear.

Within the context of the church the Holy Spirit utilizes the preached word and the word made visible in the sacraments (baptism and the Lord's Supper) to conform us more and more into the image of his Son, as well as confirm our union to his Son.[18] To use theological language, these are his

---

16. R. Michael Allen, *Justification and the Gospel: Understanding the Contexts and Controversies* (Grand Rapids: Baker Academic, 2013), 38–39.

17. To see how union with Christ relates to these metaphors, see Constantine R. Campbell, *Paul and Union with Christ* (Grand Rapids: Zondervan, 2012), 267–326.

18. For example, Calvin writes concerning the inseparability of Word and Spirit that "God works in his elect in two ways: within, through his Spirit; without, through his Word. By his Spirit, illuminating their minds and forming their hearts to the love and cultivation of righteousness, he makes them a new creation (*nova creatio*). By his Word, he arouses them to desire, to seek after, and to attain that same renewal." John Calvin, *Institutes of the Christian Religion*, ed. John T. McNeil, trans. Ford Lewis Battles, LCC, vols. 20–21 (Philadelphia: Westminster, 1960), 2.5.5.

means of grace by which he sanctifies his elect. As Michael Horton says, "Faith is not something we can manufacture within ourselves; it is a gift of the Spirit, which he gives us through tangible, unspectacular earthly means: another sinner's speech in the name of Christ, water, bread, and wine. What could be more common? And yet, consecrated by God, they become his means of salvation."[19] Horton's point is rooted in the Protestant Reformation. One of its hallmark doctrinal statements, the Heidelberg Catechism, asks, "Where... does that true faith come from?" Answer: "The Holy Spirit produces it [faith] in our hearts by the preaching of the holy gospel, and confirms it through our use of the holy sacraments [i.e., means of grace]" (Q. 65). As the body of Christ assembles together, the Word proclaimed in the pulpit and made visible in baptism and the Lord's Supper proves critical if the Christian is to reach full maturity in the Lord Jesus Christ.

Summary

In Scripture, God commands his children to pursue holiness, which assumes that sanctification involves our active, ongoing, and persistent effort to kill sin and strive after holiness. However, our pursuit of holiness and transformation into the image of Christ is entirely dependent upon the power of the Holy Spirit. If he is not at work in us and through us, then even our greatest effort amounts to nothing. Sanctification, in other words, is his work; sanctification is by grace. It is only because he works in us that we work for his good pleasure.

REFLECTION QUESTIONS

1. Is sanctification our work or God's work, and why?

2. In what sense can we say that sanctification is by God's grace?

3. Study Titus 2:11–14. How does the apostle Paul understand sanctification?

4. Read Hebrews 12:10. Does it surprise you that discipline is a means to holiness?

5. How does the Spirit's indwelling presence give you confidence to live for the glory of God and fight against sin?

---

19. Michael Horton, *Pilgrim Theology: Core Doctrines for Christian Disciples* (Grand Rapids: Zondervan, 2011), 345.

How Do We Die to Sin?

John Owen, one of the greatest English Puritans and writers on sanctification, once said something very profound: "be killing sin or it will be killing you."[1] Perhaps "killing" sin sounds a little intense. But sin is intense. In fact, sin is deadly. It kills spiritual life wherever it is found. So Owen is spot on: Sin will kill us. That is what sin does. It destroys us spiritually (see Question 1). Could there be a greater threat to the Christian life than sin itself?

We know this is true from personal experience. Our relationship with the Lord is going strong, we are living a life that is holy and set apart to the Lord, and then we cave in to sin. In a moment of temptation, we give in. For the Christian, it does not take long for conviction to set in (thanks to the indwelling Holy Spirit). You know that you have rebelled against your good, loving heavenly Father, and you hate it because it ruins your relationship with him. You are like a rebellious child who has done the very thing his caring father told him not to do. Your unfaithfulness is so hurtful because in that moment of sin you did not trust in the one who knows what is best for you. Instead, you went your own way, thinking you know what is best. Naturally, the guilt for your sin weighs down heavily until you run to your heavenly Father in tears of repentance, asking his forgiveness, which he gives freely through Christ (1 John 1:9).

Mortification

The ugliness, painfulness, and devastation of sin is a serious reminder—especially in the midst of a world that takes sin so lightly—that we must do battle with sin lest it triumph over us. This warfare is called—to use an

---

1. John Owen, "Of the Mortification of Sin in Believers," in *Overcoming Sin and Temptation*, ed. Kelly M. Kapic and Justin Taylor (Wheaton, IL: Crossway, 2006), 50. For an introduction to his thought on this topic, see Matthew Barrett and Michael A. G. Haykin, *Owen on the Christian Life* (Wheaton, IL: Crossway, 2015), 219–52.

old Puritan term—*mortification*. To mortify is to subdue sin by means of self-denial and self-discipline. As the story of Cain and Abel reveals, sin is crouching at the door. Its desire is for us. By God's grace, we must "rule over it" (Gen. 4:7). In the Christian life, this process of mortification means subduing sin by denying the sinful desires of the flesh and disciplining ourselves to resist temptation (James 1:14). To use biblical language, mortification means putting down the "old man," killing the sinful desires of our flesh, as well as dying to this world. Or as Paul says in Romans 8:13, "For if you live according to the flesh you will die, but if by the Spirit you put to death the deeds of the body, you will live."

Mortification is not a suggestion, but a command, one issued throughout Scripture. In Romans 6, for example, Paul explains that we have been united with Christ in his death and one day we will be united with him in a resurrection like his (6:5). On that basis, we know that "our old self was crucified with him in order that the body of sin might be brought to nothing, so that we would no longer be enslaved to sin" (6:6). Paul powerfully concludes, "For one who has died has been set free from sin" (6:7). Those who have died with Christ, Paul goes on to explain, will also live with him. Since Christ was raised, he will never die again. So death "no longer has dominion over him. For the death he died he died to sin, once for all, but the life he lives he lives to God" (6:9–10). As those who have been united to Christ by faith, what does all this mean for the Christian life? Paul tells us: "So you also must consider yourselves dead to sin and alive to God in Christ Jesus" (6:11).

It is likely that Paul is reminding the Roman Christians of their old and new identity because Paul knew they would be tempted to return to the "old self." But if these Christians have died to sin and if their old self has been crucified with Christ, then it is contrary to their new identity in Christ to return to that old man, enslaving themselves all over again. Yet, this is the temptation every Christian faces because though the dominion and reign of sin has been broken, its influence is still present in this world. It's not until we reach glorification that temptations will be no more. As we saw in Question 22, sin's *legal* claim over us and *condemnation* of us has been eliminated by God's gracious verdict in justification. Yet, until glorification, remnants of the sinful nature continue and we must do battle against them.

It makes sense, then, why Paul would then give these Christians in Rome a command: "Let not sin therefore reign in your mortal body, to make you obey its passions. Do not present your members to sin as instruments for unrighteousness, but present yourselves to God as those who have been brought from death to life, and your members to God as instruments for righteousness. For sin will have no dominion over you, since you are not under law but under grace" (6:12–14). Paul expects us to live according to who we *are* (those brought from death to life by grace), not according to who we *were* (those under the dominion of sin and law).

Paul's command in Colossians 3 is similar to Romans 6. Once again, Paul begins by reminding Christians who they are in Christ. Since the believer has been "raised with Christ," he should then "seek the things that are above, where Christ is, seated at the right hand of God" (3:1). His mind is to be set on "things that are above" (3:2).[2] Don't forget, in other words, who you are in Christ. "For you have died, and your life is hidden with Christ in God" (3:3).[3] Don't forget what is to come, either. "When Christ who is your life appears, then you also will appear with him in glory" (3:4).

Paul has hinted at it already (see 3:1–2), but in light of our new standing in Christ, what should our disposition toward sin be? Paul is quite blunt: Put sin to death! Though this list is not meant to be exhaustive, notice how Paul addresses specific sins: "Put to death therefore what is earthly in you: sexual immorality, impurity, passion, evil desire, covetousness, which is idolatry" (3:5). Neither does Paul mince words about how God perceives these sins: "On account of these the wrath of God is coming" (3:6; cf. Zeph. 1:14–15).

Again, Paul's language of mortification ("put to death") has everything to do with our identity. It is precisely because we have died with Christ (Col. 2:20; 3:3) that we can overcome sin. Paul makes a point to remind the Colossians of who they are. "In these you too once walked, when you were living in them" (3:7). In other words, these sins used to characterize you before you died and were raised with Christ. But now they no longer should characterize you. Instead, you should put them to death should they try to intrude into your life once again. As Paul says, "But now you must put them all away: anger, wrath, malice, slander, and obscene talk from your mouth. Do not lie to one another, seeing that you have put off the old self with its practices and have put on the new self, which is being renewed in knowledge after the image of its creator" (3:8–10).

One should not miss how Paul utilizes the imagery of putting on or taking off clothing ("put off" in 3:9; "put on" in 3:10, 12) to make his point. All of these evils characterized our "old self." But we "have put off the old self with its practices."[4] Having put off the "old self," that "old self" can no longer be our identity. Therefore, whenever the evils of that old self pop up once more, seeking to return and regain a foothold, they must be severely squashed. Or to use the

---

2. I do not think Paul is advocating some form of asceticism (he warns against asceticism in Colossians 2:18), nor is he teaching that one should not be concerned with responsibilities here and now. Instead, Paul is contrasting a mind that is devoted to God and his kingdom (see Matt. 6:33; Phil. 3:10; Col. 1:10; 2:6) as opposed to a mind that is consumed with thoughts of sinful pleasures that this world offers.

3. Paul may be utilizing the language of Isaiah 49:2; Psalm 27:5–6; 31:19–20.

4. The aorist tense of the participle indicates that this putting off has already happened: "have put off" or ἀπεκδυσάμενοι (*apekdusamenoi*). Likewise, consider: "have put on" or ἐνδυσάμενοι (*endusamenoi*) in v. 10. Campbell observes how ἐνδυσάμενοι (aor mid ptc masc nom pl) is causal and the "perfective aspect here implicates an antecedent action" (Constantine R. Campbell, *Colossians and Philemon: A Handbook on the Greek Text* [Waco, TX: Baylor University Press, 2013], 54).

language of mortification, they must be killed ("put to death"; 3:5). Paul's language is one of violence; mortification is warfare. Knowing what a threat it is (and we should know if we recall our "old self"), sin must be slaughtered; otherwise Satan will devour us like a wild animal devours his prey (see 1 Peter 5:8).

If we're not careful, we can neglect this active habit and battle of mortification.[5] We can let down our guard, become lazy, or slowly be seduced by sin's allure. It can be like a sickness that subtly takes over until we wake up one morning and can't get out of bed. Several different symptoms usually indicate that this is happening:[6]

1. Sin is repeatedly present, but one gets in the habit of letting it go, turning a blind eye to it, and failing to confront it and kill it.

2. Denial sets in as one refuses to acknowledge that sin is a problem, even though all evidence points to the contrary.

3. When one chooses between sin and godliness, one is consistently choosing sin.

4. When one does resist sin, one does so only because of the threat of its external, negative consequences (rather than out of a love and fear for God).[7]

5. One does not fight against sin because it doesn't appear that God will discipline him for it.[8]

6. One permits sin entirely because one has already endured God's discipline.

More symptoms could be listed, but these symptoms, if present, are clear indicators that one is habitually failing to mortify sin and is in danger of

---

5. The full verse (v. 2) reads: "Set your minds on things that are above, not on things that are on earth." We should not think that because we are Christians we don't need to actively kill sin, as if we are somehow immune from sin and its poison. Nor should we conclude that we have reached a sufficient degree of sanctification and can now just relax, as if we have somehow risen above temptation to sin. Typically, the moment we do so is followed by a fall into sin, for sin tends to strike just when we think we are no longer susceptible. David's adultery with Bathsheba is an example of such a mindset (see 2 Sam. 11).

6. Though I have put them in my own words, these six points come from John Owen, "Of the Mortification of Sin in Believers," in *The Works of John Owen* (Edinburgh: Banner of Truth, 1991), 6:56–62; cf. J. V. Fesko, *A Christian's Pocket Guide to Growing in Holiness* (Fearn, Ross-shire, Scotland: Christian Focus, 2012), 16.

7. This is not to say that external consequences should not motivate us, but if this is all that motivates us then our obedience becomes superficial and is not rooted in a heart that loves and fears God. It is not heartfelt obedience.

8. One might even go so far as to conclude that he must, then, have the freedom to sin!

grieving the Holy Spirit if he has not already (Eph. 4:30).[9] For such a person, the threat is very serious for one is either blind to the danger of sin or, and this may be worse, intentionally justifying his sinful actions. Either way, he is not seeking "the things that are above" and setting his mind "on things that are above" as opposed to "things that are on earth." He is not living as one who has "been raised with Christ," nor as one who has "died" and whose "life is hidden with Christ in God" (Col. 3:1–3).

The Remedy for Sin-Sick Souls

Mortification is hard work. Sometimes it can feel impossible. As we close this chapter, we should keep in mind that mortification is not something we do alone. Rather, God is the one who is at work within us, and he will triumph over sin and the devil in the end. We know this because, though we await our final relief from the battle with sin, even now we rest assured that sin is no longer our master for Christ conquered sin on the cross and in his resurrection. John Owen's charge is fitting: "Set faith at work on Christ for the killing of thy sin. His blood is the great sovereign remedy for sin-sick souls. Live in this, and thou wilt die a conqueror."[10]

Summary

Sanctification is warfare. The Christian is at war against sin. Unless he kills sin, it will kill him. Therefore, mortification is a daily part of the Christian's pursuit after holiness. It involves putting to death our old self and living in line with our new self, our new identity in Christ.

REFLECTION QUESTIONS

1. How would you explain mortification, in your own words?

2. Why is mortification so necessary for sanctification?

3. Read Colossians 3. How seriously does Paul take mortification?

4. In Colossians 3, what everyday imagery does Paul use to describe mortification?

5. Read Romans 6. How does a failure to kill sin violate our new identity in Christ?

---

9. To grieve the Spirit is to bring sorrow to the Spirit because one has not trusted in Christ but has instead turned to sin.
10. Owen, "Of the Mortification of Sin in Believers," in *Works*, 6:79.

How Do We Grow in Likeness to Christ?

If mortification is the act of *putting off*, then vivification is the act *putting on*. In mortification we are putting to death sin and putting off all sinful desires; in vivification we are putting on righteousness, aligning our thoughts and actions into conformity with God's Word so that we might be renewed further into the image of Christ and made holy.

Vivification

Vivification should not be underestimated; it is extremely important. It's not enough to resist sin and to empty one's heart of any corruption; one must also fill his life up with the good blessings of the Spirit and practice godliness. Take a very practical example: stealing. As important as it is not to steal, one must also make a habit of being generous, giving to others rather than taking away (Eph. 4:28–29). Certainly mortification led to vivification with Zacchaeus, even at the very start of his Christian life. While previously a notorious tax collector (Luke 19:2), once Jesus confronted him Zacchaeus gave half of his goods to the poor and anyone he had defrauded he gave them fourfold in return (19:8). Seeing his actions and knowing his heart, Jesus concluded that salvation had come to the house of Zacchaeus that day (19:9). The point is, if mortification is really having an effect, it will naturally lead to vivification. They are two sides of the same coin.

To understand vivification better, let's return to Colossians 3. One may have noticed that we never finished Paul's train of thought but ended with the concept of putting sin to death since we have put off the old self. But if we continue in the passage, we discover that Paul transitions to talk about vivification. In Colossians 3:9–10 Paul says we "have put off the old self with its practices and have put on the new self, which is being renewed in knowledge after the image of its creator." As mentioned before, this putting off of the old self and putting on of the new self is something that has already happened. And yet, Paul says that this new self "is being renewed" (present tense; *avakain-oumenon*), implying that this transformation is an ongoing, lifelong process.

What does this renewal look like practically? Utilizing the imagery of clothing once more, Paul's answer comes in the form of an imperative: "put on . . ." (3:12).

> Put on then, as God's chosen ones, holy and beloved, compas-
> sionate hearts, kindness, humility, meekness, and patience,
> bearing with one another and, if one has a complaint against
> another, forgiving each other; as the Lord has forgiven you,
> so you also must forgive. And above all these put on love,
> which binds everything together in perfect harmony. And let
> the peace of Christ rule in your hearts, to which indeed you
> were called in one body. And be thankful. Let the word of
> Christ dwell in you richly, teaching and admonishing one an-
> other in all wisdom, singing psalms and hymns and spiritual
> songs, with thankfulness in your hearts to God. And what-
> ever you do, in word or deed, do everything in the name of
> the Lord Jesus, giving thanks to God the Father through him
> (3:12–17).

It is hard to think of a better description of the Christian life than this one. As pictured in the table below, the contrast between what the believer is to "put to death" and "put away" with what the believer is to "put on" could not be greater.

Table 10
Colossians 3:5–17[1]

Put to Death / Put Away	Put On
Sexual immorality, impurity, passion, evil desire, covetousness (3:5)	Compassionate hearts, kindness, humility, meekness, patience, and forgiveness (3:12–13)
Anger, wrath, malice, slander, obscene talk (3:8)	Love (3:14)
Lying (3:9)	Peace of Christ (3:15)

---

1. In this chart I am abbreviating some of these descriptions for the purpose of contrast.

Put to Death / Put Away	Put On
	Word of Christ dwells within and is used to teach and admonish in all wisdom (3:16)
	Singing psalms, hymns, spiritual songs with thankfulness to God (3:16)
	Do everything in the name of Jesus, giving thanks to God the Father (3:17)
	Compassionate hearts, kindness, humility, meekness, patience, and forgiveness (3:12–13)

A second passage where we see vivification highlighted is Ephesians 4, where Paul uses the language of "old man" and "new man" to explain sanctification.

> Now this I say and testify in the Lord, that you must no longer walk as the Gentiles do, in the futility of their minds. They are darkened in their understanding, alienated from the life of God because of the ignorance that is in them, due to their hardness of heart. They have become callous and have given themselves up to sensuality, greedy to practice every kind of impurity. But that is not the way you learned Christ!—assuming that you have heard about him and were taught in him, as the truth is in Jesus, to put off your old self, which belongs to your former manner of life and is corrupt through deceitful desires, and to be renewed in the spirit of your minds, and to put on the new self, created after the likeness of God in true righteousness and holiness (Eph. 4:17–24).

Paul warns these Ephesian Christians not to return to the "old man" (and no doubt some of the Ephesians were!). This old man was characterized by all the sins of the world. Instead, having been united to Christ, Christians must no longer walk in such darkness and impurity, but rather in true righteousness and holiness. They are those who "put off" the "old self" and "put on the new self." In the following table, consider the explicit contrast Paul makes between the "old" and "new" self:

Table 11
Ephesians 4:17–24

"Old Self"	"New Self"
futility of mind	renewed in the spirit of your minds
darkened in understanding	created after the likeness of God in true righteousness and holiness
alienated from life of God	
ignorant	
hardness of heart	
callous	
sensual	
greedy to practice every impurity	
corrupt through deceitful desires	

It should be noted, however, that the putting on of the new self, for Paul, is no abstract matter. Instead, it takes on very practical implications. In fact, in the verses that directly follow (4:25–32) Paul gives very practical examples of what it looks like to "put off" and "put on." Consider the following comparison:

Table 12
Putting Off and Putting On in Ephesians 4:25–32

"Put Off"	"Put On"
falsehood	speak the truth
anger	peace/reconciliation[2] (do not let the sun go down on your anger)
stealing	honest work (result: generous sharing/giving)
corrupt talk	talk that builds up (talk that gives grace to hearers)
bitterness, wrath, anger, clamor, slander, malice	kind, tenderhearted, forgiving one another

---

2. "Peace" and "reconciliation" are not named by Paul, but seem to be what is implied in the phrase "do not let the sun go down on your anger." In other words, rather than staying angry, go to the person and reconcile with him or her, resulting in peace between the two of you.

Already we noted the example of Zacchaeus, but here Paul puts his finger on the issue as well: One must put off stealing (which involves deceit) and instead do honest work so that he can give and share with others. Or consider lying. Paul says to put off lies and to put on truth telling; put off corrupt talk and put on speech that builds up. After all, we are brothers and sisters with one another, united together in the same body. Apparently, Paul believes vivification has much to do with life together in the church. Putting on the new man takes practical effect in how we treat one another.

In summary, both mortification and vivification are key aspects to sanctification. It's not enough to put off the old man; we must put on the new man.

Renewed into the Image of Christ

As we conclude our discussion of vivification, it is critical that we not forget the goal in this process—namely, renewal into the image of Christ. As mentioned in Question 8, each aspect of the order of salvation (*ordo salutis*) flows out of union with Christ. This is no less true with sanctification (Eph. 4:15; 1 Cor. 1:30). Naturally, then, the pattern of our sanctification is renewal into Christ's likeness.[3] Vivification, in other words, is to result in likeness to Christ.

Remember, Jesus is the true and perfect image of God (John 14:8–9; 2 Cor. 4:4; Col. 1:15; Heb. 1:3). As those who are in Christ, we are being made more and more, by the power of the Spirit, into his likeness. Yes, sin has terribly distorted the image of God within us. But thanks to the cross and empty tomb, as well as the indwelling presence of the Holy Spirit, that image is being restored. This process started at regeneration (see Question 15) and continues throughout the Christian life. One day, when we are glorified, that image will finally be renewed in full.

Until then, the Spirit is continually at work upon us and within us to renew that image. Very practically, we are being made more and more like Jesus. Paul goes so far as to say that this is the fruit of our election. Those whom the Father "predestined" he "predestined to be *conformed to the image of his Son,* in order that he might be the firstborn among many brothers" (Rom. 8:29). Being conformed into the image of Christ was God's plan in eternity and is the goal of our election.[4]

Furthermore, though this reality will not be completed until glory, even now the future has broken into the present as Christians reflect the glory of Christ, albeit imperfectly. Paul can say to the Corinthians, "And we all, with

---

3. This language of "pattern" comes from Anthony A. Hoekema, *Saved by Grace* (Grand Rapids: Eerdmans, 1989), 197.
4. Ryle adds, "We must be holy, because this is one grand end and purpose for which Christ came into the world"(J. C. Ryle, *Holiness: Its Nature, Hindrances, Difficulties, and Roots* [Moscow, ID: Charles Nolan, 2011], 49).

unveiled face, beholding the glory of the Lord, are being transformed into the same image from one degree of glory to another." Paul concludes that this has "come from the Lord who is the Spirit" (2 Cor. 3:18). The day is coming when this transformation will reach its full potential and on that day the new heavens and earth will be full of God's elect sons and daughters who, by his grace, have been made into the image of his Son.

Summary

If mortification is the act of putting off, then vivification is the act putting on. In mortification we are putting to death sin and putting off all sinful desires; in vivification we are putting on righteousness, aligning our thoughts and actions into conformity with God's Word so that we might be renewed further into the image of Christ and made holy.

REFLECTION QUESTIONS

1. What is vivification, and why isn't mortification enough?

2. Read Colossians 3. What does Paul say should be put away, and what should be put on?

3. Read Ephesians 4. How does the "old self" compare to the "new self," and which of these characterizes you?

4. What specific sin in Ephesians 4:25–32 do you find yourself needing to "put off"? What then do you need to "put on"?

5. What does vivification have to do with being renewed into the image of Christ?

QUESTION 33

Will We Ever Reach Perfection in This Life?

In the history of the church, some have believed that a Christian can attain some form of perfection in this life.[1] For example, the great eighteenth century preacher John Wesley has become known for his work *A Plain Account of Christian Perfection*.[2] This is the view that a Christian can attain a state of "entire sanctification." Contemporary Wesleyan theologian Melvin Dieter defines entire sanctification as a "personal, definitive work of God's sanctifying grace by which *the war within oneself might cease and the heart be fully released from rebellion into wholehearted love for God and others*." It is a "*total death to sin* and an entire renewal in the image of God."[3] Entire sanctification, which is said to be an instantaneous experience, involves the complete

---

1. There are many different views on sanctification. I have chosen to focus my attention on responding to just one, the Wesleyan view of entire sanctification, since it poses as the most popular alternative to an Augustinian/Reformed view. However, one might also consider the influence of Keswick teaching in the last century. For two helpful critiques, see J. I. Packer, *Keep in Step with the Spirit: Finding Fullness in Our Walk with God*, 2nd ed. (Grand Rapids: Baker, 2005), 120–33; Andrew David Naselli, *No Quick Fix: Where Higher Life Theology Came From, What It Is, and Why It's Harmful* (Bellingham, WA: Lexham, 2017).
2. John Wesley, *A Plain Account of Christian Perfection* (New York: G. Lane and P. P. Sandford, 1844). Also see idem, "Brief Thoughts on Christian Perfection," in vol. 11 of The Works of John Wesley, 3rd ed. (1892; Peabody, MA: Hendrickson, 1984). Today many diverse denominations would fall within the stream of perfectionist teaching, including the Wesleyan Methodist Church, the Free Methodist Church, the Salvation Army, the Church of God, the Christian and Missionary Alliance, the Nazarene Church, the Pilgrim Holiness Church, etc. See George M. Marsden, *Fundamentalism and American Culture* (New York: Oxford University Press, 1980), 75.
3. Melvin Dieter, "The Wesleyan Perspective," in *Five Views on Sanctification*, ed. Stanley Gundry (Grand Rapids: Zondervan, 1987), 17 (emphasis added).

destruction of man's sinful nature. To quote Wesley himself, it means that "all inward sin is taken away."[4]

However, this affirmation of perfectionism is often qualified. For example, Wesley defined "sin" as a "*voluntary* transgression of a *known* law." Wesley is not talking about "*involuntary* transgression of a divine law, known or unknown."[5] Wesley does not call involuntary transgression sin. Entire sanctification does not include those thoughts or actions that are involuntary transgressions, but only conscious, voluntary violations of known commands. In short, one must recognize something to be a sin for it to really be a sin.[6] Should one do something wrong without knowing it was wrong, then it does not count as a voluntary sin and one can remain in a state of entire sanctification. With such a qualification in mind, Wesleyans have shied away from using phrases like "sinless perfection" to describe their view.[7]

However, those outside the Wesleyan tradition have rejected the doctrine of entire sanctification because they believe it to be inconsistent with the biblical witness. As we will argue in this chapter, Scripture teaches that one will not reach perfection until glory, even if we mean by that merely freedom from voluntary sins. Though the Christian is no longer under the dominion of sin, nevertheless, the fight against sin continues until death, with wins and losses along the way. Sanctification is never complete but is a progressive process.

Arguments for Entire Sanctification

There are several arguments made for entire sanctification.[8] First, appeal is made to examples in the Bible of individuals believed to have achieved perfection (as defined above): Noah, Job, Zacharias, Elisabeth, Nathanael, and the "mature" in many of Paul's epistles (1 Cor. 2:6; Phil. 3:15).[9] Also, appeal is especially made to 1 John.[10] In 3:9 we read, "No one born of God makes a practice of sinning, for God's seed abides in him, and he cannot keep on sinning because he has been born of God." And in 5:18 we read, "We know that

---

4. "A Plain Account," in *Works*, 11:387. For other similar descriptions, see H. Orton Wiley, *Christian Theology* (Kansas City, MO: Beacon Hill, 1958), 2:446; Donald Metz, *Studies in Biblical Holiness* (Kansas City, MO: Beacon Hill, 1971), 250; Kenneth J. Grider, *Entire Sanctification* (Kansas City, MO: Beacon Hill, 1980), 27.

5. "A Plain Account," 11:396. Similarly, see Metz, *Biblical Holiness*, 79.

6. Speaking of involuntary transgressions, Wesley refused to call them sins: "You may call [involuntary transgressions] sins, if you please: I do not" ("A Plain Account," *Works*, 11:396).

7. E.g., J. Sidlow Baxter, *A New Call to Holiness* (Grand Rapids: Zondervan, 1973), 121; Kenneth J. Grider, *Entire Sanctification* (Kansas City, MO: Beacon Hill, 1980), 36; Metz, *Biblical Holiness*, 228; Dieter, "The Wesleyan Perspective," 91.

8. This chapter is indebted to the excellent work of Anthony Hoekema, whose outline and argument I follow. See *Saved by Grace* (Grand Rapids: Eerdmans, 1989), 214–25.

9. Wiley, *Christian Theology*, 2:515. Also see Wesley, "A Plain Account," in *Works*, 11:441–42.

10. Wesley, "A Plain Account," 11:375; Metz, *Biblical Holiness*, 250; Richard Taylor, *Exploring Christian Holiness* (Kansas City, MO: Beacon Hill, 1985), 3:62.

everyone who has been born of God does not keep on sinning." These passages, it's argued, assume that entire sanctification is a real, attainable state.

Additionally, Paul prays in 1 Thessalonians 5:23–24 that God himself would "sanctify you completely" and that "your whole spirit and soul and body be kept blameless at the coming of our Lord Jesus Christ." Paul then concludes, "He who calls you is faithful; he will surely do it." Now why would Paul pray this way if he didn't think God completely sanctifies Christians in this life, prior to death? Surely Paul expects his prayer to be answered.[11] But Scripture not only issues prayers for perfection but commands as well. For example, Jesus says in Matthew 5:48, "You therefore must be perfect, as your heavenly Father is perfect." Why would Jesus and the apostles give such commands if perfection were not attainable?

Problems with Entire Sanctification

Despite these arguments, Anthony Hoekema gives several reasons why they remain unconvincing. To begin with, the persons listed as examples cannot be said to have reached a state of entire sanctification.[12] As exemplary as they may have been, individuals like Job and Noah were far from it. Job despised himself, even repenting of his sin (Job 42:6), and Noah, though praiseworthy for being a just man, became drunk not long after the flood (Gen. 9). And when Paul refers to the "mature" in 1 Corinthians 2:6, it is reading into the text to say that "mature" here must mean perfect. Actually, "mature" refers to believers who are spiritually obedient and wise in comparison to brand-new Christians who have much to learn. The context says nothing about the "mature" being without voluntary transgression; nothing at all.

Also, the context of Philippians 3:15 disproves entire sanctification. In verse 12 Paul is very clear that perfection has *not* been attained: "Not that I have already obtained this or am already perfect, but I press on to make it my own, because Christ Jesus has made me his own." It's fair to say that if the apostle Paul did not think he had reached that "perfect" state, no one has. Instead, Paul says, he presses on toward the "goal for the prize of the upward call of God in Christ Jesus" (3:14). As it turns out, being "mature" means being conscious that one has *not* reached perfection and must still press on to the goal. A better approach to men and women in the Bible is to recognize that even the most godly of these individuals recognized their ongoing fight against sin and continual, neverending need to repent and seek further sanctification, knowing that they would not reach that perfect state until heaven. They all agreed that Jesus alone lived in a state of perfect obedience.

---

11. See Baxter, *A New Call to Holiness*, 107, 115, 147; Grider, *Entire Sanctification*, 96, 140; W. T. Purkiser, *Exploring Christian Holiness* (Kansas City, MO: Beacon Hill, 1983), 1:205.
12. My argument here is indebted to Hoekema, *Saved by Grace*, 218–25.

But what about texts like 1 John 3:9 and 5:18? It is a mistake to read perfection into these verses. Instead, John is saying that those who have been truly born again do not live in sin. Or as Hoekema puts it, they do not go on "doing and enjoying sin with complete abandon."[13] This fits the context of the entire letter. Furthermore, to say that these verses teach entire sanctification would mean that John is contradicting himself, for he very clearly says at the opening of his letter, "If we say we have no sin, we deceive ourselves, and the truth is not in us. . . . If we say we have not sinned, we make him a liar, and his word is not in us" (1:8, 10). A stronger denial of perfectionism is hard to come by in Scripture.

On close examination, prayers and commands for perfection don't prove to be proof texts for entire sanctification either. In 1 Thessalonians 5:23 it is true that Paul is praying for the completion of sanctification when he says, "may the God of peace himself sanctify you completely." But remember, this is a prayer, not a dogmatic assertion. It's a step too far to assume that Paul is saying that such a sanctifying work will happen at some definitive point in one's lifetime (something similar could be said of Matthew 5:38). Rather, Paul is summarizing the work of God over the entirety of one's lifetime, culminating in the return of Christ.

Moreover, context would rule against such an assumption, for the rest of the verse indicates that Paul has in mind that time when Christ comes back. Paul prays that the Christian would be "kept blameless at the coming of our Lord Jesus Christ." Paul is not talking about a second blessing experienced at a definitive point in one's life, subsequent to conversion; instead, he is praying that Christians would not compromise but would remain faithful, being persistently characterized by holiness and steadfastness, until the Lord's return. Notice also that the Christian's confidence is grounded not in attaining a state of entire sanctification, but in God's faithfulness to preserve his elect until his Son's second coming. For this reason Paul can say, "He who calls you is faithful; he will surely do it." Yes, entire sanctification will come, but it will come when Christ returns in glory. It is not something already attained, but something we hope for and long for, knowing that it will be given to us in the life to come. Paul's hopeful gaze is set on the world yet to come, not on the one already in hand.[14]

Misunderstanding Sanctification and the Ongoing Struggle against Sin

There are also broader theological problems with entire sanctification. Anthony Hoekema points out several that must be taken into consideration.[15]

---

13. Ibid., 218.
14. On this point, see B. B. Warfield, *Perfectionism*, ed. Samuel C. Craig (Philadelphia: P&R, 1958), 462–63.
15. Hoekema, *Saved by Grace*, 220–25.

First, *entire sanctification assumes an inadequate definition of sin.* As we saw, for the Wesleyan only deliberate transgression of a known law counts as sin. One could violate God's law, but if that individual doesn't know it then one's entire sanctification is not violated. But as we saw in Question 1, sin is sin whether one realizes it or not. Whether it is a sin of omission or commission, all transgression of God's holy law counts as sin. A failure to be conscious of one's own anger, covetousness, lust, etc., does not somehow excuse one from being guilty. In fact, the process of sanctification seems to assume that one will *not* be aware of one's own sin. That is the point. The Holy Spirit makes us more and more aware, convicting us of our wrongdoing, wrongdoing that we previously may not have even considered sinful. And as the Spirit opens our eyes, we see just how deeply our hearts must be cleansed. Ignorance, therefore, is never acceptable in God's sight. Sin is sin, and whether we know it or not, there is no question that God is aware.

Second, *entire sanctification lowers the standard of perfection.* Entire sanctification only requires the absence of known and deliberate transgression; unknown and undeliberate transgression does not disqualify oneself from remaining in the state of entire sanctification. "The highest perfection which man can attain, while the soul dwells in the body," says Wesley, "does not exclude ignorance, and error, and a thousand other infirmities,"[16] nor does it exclude "involuntary transgression of a divine law, known or unknown."[17]

But is this the biblical standard of perfection? It is not. One is hard-pressed to find any qualification of perfection in this Wesleyan sense in Scripture at all. Scripture never tries to lower the bar or the standard of perfection. It will not settle, as the Wesleyan does, for an imperfect perfection.[18] No, perfect *means* perfect, which is why, as long as we remain in the body, we will not experience such perfection until final glorification.

Third, Scripture teaches that there always remains an ongoing, conscious struggle with sin since sanctification is a progressive work. Consider the numerous ways Scripture attests to the ongoing, progressive, and unfinished work of sanctification:

- The Christian has an ongoing fight with his own flesh (Gal. 5:16–17).
- The Christian is to cleanse himself from any and every defilement (2 Cor. 7:1).
- Temptation is still an ongoing, real threat to the Christian (Rom. 7:7; James 1:14; 1 Peter 2:11; 1 John 2:16).

---

16. Wesley, "Sermon 76. On Perfection," in *Works*, 6:412.
17. Wesley, "Plain Account," 11:396.
18. E.g., Metz, *Biblical Holiness*, 228.

- Scripture assumes that the sanctifying process is progressive, not completed at a specific point in the Christian's life (Rom. 12:2; Eph. 4:11–16; 1 Peter 2:2; 2 Peter 3:18).
- No Christian can claim to be without sin (1 Kgs. 8:46; Ps. 130:3; Prov. 20:9; James 3:2; 1 John 1:8).
- Even the most impressive Christians claim to still be the chief of sinners (1 Tim. 1:15) and in need of repentance and forgiveness (Job 42:6; Ps. 32:5; 130:3–4; Isa. 6:5; 64:6; Dan. 9:15–16; Mic. 7:18–19; 1 John 1:9).
- Jesus assumes confession of sin will be a part of the daily life of his followers (Matt. 6:12).
- The Christian always lives in the continual tension between the *already/not yet* of sanctification, being no longer enslaved by the flesh (Rom. 8:9), yet still having to fight the desires of the flesh (Gal. 5:16–17); having crucified the flesh (Gal. 5:24) and died to sin (Rom. 6:2, 11); yet still needing to put to death the deeds of the body (Rom. 8:13); having been crucified to the world (Gal. 6:14), yet resisting conformity to this world (Rom. 12:2); being unleavened, yet exhorted to cleanse out the old leaven (1 Cor. 5:7).[19]
- The Christian is continually commanded to seek holiness rather than assume he has already reached such a perfect state (2 Cor. 7:1; Phil. 3:13–14; Heb. 12:14; 1 Peter 1:16).

The Danger of Two-Tiered Christianity

In closing, a practical-pastoral word is necessary. While we can admire the great zeal for holiness that characterizes the Wesleyan view, we must acknowledge that perfection teaching has the potential to be harmful in the ministry of the church. The reason is simple enough. The doctrine of entire sanctification results in two types of Christians, those perfected and those not. The consequence is a two-tiered Christianity, with some Christians being far superior to others.

As some can bear witness from personal experience, this doctrine can leave those without this "second blessing" of entire sanctification utterly depressed, discouraged, and hopeless. No matter how hard they try, they still find sin in their lives, while others have apparently reached the higher state.

So it is critical to understand that the Christian life is not one in which perfection is achieved here and now. To think this way is to forget that Scripture portrays the Christian life as an ongoing battle against indwelling sin (Rom. 7:20–23; Heb. 12:1; 1 John 1:8). J. I. Packer warns against those evangelicals who teach others that "once we become Christians, God's power in us will immediately cancel out defects of character and make our whole lives plain

---

19. For a helpful overview of this tension, see Hoekema, *Saved by Grace*, 222–25.

sailing." On the one hand, says Packer, "God sometimes works wonders of sudden deliverance from this or that weakness at conversion." However, "every Christian's life is a constant fight against the pressures and pulls of the world, the flesh, and the devil." In other words, we are engaged in a battle (see Matt. 26:41; Rom. 7:20; Gal. 5:17; Heb. 12:3–4). It's a battle, Packer concludes, for "Christlikeness (that is, habits of wisdom, devotion, love, and righteousness" and it is "as grueling as it is unending."[20]

So what shall we conclude? We must conclude that sanctification is always progressive and unfinished until glory. While victory is guaranteed (a point we will explore in the next two chapters), this side of glorification the battle rages on, and as God's soldiers we take up our sword to fight against sin and Satan. We dare not assume the battle is over until Christ brings us home and we can, finally, retire our weapons of warfare.

Summary

Sanctification is always progressive and unfinished until glory. The Bible always assumes that the Christian must fight against sin and that fight is not complete until glorification. Scripture never teaches that subsequent to conversion one will experience a second blessing whereby one reaches a state of entire sanctification. Rather, there always remains an ongoing, conscious struggle with sin since sanctification is a progressive work.

REFLECTION QUESTIONS

1. What are the most significant arguments for and against entire sanctification?

2. In what ways does entire sanctification change our definition of sin and transgression?

3. In what ways does entire sanctification change the definition of "perfection"?

4. Read Galatians 5:16–17. How does Scripture describe our ongoing fight against sin?

5. What are some practical pitfalls that can result from perfectionism teaching in the church?

---

20. Packer, *Keep in Step with the Spirit*, 26. I have limited our discussion to entire sanctification. However, other movements that have emphasized a second experience include the Keswick movement, though it differs from Wesleyan theology in significant ways. For a critique, see ibid., 120–37.

Can We Lose Our Salvation? (Part 1)

Can a sinner who has genuinely been born again, converted by the Spirit, and justified by God's grace lose his/her salvation and suffer eternal punishment in hell?[1] Few questions strike closer to home than this one. Here we come to not only a doctrinal question but a pastoral one, for one's answer will have untold consequences for how one lives the Christian life. So what's the answer? In this chapter, we will learn that all those whom God has predestined, regenerated, converted, and justified, he *will* sanctify and glorify. In short, God will never permit anyone who has genuine faith in Christ to lose his/her salvation. Those he has united to Christ will stay united to Christ to the very end.[2]

This fundamental truth does not make light of the very real fact that Christians will experience incredible hardship and failure. Satan and the world will tempt the Christian and, at times, due to the corruption that remains within the believer this side of heaven, the Christian will sin. As the Westminster Confession of Faith says, he will "neglect the means" of his "preservation" and "fall into grievous sins," and for a time "incur God's displeasure," even grieving the Holy Spirit (17.3). As a result, that divine grace and comfort that previously felt so real and close will feel so far away. The heart has been hardened and the conscience wounded. And God may even decide to exercise his loving discipline. Nevertheless, the Christian remains God's child still. And though these times of sin and discipline are incredibly painful, God will nonetheless sustain his children through them, so that they

---

1. Notice the qualifications in this sentence. We are talking about real, authentic, genuine born-again Christians. This is not to deny that there are some who look like Christians but in time it becomes apparent that they were not Christians after all.

2. As I state in the preface to the book, my purpose is not to explore all the various views on this topic, but rather to focus in on what Scripture itself teaches. Nevertheless, for treatments that do critique those who reject the eternal security of the believer, see the bibliography.

do not finally fall away from the "state of grace, but shall certainly persevere" to the very end and be "eternally saved" (17.1).

God's Omnipotent Faithfulness to His Covenant Promises

The first thing to understand about the security of our salvation is that it is rooted first and foremost in our doctrine of God. It is precisely because God is truthful, faithful, all-powerful, and unchanging that he will not go back on his promise nor allow anyone or anything to remove us from the kingdom of his beloved Son. The point is this: Our eternal life does not finally depend upon our willpower, strength, and effort, but upon God himself. Again, the WCF says it beautifully: "This perseverance of the saints depends not upon their own free will, but upon the immutability of the decree of election, flowing from the free and unchangeable love of God the Father; upon the efficacy of the merit and intercession of Jesus Christ, the abiding of the Spirit, and of the seed of God within them, and the nature of the covenant of grace: from all which arises also the certainty and infallibility thereof" (17.2). Our eternal security depends upon the *character* and the *power* of God. Let's consider each.

First, the character of God guarantees the preservation of the saints. How do we know that God will not go back on his covenant promise to save? This question has to do with God's character, specifically whether or not his word is *truthful* and whether or not he will be *faithful* to his word.[3] How do we know that God will not change his mind? This question also has to do with God's character, specifically whether or not the God of the Bible is *immutable*.

Scripture is reassuring. God is not only said to be the true God (Ps. 96:5; 97:7; 115:4–8; Isa. 44:9–10; John 14:6; 1 Thess. 1:9), the standard of truth (John 17:17; Rom. 3:34), and therefore the one whose word is truthful (Ps. 12:6; Heb. 6:18), but God is said to be unchanging in his:

1. Nature: God will never be wiser, holier, more loving, more powerful, more eternal, more omnipresent, etc. than he is already (Exod. 3:14; Ps. 102:25–27; Mal. 3:6; Heb. 13:8; James 1:17).

2. Character: God does not change ethically-morally, becoming better or worse (Mal. 3:6; James 1:17).

3. Purpose (Will): God is sovereign and his eternal purposes cannot be thwarted (Job 23:13; Ps. 33:11; Prov. 19:21; Isa. 14:24; 46:8–11; Matt. 13:35; 25:34; Eph. 1:4, 11; 3:9, 11; 2 Tim. 2:19; 1 Peter 1:20; Rev. 13:8).

---

3. Truthfulness, according to Scripture, can also mean "faithfulness" (in Hebrew the word for truth is *'emeth*, which can mean faithfulness). So when we say God is truthful we also mean God is faithful. For an extensive treatment of God's faithfulness to his covenant word, see Matthew Barrett, *God's Word Alone: The Authority of Scripture* (Grand Rapids: Zondervan, 2016).

4. Promises: God does not break his promises, nor go back on his word (Num. 23:19; 1 Sam. 15:29; Mal. 3:6; Rom. 8:28; Eph. 1:11; 2 Tim. 2:13; Heb. 6:17).[4]

Points three and four are especially notable, because one of God's "purposes" and one of his "promises," as we will see below, is that he will not lose anyone who has been born again and converted to Christ.

Second, the power of God guarantees the preservation of the saints. Hypothetically, God might be truthful, he might even be faithful, but he might not be powerful enough to make his word happen. In other words, he might have all the wisdom in the world, but be impotent to effect his plan. In this scenario, it wouldn't matter how truthful, faithful, or wise God is; he remains incapable of bringing about his will.

Thankfully, this is not true of the God of the Bible. He is said not only to be all-wise (Ps. 104:24; Rom. 16:27), but all-powerful (omnipotent), too (Gen. 18:14; Job 42:1–2; Ps. 24:8; Isa. 14:24, 27; 40:12; 46:10; 55:11; Jer. 32:17–19; Dan. 4:35; Mark 10:27; Luke 1:37; Rev. 4:8; 11:17). He is said not only to be faithful and true to his promises but sovereign in the execution and delivery of those promises for the salvation of his people (Rom. 1:16; 2 Cor. 1:22–24; Eph. 3:20–21).

All that to say, the God who guarantees that he will not lose any of his elect (a point biblically supported below) has all the credibility in the world since his very character demonstrates that he is true and trustworthy, faithful and wise, as well as all-powerful and sovereign to fulfill what he has promised—namely, the final redemption of his covenant people.

Election, Christ, and Perseverance

It's not just the doctrine of God, however, that buttresses our final perseverance and glorification. As Louis Berkhof points out, many other aspects of our salvation do the same.[5]

First, God's unconditional election in eternity guarantees that none of his elect will be lost. As we saw in Questions 10–11, election does not merely make the salvation of God's elect a possibility; rather, final salvation is secure. Those whom God elects cannot lose their election.

Second, the covenant of redemption solidifies the believer's final salvation. In this covenant God has a certain people he is sending his Son to die for. By fulfilling the covenant of redemption, the Son receives this chosen people as his reward. As Berkhof explains, "In the covenant of redemption God gave His people to His Son as the reward for the latter's obedience and suffering.

---

4. Though adapted and modified, these four points are indebted to Stephen Wellum's lectures on the doctrine of God.
5. Here I am following the lead of Louis Berkhof, *Systematic Theology* (Edinburgh: Banner of Truth, 2003), 547–48, though with some modifications.

This reward was fixed from eternity and was not left contingent on any uncertain faithfulness of man. God does not go back on His promise, and therefore it is impossible that they who are reckoned as being in Christ, as forming a part of His reward, can be separated from Him (Rom. 8:38, 39), and that they who have entered the covenant as a communion of life should fall out."[6]

Third, the intercession of Christ certifies the salvation of God's elect. In fulfilling the covenant of redemption, Christ not only paid the penalty for sin but he rose on the third day and sits at the right hand of the Father where he intercedes on our behalf with the Father. And we know from Scripture that the intercession of the Son is always effectual. The author of Hebrews says that since Jesus holds his priesthood permanently, "he is able to save to the uttermost those who draw near to God through him, since he always lives to make intercession for them" (Heb. 7:25).

Fourth, the Spirit will not abandon those whom he has united to Christ. Remember, in effectual calling and regeneration the believer has been united to Christ (see Questions 8–9). Scripture gives no indication that the Spirit will then leave this work of union incomplete. Rather, it is everywhere assumed that those united to Christ at the start of their Christian life will be preserved until they see Christ face to face. That the bond of this union with Christ will not be broken depends upon the faithfulness and omnipotence of the Holy Spirit, which brings us full circle. He has not called, regenerated, justified, only to fail in his work to sanctify. In conversion he put before the believer eternal life (John 3:36; 5:24; 6:54); the Spirit will in no way fail to see the believer receive that life eternal in full.

Biblical Support from the Gospels

Now that we've established that our security is rooted in the very character of God, as well as the intercessory work of Christ and the efficacious application of Christ's work by the Spirit, where in Scripture do we see promises made by God that he will not abandon, forsake, or lose any of his children? We see such promises in both the Gospels and the Epistles.

In Luke 22:31–32, Jesus gives us a behind the scenes look at spiritual warfare, in this case Satan's attempt to destroy Simon (Peter). "Simon, Simon, behold, Satan demanded to have you that he might sift you like wheat, but I have prayed for you that your faith may not fail. And when you have turned again, strengthen your brothers." Notice, first of all, that Satan must ask permission to even touch one of God's children. God has full control over his saints what can and cannot happen to them (cf. Job 1). But more to the point, the sifting like wheat refers to Peter's forthcoming denial of Jesus (22:33–34; cf. 22:54–62). Satan's desire is to destroy the faith of Peter through this intense testing. However, Jesus then says that he has

---

6. Ibid., 547.

prayed for Peter that his faith may not fail. Jesus knows his prayer will be effective, for he then assumes Peter will be restored when he instructs Peter to strengthen his fellow disciples after he has repented ("turned again"; *epistrepsas*) and turned back to Christ.

Therefore, when Jesus says he has prayed that Peter's faith would "not fail" (*mē eklipē*), Jesus means: not fail totally, finally, or completely. Yes, Peter does fail the initial test, for he denies knowing Jesus three times. However, there is a bigger test, as to whether or not Peter will abandon following and believing in Jesus altogether. This is a test Peter does not fail, as proven through his repentance. Of course, such repentance and turning back to Jesus is not ultimately due to Peter but to the grace of God. And here, in Luke 22, we see that it is due to the efficacy of Jesus' own prayer.

We, as children of God, can rest assured that Jesus does the same for us. Though we, too, may fail when tempted, Jesus, as our mediator and intercessor, prays for us so that we will not finally fall away but turn back and be restored. As Hebrews 7:25 makes especially clear, since Jesus holds his priesthood permanently, "he is able to save to the uttermost those who draw near to God through him, since he always lives to make intercession for them."

The efficacy of Jesus' prayer in Luke 22 is only further solidified when we turn to the Gospel of John. Consider these many promises from the lips of Jesus himself:

> For God so loved the world, that he gave his only Son, that whoever believes in him should not perish but have eternal life (John 3:16).

> Jesus said to her [the Samaritan woman], "Everyone who drinks of this water will be thirsty again, but whoever drinks of the water that I will give him will never be thirsty again. The water that I will give him will become in him a spring of water welling up to eternal life" (John 4:13–14).

> Truly, truly, I say to you, whoever hears my word and believes him who sent me has eternal life. He does not come into judgment, but has passed from death to life (John 5:24; cf. 1 John 5:11–13).

> I [Jesus] am the living bread that came down from heaven. If anyone eats of this bread, he will live forever. And the bread that I will give for the life of the world is my flesh (John 6:51).

> I am the resurrection and the life. Whoever believes in me,
> though he die, yet shall he live, and everyone who lives and
> believes in me shall never die (John 11:25–26).

Do not pass too quickly over these promises, lest you miss the finality and guarantee of eternal life once one has trusted in Christ. Countless times Jesus promises that new birth and conversion result in a permanent break with condemnation, as well as an irreversible union with Christ, his kingdom, and the everlasting life he alone gives. This transfer from death to life is never qualified or considered reversible.

As we saw in Questions 13–14, John 6 is a powerful passage in support of effectual calling. However, Jesus, in John 6, not only has something to say about that initial call, but he also has something to say about the believer's eternal security. He says to his listeners, "All that the Father gives me will come to me, and whoever comes to me I will never cast out" (6:37). Notice, not only does Jesus guarantee that the elect will be drawn to Jesus, but when they do come Jesus promises that he will never throw them out. He then goes on to explain how he has come to do the Father's will, and the Father's will is that "I should lose nothing of all that he has given me, but raise it up on the last day." Jesus is very straightforward: He will accomplish the Father's will, and the Father's will is that he not lose any that the Father has entrusted to him. And by "lose" Jesus has in mind being condemned, the very opposite of eternal life.

That eternal life and death hang in the balance is plain in what Jesus promises next: "For this is the will of my Father, that everyone who looks on the Son and believes in him should have eternal life, and I will raise him up on the last day" (6:40). By definition, eternal life is forever. It's not as if one receives *eternal* life, only to discover (perhaps due to a lack of faith) that the eternal life he/she had is not so eternal after all. No, eternal life is what it sounds like. And here Jesus promises that if one has believed in the Son, he possesses this eternal life. Not only that, but Jesus promises the future resurrection from the grave to such persons as well. Jesus could not provide believers with a stronger guarantee of eternal security than resurrection. And he is credible to give such a guarantee since he is the resurrection and the life, and by his own resurrection proves to be the firstfruits of the great harvest to come (1 Cor. 15).

As clear and as straightforward as Jesus is in John 6 concerning the believer's security, he is even more so in John 10:27–29: "My sheep hear my voice, and I know them, and they follow me. I give them eternal life, and they will never perish, and no one will snatch them out of my hand. My Father, who has given them to me, is greater than all, and no one is able to snatch them out of the Father's hand." To say that Christians can lose their salvation undercuts the entire thrust of this passage, which places the believer safely in the hands of the Son and the Father. Notice what is being taught here:

- The Christian is given eternal life by Christ.
- The Christian will never perish.
- No one can snatch the Christian from the hand of Christ.
- The Father has given the Christian to his Son for safekeeping.
- If the Son's hold on the Christian is secure, so is the Father's, for he is the one who gave the Christian to the Son in the first place.

We should conclude, then, that the "security of believers is thus not dependent on their hold of Christ, but on Christ's hold on them."[7]

Summary

Jesus himself promises and guarantees that he will not lose any child of God, not even one. Those who have been born again and converted to Christ will not fall away from the faith. They are kept safe due to the omnipotent faithfulness of God to his covenant promises.

REFLECTION QUESTIONS

1. What divine attributes play an important role in how we understand the believer's eternal security and why?

2. As you read the story of the Bible, where do you get a constant impression that this God is one who is faithful to his saving, covenant promises?

3. Read Luke 22:31–32. What does Jesus say to Peter that guarantees Peter's preservation?

4. Study John 6:37–40. What role does Jesus play in the final salvation of the believer?

5. How does John 10:27–29 strengthen your assurance of salvation?

---

7. Hoekema, *Saved by Grace*, 239. Some argue that while Christ will not lose his sheep, nonetheless, the sheep may let go of Christ. Cf. Robert Shank, *Life in the Son* (Springfield, MO: Westcott, 1960), 56–60; Grant R. Osborne, "Exegetical Notes on Calvinist Texts," in *Grace Unlimited*, ed. Clark H. Pinnock (Minneapolis: Bethany Fellowship, 1975), 179; Dale Moody, *The Word of Truth* (Grand Rapids: Eerdmans, 1981), 356–57. Hoekema counters: "The 'no one' to whom Jesus alludes must include believers themselves. Our hold on Christ may sometimes be very weak, but Christ's hold on us is strong and unbreakable. Further, does it make sense to understand Jesus' words as meaning, My sheep, some of whom may indeed perish, will never perish?"

Can We Lose Our Salvation? (Part 2)

In the last chapter we saw that Jesus himself promises and guarantees that he will not lose any child of God, not even one. Those who have been born again and converted to Christ will not fall away from the faith. In many ways the teaching of Jesus on this subject reflects the teaching of the Old Testament. For example, David writes in Psalm 37, "For the LORD loves justice; he will not forsake his saints. They are preserved forever, but the children of the wicked shall be cut off" (37:28). But is the preservation of the saints also something that is taught by Jesus' apostles? That is the question we will answer in this chapter.[1]

Paul's Golden Chain

Perhaps the place to start is with Paul's epistle to the Romans. In Question 14 we saw how Romans 8:28–29 referenced the effectual call. But if we read this text to the end, we will also notice that God's preservation of his elect is assumed as well. Paul begins by affirming the doctrine of predestination (8:29), only to then say that those whom God has predestined he has also called (8:30). However, Paul doesn't stop there—if he did, we might wonder whether someone who is predestined and called could lose such privileges. Instead, he continues, linking together that golden chain. Those predestined and called, he also justifies, and those justified he also glorifies (8:30). It doesn't appear that Paul leaves any room in this order for falling away, as if one could be predestined, called, and justified, but fail to then be glorified. No, for Paul one step in this order irreversibly leads to the next.

---

1. In this chapter our focus will be on those many passages that affirm God's preservation of his saints. It should be acknowledged, however, that there are other passages of Scripture which might, on first appearance, give the impression that a believer *can* lose his/her salvation. Though tempting to address such passages here and now, we will wait and address them in Questions 38–39. But suffice it to say that these passages are warnings against falling away, and these warnings are God's ordained means to create a healthy fear within, a fear that serves to keep his elect from falling away.

Table 13
Order of Salvation
(Ordo Salutis)

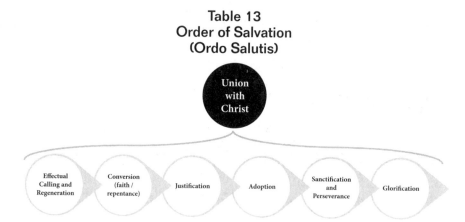

The Love of Jesus

If this was ever in doubt, all doubt is removed when we come to Romans 8:38–39. Directly after this golden chain of salvation Paul asks whether there is anything that can separate us from the "love of Christ" (8:35). Notice how confident Paul is in his response:

> What then shall we say to these things? If God is for us, who can be against us? He who did not spare his own Son but gave him up for us all, how will he not also with him graciously give us all things? Who shall bring any charge against God's elect? It is God who justifies. Who is to condemn? Christ Jesus is the one who died—more than that, who was raised—who is at the right hand of God, who indeed is interceding for us. Who shall separate us from the love of Christ? Shall tribulation, or distress, or persecution, or famine, or nakedness, or danger, or sword? . . . No, in all these things we are more than conquerors through him who loved us. For I am sure that neither death nor life, nor angels nor rulers, nor things present nor things to come, nor powers, nor height nor depth, nor anything else in all creation, will be able to separate us from the love of God in Christ Jesus our Lord (Rom. 8:31–35, 37–39).

Paul is emphatic: Nothing in all the world can separate us from the love of Jesus. Absolutely nothing. And notice Paul's basis for saying so: It is because God gave up his own Son. In other words, it is because Christ died, was raised, and is now interceding on our behalf that we can rest assured that nothing and no one will be able to divorce us from the love of our Savior. Out of all Paul's statements, Romans 8:31–39 might just be the most powerful passage affirming the eternal security of the believer.

Paul affirms the same elsewhere as well. For example, consider the start of his first letter to the Corinthians. We know from the rest of the book that the Corinthians were a mess. They struggled with all kinds of sins: divisions in church (1:10–17; 3:1–23), sexual immorality (5:1–12; 6:12–20), lawsuits against one another (6:1–11), etc. Yet, Paul opens his letter addressing these Corinthians as those "sanctified in Christ Jesus" and "called to be saints" (1:2). Paul goes on to say that the "testimony about Christ was confirmed" among these Corinthians (1:6). But then Paul says something of great importance. He says that the Corinthians are waiting for the "revealing of our Lord Jesus Christ," and this same Christ is the one who "will sustain you to the end, guiltless in the day of our Lord Jesus Christ" (1:8). Paul powerfully concludes, "God is faithful, by whom you were called into the fellowship of his Son, Jesus Christ our Lord" (1:9).

Clearly, the Corinthians had tons of problems, but Paul gives them every assurance that God will not let them fall away. The Lord Jesus, he says, will sustain the Corinthians to the very end, so that on the day of judgment they will stand before God blameless. While it is critical that the Corinthians persevere in the faith (a point we will stress in the chapters to come), their ultimate hope and confidence is not found in themselves but in the power of God to sustain them. Furthermore, this confidence is grounded in the very character of God: "God is faithful" (1:9). The God who "called" the Corinthians into "fellowship" with his "Son, Jesus Christ our Lord" (1:9) will be faithful to sustain the Corinthians to the end.

The Guarantee of Our Inheritance: The Holy Spirit

In his second letter to the Corinthians, Paul again emphasizes such security, but this time with reference to the Holy Spirit. God, says Paul, has "put his seal on us and given us his Spirit in our hearts as a guarantee" (1:22). Perhaps turning to the book of Ephesians will shed further light on what Paul means. To the Ephesians Paul writes, "In him we have obtained an inheritance, having been predestined according to the purpose of him who works all things according to the counsel of his will, so that we who were the first to hope in Christ might be to the praise of his glory. In him you also, when you hear the word of truth, the gospel of your salvation, and believed in him, were sealed with the promised Holy Spirit, who is the guarantee of our inheritance until we acquire possession of it, to the praise of his glory" (1:11–13).

Pay attention to the language of predestination and inheritance. God has predestined certain sinners for salvation (Eph. 1:4, 11) and therefore his elect possess an "inheritance" (1:11), that is, an eternal inheritance (i.e., eternal life). But Paul also explains how God's predestination took effect in time and space. When the Ephesians heard the gospel, they were "sealed with the promised Holy Spirit" (1:13). The Spirit, he explains, is the "guarantee" that the Ephesians will one day receive this promised inheritance (1:14). Though debated, this sealing entails that the Spirit preserves Christians so that they obtain this inheritance (an interpretation supported by 2 Cor. 1:22; Eph. 4:30; 1 Peter 1:5; Rev. 7:2–3).[2] This same point that is made by Paul in 2 Corinthians 1:22 when he says God has "put his seal" on believers, giving them his Spirit in their hearts as a "guarantee."

This language of "guarantee," both in 2 Corinthians and Ephesians, is crucial. It's like a down payment (think of how a down payment, for example, secures buying a house or car), a down payment that secures the believer's placement in God's everlasting kingdom. Of course, the believer, this side of heaven, has yet to obtain that inheritance. Nevertheless, it is guaranteed that he/she will. And if we ask how we know it is guaranteed, the answer is that God has given to us the Spirit. The fact that we have the Spirit and have been sealed by the Spirit proves that we will acquire this inheritance. The Spirit himself, in other words, is our guarantee! As Paul can say later on in his letter to the Ephesians, "And do not grieve the Holy Spirit of God, *by whom you were sealed for the day of redemption*" (4:30).[3] In each of these passages we have in the language of "inheritance," "sealing," and "guarantee" a remarkably strong affirmation of God's preservation of his elect. This language highlights God's ownership of his elect.

Completion and Rescue

Paul begins his letter to the Philippians thanking God for the Philippians because of their "partnership in the gospel" (1:5). Then Paul expresses his confidence in God: "And I am sure of this, that he who began a good work in you will bring it to completion at the day of Jesus Christ" (1:6). Paul has no doubt whatsoever that the God who started this work of salvation in the Philippians will finish it. As a result, the Philippians can rest assured that God will not abandon them, but will complete what he first begun. Again, notice where the believer's confidence rests. Though Paul expects the Philippians to stand firm (1:27), their confidence is ultimately grounded in the guarantee that *God* will bring to completion this good work. On that day when Jesus returns (Phil. 2:16), the believer will receive the promised inheritance.

---

2. Another interpretation says this sealing refers to a certifying by the Spirit, meaning that the Spirit certifies God's approval of the believer. This interpretation gains support from John 3:33 and Acts 10:44, 47. However, the context of Ephesians 1 and 1 Corinthians 1:22 seems to rule against this interpretation. Regardless, either interpretation does not preclude but only supports the doctrine of divine preservation.

3. Ephesians 4:30 is especially insightful. In context, Paul is correcting the Ephesians for various sins (e.g., anger, stealing, corrupting talk). He warns the Ephesians how giving in to these sins can result in grieving the Spirit. However, though Christians may at times (sadly) grieve the Spirit, this grieving does not result in a loss of salvation. As Paul makes clear in 4:30, the Spirit has sealed the Christian for the day of redemption. This knowledge should lead the Christian all the more to guard himself against grieving the very one who has sealed him.

Paul can express a similar confidence in his second letter to Timothy saying, "The Lord will rescue me from every evil deed and bring me safely into his heavenly kingdom" (4:18). Certainly Paul must have known that he would eventually be put to death for his faith. His prayer is not one of deliverance from physical death. He understands that he must be willing to die for the sake of Christ. However, Paul does pray for another type of deliverance, namely, the deliverance from sin. Sin is dangerous, threatening one's salvation. Paul, however, puts his confidence in the Lord, whom he says will rescue him from evil deeds. Paul has no doubt in his mind that such a rescue will result in an eternal safety, that of God's heavenly kingdom.

An Imperishable Inheritance

Paul, however, is not the only one who expresses such bold confidence in God. Peter does as well. Listen to 1 Peter 1:3–5:

> Blessed be the God and Father of our Lord Jesus Christ! According to his great mercy, he has caused us to be born again to a living hope through the resurrection of Jesus Christ from the dead, to an inheritance that is imperishable, undefiled, and unfading, kept in heaven for you, who by God's power are being guarded through faith for a salvation ready to be revealed in the last time.

Imperishable, undefiled, unfading, kept in heaven—this is the type of inheritance that belongs to the Christian. To say that we can lose our salvation is to deny that this inheritance is imperishable, undefiled, and unfading. Even the reference to where this inheritance is kept is significant (i.e., heaven), the point being that it is safe, guaranteed, and from God. Nothing and no one can destroy it.

It's also critical to observe not only what type of inheritance this is (imperishable, undefiled, unfading) and where it is kept (in heaven), but what the text says God is doing in relation to the believer himself. The Christian, Peter says, is one who "by God's power" is being "guarded (*phrouroumenous*) through faith for a salvation ready to be revealed in the last time" (1:5). In other words, not only is the Christian's inheritance being kept safe, but the Christian himself is being kept safe.[4] This does not mean he is passive—the text says this guarding happens "through faith." But it does mean that God himself, by his divine power, is guarding his children. Could there be a greater guarantee of our eternal protection than the power of God?

---

4. Hoekema fittingly titles this a "double security" (Anthony A. Hoekema, *Saved by Grace* [Grand Rapids: Eerdmans, 1989], 244).

Divine Preservation and Christian Assurance

One of the many practical benefits of God's sovereign promise to keep his elect safe has to do with Christian assurance. Whether one is sick and near death, whether one is discouraged from a failure to overcome sin, or whether one is frightened by threats of persecution in the world, the fear of falling away can be real. In these moments one might struggle to find the assurance he/she once enjoyed. One might even begin to worry whether he/she will make it to the Celestial City (to borrow imagery from John Bunyan's *Pilgrim's Progress*).

God's preservation of his elect is a great comfort and hope in such times of hardship and anxiety. Certainly the words of Jesus are warm and reassuring when it appears as though the wind and waves of life will deal a crushing blow: "I give them eternal life, and they will never perish, and no one will snatch them out of my hand" (John 10:28). These assuring words remind us that the safety of our soul does not ultimately depend upon us, but upon Christ. And as the one who has overcome, having risen from the grave, defeating both sin and death, we can rest assured—even in the midst of the greatest storm—that our Savior will not fail to save us to the very end. The great hymn, "How Firm a Foundation" (1781), summarizes the message of this chapter best:

> Fear not, I am with thee, oh, be not dismayed,
> For I am thy God and will still give thee aid;
> I'll strengthen thee, help thee, and cause thee to stand,
> Upheld by My righteous, omnipotent hand.
>
> When through the deep waters I call thee to go,
> The rivers of sorrow shall not overflow;
> For I will be with thee thy troubles to bless
> And sanctify to thee thy deepest distress.
>
> When through fiery trials thy pathway shall lie,
> My grace, all-sufficient, shall be thy supply.
> The flames shall not hurt thee; I only design
> Thy dross to consume and thy gold to refine.
>
> The soul that on Jesus hath leaned for repose
> I will not, I will not, desert to his foes;
> That soul, though all hell should endeavor to shake,
> I'll never, no never, no never, forsake!

Summary

According to the apostle Paul, nothing can separate us from the love of Christ. God has sealed us with his promised Holy Spirit, the guarantee of our inheritance. The work God has begun, he will bring to completion. Likewise,

Peter stresses that this inheritance is an imperishable one and by God's power we are being guarded through faith for a salvation yet to come. Divine preservation, therefore, proves to be a great comfort to the Christian, especially in times of hardship.

REFLECTION QUESTIONS

1. What biblical passage in the Epistles lends the greatest support to God's preservation of his elect, and why?

2. Does God's promise to preserve the Corinthian church—a church that had serious problems—give you hope when you become frustrated with sin in the church?

3. Read 2 Corinthians 1:11–13, 22, as well as Ephesians 1:1–14. Who is the guarantee of the inheritance that awaits us?

4. Study 1 Peter 1:3–5. How does Paul's language here add support to the doctrine of divine preservation?

5. Do you struggle with assurance? If so, how does divine preservation affect your Christian assurance?

Is Perseverance in the Faith Necessary? (Part 1)

In the last chapter we saw from numerous passages that those whom God has effectually called, regenerated, and justified, he will not fail to preserve until final glorification. And we learned what a tremendous comfort it is to know that our Father does not and will not lose his elect; our eternal inheritance is secure.

However, this should not lead us to think, then, that we, as Christians, need not persevere in the Christian life. It could be tempting to think that since our eternal inheritance is secure in Christ, we can be lax, sin as we want, and coast through life. Quite the contrary, Scripture exhorts us to persevere. In fact, Scripture even says perseverance is *necessary* and *essential* if we are to one day receive that eternal inheritance promised to us.[1]

This is a reminder that divine sovereignty and human responsibility go together. Yes, God is sovereign and his sovereignty is exhaustive, meticulous, and unbreakable. No one can thwart his will. Not even Satan can break God's grip on us or stop his plan of salvation from going forward. Yet, at the same time, God uses *means* to accomplish this goal, to bring us to final glorification (we will see in Questions 38–39 that "warnings" are one means God uses). God has chosen, in his great wisdom, to involve us in the process and progress of sanctification (what a privilege!).

---

1. The Heidelberg Catechism (1563) stresses this point: "Can those be saved who do not turn to God from their ungrateful and impenitent ways? By no means. Scripture tells us that no unchaste person, no idolater, no adulterer, no thief, no covetous person, no drunkard, slanderer, robber, or the like is going to inherit the kingdom of God" ("The Heidelberg Catechism," in *Reformed Confessions of the Sixteenth Century and Seventeenth Centuries in English Translation, Volume 2, 1552–1566,* ed. James T. Dennison Jr. [Grand Rapids: Reformation Heritage, 2010], Q/A 87).

So perseverance, as we'll see, is critical. Without it, the link between justification and glorification is broken. Without perseverance, sanctification is incomplete and impossible. And apart from it, heaven will not be reached. Perseverance, in other words, is the path by which God brings us from this life to the next. Therefore, it is not a surprise that we should encounter many exhortations to persevere in the Bible, for without perseverance we will not inherit the kingdom.

In this chapter, we will explore what Scripture says about perseverance, specifically how it repeatedly exhorts new Christians to persevere in the faith.

Continue in the Faith: The Book of Acts

Some of the greatest exhortations to persevere can be seen in the book of Acts. This makes sense. The gospel was preached, many repented and believed, and so they were then exhorted to persevere, especially in light of the persecution they would undoubtedly face.

For example, in Acts 11:19 we read that when persecution came, many traveled as far as places like Antioch. Persecution had the opposite effect; when scattered, the gospel only spread. So in Antioch Jesus was preached (Acts 11:20), and as a result many believed and turned to the Lord (11:21). The church in Jerusalem heard the news and sent Barnabas to Antioch to see this great harvest for himself (11:22). Upon arriving, Barnabas saw "the grace of God" and the text says "he was glad" (11:23). So what did Barnabas do? Did he say: "Wonderful! You all are eternally secure. Everything is done then. I'll be on my way"? Not at all. Instead we read that: "he exhorted [*parekalei*] them all to remain faithful [*prosmenein*] to the Lord with steadfast purpose" (11:23).

In other words, Barnabas exhorted these new Christians to persevere. If persecution had come once, it would come again, and these new believers might be tempted to abandon Christ and apostatize. Barnabas encourages them, even commands them, to stay faithful to Jesus. On the one hand, Barnabas knew that these individuals were converted by God's grace alone; the text says he "saw the grace of God" (11:23a). This did not stop him, though, from admonishing them to persevere in this new found faith. Indeed, God's grace is the basis and foundation on which these new converts could persevere.[2]

We see something similar in Acts 13. Paul and Barnabas went to Antioch in Pisidia, and once again they were given an opportunity to share the good news about Jesus. In Acts 13:42 it appears that some believed. Paul and Barnabus then "urged [*epeithon*] them to continue [*prosmenein*] in the grace of God" (13:43). Notice, Acts 11:23 says Barnabas "exhorted" [*parekalei*];

---

2. Thomas R. Schreiner, *Run to Win the Prize: Perseverance in the New Testament* (Wheaton, IL: Crossway, 2010), 17.

here, in 13:43, it says they "urged" or "persuaded" [*epeithon*]. Both of these verbs, Schreiner observes, demonstrate the "seriousness of the admonition . . . showing that vigilance is mandated for new believers."[3] Moreover, Acts 13:43 uses the same verb we saw in Acts 11:23: Believers are "to continue" (*prosmenein*) in the grace of God. The point seems to be the same as it was in Acts 11:23: believers must persevere, press on, continue, and remain faithful. Of course, this can only be done by God's grace. Paul and Barnabas urge these new converts to continue "in the grace of God" (13:43). This is a reminder that perseverance is not a disguised form of works-righteousness but is accomplished only by depending upon God's assistance.[4]

This theme of perseverance continues throughout the book of Acts. In Acts 14 Paul is stoned at Lystra and left for dead outside the city. Recovered by the disciples, Paul then traveled with Barnabas to Derbe. As a result of preaching the gospel, many believed. They then returned to Lystra and Iconium and Antioch. But it's their reason for doing so that draws our attention. They returned to these areas "strengthening the souls of the disciples, encouraging them to continue [*emmenein*] in the faith, and saying that through many tribulations we must enter the kingdom of God" (14:22). Once again, hardship is real, and when it comes, the Christian faces a real temptation to abandon the faith. Jettisoning the faith would return one to a state of peace, after all. But should they turn back, they will not inherit eternal life. They *must* press on; only then will they enter into God's kingdom.

No One Be Moved (1 Thessalonians 3:1–5)

The hardship we saw in the book of Acts can also be sensed in Paul's epistles. In 1 Thessalonians Paul writes to these converts, whom he considers his "crown of boasting" before the Lord (2:19). Paul was no doubt mindful of the fact that this recently established Thessalonian church was facing hard times. Apparently becoming a Christian did not mean one escaped trials. And the Thessalonians had to endure many of them, which Paul warned them would be the case when he was with them (1 Thess. 3:4). This is why, explains Paul, he sent Timothy, "to establish and exhort you in your faith, that no one be moved by these afflictions" (1 Thess. 3:2–3). Paul goes on to explain how eager he was to learn about their faith, "for fear that somehow the tempter had tempted you and our labor would be in vain" (3:5). In other words, Paul was fearful that the Thessalonians would give up the faith when persecuted. Paul knew how vicious Satan could be (1 Thess. 2:18) and how Satan would try to draw the Thessalonians away from Jesus to an easier path. Should this have

---

3. Ibid.
4. "We are reminded of what Paul taught in Galatians 3:3. We continue in the Christian life the same way we began, for we do not initiate the Christian life in the Spirit and then progress in it by means of the flesh" (ibid.).

happened, the church Paul planted would have perished and his labor would have been in vain.

For Paul it is not enough to be converted, as important as conversion may be. Conversion is just the start. The Thessalonians (and we by implication, too) must not only embrace the faith at conversion but persist in that faith until glorification. Should we do so, then it will be clear that our faith is real, not fake.[5]

Perseverance and Christian Ministry

Pastorally, this is an important word every new believer should hear. Just as Paul was concerned about his newly converted Thessalonians, so should we be concerned about those we have seen trust in Jesus for the first time. Conversion is exciting, and we should not dampen that exciting moment. At the same time, it is not long after conversion that we, as more experienced Christ-followers, should come alongside new believers and warn them in advance that trials will come and when they do come they will be tempted to abandon Jesus. Our exhortation should be that of the apostle Paul: Continue in the faith, and do so by trusting in the grace of God.

Summary

It could be tempting to think that since our eternal inheritance is secure in Christ, we can be lax, sin as we want, and coast through life. Yet Scripture exhorts us to persevere, and even says perseverance is *necessary* and *essential* if we are one day to receive that eternal inheritance promised to us. Without perseverance, the link between justification and glorification is broken. Without perseverance, sanctification is incomplete and impossible. And apart from it, heaven will not be reached. Perseverance, in other words, is the path by which God brings us from this life to the next. Therefore, it is not a surprise that we should encounter many exhortations to persevere in the Bible, for without perseverance we will not inherit the kingdom.

REFLECTION QUESTIONS

1. Do you ever experience temptations to abandon Christianity? What has kept you following Christ?

---

5. "Paul did not assume that the Thessalonians were truly believers merely because they had embraced the faith when he first preached to them. The authenticity of their faith manifested itself in their response to trials, so that their persistence in faith demonstrated that their faith was genuine" (ibid., 19).

2. How can others in the church help struggling believers continue to persevere?

3. Given Paul's constant practice of encouraging his churches to persevere, should pastors make such a responsibility a major priority?

4. How do the many exhortations to persevere kick against the tendency to dismiss good deeds from the Christian life?

5. What temptations might lead a new believer to abandon the faith?

Is Perseverance in the Faith Necessary? (Part 2)

In the last chapter, Scripture taught us just how important it is for newly converted believers to be exhorted to persevere in the faith. Typically, the new convert has yet to experience persecution for the gospel or temptation to abandon Christ and return to the pleasures of the world. But now that he has been converted, it is only a matter of time until such temptations come. The excitement that accompanies conversion will, in time, mellow down as the trials of life set in. If that new convert is to finish the race, then he must be encouraged and at times even exhorted by fellow Christ-followers in the church to press on, continue in the faith, and persevere to the end when hardship comes.

But it would be a mistake to think that the exhortation to persevere is only applicable to new converts. Actually, it is one that even the most experienced Christian needs to hear again and again. Satan plays no favorites; he will go after those who appear the most mature in their faith. At no point can a Christian let down his guard.[1] The moment he does so is the moment Satan pounces. He is like a lion on the prowl, hiding silently in the tall grass, just waiting for the right moment to pounce and devour us (1 Peter 5:8).

With that image in mind, this chapter will explore how Scripture also exhorts experienced Christians to persevere in the faith.

---

1. If we have been Christians a long time, we may be especially prone to this mistake. We tend to think we have everything figured out, that we are above sins a new convert might struggle with, and that Satan isn't really concerned with us "stable" Christians anyhow. This would be to underestimate Satan. His silence should not necessarily be interpreted as his absence or total retreat. He often waits until you think he is gone, and then finds the most opportune moment to attack. It is typically in those moments when we think we are victorious, above temptation, that he then launches his assault, for in that moment we have stopped relying on God's grace and instead are relying upon our own achievement.

Hold Fast to the Word of Life (Philippians 2:16)

In Philippians Paul has much to say about salvation—past, present, and future. In the latter half of Philippians 2, however, the focus is on the present. Paul instructs the Philippians to "work out your own salvation with fear and trembling, for it is God who works in you, both to will and to work for his good pleasure" (2:12–13). While this passage is well known, it is the one that directly follows that is especially relevant for our purposes. Paul writes:

> Do all things without grumbling or disputing, that you may be blameless and innocent, children of God without blemish in the midst of a crooked and twisted generation, among whom you shine as lights in the world, holding fast to the word of life, so that in the day of Christ I may be proud that I did not run in vain or labor in vain (Phil. 2:14–16).

Paul assumes the Christian should be striving to be blameless and innocent. This is not easy to do since the Christian lives in the midst of a world that is crooked and twisted. But he does it by "holding fast to the word of life" (2:16). While some have translated and interpreted the participle (*epexontes*) evangelistically (as if Christians are "holding forth" the word of life to a lost world [i.e., proclamation]), it is better translated and interpreted as a reference to perseverance ("holding fast"),[2] which means that Paul is commanding the

---

2. For an evangelistic translation-interpretation, see Robert L. Plummer, *Paul's Understanding of the Church's Mission: Did the Apostle Paul Expect the Early Christian Communities to Evangelize?*, Paternoster Biblical Monographs (Waynesboro, GA: Paternoster, 2006), 74–77. For someone who tries to hold to both, see Vern S. Poythress, "'Hold Fast' Versus 'Hold Out' in Philippians 2:16," *WTJ* 63 (2002): 45–53. While sympathizing with Poythress, Schreiner gives several reasons for a perseverance view: "First, twice Paul considers the possibility of believers not continuing in the faith. Second, the warning against grumbling and complaining (Phil. 2:14) harks back to the OT and the grumbling of the wilderness generation (Exod. 16:7–9, 12; Num. 17:5, 10) and their failure to enter the promised land. The land promise in Exodus becomes a type of the future inheritance in Paul, and hence a connection is forged between Israel's failure to enter the land of promise and the warning directed to believers. Third, the words 'blameless,' 'innocent,' and 'without blemish' are in the same semantic range and are used elsewhere in Paul to denote the godly character needed to obtain the final reward. Fourth, the expression 'that you may be . . . children of God' (Phil. 2:15) has an eschatological reference, designating the truth that those who continue to believe will be God's children on the day of Christ. Such an interpretation is confirmed by the allusion to Deuteronomy 32:5, which again considers the rebellion of Israel. . . . Notice that Israel's sin demonstrates they are not God's children, but Paul admonishes the Philippians to hold fast to the word of life so that they will be God's children. Moreover, Israel was blemished, but the church should remain unblemished. Finally, Israel was 'a crooked and twisted generation,' but the Philippians are to distinguish themselves as righteous in the midst of an evil generation. The many points of contact between Deuteronomy 32:5 and Philippians 2:15 indicate that we have a call to perseverance in these verses. Finally, the call to 'shine as lights in the world' probably alludes to Daniel 12:3, where believers are to shine

Philippians (and all Christians for that matter) to hold fast, i.e., be obedient and faithful by their conduct. To hold fast is to obey the word of God in the midst of a generation who disobeys, violates, and despises the word of God. If they do not, then Paul's labor will have been for naught. Of course, Paul puts himself forward as an example of perseverance (Phil. 3:17). He is not perfect (3:12) but presses on "toward the goal for the prize of the upward call of God in Christ Jesus" (3:14). Certainly Paul understood perseverance as necessary if the prize is to be one day attained.

Obtain the Grace of God (Hebrews 12:15)

One of the most powerful passages affirming perseverance is Hebrews 12, where the author uses the imagery of a runner in a race. The chapter begins by instructing believers to "lay aside every weight, and sin which clings so closely"—anything that might slow you down in the race and keep you from finishing. This is what sin does; it impedes the Christian just as a weight would an athlete (cf. 1 Cor. 9:24–27; 2 Tim. 4:7–8). The Christian, like the athlete, is to run with "endurance" the race God has put before him (Heb. 12:1). It is hard to think of better imagery for perseverance. Endurance is at the very essence of what it means to persevere. If a runner cannot endure, he will not get very far at all. This is why athletes train; they are teaching their body how to endure when tired and how to endure under hard circumstances in the arena. So, too, with the Christian. If the Christian life is like running a race, endurance must characterize the Christian if he is to reach the finish line rather than be disqualified.

Paul, however, does not leave us looking within to somehow muster up endurance. No, we are to look to Jesus, "the founder and perfecter of our faith, who for the joy that was set before him endured the cross, despising the shame" (12:2). We are to consider "him who endured from sinners such hostility against himself, so that you may not grow weary or fainthearted" (12:3).

If we skip ahead to Hebrews 12:15, we will note, however, that a warning is in view. The author says something very sobering: "See to it that no one fails to obtain the grace of God." What does the author mean here by failure? It is not the case that he has in mind a mere lack of fruitfulness in the Christian life; instead, he has apostasy in mind. Or to return to the sports imagery: The runner who does not run with endurance does not finish the race. We know this because the author goes on to enlist Esau as an example of one who fails to obtain the grace of God (12:16–17). Final salvation or final destruction is

---

like lights. Those believers who shine like lights will 'be delivered' (Dan. 12:1). They will rise 'to everlasting life' (Dan. 12:2). Hence we have another piece of evidence supporting the claim that Paul exhorts the Philippians to continue in the faith to the end in order to receive the end-time reward of eternal life" (Thomas R. Schreiner, *Run to Win the Prize: Perseverance in the New Testament* [Wheaton, IL: Crossway, 2010], 22–23).

the context.[3] The point is this: Perseverance is necessary if one is to reach final salvation. Faith must endure if Christian runners are to obtain the reward at the end of the finish line.

Before moving on, it is imperative to observe that holy living is key to such perseverance in Hebrews 12. While external persecution was a test for first-century Christians (see Heb. 12:3), another was temptation to sin, sin that would lead them to abandon Christ. The fight the Christian has, in other words, is a fight against his own sinful nature. If we look closely, this is what Hebrews 12:4 says, "*In your struggle against sin* you have not yet resisted to the point of shedding your blood" (emphasis added). The author then progresses to discuss the loving, fatherly discipline of God, specifically how God disciplines us, his children, for our "good," so "that we may share his *holiness*" (12:10). While discipline is painful, it "yields the peaceful fruit of *righteousness* to those who have been trained by it" (12:11).

Firm in Your Faith (1 Peter 5:8–12)

At the start of this chapter Satan was compared to a lion. The apostle Peter is the one who uses this imagery, and he does so in order to exhort his readers to perseverance in the midst of much suffering and severe trials (see 1 Peter 3:8–22; 4:12–19). Peter calls Christians to be "sober-minded" and "watchful." Why? Because they have an adversary, the devil himself. Like a lion, he "prowls around," "roaring," just looking for someone "to devour" (5:8). With this roaring lion on the prowl, how are Christians to respond? "Resist him, firm in your faith, knowing that the same kinds of suffering are being experienced by your brotherhood throughout the world" (5:9). Peter goes on to provide tremendous confidence and hope: "And after you have suffered a little while, the God of all grace, who has called you to his eternal glory in Christ, will himself restore, confirm, strengthen, and establish you" (5:10). In other words, the perseverance of the believer is grounded in a confident promise—namely, that suffering will be followed by the comfort and strength of God.

It is crucial to observe how Peter concludes his letter. Peter tells his readers why he has written: "I have written briefly to you, exhorting and declaring that this is the true grace of God. Stand firm in it" (5:12). Peter's readers are to stand firm (or stand fast) in the grace of God when times of testing come. Though the devil roars, hungry for apostasy, believers stand firm in their faith (5:9, 12), continuing to trust in the God who has promised to restore them and strengthen them (5:10).

---

3. Likewise, see 2 Corinthians 6:1: "Working together with him, then, we appeal to you not to receive the grace of God in vain."

Keep Yourselves in the Love of God (Jude 21)

Finally, we close with the short letter of Jude. Jude, addressing those called by God and "kept for Jesus Christ" (Jude 1; note the stress on eternal security), reminds his readers that in the last days there will be "scoffers, following their own ungodly passions" (Jude 18), and they will come from within the church itself (see Jude 3–4, 19). They are divisive, "worldly people, devoid of the Spirit" (Jude 19). They are a serious threat to real, true believers in the church. In contrast to them, Jude tells his readers to build themselves up in the faith and pray (Jude 20). And then he commands them, "keep yourselves in the love of God, waiting for the mercy of our Lord Jesus Christ that leads to eternal life" (Jude 21). In the midst of churchgoers and church leaders who are leading the people astray into false doctrine and immorality, Jude essentially says, "Don't do it! Don't go down that path, abandoning biblical doctrine. Don't let them lead you into sinful, pagan behavior." Instead, keep yourselves in the love of God. Notice, this is no light matter for Jude. There are but two options: (a) follow these false teachers and go to hell, or (b) keep following God and receive eternal life.[4] Nothing greater could be at stake.

One cannot miss Jude's doxology, for in it he undergirds everything he has just said. "Now to him who is able to keep you from stumbling and to present you blameless before the presence of his glory with great joy, to the only God, our Savior, through Jesus Christ our Lord, be glory, majesty, dominion, and authority, before all time and now and forever. Amen" (Jude 24–25). We, as Christians, are to persevere, but Jude reminds us that we do not persevere in our own strength. Rather, we persevere by depending upon God who keeps us from stumbling. We rely on God who presents us blameless in his sight.

Summary

The exhortation to persevere is not only applicable to new converts but is one that even the most experienced Christian needs to hear. Paul, Peter, the author of Hebrews, and Jude command the Christian to work out his salvation, obtain the grace of God, stand firm in his faith, and to keep himself in the love of God. At the same time, while we are commanded to persevere, we cannot forget that we persevere by depending upon the grace of God, for he is the one that keeps us from stumbling.

REFLECTION QUESTIONS

1. How long have you been a Christian? As you look back, were there moments when the Bible passages in this chapter helped you persevere?

---

4. "Jude does not merely give helpful advice on growth in the Christian life. Keeping oneself in the love of God is essential for receiving eternal life on the final day" (ibid., 19).

2. If perseverance is necessary to obtain eternal life, how seriously should we take temptation to sin?

3. Read Jude 24–25. What role does God's grace have in our perseverance?

4. In what ways does perseverance compare to an athletic race?

5. As you look out on your church, do you think other Christians understand how essential perseverance is?

What Role Do the Warning Passages Play in Our Perseverance? (Part 1)

In Questions 34–35 we learned a very comforting truth: God will not lose any of his children.[1] Or to use Pauline language: Those whom God has predestined, called, and justified, he will glorify (Rom. 8:30). Likewise, Jesus assures us that no one can snatch us out of his hand (John 10:28) or his Father's hand (10:29). And yet, as we saw in Questions 36–37, the path God puts us on to bring his justified children to glorification is the road of perseverance. It is necessary to press on and endure, otherwise one will not enter into the kingdom on that final day (Acts 11:23; 13:43; 14:22–23; 2 Cor. 6:1; 1 Thess. 3:1–5; 1 Peter 5:12; Jude 21; Heb. 12:15).

Undoubtedly, these two twin truths (eternal security and perseverance) present a mysterious tension, though a very biblical one. This tension is only intensified when one encounters severe warning passages in Scripture, passages that threaten eternal damnation if one does not persevere. While these warnings have been interpreted differently in the history of the church, we will argue in this chapter and the next that it is most biblical to interpret these warnings (a) as addressed to God's elect (i.e., real, authentic Christians) who are guaranteed eternal life and (b) as God's ordained *means* by which Christians persevere in the faith.[2] These warnings act as means to keep the believer from

---

1. I am very grateful for the pioneering work of Thomas Schreiner on this topic. This chapter and the next is indebted to his argument and outline in *Run to Win the Prize: Perseverance in the New Testament* (Wheaton, IL: Crossway, 2010).

2. Space does not permit us to present and critique the various views. Nevertheless, the reader should be aware of them. Consider four views:

   (1) In the Arminian and Wesleyan-Arminian traditions, some have said that these warning passages are addressed to believers and therefore it is possible for a Christian to lose his salvation and apostatize. John Wesley, *Explanatory Notes Upon the New Testament* (London: The Epworth Press, 1952), 551; I. H. Marshall, *Kept by the Power of God: A Study*

eternal damnation. They are not retrospective, but prospective. Their purpose, in other words, is to protect believers from falling away from Jesus.

Consider two illustrations. When I lived in Southern California there was a windy road I had to drive down in order to get home. This road frightened me because on one side was an enormous cliff and it would be very easy to drive too fast and slide off the road to my death. However, each time I approached this windy road, there was a big yellow sign that said in giant letters: "SLOW DOWN. CLIFF AHEAD." As soon as I saw that sign, my foot hit the

---

of Perseverance and Falling Away (1969; reprint, Minneapolis: Bethany Fellowship, 1974); Scot McKnight, "The Warning Passages of Hebrews: A Formal Analysis and Theological Conclusions," *TJ* 13 (1992): 21–59; Grant R. Osborne, "A Classical Arminian View," in *Four Views on the Warning Passages in Hebrews*, ed. Herbert W. Bateman IV (Grand Rapids: Kregel, 2007), 86–128; Gareth Lee Cockerill, "A Wesleyan Arminian View," in *Four Views on the Warning Passages in Hebrews*, 257–92. We saw in Questions 34–35, however, that such a view is contrary to Scripture which affirms the eternal security of the believer.

(2) Or consider the "loss of rewards" view. Advocates argue that the warnings are addressing genuine Christians, but the warning is not referring to a loss of salvation but to a loss of rewards that the Christian would otherwise receive. This view affirms eternal security, concluding that such warnings cannot mean a loss of salvation or eternal life. Instead, the warnings mean a loss of higher status and/or blessings in heaven. Charles Stanley, *Eternal Security: Can You Be Sure?* (Nashville: Thomas Nelson, 1990); R. T. Kendall, *Once Saved, Always Saved* (Chicago: Moody Press, 1983); Zane C. Hodges, *The Gospel under Siege: A Study on Faith and Works* (Dallas: Redención Viva, 1981); idem, *Absolutely Free: A Biblical Reply to Lordship Salvation* (Dallas: Redención Viva, 1989; Grand Rapids: Zondervan, 1989); Michael Eaton, *No Condemnation: A New Theology of Assurance* (Downers Grove, IL: InterVarsity Press, 1995); Randall C. Gleason, "A Moderate Reformed View," in *Four Views on the Warning Passages in Hebrews*, 336–77.

(3) Others, taking a classical Reformed perspective, have argued that these warning passages do not refer to actual Christians but instead refer to those who merely appear to be believers but in reality are not. So while this view agrees with the Arminian view that it is not merely "rewards" but final salvation that is being threatened, they do not agree on the recipients of the warnings. In the end, no believer loses his salvation, for these warnings do not address authentic Christ-followers. John Owen, *Hebrews: The Epistle of Warning* (Grand Rapids: Kregel, 1953), 96–98; Roger Nicole, "Some Comments on Hebrews 6:4–6 and the Doctrine of the Perseverance of God with the Saints," in *Current Issues in Biblical and Patristic Interpretation: Studies in Honor of Merrill C. Tenney Presented by His Former Students*, ed. Gerald F. Hawthorne (Grand Rapids: Eerdmans, 1975), 355–64; Wayne Grudem, "Perseverance of the Saints: A Case Study from the Warning Passages in Hebrews," in *Still Sovereign: Contemporary Perspectives on Election, Foreknowledge, and Grace*, eds. Thomas R. Schreiner and Bruce A. Ware (Grand Rapids: Baker, 2000), 133–82; Buist M. Fanning, "A Classical Reformed View," in *Four Views on the Warning Passages in Hebrews*, 172–219.

(4) Finally, others within the Reformed tradition have affirmed eternal security but simultaneously argued that these warnings really are addressed to Christians, and are God's means by which he preserves his elect and keeps them persevering. This view is represented by Thomas R. Schreiner and Ardel B. Caneday, *The Race Set Before Us: A Biblical Theology of Perseverance and Assurance* (Downers Grove, IL: InterVarsity Press, 2001). This is the view I will argue for in this chapter and the next.

brakes. Warnings in Scripture act like that big yellow sign. God warns us, "If you go this way, you will die!" The warning is his means to keep us from spiritual death, and just like that yellow sign, God's warning works.

Or suppose you are on a tour, walking through a beautiful but deep canyon.[3] Suddenly, the tour guide stops you and he has a very grave look on his face. He says to you, "Be careful to follow me. Around this corner is a very deep precipice and if you slip and fall you will be dashed to pieces." How do we respond? First of all, we thank him for the warning. Second, we watch our every step, making sure we are following his instructions exactly. What has this serious warning accomplished? It has acted as a means to keep us from death. One might also appeal to speech-act theory to make this point. Words in the form of a warning are not mere words. Rather, they do something, creating a response and a desired effect. If this is true of our words, how much more so with God's words? They keep us on the road of perseverance, instilling within us a healthy fear and caution.[4]

That said, if we were to summarize where we are thus far in our discussion of perseverance and capture the tension that we see in Scripture, we might put it all together like this:

1. God's elect are eternally secure due to his sovereign care and preservation (Questions 34–35).

2. God's elect must persevere in the faith if they are to enter into eternal life (Questions 36–37).

3. God uses "warnings" as his means to keep his elect persevering in the faith and from committing apostasy (Questions 38–39).

It is the third point in this formula that we will now explore more thoroughly in this chapter and the next. We will discover that:

1. The warnings are addressed to genuine believers.

2. The warnings warn of what will happen to the believer, should he abandon Christ.

---

3. Parts of this illustration are indebted to C. H. Spurgeon, "Final Perseverance," in *The New Park Street Pulpit,* http://www.spurgeon.org/sermons/0075.htm.

4. If you are a parent, you know this well. You might say to your child, pointing to a poisonous bottle of cleaning solution, "Do not touch! If you drink that, you will die!" Your words create fear within the heart of your little one, keeping them away. However, in the Christian life these warnings not only move us to fear but to prayer and dependence upon God for his grace and help.

3. The warnings do not contradict the doctrine of eternal security but actually are the very means that keep the Christian eternally secure.

The Warnings of Jesus

Christians tend to caricature Jesus as "meek and mild." However, reading through the Gospels tells us otherwise. Jesus has some very stern words, not only for those who are unbelievers but also for those who are his own followers.

In Matthew 10:32–33 Jesus says, specifically to his own disciples (see 10:1, 5), "So everyone who acknowledges me before men, I also will acknowledge before my Father who is in heaven, but whoever denies me before men, I also will deny before my Father who is in heaven."[5] The context of the passage is persecution. In Matthew 10:16–25 Jesus told his disciples very plainly that persecution would come and when it does it will be brutal (e.g., brother delivering brother over to death). Jesus promised his disciples that they would be "hated by all for my name's sake." "But," said Jesus, "the one who endures to the end will be saved" (10:22).

Jesus recognizes that when persecution comes, the temptation his disciples will face is to deny being a follower of Jesus. Such a denial will allow one to keep his life. But the true disciple, says Jesus, will endure persecution, fearing God rather than death (cf. 10:28). Knowing this temptation will come, Jesus gives a warning. Only those who persevere to the end will be saved (10:22); those who deny Jesus will be denied by Jesus himself before the Father in heaven (10:33). So the cost is clear: One must take up his cross and follow Jesus, willing to lose his life in order to gain it; anything less means one is not worthy of Jesus (10:38–39). Certainly this context demonstrates that nothing less than eternal life and eternal damnation are on the line.

Similarly, consider John 15, that famous passage about abiding in the vine. In this garden illustration, believers are the branches who are to abide in Jesus, the vine (cf. 15:1). We know these branches must be believers because in 15:2 Jesus refers to them as "in me," something not true of unbelievers. So what does Jesus have to say about believers abiding in him?

1. Any branch not bearing fruit (i.e., good works) the Father (the vinedresser; 15:1) prunes so that it will bear more fruit (15:2).

2. A branch cannot bear fruit unless it abides in Jesus, the vine (15:4–5).

3. If any branch does not abide, it will be destroyed (15:6).

---

5. What is fascinating about this particular passage is that it follows a very firm affirmation by Jesus himself of the believer's security in the hands of God (10:30–31). Apparently the marriage of exhaustive, meticulous divine sovereignty and the believers' responsibility to persevere was not problematic for Jesus.

It is this third point that is particularly important. "If anyone does not abide in me," warns Jesus, "he is thrown away like a branch and withers; and the branches are gathered, thrown into the fire, and burned" (15:6). It will not do to argue that "rewards" are in view since Jesus uses the imagery of judgment and eternal damnation ("fire," "burned"). Also, John 15:6 is a *warning*, as the "if" at the start of the verse hints at. If one does not abide, he warns, then he will be burned.

Further Warnings from the Apostles

Jesus' apostles likewise picked up his teaching and applied it to Christians in the church. Consider Peter, for example. Peter begins his second letter addressing "those who have obtained a faith of equal standing with ours by the righteousness of our God and Savior Jesus Christ" (2 Peter 1:1b). By this language it very much appears that Peter has Christian recipients in mind. If this were in question, it is no longer once Peter includes himself in this address:

> His divine power has granted to us all things that pertain to life and godliness, through the knowledge of him who called us to his own glory and excellence, by which he has granted to us his precious and very great promises, so that through them you may become partakers of the divine nature, having escaped from the corruption that is in the world because of sinful desire (2 Peter 1:3–4).

Certainly the elect are in view when Peter addresses his readers as those whom God "called," those whom God "granted" his "precious and very great promises," and those who may partake of the "divine nature."

Such confidence in receiving the promises of God or partaking in the divine nature, however, does not keep Peter from issuing a warning. He says in the very next verses: "For this very reason, make every effort to supplement your faith with virtue, and virtue with knowledge, and knowledge with self-control, and self-control with steadfastness, and steadfastness with godliness, and godliness with brotherly affection, and brotherly affection with love" (1:5–7). Now why would Peter stress such virtues? He explains:

> For if these qualities are yours and are increasing, *they keep you from being ineffective or unfruitful* in the knowledge of our Lord Jesus Christ. *For whoever lacks these qualities is so nearsighted that he is blind, having forgotten that he was cleansed from his former sins.* Therefore, brothers, be all the more diligent to confirm your calling and election, for *if* you practice these qualities you will *never fall*. For in this way there will be richly provided for you an *entrance into the*

eternal kingdom of our Lord and Savior Jesus Christ (1:5–11, emphasis added).

It is unlikely that a greater motivation to cultivate virtue in the Christian life could be given.[6] Are these virtues necessary? Absolutely. Without them, warns Peter, one will be ineffective (unfruitful), nearsighted (blind), and forgetful (that he's been cleansed of sin). But more to the point, it is imperative that one "confirm" his "calling and election," because "if" one practices these qualities he "will never fall" and will enter into the eternal kingdom. The assumption, in the opposite direction, of course, is that "if" one does not practice these qualities he will fall and he will not enter the eternal kingdom. Apparently bearing fruit is absolutely necessary if one is to enter the kingdom. Again, the language here has to do with two opposing destinies: eternal life and eternal damnation. And the roads to each are clearly marked by certain qualities or characteristics. The kingdom itself is at stake in one's choices.[7]

Or consider John, both in his second epistle and in Revelation. Let's start with John's second letter. To begin with, notice that John addresses the church, who is referred to as the "elect lady" (2 John 1). John rejoices that "some of your children" are "walking in the truth" (v. 4) and he exhorts them to love one another, which is manifested in obedience (v. 6).

Nevertheless, the church faces a challenge: There are "many deceivers" who "do not confess the coming of Jesus Christ in the flesh" (v. 7). Some form of Docetism (a denial of Jesus' humanity) was a real problem, leading people into false doctrine. For this reason John issues a warning: "Watch yourselves, so that you may not lose what we have worked for, but may win a full reward" (v. 8). He then concludes, "Everyone who goes on ahead and does not abide in the teaching of Christ, does not have God. Whoever abides in the teaching has both the Father and the Son" (v. 9).

While it may be tempting to interpret "full reward" in verse 8 as something beyond eternal life (i.e., the reception of special blessings in heaven for believers), such a reading does not fit the context. Remember, verse 7 refers to deceivers and antichrists who are heretical in their Christology. Certainly John does not think this is an error that merely results in a lower heavenly status but is instead a heresy that leads to damnation (hence the labels "deceiver" and "antichrist"). Additionally, if one doubted John had eternal life or damnation in view, there can be no question by the time one arrives at verse

---

6. One might be wondering whether Peter, then, is teaching works-righteousness. It should be observed that these virtues are the result of God's power (1:3–4) and faith (1:5). So no, Peter is not teaching works-righteousness.

8. Schreiner observes, "Such a reading fits with the whole of 2 Peter, for the false teachers and their followers are clearly destined for final judgment (see 2 Peter 2:1–3, 20–22). Hence in 2 Peter 1:8–11 a reference to eschatological salvation accords with the entire message of 2 Peter" (*Run to Win the Prize*, 37).

9, which says that those who adopt this Christological heresy do not abide in Christ's teaching and do not have God. To not "abide in Christ" (as we saw in John 15:6) and to "not have God" is to bring eternal judgment down on one's head. So the context, verses 7 and 9, has everything to do with the contrast between eternal life and damnation. Given how serious the danger is, then, it makes very good sense that John, who is deeply concerned for the church, would give a stern, even fierce warning so that the "elect Lady" is not tempted to buy into this damning heresy. So he warns them not to forfeit what they've worked for, lest they lose the "full reward" of heaven itself.

John, and Jesus through him, also issues warnings to believers in churches throughout the book of Revelation (e.g., Rev. 2:5–7, 11, 17, 26; 3:5, 12, 21). That he has true Christians in mind is apparent at the start of the book when he says repeatedly, "He who has an ear, let him hear what the Spirit says to the churches" (2:7, 11, 17, 29; 3:6, 13, 22). Likewise John opens his revelation addressing those who have been "freed" from their "sins by his [Jesus'] blood," and made into a "kingdom" of "priests" (1:5–6). These churches are under extreme duress, facing persecution from the "beast," likely a reference to the Roman Empire. John writes to encourage these churches not to cave in but to endure knowing that a day is coming when God will judge his enemies.

At the start of the book, Jesus (through John) finds it necessary to warn these churches of what will happen should they not listen to God. He also finds it necessary to remind them of the life ahead should they listen and obey. For example, Jesus praises the church in Ephesus because they will not tolerate "those who are evil" but "have tested those who call themselves apostles and are not," finding them "to be false" (Rev. 2:2). He also praises them for "enduring patiently and bearing up for my name's sake"; they have "not grown weary" (2:3). Nevertheless, he does have one thing against them: "you have abandoned the love you had at first" (2:4). So he commands them to repent and do the works they used to do (2:5). And then comes the warning: "If not, I will come to you and remove your lampstand from its place, unless you repent. . . . To the one who conquers I will grant to eat of the tree of life, which is in the paradise of God" (2:5, 7). This reference to the "tree of life" (echoing Eden) demonstrates that eternal life is on the line (cf. 22:2, 14, 19).

Or consider the church in Smyrna, a church that is experiencing "tribulation" and "poverty," though in reality they are "rich" before God (Rev. 2:9). He warns them that Satan is about to "throw some of you into prison, that you may be tested" (2:10a). If they are faithful, Jesus promises he will give them "the crown of life" (2:10). And the one who "conquers will not be hurt by the second death" (2:11b), which refers to the final judgment, the "lake of fire" (20:14; cf. 20:6; 21:8). There is an implicit warning here: Should they fail to "conquer," they will be "hurt by the second death." Should they fail to overcome, then they will not receive the "crown of life." Being thrown into prison (2:10) does not begin to compare with being "thrown into the lake of fire" (20:15). The point is this: Perseverance is absolutely necessary if one is to receive eternal life rather than eternal fire, and these warnings in Revelation serve to help the church conquer in the face of persecution.[8]

Summary

The warnings in Scripture are (a) addressed to God's elect (i.e., real, authentic Christians) who are guaranteed eternal life and (b) prove to be God's ordained *means* by which Christians persevere in the faith. These warnings act as means to keep the believer from eternal damnation. They are not retrospective, but prospective. Their purpose, in other words, is to protect believers from falling away from Jesus.

REFLECTION QUESTIONS

1. How have biblical warnings kept you from abandoning the faith in the past?

2. How do warnings create a godly fear within the believer?

3. Study the passages discussed in this chapter. Do you think they are retrospective (looking back on those who proved not to be Christians after all), or prospective (looking ahead at what one's fate will be should he/she abandon Christ?

4. Do the warnings contradict the doctrine of eternal security?

5. If you see a fellow Christian living in sin, how can these biblical warnings be used to bring your brother or sister back to Christ?

---

8. This language of "conquering" is significant. Only those who conquer will wear white garments (garments necessary to enter God's presence) and avoid being erased from the book of life (Rev. 3:5). The conqueror gets to reign with Jesus (3:21). This reward is not for the best of believers but is promised to all believers, for they are the ones who conquer. See Schreiner, *Run to Win the Prize*, 39–40. On this conquer language, see Richard Bauckham, *The Theology of the Book of Revelation* (Cambridge: Cambridge University Press, 1993), 14.

What Role Do the Warning Passages Play in Our Perseverance? (Part 2)

In the last chapter we argued that the warnings in Scripture are (a) addressed to God's elect (i.e., real, authentic Christians) who are guaranteed eternal life and (b) prove to be God's ordained *means* by which Christians persevere in the faith. In addition, we made such a case by appealing to the warnings Jesus issues both in John's gospel and in the book of Revelation. In this chapter we continue to argue for this interpretation of the warning passages, but this time we will focus our attention first on the apostle Paul, and then on the famous warnings in the book to the Hebrews.

The Kindness and the Severity of God: Pauline Warnings

In Romans 11 Paul issues a sobering warning to Gentile Christians. These Gentile Christians have been grafted on to the "olive tree," which is symbolic for the people of God. While these Gentile branches were grafted on, Jewish branches were removed due to their unbelief (11:19–20). Lest the Gentiles become arrogant, however, Paul reminds them that if they do not stand fast in their faith (11:20), God will remove them. "For if God did not spare the natural branches, neither will he spare you" (11:21). Paul continues, "Note then the kindness and the severity of God: severity toward those who have fallen, but God's kindness to you, provided you continue in his kindness. Otherwise you too will be cut off" (11:22). If the Gentiles continue in faith, they will experience God's kindness. But if they do not, then they will experience his severity. What is this severity, exactly? Answer: being "cut off." No mere loss of rewards is in view but eternal destruction, being cut off from God's people and from God himself. Paul's point isn't merely to frighten the Gentiles but to cultivate a godly humility by this warning so that they continue in the faith, fearing God's judgment should they become arrogant and fail to repent and trust in Christ.

Paul also issues a warning as a means to perseverance in 1 Corinthians 6. The Corinthians struggled with many different sins such as schism over church leaders (1:10–17; 3:1–23) and sexual immorality (5:1–13; 6:12–20). They also displayed a poor witness by pursuing lawsuits against one another (6:1–11). Rather than resolving their disagreements with one another, they took each other to court, airing their grievances before the unbelieving world. Paul calls this a "defeat" (6:7). "Why not rather suffer wrong? . . . But you yourselves wrong and defraud—even your own brothers!" (6:8). Paul does not merely slap the Corinthians on the hand. Instead, he threatens them with taking away the kingdom itself.[1] "Or do you not know that the unrighteous will not inherit the kingdom of God?" (6:9). Paul promises that those who practice wickedness (sexual immorality, greed, revilers, swindlers, etc.) will not "inherit the kingdom of God" (6:10). Here is a prospective warning. This is not the identity of the Corinthians. As Paul must remind them, they are those who have been "washed," "sanctified," and "justified" by the Spirit (6:11). However, if they continue to act in this way, Paul warns, they will not receive eternal life, which is what it means to fail to inherit the kingdom (Gal. 5:21; Eph. 5:5). Again, the point of this severe warning is to strike fear into the Corinthians so that they sober up spiritually, correct their lifestyle with one another, and live in accordance with the commands of Christ, thereby persevering in the faith rather than returning to their unregenerate days.

Paul also has some very stern, scary words for those Christians in Galatia who are being tempted to turn to works of the law for justification. As the context of the book reveals, they were being tempted to make circumcision a requirement for justification.[2] It doesn't appear they have done it, yet. This is why Paul can say, in Galatians 5:2, "*if* you accept circumcision." But they are being tempted to nonetheless. And Paul is very distressed to hear this. To accept circumcision as a requirement for salvation would then mean that one is required to keep the entire law in order to be saved (5:3). Paul recognizes just how dangerous it is to return to the Sinai law for justification since the requirement of the law is nothing less than perfection (see 3:10). Furthermore, if justification through the law can be attained by sinful man, or if forgiveness could be found through the law, then Christ's death was pointless (see 2:21; 5:2). Such a return to the law misunderstands the purpose of the Old Testament sacrifices, which were meant to typologically point to the final sacrifice, Christ, the Lamb of God, and the free gift of salvation he gives to those who trust in him.

---

1. "The link in the *adik* words demonstrates that the warning is addressed to the same persons engaged in the lawsuits" (Thomas R. Schreiner, *Run to Win the Prize: Perseverance in the New Testament* [Wheaton, IL: Crossway, 2010], 33; cf. Gordon D. Fee, *The First Epistle to the Corinthians*, NICNT [Grand Rapids: Eerdmans, 1987], 242).

2. That justification in view, see 5:4, as well as the rest of the letter.

In order to stop the Galatians, Paul gives a fierce warning: "If you accept circumcision, Christ will be of no advantage to you" (5:2). Paul clearly spells out the consequences: "You are severed from Christ, you who would be justified by the law; you have fallen away from grace" (5:4). Two points should be noted: (1) Paul has in mind eternal judgment and condemnation, as his words "severed from Christ" and "fallen away from grace" make plain. To seek justification through the law is to cut oneself off from Christ and the eternal life he brings. (2) One should not read this statement and think that this dark reality has already transpired. Rather, Paul is speaking *prospectively* in this warning.[3] It's as if he said, "If you do this, then you will fall away from grace." And the reason is obvious: justification by works is absolutely antithetical to the gospel and the free grace of God through Christ (Gal. 1:4; 2:21; 3:1, 13; 4:4–5; 5:11; 6:12–17).

Finally, we should not miss the purpose of the warning itself: to keep these Galatians from accepting circumcision, which would result in being cut off from salvation in Christ. Paul's words must be firm if they are to act as a means to keep the Galatians from damnation.[4]

Warnings in Hebrews

There are many warning passages in the book of Hebrews and we cannot address them all here.[5] Nevertheless, several stand out and deserve our attention.

First, notice that Christians are the recipients of these warnings.[6] Throughout Hebrews the author identifies himself with the Christians he is addressing, as if he, too, is a recipient of each warning. He consistently and repeatedly uses "we" and "us" when warning against drifting away and being condemned (2:1; 3:12–4:13; 5:11–6:12; 10:26; 12:28), and at other times he uses the word

---

3. Note the aorist verbs in 5:4. "The aorist verbs 'severed' (*katērgēthēte*) and 'have fallen' (*exepesate*) in Galatians 5:4 have a gnomic sense" (Schreiner, *Run to Win the Prize*, 30). Also see J. B. Lightfoot, *The Epistle of St. Paul to the Galatians with Introductions, Notes and Dissertations* (Grand Rapids: Zondervan, 1957), 204; F. F. Bruce, *The Epistle to the Galatians: A Commentary on the Greek Text*, NIGTC (Grand Rapids: Eerdmans, 1982), 231.

4. For other Pauline texts where Paul issues warnings as a means to persevering, see Romans 8:13; 1 Corinthians 9.

5. Hebrews 2:1–4; 3:12–4:13; 5:11–6:12; 10:19–39; 12:25–29. It should be noted from the start that all of these warnings should be read together, in continuity, synoptically. These warnings do not contradict each other, nor does the author have different purposes in mind when writing each. So we should not isolate one from another; rather, they are a coherent, consistent whole. After all, Hebrews is a sermon to the church (13:22) and so these warnings build off of one another with the purpose, as we shall see, of keeping the church on the narrow road. This point is stressed by Schreiner, *Run to Win the Prize*, 40–41; contra Osborne, "A Wesleyan Arminian View," 275–76.

6. The following three points are indebted to Schreiner, *Run to Win the Prize*, 42–48, though I utilize them in a different order and at times with different emphases.

"brothers" when warning his readers not to fall away (3:12). In other words, the writer, who is a Christian, places himself under these warnings about damnation when he is addressing other Christians in the church. This cannot be emphasized enough.

But what about Hebrews 6:4–6a: "For it is impossible, in the case of those who have once been enlightened, who have tasted the heavenly gift, and have shared in the Holy Spirit, and have tasted the goodness of the word of God and then the powers of the age to come, and then have fallen away, to restore them again to repentance"? How can this verse have authentic Christians in mind? It is understandable why someone might think these cannot be Christians, since these individuals are connected to falling away. However, the text itself shows signs that only believers are in view. Possessing the Spirit in the New Testament is at the very essence of what it means to be a Christian (see Acts 15:7–11; Gal. 3:1–5). Similarly, to be "enlightened" and to have "tasted" refers to no mere superficial affiliation with Christ (like an unbeliever looking on in mere interest), but rather to those who have had their eyes miraculously opened and have started feasting.

Second, these warning passages have everything to do with eternal life and eternal death; they are warnings against apostasy, nothing less. For example, Hebrews 1:14 has in mind those who are to "inherit salvation." In light of the revelation concerning the Son, Christians must "pay much closer attention" to what they have heard and been taught about Jesus, lest they should "drift away from it" (2:1). The author then warns that if those under the Mosaic law ("the message declared by angels"; cf. 2:2) resulted in retribution for its lawbreakers, how much more so for those who neglect the salvation that has come through Jesus (2:3)? Surely they will not escape.

In Hebrews 3 the author appeals to Psalm 95:7–11 to show how Israel hardened her heart in the wilderness, putting God to the test. The result? "As I swore in my wrath, 'They shall not enter my rest'" (Heb. 3:11; cf 3:18) Here we have a vivid picture of the wrath of God. Not to enter into God's rest is to experience his judgment.

Hebrews 10:26–27 strikes just as much fear in its warning. The author warns believers that *if* they go on "sinning deliberately," no sacrifice remains for their sins but only "fearful expectation of judgment, and a fury of fire that will consume the adversaries." The fire that consumes adversaries is the fire of hell, where God's enemies will spend an eternity under his wrath. Any Christian who is being tempted to apostatize should keep in mind that if he/she tramples underfoot the Son of God, profaning the blood of the covenant, he will undergo the vengeance of the Lord (10:29–30; cf. Deut. 32:35–36; Ps. 5:4; 135:14). Indeed, it "is a fearful thing to fall into the hands of the living God" (10:31). The author has in mind a fixed rejection of Jesus on the person's part; he has in mind apostasy and he labors to warn against it.

Many other passages in Hebrews teach the same (see 4:3, 5, 11; 6:4, 6; 6:7–8; 12:25), each of which emphasizes how eternal destruction will await anyone who chooses to abandon the faith.[7]

Third, as real warnings to Christians, these warnings are prospective in nature, acting as means to keep believers from falling away in the future. Hebrews 6 is especially important in this regard. The reference to falling away in 6:6 is not describing something that has already happened (retrospective)—as if (1) Christians are in view but they have lost their salvation,[8] or (2) individuals who appear to be Christians are in view but, as it turns out, they really were not after all because they have "fallen."[9] Rather, genuine Christians are being addressed, but Hebrews 6:4–6 is a statement (and by implication a warning) about what will happen or what would happen should one reject Christ (prospective). "Some understand the participle here (*parapesontas*), given the use of the preceding participles in verses 4–5, to say that the readers have already fallen away." However, explains Schreiner, such a reading "does not fit with all the other admonitions in Hebrews, for the author does not chide the readers because they have fallen away but admonishes them so that they will not fall away."[10] This becomes all the more clear in verses 11–12 when the author expresses his desire that these Christians "show the same earnestness to have the full assurance of hope until the end, so that you may not be sluggish, but imitators of those who through faith and patience inherit the promises." The warning in verses 4–6 is meant to move these believers to take hold of the inheritance on the last day.

Hebrews 10:26–31 also proves our point. Perhaps it is accurate to say that out of all passages the threat of God's wrath is most vivid in this passage (especially 10:27, 30). As we saw, the Christian (cf. 10:29: the "sanctified" person) who goes on sinning deliberately "after receiving the knowledge of the truth" (10:26) is threated with "judgment," the "fury of fire that will consume the adversaries," the "vengeance" of the Lord who "will judge," and "falling" into the "hands of the living God" (10:27–30). The reason he is threatened is not because this judgment has come, but because it will come should he trample "underfoot the Son of God" and profane the "blood of the covenant" (10:29). In other words, the warning is prospective and its purpose is to keep the "sanctified" on the road of faith. Hence, the author can conclude Hebrews 10 on a note of perseverance. "But we are not of those who shrink back and are destroyed, but of those who have faith and preserve their souls" (10:39).

---

7. In the New Testament, "destruction" refers to end-time judgment and eternal punishment (Matt. 7:13; John 17:12; Acts 8:20; Rom. 9:22; Phil. 1:28; 3:19; 2 Thess. 2:3; 1 Tim. 6:9; 2 Peter 2:1, 3; 3:7, 16; Rev. 17:8, 1). See ibid., 47.
8. I.e., Arminianism and Wesleyanism.
9. I.e., the more traditional Reformed view.
10. Schreiner, *Run to Win the Prize*, 45.

Again, many other passages could be examined (2:1; 3:7–19; 4:11; 6:1), but the point is clear: The warnings act as means that God uses to keep his elect persevering in the faith.

What Do We Make of These Warnings?

In summary, there are numerous warnings in Scripture, even more than we could discuss in these last two chapters.[11] But these warnings do not address unbelievers, nor those who merely appear to be believers but in reality are not. Rather, these warnings are addressed to genuine Christians. Furthermore, these warnings do not speak merely about rewards in heaven, but rather address eternal life and eternal destruction, warning fiercely against the latter. And, as we've seen, these warnings are used by God (issued by God even) as means to keep his elect from falling into eternal destruction.

As we conclude we return to our original three points:

1. God's elect are eternally secure due to his sovereign care and preservation (Questions 34–35).

2. God's elect must persevere in the faith if they are to enter into eternal life (Questions 36–37).

3. God uses "warnings" as his means to keep his elect persevering in the faith and from committing apostasy (Questions 38–39).

Not one of these three can be compromised; they all go together, like three pillars upholding the edifice of Christian security and perseverance.[12]

Summary

Not only does Paul teach that warnings are means to keep the believer from eternal damnation, but so does the author of Hebrews. Hebrews reinforces that these warnings are addressed to Christians, have everything to do with eternal life or eternal death, and are prospective in nature, acting as means to keep believers from falling away in the future.

---

11. E.g., Romans 8:13; 1 Corinthians 9:24–10:13; 15:1–2; 16:22; Galatians 5:19–21; 6:8–9; Ephesians 5:5–6; Colossians 1:21–23; 3:5–6; 1 Thessalonians 4:3–8; 2 Timothy 2:11–18.
12. For answers to objections to the position presented in the last two chapters, see Schreiner, *Run to Win the Prize*, 51–112.

REFLECTION QUESTIONS

1. Read Romans 11:19–22. How does this severe warning create godly humility within you?

2. Who is the author of Hebrews addressing in his many threats of eternal destruction?

3. Read Hebrews 10:26–27. Do you think the author has in mind the loss of rewards or the loss of eternal life?

4. How can the church take these warnings in Hebrews more seriously today?

5. Which warning passage do you find the most convicting, as you think about temptations to sin in your own life?

What Will Glorification Be Like?

Death is not a subject people like to talk about, and for good reason, too. Nothing is as ugly as death. Death divorces us from everything we know and love. Death separates us from family and friends who we care for. It rips us apart from a wife, a daughter, a son—each of whom we've loved and devoted ourselves to for a lifetime.

Death is also ugly because it disconnects our soul from our body. Surely this is not natural but an unnatural and awkward division. It's not the way things are supposed to be. From the beginning God created us body *and* soul, a union not be torn asunder.

Furthermore, death itself is a hideous thing. It is painful, sometimes even torturing, putting us through much suffering and agony. The body we once knew as vibrant, resilient, and full of youth now decays and shuts down. The elderly in some societies are, sadly, neglected, put out of sight, because they remind everyone else that death is coming for them, too. Being around the sick and dying is the last thing most people want to do because it is like looking in a mirror.

In short, death is awful. It's a crisis like no other, and it's the final crisis—indeed, the greatest one, bringing everything we know to an end.[1] Is it any wonder people don't like to talk about death?

Death: The Consequence and Curse of Sin

As Christians, however, we must come to terms with death. Scripture itself has much to say about death. It acknowledges just how terrible death is. But unlike the philosophies of this world, Scripture is able to explain why death is here and where it came from.

---

1. Sinclair B. Ferguson, *The Christian Life: A Doctrinal Introduction* (Edinburgh: The Banner of Truth Trust, repr. 2009), 181.

According to Scripture, death is both the consequence and the curse of sin. Think back to Genesis 1–2. Life was good, precisely because there was only life, not death. But everything changed when Adam and Eve chose to sin. Though God warned them that the consequence of disobedience would be death, they did not listen. Their sin was the first sin of humanity, and it was the sin that would set this world in the grip of death itself. Not only was the guilt and corruption of Adam's sin inherited by all mankind, but due to Adam's sin everyone thereafter would physically die. In other words, death is not only spiritual but physical. As Scripture repeatedly reminds us, the consequence of sin is death, that is, both spiritual and physical death (e.g., Rom. 3:23; 5:12–21).

Naturally, therefore, death is not merely a consequence of sin but a curse of sin. Christians tend to skip over this side of death. We tend to talk about death as if it were a mere pathway to the life to come, and in that sense even a blessing. But such language ignores death for what it truly is. Death, as Sinclair Ferguson observes, is "disintegration," the "breaking of a union which God created," and an "ugly, destructive thing—it is 'the last *enemy*'." [2] There is no way to cover it up. The consequence and curse of Adam's sin and our own sin is death. And lest we think we will somehow escape this curse, we must remember that death takes no prisoners.

God Wins: Christ's Resurrection and Ours

So far we have come to terms with death. It's real, it's a problem, it's a crisis, it's inescapable, and it's tragic. It's sin's consequence and curse. Death, therefore, proves to be our enemy, and not just ours but God's enemy as well.

But it is not an enemy that wins. This is the great news of the gospel. In the end, sin, Satan, and death do not win; God does! But he wins in the most surprising way of all: by dying. Christ acted as our substitute, paying the penalty for our sin (i.e., the wrath of God) on the cross. As a result, sin no longer has dominion over us. Our debt has been paid on the cross.

But there's more: Not only did Christ die, he rose three days later. Perhaps the most sobering statement Paul makes in 1 Corinthians 15 is that "if Christ has not been raised, your faith is futile and you are still in your sins" (15:17). So often we limit our understanding of salvation to the death of Christ. And certainly the death of Christ, as Paul says in Romans 3:25–26, is the very basis of our justification. It is through his "one act of righteousness" (Rom. 5:18), the "propitiation by his blood" (Rom. 3:25–26), that sinners are declared righteous in God's sight. But there is much more to be said. Not only does the substitutionary death of Christ save, but so also does his resurrection. For example, Paul states in Romans 4:24–25 that we, like Abraham, are counted righteous since we believe in him "who raised from the dead Jesus our Lord, who was delivered up for our trespasses *and* raised for our justification."

---

2. Ibid., 183.

By raising Jesus from the dead, God declared his satisfaction and approval of the payment Christ made on our behalf, for our sins, on the cross. And as those who are *in Christ* (Rom. 6:6–11; Eph. 2:6; Col. 2:12; 3:1), God's approval of Christ's substitutionary death, demonstrated in raising Jesus from the dead, is likewise directed toward us so that when we believe we receive the favor of God. Therefore, our justification is a real consequence of Christ's resurrection. No wonder Paul can say that "if Christ has not been raised, your faith is futile and you are still in your sins" (1 Cor. 15:17). And if we are still in our sins, we have no confidence, no assurance of our salvation whatsoever. It is no overstatement to say, then, that the resurrection of Christ saves.

But it doesn't just save our souls; it saves our bodies as well. How practical Christ's resurrection is—precisely because Christ has been raised, we can tell those looking into the casket of their loved one that this is not the end of the story. If your loved one has trusted in Christ, then even though they have "fallen asleep," they have fallen asleep "in Christ" (1 Cor. 15:18). Since they are united to this resurrected Christ, they have not perished but their soul has gone to be with Christ (Phil. 1:23), and they await that day when they will receive their resurrected body. As Paul tells the Corinthians, Christ's resurrection is the first fruits of that great harvest to come. Though death came by the first Adam, in the second Adam "shall all be made alive" (15:22). Yes, death is real and it will come, but it comes as a "defeated foe."[3] For though we die, one day we will rise, and our soul will be reunited to our body, though this time as a body in all of its resurrected splendor.

Apart from the resurrection of Christ, we have no future hope. As Paul says in no uncertain terms, if Christ has not been raised then we, out of all people, are to be "pitied," for our hope in Christ fails to extend beyond this present life (1 Cor. 15:19). But since Christ has been raised, we are those who can look death in the face knowing that it has no final victory, no lasting sting (1 Cor. 15:54–55).

What Will Glorification Be Like?

We might ask then, in light of this great hope, what will our future glorification will be like? Now that's a hard question to answer. Scripture does not give us all the details we might want (e.g., What age will we be? Will we recognize each other?).[4] Nevertheless, Scripture is not silent either. In fact, it has much to say.[5]

---

3. Ibid., 184.
4. Ferguson helpfully notes how this subject "takes us to the outer limits of Christian knowledge, and leaves us like men standing on the shore watching a boat disappear over the horizon into an experience at which we can only begin to guess" (ibid., 191).
5. In what follows, I have not addressed the Eastern-Western debate over "deification" (cf. 2 Peter 1:4) as this would take us beyond the scope of this chapter. However, for an outstanding treatment of this issue, and one that is well balanced, see Michael Horton, *Pilgrim*

First, prior to glorification there is a heavenly in-between state after death. Theologians refer to this as the "intermediate state," which is not glorification itself but that phase just prior. When we breathe our last, it is not the case that we cease to exist or our soul goes to sleep until the time of our bodily resurrection.[6] Rather, our soul remains conscious and upon the death of our body our soul goes to be with the Lord in heaven. In other words, Scripture teaches that when we die we go directly into the presence of God (Luke 23:43; Phil. 1:23; cf. John 14:2–3). As Paul says, to be "away from the body" is to be "at home with the Lord" (2 Cor. 5:8). Scripture also says that it is at this point that the "spirits of the righteous" are "made perfect" (Heb. 12:23). Paul eagerly desired this perfect state, revealing that his "desire is to depart and be with Christ, for that is far better" (Phil. 1:23). Yet we should emphasize, at this point, that though we enter into the presence of our Lord, our salvation in its totality remains incomplete since our soul is separated from our body. Our glorification has not yet begun because we still await that day when "the perishable puts on the imperishable, and the mortal puts on immortality," and finally "death is swallowed up in victory" (1 Cor. 15:54).

Second, this heavenly in-between state will come to an end when God unites our soul to our resurrected body. Now we come to the doctrine of glorification. When will this day happen? According to Paul, "we shall all be changed, in a moment, in the twinkling of an eye, at the last trumpet." When this trumpet sounds the "dead will be raised imperishable, and we shall be changed" (1 Cor. 15:52; cf. 1 Thess. 4:16–17). On that day we shall experience the fullness of salvation, for only then will we, as whole persons, be conformed to the image of our resurrected Savior. As Paul tells the Philippians, "our citizenship is in heaven, and from it we await a Savior, the Lord Jesus Christ, who will transform our lowly body to be like his glorious body" (3:20–21). On that day, our union with Christ will reach its full potential. What predestination promised will finally come to fruition; what Christ accomplished in his death and resurrection will reach its consummation.[7]

We are not told specifics as to what this resurrected body will be like. Christ's resurrected body may be an indicator, especially since we are told that our glorification will involve the final goal of becoming like Christ, bearing his image (1 Cor. 15:49). As those united to Christ, we will receive a body that, in some way, is like Christ's resurrected body. After all, Scripture attests that the same power that raised Jesus from the dead will raise our mortal bodies

---

Theology: Core Doctrines for Christian Disciples (Grand Rapids: Zondervan, 2011), 325–41. I agree with Horton's energy-essence distinction, as well as his take on the beatific vision (via Calvin).

6. Scripture does use the language of "sleep" (e.g., 1 Cor. 15:51). However, by "sleep" it often means death itself, though not to the exclusion of the soul's afterlife.

7. John Murray, *Redemption Accomplished and Applied* (Grand Rapids: Eerdmans, 1955), 174.

from the dead as well (Rom. 6:8–10; Heb. 7:16; Rom. 8:11). And our resurrected bodies, if anything like his, will be indestructible, no longer susceptible to sickness and death, to temptation and sin. So at the very least we can say that there will be a supernatural transformation that takes place. As Paul says to the Philippians, our citizenship is in heaven, and "from it we await a Savior, the Lord Jesus Christ, who will *transform our lowly body to be like his glorious body*, by the power that enables him even to subject all things to himself" (Phil. 3:20–21, emphasis added). "Only when we share in his [Christ's] bodily resurrection," comments Peterson, "will we be truly conformed to his image as the glorified Son of God."[8]

This transformation will involve continuity and discontinuity. Presumably our future resurrected body will resemble our current body (though we're not told to what degree or at what stage), just as Jesus was recognizable when he appeared to his disciples. And yet, there will also be a degree of discontinuity. It would be a mistake to think that our resurrected body will merely be a reembodied version of our old self. According to Philippians 3:20–21, there will be an actual *transformation*. A change will take effect, and a supernatural one at that (see 1 Cor. 15:51–54).[9] No longer will it be a body of death, but a body of life. As Paul writes to the Corinthians, "What is sown is perishable; what is raised is imperishable. It is sown in dishonor; it is raised in glory. It is sown in weakness; it is raised in power. It is sown a natural body; it is raised a spiritual body" (1 Cor. 15:42–44). Paul's contrast between a natural body and a spiritual body is not a contrast between a physical and nonphysical (or immaterial) body, but a contrast between a body that only lives for a short time and a body that will be immortal due to the empowering presence of the Holy Spirit. As Paul goes on to explain (15:47–49), our natural body was tied to the first Adam, a man of the dust, but our resurrected body, which is imperishable, is tied to the second Adam, the "man of heaven," the Lord Jesus Christ.

It is this second point that gets at the essence of what it means to be "glorified." Scripture often will use the word "glory" to describe this future bodily hope. For example, Paul can promise that when "Christ who is your life appears, then you also will appear with him *in glory*" (Col. 3:4, emphasis added). Though Christ's first coming involved entering into a state of humiliation, in his second coming he will return in a state of glorification, and we will share in that glory with him.[10] In the present we pursue holiness, "waiting for our blessed hope, the appearing of the glory of our great God and Savior Jesus

---

8. David Peterson, *Possessed by God: A New Testament Theology of Sanctification and Holiness* (Downers Grove, IL: InterVarsity Press, 1995), 119.
9. Note how Scripture can apply the language of "regeneration" and "renewal" to describe this future state. In Matthew 19:28, for example, Jesus describes the "new" or "regenerated" (*palingenesia*) world to come, one in which his disciples will sit on twelve thrones judging the twelve tribes of Israel as the Son of Man sits on his "glorious throne."
10. Ferguson, *The Christian Life*, 193.

Christ" (Titus 2:13). If we must, we even suffer with Christ "in order that we may also be glorified with him" (Rom. 8:17).

Third, as those who have received resurrected bodies, we will enjoy a con-summated sonship and a new heavens and earth. Sometimes it is forgotten that not only will we, as "heirs of God and fellow heirs with Christ" (Rom. 8:17), be transformed and changed but so will the creation (Ps. 102:26; Heb. 1:11–12; 2 Peter 3:13; Rev. 21:1–8). The creation itself awaits eagerly for this day, much like a woman ready to give birth (Rom. 8:19–21, 23). On that day the mountains and hills will burst into song and dance (Isa. 55:12–13). No longer will creation be subjected to futility—a futility it's been subjected to ever since Genesis 3—but it will be set free from "its bondage to corruption" (Rom. 8:21).

In Scripture this new creation is also referred to as a "new heavens and a new earth" (Isa. 65:17; 66:22; Rev. 21:1–3).[11] When the final judgment is complete, those in Christ will have the joy and privilege of being with God in this new heavens and earth. This renewed heavens and earth—the result of a "cosmic regeneration" (2 Peter 3:12–13)—is promised by God and said to be a place "in which righteousness dwells" (2 Peter 3:13; cf. Rev. 21:27).[12] Christians are those who will inherit this new earth (Matt. 5:5).

Of course, the most important aspect about this new creation is not *what* is there but *who* is there—namely, God himself. The reason eternity will be a world of joy, beauty, and love is because we will enjoy *God*. His glory will radiate like a "rare jewel, like a jasper, clear as crystal" (Rev. 21:11). Echoing God's promise in the Old Testament, Revelation 21:3 says that in this new creation God's dwelling place will be with man, for man, and "they will be his people, and God himself will be with them as their God." The God who has kept us from "stumbling" will present us "blameless before the presence of his glory with great joy" (Jude 24). As we dwell in his presence we will "behold the beauty of the Lord" (Ps. 27:4) and experience the "fullness of joy" and "pleasures evermore" (Ps. 16:11).

Knowledge of this new creation has implications for us as God's image-bearers. As Paul says in Romans 8, not only does the creation groan, but so do we as we "wait eagerly for adoption as sons, the redemption of our bodies" (8:23). In Question 27 we discussed what it means to be adopted as sons of God. But here, in Romans 8, we see another dimension to this sonship, a future dimension. We are those who have been "predestined to be conformed to the image of his Son, in order that he might be the firstborn among many brothers" (Rom. 8:29). Here and elsewhere (Col. 1:18), Christ is called the

---

11. Debate exists as to whether this new earth refers to a totally "new" earth (the present earth being totally annihilated) or whether the present earth will be "renewed." Passages under debate include Hebrews 1:11–12; 12:26–27; 2 Peter 3:10; Revelation 20:11; 21:1.
12. The phrase "cosmic regeneration" is from Murray, *Redemption*, 179.

firstborn. He is the firstborn in his eternal sonship, but he is also the firstborn in regard to his bodily resurrection, through which he entered into glory.[13] Therefore, our sonship is inseparably based upon and modeled after him. As sons, we await our final, eschatological adoption as sons, which is nothing less than the resurrection of our bodies (Rom. 8:23). Such a sonship entails that we will be like Christ in this resurrected state. As John says, we are "children of God," and as his children we know with confidence that "when he appears we shall be like him, because we shall see him as he is" (1 John 3:2).[14]

How Then Shall We Live . . . and Die?

Should this knowledge of the glorification that awaits us as children of God change the way we live here and now, and especially the way we die? Earlier 1 John 3:2 was quoted to highlight how we will one day be conformed into the image of Christ: "We know that when he appears we shall be like him, because we shall see him as he is." But if we continue reading, John explains how this knowledge should change how we live: "And everyone who thus hopes in him purifies himself as he is pure" (3:3). Apparently John believed that this great "hope" (i.e., future conformity to Christ) should motivate us to live a life that is set apart and faithful. Holiness in life, in other words, is motivated by that ultimate conformity to Christ on that last day.[15]

Paul's eschatology also shoots back into the present. One day, he says, the perishable will put on the imperishable, and on that day we will say, "Death is swallowed up in victory" (1 Cor. 15:54). This victory has come through our Lord Jesus Christ (15:57). "Therefore," he concludes, "be steadfast, immovable, always abounding in the work of the Lord, knowing that in the Lord your labor is not in vain" (15:58). Like John, Paul believes our future hope should motivate us as we go about the "work of the Lord."

This changes everything. It changes how we live; it changes how we die. When we know that nothing, not even death itself, can separate us from the love of God in Christ Jesus our Lord (Rom. 8:38), suddenly we can boldly look death in the face and ask, "O death, where is your victory . . . where is your sting?" (1 Cor. 15:55). We live as those who set their hearts on the glory of the presence of Christ to come (Phil. 1:23), and we remember the countless blessings that await us in that glory (Heb. 12:23). Here and now we live knowing that this world is passing away (Matt. 6:19) but the world to come is eternal (Matt. 6:20–21; 1 Cor. 7:31) and full of joy (1 Peter 4:13).[16] And so we say, "Amen. Come Lord Jesus!" (Rev. 22:20). And with Job we rejoice

---

13. Ferguson, *The Christian Life*, 199.
14. I do not think "like him" means identical to him, as if we are somehow gods now. Instead, it must have to do with holiness and immortality.
15. Paul is not the only one. Also consider 2 Peter 3:11–13.
16. Ferguson, *The Christian Life*, 187–89.

confidently and declare, "I know that my Redeemer lives, and at the last he will stand upon the earth. And after my skin has been thus destroyed, yet in my flesh I shall see God" (Job 19:25–26).

Summary

After death but prior to glorification the Christian enters into a heavenly in-between state where he dwells in the presence of God. This heavenly in-between state will come to an end when God unites our soul to our resurrected body. Finally, as those who have received resurrected bodies, we will enjoy a consummated sonship and a new heavens and earth.

REFLECTION QUESTIONS

1. Why is Christ's resurrection so key to our future bodily resurrection?

2. What happens to our soul when we die?

3. What does Scripture say about our future resurrected body?

4. In light of 1 Corinthians 15:55, why is it that we can sing victoriously over death?

5. Read 1 John 3:2. How should the glory that awaits us change how we live here and now?

Select Bibliography

This book is designed to be an introduction (or primer) to the doctrine of salvation. There is far more to learn and explore when it comes to the subject. So here are some of the best resources that can help you go deeper. These resources range from beginner (B) to intermediate (I) to advanced (A).

General Studies on Salvation

Bavinck, Herman. *Reformed Dogmatics*. Vol. 3, *Sin and Salvation in Christ*. Grand Rapids: Baker Academic, 2008.   (A)

Berkhof, Louis. *Systematic Theology*. Edinburgh: Banner of Truth, 2003.   (I)

Calvin, John. *Institutes of the Christian Religion*. 2 vols. Edited by John T. McNeill. Translated by Ford Lewis Battles. Library of Christian Classics, vols. 20–21. Philadelphia: Westminster John Knox, 1960.   (I)

Frame, John. *Salvation Belongs to the Lord: An Introduction to Systematic Theology*. Phillipsburg, NJ: 2006.   (I)

Ferguson, Sinclair B. *The Christian Life: A Doctrinal Introduction*. Carlisle, PA: The Banner of Truth Trust, 1989.   (B)

_____. *The Holy Spirit*. Downers Grove, IL: InterVarsity Press, 1981.   (A)

Hoekema, Anthony A. *Saved by Grace*. Grand Rapids: Eerdmans, 1989.   (I)

Horton, Michael. *Christian Theology: A Systematic Theology for Pilgrims on the Way*. Grand Rapids: Zondervan, 2011.   (A)

_____. *Pilgrim Theology: Core Doctrines for Christian Disciples*. Grand Rapids: Zondervan, 2011.   (I)

_____. *Covenant and Salvation: Union with Christ*. Louisville: Westminster John Knox, 2007.   (A)

Murray, John. *Redemption Accomplished and Applied.* Grand Rapids: Eerdmans, 1955. (B)

Perkins, William. *Golden Chain.* Vol. 6 of *The Works of Williams Perkins,* ed. Joel R. Beeke and Derek W. H. Thomas. Grand Rapids: Reformation Heritage Books, forthcoming.

Turretin, Francis. *Institutes of Elenctic Theology.* 3 volumes. Edited by James T. Dennison Jr. Translated by George Musgrave Giger. Phillipsburg, NJ: P&R Publishing, 1992–97. (A)

Sin

Hoekema, Anthony A. *Created in God's Image.* Grand Rapids: Eerdmans, 1986. (I)

Luther, Martin. *The Bondage of the Will.* Vol. 33 of *Luther's Works.* Edited by Jaroslav Pelikan and Helmut T. Legmann. American ed. 82 vols. (projected). Philadelphia: Fortress; St. Louis, MO: Concordia, 1955-.

Plantinga Jr., Cornelius. *Not the Way It's Supposed to Be: A Breviary of Sin.* Grand Rapids: Eerdmans, 1995. (I)

Smith, David L. *With Willful Intent: A Theology of Sin.* Eugene, OR: Wipf and Stock, 1994. (I)

Union with Christ

Billings, J. Todd. *Union with Christ: Reframing Theology and Ministry for the Church.* Grand Rapids: Baker Academic, 2011. (I)

Campbell, Constantine R. *Paul and Union with Christ: An Exegetical and Theological Study.* Grand Rapids: Zondervan, 2012. (A)

Fesko, John V. *Beyond Calvin: Union with Christ and Justification in Early Modern Reformed Theology (1517–1700).* Göttingen: Vandenhoeck & Ruprecht, 2012. (A)

Letham, Robert. *Union with Christ: In Scripture, History, and Theology.* Phillipsburg, NJ: P&R, 2011. (I)

Macaskill, Grant. *Union with Christ in the New Testament.* Oxford: Oxford University Press, 2013. (A)

Peterson, Robert A. *Salvation Applied by the Spirit: Union with Christ*. Wheaton, IL: Crossway, 2015.   (I)

Smedes, Lewis B. *Union with Christ: A Biblical View of the New Life in Jesus Christ*. Grand Rapids: Eerdmans, 1983.   (I)

Covenants
Fesko, J. V. *The Trinity and the Covenant of Redemption*. Fear, Ross-shire, Scotland: Mentor, 2016.   (A)

Gentry, Peter J., and Stephen J. Wellum. *Kingdom through Covenant: A Biblical-Theological Understanding of the Covenants*. Wheaton, IL: Crossway, 2012.   (A)

_____. *God's Kingdom through God's Covenants: A Concise Biblical Theology*. Wheaton, IL: Crossway, 2015.   (I)

Election, Effectual Calling, and Regeneration
Barrett, Matthew. *Salvation by Grace: The Case for Effectual Calling and Regeneration*. Phillipsburg, NJ: P&R, 2013.   (A)

Bavinck, Herman. *Saved by Grace: The Holy Spirit's Work in Calling and Regeneration*. Edited by J. Mark Beach. Translated by Nelson D. Kloosterman. Grand Rapids: Reformation Heritage, 2008.   (A)

Calvin, John. *The Bondage and Liberation of the Will: A Defence of the Orthodox Doctrine of Human Choice against Pighius*. Edited by A. N. S. Lane. Translated by G. I. Davies. Texts and Studies in Reformation and Post-Reformation Thought. Grand Rapids, MI: Baker, 1996.

Edwards, Jonathan. *Freedom of the Will*. Vol. 1, *The Works of Jonathan Edwards*, ed. by Paul Ramsay. New Haven, CT: Yale University Press, 1970.

Horton, Michael. *For Calvinism*. Grand Rapids: Zondervan, 2011.   (I)

Peterson, Robert A. *Election and Free Will: God's Gracious Choice and Our Responsibility*. Explorations in Biblical Theology. Phillipsburg, NJ: P&R, 2007.   (I)

Peterson, Robert A., and Michael D. Williams. *Why I Am Not an Arminian*. Downers Grove, IL: InterVarsity Press, 2004.   (I)

Piper, John. *Finally Alive*. Fearn, Ross-Shire, Scotland: Christian Focus, 2009.   (B)

_____. *The Justification of God: An Exegetical and Theological Study of Romans 9:1–23*. 2nd ed. Grand Rapids: Baker, 1993.   (A)

Schreiner, Thomas R., and Bruce A. Ware, eds. *Still Sovereign: Contemporary Perspectives on Election, Foreknowledge, and Grace*. Grand Rapids: Baker Academic, 2000.   (A)

Storms, Sam. *Chosen for Life: The Case for Divine Election*. Wheaton, IL: Crossway, 2007.   (I)

Ware, Bruce A., ed. *Perspectives on Election*. Nashville: B&H, 2008.   (I)

Justification

Allen, R. Michael. *Justification and the Gospel: Understanding the Contexts and Controversies*. Grand Rapids: Baker Academic, 2013.   (A)

Barrett, Matthew, ed. *The Doctrine By Which the Church Stands or Falls: Justification in Biblical, Theological, Historical, and Pastoral Perspective*. Wheaton, IL: Crossway, 2019.   (A)

Beilby, James K., and Paul R. Eddy, eds. *Justification: Five Views*. Grand Rapids: InterVarsity Press, 2011.   (A)

Crowe, Brandon D. *The Last Adam: A Theology of the Obedient Life of Jesus in the Gospels*. Grand Rapids: Baker Academic, 2017.

Fesko, J. V. *Justification: Understanding the Classic Reformed Doctrine*. Phillipsburg, NJ: P&R, 2008.   (A)

McGrath, Alister. *Iustitia Dei: A History of the Christian Doctrine of Justification*. 3rd ed. New York: Cambridge University Press, 2005.   (A)

Oliphint, Scott K., ed. *Justified in Christ: God's Plan For Us in Justification*. Fearn, Ross-shire: Mentor, 2007.   (A)

Piper, John. *Counted Righteous*. Wheaton, IL: Crossway, 2002.   (A)

_____. *The Future of Justification: A Response to N. T. Wright*. Wheaton, IL: Crossway, 2007.   (I)

Schreiner, Thomas R. *Faith Alone: The Doctrine of Justification*. The 5 Solas Series. Edited by Matthew Barrett. Grand Rapids: Zondervan, 2015. (I)

Sproul, R. C. *Faith Alone: The Evangelical Doctrine of Justification*. Grand Rapids: Baker, 1999. (B)

Vickers, Brian. *Jesus' Blood and Righteousness: Paul's Theology of Imputation*. Wheaton, IL: Crossway, 2006. (A)

_____. *Justification by Grace through Faith: Finding Freedom from Legalism, Lawlessness, Pride, and Despair*. Phillipsburg, NJ: P&R, 2013. (I)

Waters, Guy P. *Justification and the New Perspective on Paul: A Review and Response*. Phillipsburg, NJ: P&R, 2004. (A)

Westerholm, Stephen. *Perspectives Old and New on Paul: The "Lutheran" Paul and His Critics*. Grand Rapids: Eerdmans, 2004. (A)

Adoption
Burke, Trevor J. *Adopted into God's Family: Exploring a Pauline Metaphor*, NSBT 22, ed. D. A. Carson. Downers Grove, IL: InterVarsity Press, 2006. (A)

Garner, David B. *Sons in the Son: The Riches and Reach of Adoption in Christ*. Phillipsburg, NJ: P&R, 2016. (I)

Peterson, Robert. *Adopted by God: From Wayward Sinners to Cherished Children*. Phillipsburg, NJ: P&R, 2001. (I)

Assurance
Beeke, Joel R. *The Quest for Full Assurance: The Legacy of Calvin and His Successors*. Edinburgh: The Banner of Truth Trust, 1999.

Beeke, Joel R. *Knowing and Growing in Assurance of Faith*. Fearn, Ross-shire: Christian Focus, 2017.

Sanctification and Perseverance
Allen, Michael. *Sanctification*. New Studies in Dogmatics. Edited by Michael Allen and Scott R. Swain. Grand Rapids: Zondervan, 2017. (A)

Fesko, J. V. *A Christian's Pocket Guide to Growing in Holiness: Understanding Sanctification*. Fear, Ross-shire: Christian Focus, 2012. (B)

DeYoung, Kevin. *The Hole in Our Holiness: Filling the Gap between Gospel Passion and the Pursuit of Godliness.* Wheaton, IL: Crossway, 2012.   (B)

Gundry, Stanley N., ed. *Five Views on Sanctification.* Grand Rapids: Zondervan, 1987.   (A)

Horton, Michael. *The Holy Spirit: God's Perfecting Presence in Creation, Redemption, and Everyday Life.* Grand Rapids: Zondervan, 2017.   (A)

Kapic, Kelly M., ed. *Sanctification: Explorations in Theology and Practice.* Downers Grove, IL: IVP Academic, 2014.   (A)

Naselli, Andrew David. *No Quick Fix: Where Higher Life Theology Came From, What It Is, and Why It's Harmful.* Bellingham, WA: Lexham, 2017.   (I)

Owen, John. *A Discourse Concerning the Holy Spirit.* Vol. 3 of *The Works of John Owen.* Edinburgh: Banner of Truth, 1991.   (A)

_____. *Overcoming Sin and Temptation.* Edited by Justin Taylor and Kelly Kapic. Wheaton, IL: Crossway, 2015.   (I)

Packer, J. I. *Keep in Step with the Spirit: Finding Fullness in Our Walk with God.* Grand Rapids: Baker, 2005.   (I)

Pinson, J. Matthew, ed. *Four Views on Eternal Security.* Grand Rapids: Zondervan, 2002.   (A)

Schreiner, Thomas R. *Run to Win the Prize: Perseverance in the New Testament.* Wheaton, IL: Crossway, 2010.   (B)

_____. *40 Questions about Christians and Biblical Law.* Grand Rapids: Kregel, 2010.   (I)

Schreiner, Thomas R., and Ardel B. Caneday. *The Race Set Before Us: A Biblical Theology of Perseverance and Assurance.* Downers Grove, IL: InterVarsity Press, 2001.   (A)

Storms, Sam. *Kept for Jesus: What the New Testament Really Teaches about Assurance of Salvation and Eternal Security.* Wheaton, IL: Crossway, 2015.   (I)

Warfield, B. B. *Perfectionism.* Edited by Samuel C. Craig. Philadelphia: P&R, 1958.   (I)